في ذكرى

مارك لينز

Gingko-St Andrews Series

Series Editor
Ali Ansari

The Age of Aryamehr

Late Pahlavi Iran and its Global Entanglements

Edited by Roham Alvandi

First published in 2018 by
GINGKO
4 Molasses Row
London SW11 3UX

This paperback edition published 2024

A CIP catalogue record for the book is available from the British Library.

The authorised representative in the EEA is:
Haus Publishing
Casella Postale 32
50037 San Piero a Sieve (Fi)
Italy
(*gpsr@gingko.org.uk*)

ISBN 978-1-914983-28-3
eISBN 978-1-909942-19-6

Typeset in Times by MacGuru Ltd
Printed and bound by CPI Group (UK) Ltd, Croydon CR0 4YY

www.gingko.org.uk
@GingkoLibrary

Contents

Acknowledgements

An editor's task, I was warned, is akin to herding cats. Luckily, it was my pleasure to work with an extraordinarily patient and dedicated group of colleagues to produce this volume. I am deeply grateful to each of them for their forbearance through multiple rounds of review and revision.

The chapters in this volume were initially presented at a workshop entitled, 'Pahlavi Iran, 1941–1978: A Global History Workshop', hosted by the Middle East Centre at the London School of Economics and Political Science on 19 May 2016. I thank the LSE Kuwait Programme and the British Institute of Persian Studies for generously sponsoring the workshop, and my colleagues at the LSE Middle East Centre, particularly Toby Dodge and Ian Sinclair, for their kind support.

My thanks also to our workshop commentators – Ali Ansari, Houchang Chehabi, Stephanie Cronin, Louise Fawcett, and Cyrus Schayegh – for providing invaluable feedback that greatly enriched the chapters in this volume.

Finally, I find myself even more indebted to Houchang Chehabi, in this instance for his invaluable help with the transliteration and copy editing of this volume.

R. Alvandi
London
May 2018

'*The Age of Aryamehr* succeeds in contributing to "the globalisation of the historiography of modern Iran", and reveals the emerging interpretive schisms in that historiography… the rich bibliographies display how these scholars so ably globalize the history of late Pahlavi Iran… the chapters make a compelling case for globalizing the historiography of modern Iran, and the book makes an important intervention by adding the Iranian case to international histories of the 1960s and 1970s. Both are welcome developments.'

Dr. Matthew Shannon, Associate Professor of History at Emory & Henry College, Virginia

'Iran under the Pahlavi regime has often been examined through the prism of national concerns and interests, even when its relationships with the outside world are studied. Roham Alvandi's aim as editor of this book is to write Iran into global history; in other words, to examine the history of the Pahlavi regime within the transnational context… This is a timely and insightful work, providing a rich and fresh account of how Iran engaged with the globalising world. The volume's main contribution to scholarship is to examine the Aryamehr regime's geopolitical ambitions and economic and cultural projects within a global framework. It also throws light on the link between economic development and the global bent of cultural events and on simmering socio-political movements in Iranian society that finally led to the 1979 Revolution. In fact, it is not so much about the Shah's 'global' projects as it is a study of the Aryamehr regime in the context of global developments and concerns in the light of the universal process of globalisation.'

Dr Hormoz Ebrahimnejad, Lecturer in History at the University of Southampton

Introduction

Iran in the Age of Aryamehr

Roham Alvandi

The reign of the last shah of Iran, Mohammad Reza Pahlavi (r. 1941–1979), marked the high-point of Iran's global interconnectedness. Never before had Iranians felt the impact of global political, social, economic, and cultural forces so intimately in their national and daily lives. Iranian artists, clerics, intellectuals, statesmen, students, technocrats, and workers found themselves entangled with global processes in which they participated and which in turn shaped and coloured the long and painful process of defining what it meant to be Iranian in an era of the Cold War and decolonisation.

The history of late Pahlavi Iran has traditionally been written as prologue to the 1978–79 Iranian Revolution.[1] These histories firmly locate the political, social and cultural origins of the revolution within a national context, into which global actors intruded and Iranian actors retreated. While engaging with Iran's national history, *The Age of Aryamehr* is concerned with the international and transnational threads that connected the country to the world, from Iran's place in the global arts scene or the international narcotics trade, to the adoption by Iranian technocrats of global models of development, or the encounter of European intellectuals with the Iranian Revolution.[2] In doing so, this volume aims to write Iran into the global history of these three decades, while also writing the global into Iran's history during the reign of Mohammad Reza Shah.

1 See, for example, Abrahamian, E., *Iran between Two Revolutions*, Princeton 1982; Keddie, N. R., *Roots of Revolution: An Interpretive History of Modern Iran*, New Haven 1981.
2 The title of 'Aryamehr' or 'Light of the Aryans' was conferred upon the shah by the Iranian Parliament in 1965.

In this chapter, I explore the impact of the Cold War and decolonisation on late Pahlavi Iran and the response of the Pahlavi state to those two major global processes. Both Mohammad Reza Shah and his opponents saw themselves as engaged in not only a local struggle for the future of Iran, but in a global struggle between communism and capitalism, between empire and independence. This chapter not only provides historical context for the chapters that follow, but also highlights the ways in which Iranians embraced, interpreted, and debated ideas such as modernisation, anti-imperialism, and Third Worldism, which had gained currency across the world in the 1960s and 1970s. I further examine how Iranians adopted the language and divisions of the global Cold War and decolonisation, developing contending narratives of 'Westoxification' and the 'Great Civilisation', which in turn shaped global history with the shock of the Iranian Revolution.

The Cold War and Iran's Modernisation

The global phenomena of the Cold War and decolonisation converged in Iran in August 1953 when Britain and the United States backed a royalist coup that toppled the popular prime minister, Mohammad Mosaddeq, who had championed the nationalisation of the British-owned Anglo-Iranian Oil Company. The coup was neither the first, the last, nor indeed the most violent global shock that Iran suffered in the twentieth century. It marked, however, the end of a consensus that had prevailed since Iran's Constitutional Revolution at the turn of the century, when the country's political and intellectual elite had looked to the West as the loadstar of Iran's path out of centuries of decline and into the sunlit uplands of what Ali Ansari has characterised as an 'Iranian Enlightenment'.[3] The decision by the Eisenhower administration to violate Iran's national sovereignty and to topple a liberal constitutional government in the name of defeating communism led to a widespread Iranian disillusionment with the United States, which was seen to have betrayed the liberal principle of national self-determination contained in President Woodrow Wilson's Fourteen Points and President Franklin Roosevelt's Atlantic Charter. Iranian nationalists had hoped that the United States would defend Iran's sovereignty against British imperialism during the Anglo-Iranian oil crisis, just as the Truman administration had done in 1946 when the Soviet Union had refused to withdraw from northern Iran, but the secret collusion between London and Washington to depose Mosaddeq in the 1953 coup marked an end to Iran's

3 Ansari, A., *The Politics of Nationalism in Modern Iran*, Cambridge 2012, pp. 36–109.

'Wilsonian moment'.[4] Iran was a front-line state in the global Cold War between the United States and the Soviet Union, which was recognised not only as a great-power struggle between two modern empires, but a world-wide contest of ideas for the very 'soul of mankind'.[5] What was at stake in Iran in 1953, and throughout the subsequent decades of the Cold War, was not simply which of the two superpowers would supplant Britain's monopoly over Iranian oil, but which model of Enlightenment modernity – capitalist or communist – would triumph in Iran and the post-colonial Middle East.[6]

The young Mohammad Reza Shah had fled the country in the midst of the political crisis of August 1953, only to be brought back and handed the reins of power thanks to a royalist coup backed by Britain and the United States. The perception that the shah had saved his throne by collaborating with foreign powers to subvert Iran's national sovereignty severely undermined the monarch's claim to embody the Iranian nation. The shah had to somehow repair this breach with many of his subjects, who viewed him as having betrayed their long struggle for national sovereignty and a constitutional government. The bargain that the shah tried to strike took the form of what Cyrus Schayegh has called the 'politics of material promise', an alternative nationalist vision for Iran that rejected Mosaddeq's liberal constitutionalism in favour of an American model of modernisation that sought to inoculate the country against communism through economic development.[7] In exchange for their loyalty and obedience to the shah, Iranians would partake in the comforts, welfare and opportunities of a developing consumer economy, while enjoying the security and stability provided by the United States against the threat of Soviet invasion or communist subversion.[8]

4 See Manela, E., *The Wilsonian Moment: Self-Determination and the International Origins of Anticolonial Nationalism*, New York 2007.

5 Leffler, M. P., *For the Soul of Mankind: The United States, the Soviet Union, and the Cold War*, New York 2008.

6 See Westad, O. A., *The Global Cold War: Third World Interventions and the Making of Our Times*, Cambridge 2007.

7 For a discussion of the history of liberalism in Iran see Siavoshi, S., *Liberal Nationalism in Iran: The Failure of a Movement*, Boulder 1990; Gheissari, A., and Nasr, V., *Democracy in Iran: History and the Quest for Liberty*, New York 2006. On the American model of modernisation see Cullather, N., 'Development and Technopolitics', in Castigliola, F., and Hogan, M. J. (eds.), *Explaining the History of American Foreign Relations*, Third Edition, Cambridge 2016, pp. 102–118; Latham, M. E., 'Modernization', in Porter, T. M., and Ross, D. (eds.), *The Cambridge History of Science, Volume 7: The Modern Social Sciences*, Cambridge 2008, pp. 721–734.

8 Schayegh, C., 'Iran's Karaj Dam Affair: Emerging Mass Consumerism, the Politics of Promise, and the Cold War in the Third World', in *Comparative Studies in Society and History*, vol. 54, no. 3, 2012, pp. 612–643.

As rising Cold War tensions over Berlin and Cuba seemed to spill over into the Middle East in 1958, the shah saw the hidden hand of the Soviet Union behind unrest in Lebanon, Jordan, and neighbouring Iraq, where the overthrow of the Hashemite monarchy in a bloody military coup was applauded by Soviet leader Nikita Khrushchev.[9] A failed coup plot that same year by the head of Iranian army intelligence, General Valiollah Qarani, who had sought Washington's help in overthrowing the shah, did not portend well for the survival of the Pahlavi monarchy.[10] Whereas Mosaddeq had pursued an early form of non-alignment with his foreign policy of *movāzeneh-ye manfi* (negative equilibrium), which rejected the idea of balancing competing foreign interests in Iran, the shah regarded an entangling alliance with the United States as the only way to preserve his throne and his country's independence. By having Iran participate in the anti-communist Baghdad Pact in 1955, alongside Britain, Iraq, Pakistan, and Turkey, the shah had hoped to secure a Western guarantee for the survival of Pahlavi Iran, but Washington's refusal to join the Pact undermined the alliance's efficacy. Hedging his bets, the shah flirted with the idea of a non-aggression pact with the Soviet Union, while at the same time negotiating and ultimately signing a bilateral defence agreement with the United States in 1959.[11]

American economic and military assistance, combined with expansionary monetary and credit policies, fuelled modernisation in 1950s Iran. The shah hoped to satisfy Iran's growing urban middle class with rising living standards and the comforts of a modern consumer society, while at the same time securing American support for his increasingly arbitrary rule by acting as a bulwark against communist penetration into the oil-rich Persian Gulf. In practice, his economic policies overheated the Iranian economy, leading to an economic crisis in the late 1950s, while his intolerance of dissent and his dependence on the United States radicalised Iranian politics. By 1961, the shah had been forced to annul the results of elections for parliament due to a public outcry over vote-rigging and he faced public protests by teachers against their declining real wages.[12] From the

---

9 See Fursenko, A., and Naftali, T., *Khrushchev's Cold War: The Inside Story of an American Adversary*, New York 2006, pp. 158–184.

10 See Gasiorowski, M. J., 'The Qarani Affair and Iranian Politics', in *International Journal of Middle East Studies*, vol. 25, no. 4, 1993, pp. 625–644.

11 See Alvandi, R., 'Flirting with Neutrality: The Shah, Khrushchev, and the Failed 1959 Soviet-Iranian Negotiations', in *Iranian Studies*, vol. 47, no. 3, 2014, pp. 419–440.

12 See Young, T. C., 'Iran in Continuing Crisis', in *Foreign Affairs*, vol. 40, no. 2, 1962, pp. 275–292; Gasiorowski, M. J., *U.S. Foreign Policy and the Shah: Building a Client State in Iran*, Ithaca 1991, pp. 175–181.

perspective of both superpowers, the shah's days were numbered. At their summit meeting in Vienna in June that year, President John F. Kennedy could only agree with Khrushchev's assessment that Iran had become a 'volcano' and that 'the Shah will certainly be overthrown' unless he enacted meaningful reform.[13]

Kennedy, more so than any other American president during the Cold War, pushed the shah to implement social and economic reforms to pre-empt a popular revolution in Iran.[14] To placate the rising tide of domestic opposition and to secure continuing American economic and military assistance, the shah appointed the liberal Ali Amini as prime minister in 1961, who set in motion a radical programme of land reform.[15] But the shah was unable to tolerate an independent prime minister for long and dispensed with Amini in 1962, while retaining his policy of land reform as part of his own 'White Revolution' of modernising reforms the following year.[16] Kennedy applauded the shah's policies, despite the absence of any political liberalisation, and told the monarch that the protests against his White Revolution in the summer of 1963 were nothing more than 'unfortunate attempts to block your reform programs'. After the violent crackdown on these protests by the security forces, the president reassured the shah that 'such manifestations will gradually disappear as your people realize the importance of the measures you are taking to establish social justice and equal opportunity for all Iranians'.[17]

---

13 Memorandum of Conversation, 3 June 1961, in Sampson, C. S., and Joyce, J. M. (eds.), *Foreign Relations of the United States, 1961–1963, Volume V: Soviet Union*, Washington, DC 1998, Document 85.

14 See Collier, D. R., 'To Prevent a Revolution: John F. Kennedy and the Promotion of Democracy in Iran', in *Diplomacy & Statecraft*, vol. 24, no. 3, 2013, pp. 456–475; Goode, J. F., 'Reforming Iran During the Kennedy Years', in *Diplomatic History*, vol. 15, no. 1, 1991, pp. 13–29; Nemchenok, V. V., 'In Search of Stability Amid Chaos: US Policy Toward Iran, 1961–63', in *Cold War History*, vol. 10, no. 3, 2010, pp. 341–369; Popp, R., 'Benign Intervention? The Kennedy Administration's Push for Reform in Iran', in Berg, M., and Etges, A., *John F. Kennedy and the 'Thousand Days': New Perspectives on the Foreign and Domestic Policies of the Kennedy Administration*, Heidelberg 2007, pp. 197–219; Summit, A. R., 'For a White Revolution: John F. Kennedy and the Shah of Iran', in *Middle East Journal*, vol. 58, no. 4, 2004, pp. 560–575; and Warne, A., 'Psychoanalyzing Iran: Kennedy's Iran Task Force and the Modernization of Orientalism, 1961–3', in *The International History Review*, vol. 35, no. 2, 2013, pp. 396–422.

15 See Hooglund, E. J., *Land and Revolution in Iran, 1960–1980*, Austin 1982; Lambton, A. K. S., *The Persian Land Reform 1962–1966*, Oxford 1969.

16 See Ansari, A., 'The Myth of the White Revolution: Mohammad Reza Shah, 'Modernization' and the Consolidation of Power', in *Middle Eastern Studies*, vol. 37, no. 3, 2001, pp. 1–24; Milani, A., *The Persian Sphinx: Amir Abbas Hoveyda and the Riddle of the Iranian Revolution*, Washington, DC 2001, pp. 135–151; Milani, A., *The Shah*, New York 2011, pp. 279–308.

17 Telegram from the Department of State to the Embassy in Iran, 16 July 1963, in Noring,

Iran hence became one of a number of American client states in the Third World where the United States encouraged reform and modernisation, with the aim of satisfying the needs and aspirations of the country's peasant masses and addressing issues of poverty and inequality that could be exploited by communist forces to foment unrest.[18] With the support of the United States, authoritarian modernisation triumphed over liberalism in Iran under the banner of the White Revolution.

Between 1963 and 1977, Iran's economy experienced the largest growth in GDP in the nation's recorded history, averaging 10.5 percent per year in real terms, making Iran one of the fastest growing economies in the world. This remarkable growth was not simply a reflection of rising oil revenues, as non-oil GDP grew at a higher annual average rate (11.5 percent) than that of GDP including oil.[19] As the shah frequently boasted, his country was closing the gap with average income levels in Western Europe. A whole generation of Iranians experienced unprecedented, yet increasingly unequal, levels of prosperity and opportunity throughout the 1960s and 1970s. A new, largely American- and European-educated, technocratic middle class emerged within the state institutions of Pahlavi Iran who shared the shah's aspirations for a modern and powerful Iran and were willing to work within the Pahlavi state, despite any reservations they harboured about the shah's arbitrary rule.[20] They were granted limited autonomy by the shah to manage Iran's economic development, because of their technocratic expertise, so long as they did not openly challenge or criticise the shah's rule.[21]

N. J. (ed.), *Foreign Relations of the United States, 1961–1963, Volume XVIII: Near East, 1962–1963*, Washington, DC 1995, Document 297.

18 See Fisher, C. T., '"Moral Purpose is the Important Thing": David Lilienthal, Iran, and the Meaning of Development in the US, 1956–63', in *The International History Review*, vol. 33, no. 3, 2011, pp. 431–451; Latham, M. E., *The Right Kind of Revolution: Modernization, Development, and U.S. Foreign Policy from the Cold War to the Present*, Ithaca 2011, pp. 123–156; Nemchenok, V. V., '"That so Fair a Thing Should Be so Frail": The Ford Foundation and the Failure of Rural Development in Iran, 1953–1964', in *Middle East Journal*, vol. 63, no. 2, 2009, pp. 261–284; Popp, R., 'An Application of Modernization Theory during the Cold War? The Case of Pahlavi Iran', in *The International History Review*, vol. 30, no.1, 2008, pp. 76–98.

19 Pesaran, M. H., 'Economy ix. In the Pahlavi Period', in *Encyclopaedia Iranica*, available at: <http://www.iranicaonline.org/articles/economy-ix>.

20 Paper prepared by William G. Miller of the Policy Planning Staff of the U.S. Department of State, 'The "New Men" and their Challenge to American Policy in Iran', 7 August 1964, National Security Files, Files of Robert W. Komer, Box 27, Lyndon B. Johnson Presidential Library, Austin, Texas.

21 See Ashraf, A., and Banuazizi, A., 'Class System vi. Classes in the Pahlavi Period', in *Encyclopaedia Iranica*, available at: <http://www.iranicaonline.org/articles/class-system-vi>; Bostock, F., and Jones, G., *Planning and Power in Iran: Ebtehaj and Economic*

Ramin Nassehi's contribution to this volume examines how these technocrats borrowed economic ideas from both American modernisation theory and Latin American protectionism to design an import-substitution policy that produced the 'economic miracle' that propelled Pahlavi Iran into the ranks of the world's fastest growing economies, alongside Brazil, Mexico, Taiwan and South Korea. In his chapter, Nassehi traces the introduction of modernisation theory to Iran to the 1950s via the Plan Organisation under the leadership of Abol Hassan Ebtehaj, and the later introduction of Latin American protectionism in the 1960s through the United Nations Conference on Trade and Development. Under the Third Five-Year Development Plan (1963–1968), the Pahlavi state used its rising oil revenues to encourage the creation of industrial conglomerates that, Nassehi argues, increasingly resembled South Korea's *chaebol*s. While the United States supported Iran's centrally-planned protectionist economy, Iran's growing prosperity afforded the shah increasing autonomy from his American patrons.[22] In fact, in 1967 the United States stopped designating Iran as a 'less developed country' and ended all direct economic aid to the country.[23] The shah demonstrated this autonomy by turning to the Soviet Union to fulfil his ambitions for Iran's heavier industries. Just as the Karaj Dam had symbolised modernisation in the 1950s, Isfahan's Aryamehr Steel Mill, completed in 1973 with Soviet assistance, embodied the same aspirations for modernity and independence that were the professed goals of the White Revolution in the 1960s.[24]

'Westoxification' and Iranian Anti-Imperialism

The state's increasing oil rent not only afforded Mohammad Reza Shah greater autonomy from the United States, but also from his own people, on whose taxes the state did not need to rely to finance its expenditure. Instead, it was the Iranian people who depended more and more on the Pahlavi state for employment,

Development under the Shah, London 1989; Nasr, V., 'Politics within the Late-Pahlavi State: The Ministry of Economy and Industrial Policy, 1963–69', in *International Journal of Middle East Studies*, vol. 32, no. 1, 2000, pp. 97–122.

22 Esfahani, H. S., and Pesaran, M. H., 'The Iranian Economy in the Twentieth Century: A Global Perspective', in *Iranian Studies*, vol. 42, no. 2, 2009, p. 189.

23 Johns, A. L., 'The Johnson Administration, the Shah of Iran, and the Changing Pattern of U.S.-Iranian Relations, 1965–1967: "Tired of Being Treated like a Schoolboy"', in *Journal of Cold War Studies*, vol. 9, no. 2, 2007, p. 88. See also, Castiglioni, C., 'No Longer a Client, Not Yet a Partner: The US-Iranian Alliance in the Johnson Years', in *Cold War History*, vol. 15, no. 4, 2015, pp. 491–509.

24 Ramazani, R. K., *Iran's Foreign Policy 1941–1973: A Study of Foreign Policy in Modernizing Nations*, Charlottesville 1975, pp. 334–336.

subsidies and welfare.[25] Political power was concentrated in the person of the *shāhanshāh* (king of kings) *Āryāmehr* (light of the Aryans). Indeed, the 'sultanistic' nature of the Pahlavi monarchy has invited unflattering comparisons with the highly personalised and arbitrary regimes of Duvalier's Haiti, Ceauşescu's Romania, or Mobutu's Zaire, rather than the Western liberal democracies with which the shah aspired to reach parity.[26] From the mid-1960s onwards, the shah's public image in the West as a modernising monarch was undermined by reports of human rights violations that made their way into the American and European press, thanks to the efforts of a transnational network of students, dissidents, and human rights organisations.[27] Meanwhile, at home, Jalal Al-e Ahmad's highly influential 1962 essay, *Gharbzadegi* (Westoxification), politicised and popularised ideas of nativism and anti-Westernism that had been developed by post-war Iranian intellectuals such as Seyyed Fakhreddin Shadman and Ahmad Fardid. This narrative of *gharbzadegi* constituted a direct assault by Iran's intellectuals against the shah, whom they denounced as an illegitimate ruler imposed on Iran by the United States, and against the technocratic elite of the Pahlavi state, whom intellectuals accused of collaborating with the shah's regime to blindly impose alien Western culture and technology on Iran in order to promote the country's dependence on and subjugation to American imperialism.[28]

In chapter three of the present volume, Maziyar Ghiabi argues that the Pahlavi state's regulation and prohibition of opium consumption in Iran, in line with global efforts to tackle the international traffic in drugs, came to be seen as a clear example of Westoxification. Addiction and opium were regarded by the Pahlavi state as hallmarks of Iran's backwardness that would need to be eliminated on the road to modernity. Opium use was a common practice in traditional Iranian society,

25 See Gasiorowski, M. J., *U.S. Foreign Policy*, pp. 130–196; Katouzian, H., *The Political Economy of Modern Iran: Despotism and Pseudo-Modernism, 1926–1979*, London 1981.
26 See the various chapters in Chehabi, H. E., and Linz, J. J. (eds.), *Sultanistic Regimes*, Baltimore 1998.
27 Shannon, M. K., *Losing Hearts and Minds: American-Iranian Relations and International Education during the Cold War*, Ithaca 2017, pp. 117–140; Dorman, W. A., and Farhang, M., *The U.S. Press and Iran: Foreign Policy and the Journalism of Deference*, Berkeley 1987, pp. 141–147.
28 Boroujerdi, M., *Iranian Intellectuals and the West: The Tormented Triumph of Natavism*, Syracuse 1996, pp. 52–76; Gheissari, A., *Iranian Intellectuals in the 20th Century*, Austin 1998, pp. 74–108; Mirsepassi, A., *Transnationalism in Iranian Political Thought: The Life and Times of Ahmad Fardid*, Cambridge 2017; Navabi, N., *Intellectuals and the State in Iran: Politics, Discourse, and the Dilemma of Authenticity*, Gainesville 2003, pp. 68–69. For an example of this discourse see Nirumand, B., *Iran: The New Imperialism in Action*, New York 1969.

transcending boundaries of class. However, as Ghiabi argues, the state's efforts to wean Iranians off opium only encouraged an illicit traffic in heroin, fuelled by the urbanisation of Iran's traditionally rural society thanks to the White Revolution. Modernisation did not mean the elimination of drug culture, rather it facilitated the introduction of a Western heroin counterculture to Iranian youth which replaced the traditional opium consumption of previous generations. Ghiabi points out that the Pahlavi state recognised the failure of prohibition and instead adopted a progressive system of opium distribution for registered addicts in 1969, based on a similar system introduced by the National Health Service in Britain. Nonetheless, the shah won few plaudits for his attempts to limit drug addiction in Iran. Instead, his opponents exploited sensational rumours of drug use and trafficking by members of the royal family to highlight the decadence, moral corruption, and Westoxification of the court. When the shah visited UCLA during his June 1964 trip to the United States, protesting students distributed copies of a letter from the International Federation for Narcotic Education accusing the shah of bringing 'narcotic addiction to the people of Iran'.[29] A small plane flew over the graduation ceremony, where the shah was to receive an honorary doctorate and deliver the commencement address, towing a banner that read: 'Need a Fix? See the Shah!'[30]

In this constant struggle between state modernisation and opposition nativism, both the shah and his critics came to reject Western liberalism. In the aftermath of the 1953 coup, a younger generation of Iranians had come to associate the West with American imperialism and support for the shah's dictatorship, rather than liberty and modernity. In doing so, they were deeply influenced by a transnational counterculture of youth alienation and protest that gripped Europe and the United States in the 1960s. This counterculture questioned the legitimacy of Western democracies, which were accused of enshrining gender inequality and racial oppression, and rejected the global Cold War order, which was viewed as responsible for the persistence of neo-colonial exploitation.[31] Iran was integrated into this transnational counterculture by the thousands of Iranian students who fanned out across Western Europe and the United States in the 1960s and made common cause with fellow students to support Third World liberation movements in Algeria, Cuba, Palestine, South Africa, Vietnam, and elsewhere.[32] Although

29 Offiler, B., *US Foreign Policy and the Modernization of Iran: Kennedy, Johnson, Nixon, and the Shah*, New York 2015, p. 78.

30 Matin-Asgari, A., *Iranian Student Opposition to the Shah*, Costa Mesa 2002, p. 75.

31 See Suri, J., 'The Rise and Fall of an International Counterculture, 1960–1975', in *The American Historical Review*, vol. 114, no. 1, 2009, pp. 45–68.

32 See Matin-Asgari, A., *Iranian Student Opposition*, pp. 96–111; Nasrabadi, M., '"Women

Iran had been deeply penetrated by both the British and Russian empires in the nineteenth century, the Iranian experience did not fit comfortably into this global anti-imperial struggle, as Iran was one of a handful of Asian countries that had never been formally colonised by the European empires. However, for these students the Pahlavi state was, in Afshin Marashi's words, a 'surrogate colonial state' because of the American intervention in Iran in 1953.[33]

As it became increasingly dangerous for these students to challenge the shah in Iran, where politics as a contest for power had effectively ceased since the shah's dismissal of Amini in 1962, they exported their opposition to the West. Nowhere was this more evident than during the mass protests by German and Iranian students against the shah's visit to West Berlin on 2 June 1967, when a 26-year old German student, Benno Ohnesorg, was killed by a West Berlin Police officer. The anger and violence that the shah's visit provoked on the streets of Berlin marked a dramatic turning point in Pahlavi Iran's relationship with the West. The death of Ohnesorg at the hands of the police radicalised the West German student movement, whose most extreme elements would evolve into the violent revolutionary Red Army Faction in the 1970s.[34] The word *Jubelperser* (cheering-Persians), used to describe the pro-shah counterdemonstrators organised by the Iranian Embassy to confront the protesting students in Germany, entered into the German lexicon as a word for any rent-a-crowd. For the West's New Left generation, the shah would join the pantheon of American-backed right-wing hate figures, alongside Indonesia's Suharto or Chile's Pinochet. Half a century later, the United States's support for that 'terrible dictator', Mohammad Reza Shah, would still be invoked by Senator Bernie Sanders, a 75-year old veteran of that generation, as an example of the moral failures of American foreign policy.[35]

While the shah's opponents accused the Pahlavi elite of Westoxification, they

---

Can Do Anything Men Can Do": Gender and the Effects of Solidarity in the U.S. Iranian Student Movement, 1961–1979', in *WSQ: Women's Studies Quarterly*, vol. 42, no. 3–4, 2014, pp. 127–145; Shannon, M. K., '"Contacts with the Opposition": American Foreign Relations, the Iranian Student Movement, and the Global Sixties', in *The Sixties*, vol. 4, no. 1, 2011, pp. 1–29.

33 Marashi, A., 'Paradigms of Iranian Nationalism: History, Theory, and Historiography', in Aghaie, K. S., and Marashi, A. (eds.), *Rethinking Iranian Nationalism and Modernity*, Austin 2014, p. 18.

34 See Matin-Asgari, A., *Iranian Student Opposition*, p. 97; Slobodian, Q., *Foreign Front: Third World Politics in Sixties West Germany*, Durham 2012, pp. 100–134; Suri, J., *Power and Protest: Global Revolution and the Rise of Détente*, Cambridge, MA 2003, pp. 176–178.

35 Transcript of the Democratic Presidential Debate in Milwaukee, 11 February 2016, *The New York Times*, available at: <https://www.nytimes.com/2016/02/12/us/politics/transcript-of-the-democratic-presidential-debate-in-milwaukee.html?_r=0>.

were themselves intoxicated by the counterculture that they encountered in the West. Iranian intellectuals idolised Jean-Paul Sartre as the politically engaged European intellectual *par excellence* and embraced the language of commitment (*ta'ahhod*) when debating the role of the intellectual in society. The publication in Persian of Frantz Fanon's *Wretched of the Earth* in 1966, translated by Shariati and a group of fellow Iranian students in Paris, did much to introduce the vocabulary of cultural imperialism and the need for a 'return to self' to Iranians.[36] The meaning of this authentic Iranian self was fiercely debated amongst a plethora of leftist, Islamist, and nationalist intellectuals, activists and groups. Nonetheless, the same romantic Third Worldism that had enchanted the youth of Europe and the United States also seduced the youth of Iran. Rather than demanding that the shah should reign and not rule, as Mosaddeq had done, this new generation called for the overthrow of the monarchy and revolutionary social change. As Ali Ansari argues, this 1960s generation of Iranian anti-imperialists came to regard the older generation of Iranian liberal constitutionalists as 'dangerously naïve in their engagement not only with Western powers but with the very ideas that underpinned the idea of the West'.[37] They denounced Hasan Taqizdeh, a distinguished liberal statesman who had been one of the leaders of the Constitutional Revolution, as Westoxified for calling on his compatriots to embrace the Enlightenment values of European civilisation.[38] They heaped scorn on political moderates like Khalil Maleki, an anti-Soviet socialist and loyal ally of Mosaddeq, because of his willingness to meet and talk with the shah within the framework of Iran's constitutional monarchy.[39] By the early 1970s, Iranian student organisations in Europe and the United States were mired in debates between Marxists of every variety over the best path to revolution in Iran, while Iranian university campuses served as recruiting grounds for the Marxist-Leninist Fadaiyan-e Khalq (Self-Sacrificers for the People) and the

36 Nabavi, N., *Intellectuals and the State in Iran: Politics, Discourse, and the Dilemma of Authenticity*, Gainesville 2003, pp. 67–106; Rahnema, A., *An Islamic Utopian: A Political Biography of Ali Shari'ati*, London 2014, pp. 117–130.
37 Ansari, A., *The Politics of Nationalism*, p. 141.
38 Ansari, A., 'Taqizadeh and European Civilisation', in *Iran: Journal of the British Institute of Persian Studies*, vol. 65, no. 1, 2016, pp. 47–58; Katouzian, H., 'Seyyed Hasan Taqizdeh: Three Lives in a Lifetime', in *Comparative Studies of South Asia, Africa and the Middle East*, vol. 32, no. 1, 2012, pp. 195–213.
39 Katouzian, H., 'Khalil Maleki: The Odd Intellectual Out', in Nabavi, N. (ed.), *Intellectual Trends in Twentieth-Century Iran: A Critical Survey*, Gainesville 2003, pp. 24–52; Milani, A., 'Khalil Maleki', in his *Eminent Persians: The Men and Women Who Made Modern Iran, 1941–1979, Volume One*, Syracuse and New York 2008, pp. 220–228. See also, Katouzian, H., *Khalil Maleki: The Human Face of Iranian Socialism*, London 2018.

Marxist-Islamist Mojahedin-e Khalq (Holy Warriors of the People), both underground guerrilla organisations that waged an 'armed struggle' to topple the Pahlavi state.[40] Islamist groups like the Muslim Students Association and the Liberation Movement of Iran were similarly radicalised, as moderate liberal Islamists like Mehdi Bazargan lost their appeal to the religious youth while more revolutionary figures like Ayatollah Khomeini gained in popularity.[41] In the age of Aryamehr, the liberalism that had defined Iranian nationalism during the Constitutional era gave way to utopian visions of revolution, both White and Red.[42]

Despite their obvious differences, the shah shared his opponents' disdain for liberalism. Since the early 1960s, he had toyed with the idea of a strictly controlled form of parliamentary democracy, but by the mid-1970s he was firmly convinced that democracy was synonymous with anarchy.[43] Both in public and in private he lectured Americans and Europeans on the need for 'social discipline' and chastised them for becoming 'lazy, undisciplined, and permissive'.[44] The shah shared the paternalism of American and European elites, who bemoaned student radicalism as symptomatic of the moral decline of the West. In Charles Maier's words, these guardians of the status quo spoke in 'tones of self-conscious and somewhat sententious adulthood: the reassertion of grownups, the calm stewards of social and political rationality, who sought to reign in a society that celebrated infantile urges under the guise of an infatuation with youth'.[45] When President Richard Nixon visited Tehran on his way home from Moscow in May 1972, he spoke to the shah of his fear that a large number of Iranian students in the United States would be radicalised. 'Are your students infected?' Nixon asked the shah, 'Can you do anything?'[46] There was indeed a great deal the shah could do.

---

40 See Abrahamian, E., *Radical Islam: The Iranian Mojahedin*, London 1989; Behrooz, M., *Rebels with a Cause: The Failure of the Left in Iran*, London 1999; Vahabzadeh, P., *A Guerrilla Odyssey: Modernization, Secularism, Democracy, and the Fadai Period of National Liberation in Iran*, Syracuse 2010.

41 Chehabi, H. E., *Iranian Politics and Religious Modernism: The Liberation Movement of Iran under the Shah and Khomeini*, Ithaca 1990, pp. 214–220.

42 Ansari, A., *The Politics of Nationalism*, p. 115.

43 On the shah's flirtations with political liberalisation see Chehabi, H. E., 'The Shah's Two Liberalizations: Re-Equilibration and Breakdown', in Chehabi, H. E., et al (eds.), *Iran and the Challenges of the Twenty-First Century: Essays in Honor of Mohammad-Reza Djalili*, Costa Mesa 2013, pp. 24–49; Milani, *The Shah*, pp. 379–381.

44 Bill, J. A., *The Eagle and the Lion: The Tragedy of American-Iranian Relations*, New Haven 1988, p. 192.

45 Maier, C. S., 'Malaise', in Ferguson, N., et al (eds.), *The Shock of the Global: The 1970s in Perspective*, Cambridge, MA 2010, p. 41.

46 Memorandum of Conversation, Tehran, 31 May 1972, 10.30am to 12.00pm, in Belmonte,

When dealing with the opposition, the shah's first preference was to co-opt those who were willing to embrace depoliticisation. The ranks of the Pahlavi state's cultural institutions, particularly the universities and the National Iranian Radio and Television, were filled with former leftists who had abandoned their opposition to the shah.[47] However, those who were not willing to reach an accommodation with the state, whether out of conviction or fear of the opprobrium of their erstwhile comrades, faced a variety of repressive measures. These ranged from the censorship of intellectuals to more violent methods of imprisonment, torture, public recantations, and executions at the hands of the national security and intelligence service, SAVAK.[48] The shah's authoritarianism reached its peak in 1975 when he established a one-party state under the Hezb-e Rastakhiz-e Mellat-e Iran (Iranian Nation's Resurgence Party) and advised anyone who did not want to join the party to leave the country.[49] While these coercive methods generated a great deal of negative publicity for the shah, less noticed were the efforts of the Pahlavi state to develop a cultural and ideological riposte to the narrative of *gharbzadegi*. The shah had inherited a state ideology that drew on much earlier historiographical ideas about the glory of Iran's ancient Persian civilisation and the decline of Iran after the Arab-Islamic conquest, as well as the privileging of a secular 'Aryan' Iranian identity – anchored linguistically and racially to the European Occident – rather than an Islamic Iranian identity embedded in the Muslim Orient.[50] These ideas were deemed inadequate, however, in the post-liberal age of Aryamehr and the post-colonial global 1970s. What was needed was an ideology

---

M. (ed.), *Foreign Relations of the United States, 1969–1976, Volume E-4, Documents on Iran and Iraq, 1969–1972*, Washington, DC 2006, Document 201.

47 See Afkhami, G. R., *The Life and Times of the Shah*, Berkeley 2009, pp. 402–403; Zonis, M., *The Political Elite of Iran*, Princeton 1971, pp. 40–44; Abbas Milani, 'Reza Ghotbi', in his *Eminent Persians: The Men and Women Who Made Modern Iran, 1941–1979, Volume One*, Syracuse and New York 2008, p. 168.

48 Abrahamian, E., *Tortured Confessions: Prisons and Public Recantations in Modern Iran*, Berkeley 1999, pp. 101–119; Karimi-Hakkak, A., 'Protest and Perish: A History of the Writer's Association of Iran', in *Iranian Studies*, vol. 18, no. 2–4, 1985, pp. 189–229.

49 See Amini, P. M., 'A Single Party State in Iran, 1975–78: The Rastakhiz Party – the Final Attempt by the Shah to Consolidate his Political Base', in *Middle Eastern Studies*, vol. 38, no. 1, 2002, pp. 131–168; Afkhami, G. R., *The Life and Times*, pp. 432–440; Milani, A., *The Persian Sphinx*, pp. 275–279.

50 See Ansari, A., *The Politics of Nationalism*, pp. 65–109; Marashi, A., *Nationalizing Iran: Culture Power, & the State, 1870–1940*, Seattle 2008; Motadel, D., 'Iran and the Aryan Myth', in Ansari, A. (ed.), *Perceptions of Iran: History, Myths and Nationalism from Medieval Persia to the Islamic Republic*, London 2014, pp. 119–145; Zia-Ebrahimi, R., *The Emergence of Iranian Nationalism: Race and the Politics of Dislocation*, New York 2016.

that would allow the shah to emerge from the shadow of Mosaddeq, Iran's anti-colonial national hero, and for Iranians to reimagine the American-backed Pahlavi monarchy as a champion of Iranian nationalism against the West.

The Shah's 'Great Civilisation'

This new state ideology emerged as a codified 'Pahlavism' in the late 1960s and 1970s, which reaffirmed the Pahlavi monarchy as authentically Iranian. Pahlavism claimed some ancient Iranian affinity for monarchy, grounded in an age-old Persian royal tradition, and proclaimed an Iranian renaissance under the Pahlavi dynasty, following centuries of decline. Given its native roots in Iranian history and culture, monarchy was presented as the most appropriate political system (as opposed to permissive democracy or atheistic communism) for Iran to overcome reactionary Islamic obscurantism and achieve what the shah termed the *tamaddon-e bozorg* or 'Great Civilisation'.[51] Pahlavi Iran was hardly unique amongst sultanistic regimes of the era in seeking legitimisation through such invented forms of nativism. For example, contemporaneous with the development of Pahlavism in Iran, President Mobutu Sese Seko of Zaire embraced the ideology of '*authenticité*' and 'Mobutism', which drew on the myth of native African 'Bantu' values to legitimise his personal rule. Just a year before the establishment of the Rastakhiz Party in Iran, Mobutu declared a one-party state under his *Mouvement Populaire de la Révolution*. Just as the shah wanted to escape the shadow of Mosaddeq, the staunchly anti-communist and pro-American Mobutu resented the memory of Congo's murdered independence leader, Patrice Lumumba.[52] Pahlavism and Mobutism were both attempts to recast Cold War autocrats as embodiments of the nation.

As Cyrus Schayegh argues in his concluding chapter to this volume, the shah's notion of Iran as a 'Great Civilisation' had both a domestic and a global projection. At home it was projected as an 'economically successful welfare state', and thus the culmination of the shah's White Revolution of social and economic reforms. The shah may well have borrowed the language of the Great Civilisation from President Lyndon Johnson's poverty-elimination programmes of the

51 Ansari, A., *The Politics of Nationalism*, 170–172; Shakibi, Z., 'Pahlavism: The Ideologization of Monarchy in Iran', in *Politics, Relgion & Society*, vol. 14, no. 1, 2013, pp. 114–135.

52 Chehabi, H. E., and Linz, J. J., 'A Theory of Sultanism 1: A Type of Nondemocratic Rule', in Chehabi, H. E., and Linz, J. J. (eds.), *Sultanistic Regimes*, Baltimore 1998, p. 13; Young, C., and Turner, T., *The Rise and Decline of the Zairian State*, Madison 1985, pp. 168–220.

1960s, which Johnson dubbed the 'Great Society'.[53] All Iranian classes benefitted from the country's rapid economic growth, including the working class, as material standards of living rose in absolute terms throughout the 1960s and 1970s.[54] For example, the Literacy Corps, an educational programme established under the White Revolution, recruited urban Iranian youth to go into the provinces and help alleviate illiteracy as an alternative to a 2-year military service in the army. Between 1966 and 1979, the rate of illiteracy was reduced from 67.2 to 44.2 percent for men and from 87.8 to 53 percent for women.[55] However, the benefits of the 'Great Civilisation' were not evenly felt across, or indeed within, social classes, generating resentments and grievances that undermined the claims of Pahlavism. For example, when it came to distributing credit subsidies to the private sector, the state seemed to favour the modern middle class, who embraced Western technology and lifestyles and were connected to the Pahlavi elite, over the traditional middle class, particularly bazaar merchants, who retained a strong religious identity and close ties to the Shia clergy.[56] Similarly, public sector blue-collar *kārgar*s (workers) resented the significantly better salaries, working conditions and benefits enjoyed by white-collar *kārmand*s (civil servants) in the National Iranian Oil Company.[57]

The global projection of Pahlavism drew on a much older idea of Iran as not only a 'run-of-the-mill nation-state', but as an 'age-old civilisation' that constituted, in Schayegh's view, the 'cultural framework for an imperial project'. The shah's claims about Iran's civilisation echoed the 'standard of civilisation' employed by Europeans to legitimise their imperialism in the nineteenth century.[58] Indeed, in the Persian Gulf, it seemed that a declining British Empire was being supplanted by Iran's rising 'Great Civilisation'. Iran's Arab neighbours watched on nervously as a bankrupt Britain withdrew its forces from the region in 1971, while an oil-rich Iran seized the disputed islands of Abu Musa and the Tunbs, deployed Iranian troops to defeat a Marxist rebellion against the Sultan of

53 I am grateful to Ali Ansari for drawing this parallel to my attention.
54 See Hakimian, H., 'Industrialization and the Standard of Living of the Working Class in Iran, 1960–79', in *Development and Change*, vol. 19, no. 1, 1988, pp. 3–32.
55 Sabahi, F., 'Literacy Corps', in *Encyclopaedia Iranica*, available at: <http://www.iranicaonline.org/articles/literacy-corps-1>. See also, Sabahi, F., *The Literacy Corps in Pahlavi Iran (1963–1979): Political, Social and Literary Implications*, Lugano 2002.
56 See Salehi-Isfahani, D., 'The Political Economy of Credit Subsidy in Iran, 1973–1978', in *International Journal of Middle East Studies*, vol. 21, no. 3, 1989, pp. 359–379.
57 See Jafari, P., 'Reasons to Revolt: Iranian Oil Workers in the 1970s', in *International Labour and Working-Class History*, vol. 84, 2013, pp. 195–217.
58 See Gong, G. W., *The Standard of 'Civilization' in International Society*, Oxford 1984.

Oman in Dhofar, and armed and financed a Kurdish insurgency in northern Iraq against a succession of Arab nationalist governments in Baghdad.[59] As Schayegh is careful to point out, the shah harboured no ambitions for territorial conquest. For example, he peacefully relinquished Iran's historic claim to Bahrain in 1970.[60] Rather, what he claimed for Iran was a great-power status that troubled friend and foe alike. Indeed, even in Washington, the shah's American allies became increasingly alarmed by the extent of his ambitions, as he poured money into a full-scale nuclear energy programme and spoke of Iran as an Indian Ocean power whose interests stretched as far afield as Australia and South Africa.[61] In 1974, *Newsweek* magazine disparaged the shah as a 'Frankenstein monster' who 'with visions of Persia's grandeur dancing in his head… has set out to convert his immense oil wealth into geopolitical clout'.[62] Such exaggerated fears of the shah's latent Persian imperialism even penetrated into popular American culture, as evidenced by Paul Erdman's apocalyptic pulp fiction novel with the prescient title, *The Crash of 79*, which imagined the end of the world in 1979 in a nuclear war between Iran and Saudi Arabia.[63]

No single event was more closely associated with the global projection of Pahlavism than the lavish celebrations of 2,500 years of Iranian monarchy that the shah hosted at the ruins of the ancient Achaemenid capital of Persepolis in 1971. Attended by heads of state from around the world, the event is best remembered for the shah's oration at the tomb of the founder of the Persian Empire, Cyrus the Great, where Mohammad Reza Shah bid his illustrious predecessor to 'sleep easy, for we are awake'. This attempt to present the shah as a modern Cyrus and to reimagine the monarchy as synonymous with Iranian nationalism was mocked by the Iranian opposition, given that virtually all the materials, food and wine for the event were imported at great expense from the finest French ateliers, chefs,

59 See Alvandi, R., *Nixon, Kissinger, and the Shah: The United States and Iran in the Cold War*, New York 2014, pp. 65–125; Goode, J. F., 'Assisting Our Brothers, Defending Ourselves: The Iranian Intervention in Oman, 1972–75', in *Iranian Studies*, vol. 47, no. 3, 2014, pp. 441–462.

60 See Alvandi, R., 'Muhammad Reza Pahlavi and the Bahrain Question, 1968–1970', in *British Journal of Middle Eastern Studies*, vol. 37, no. 2, 2010, pp. 159–177.

61 See Alvandi, R., *Nixon, Kissinger, and the Shah*, pp. 126–171; Bookmiller, R. J., *Engaging Iran: Australian and Canadian Relations with the Islamic Republic*, Dubai 2009, pp. 30–33; Chehabi, H. E., 'South Africa and Iran in the Apartheid Era', in *Journal of South African Studies*, vol. 42, no. 4, 2016, pp. 699–701; Ramazani, R. K., 'Iran's Search for Regional Cooperation', in *Middle East Journal*, vol. 30, no. 2, 1976, pp. 173–186.

62 'The Master Builder of Iran', *Newsweek*, 14 October 1974.

63 Erdman, P. E., *The Crash of '79*, New York 1976.

and vineyards for the consumption of the shah's foreign guests, while the Iranian people, whose history was being celebrated, were conspicuously absent from the celebrations. Yet, as Robert Steele argues in his contribution to this volume, the celebrations were far from a total failure. The celebrations broadcast to the world the message that Iran had not only arrived on the global stage, but that Iran had *returned* to its *rightful* place as a global power under the leadership of the shah. Despite all of its much-criticised lavishness and theatrics, the presence of the leaders from most Western states, virtually the entire communist bloc, and much of the Third World, placed Iran and the shah at the centre of the world and signalled global recognition of Iran's newfound status. To this extent, Steele argues, the celebrations were a success, albeit a mixed one, given the criticism that the event generated both at home and abroad for its opulence.

Pahlavi Third Worldism

Although Mohammad Reza Shah had firmly sided with the United States in the Cold War and rejected non-alignment, he had never felt comfortable with the popular perception that he was dependent on the West, especially the United States, for the security of his throne and the defence of his realm. Instead, the Pahlavi state sought to project an image of a resurgent Iran as an autonomous actor within the Western bloc; some British diplomats disparagingly called him the 'de Gaulle of the Middle East'.[64] By the mid-1970s the shah recognised that the Cold War consensus in the United States was breaking down in the era of Vietnam and Watergate and that a new global order was emerging based, in his words, on 'the deep interdependence of the fate of all countries and the peoples of the world'.[65] The world would no longer be so firmly divided by the Cold War between the communist East and the capitalist West. Instead, as a result of decolonisation another fault line had appeared between the rich post-industrial post-imperial North and the poor industrialising post-colonial South. Oil-rich Pahlavi Iran did not fit comfortably into either camp, but could instead serve as a bridge between East and West, North and South. As Schayegh argues, the shah envisaged that Iran's 'civilisational-developmental model' could provide an alternative to both capitalism and communism for the Third World. Consequently, Pahlavism was

64 Alvandi, R., *Nixon, Kissinger, and the Shah*, p. 32. On the shah's admiration for and relationship with Charles de Gaulle see Fath, S., *L'Iran et de Gaulle: Chronique d'un Rêve Inachevé*, Neuilly 1999.

65 As quoted in Shakibi, Z., 'Pahlavism: The Ideologization of Monarchy in Iran', in *Politics, Religion & Society*, vol. 14, no. 1, 2013, p. 133.

grafted on to the global project and ideology of 'Third Worldism' so as to buttress the shah's claims to being an authentic nationalist leader and to rebut the *gharbzadegi* critique of his anti-imperialist opponents.[66]

By the late 1960s, Third Worldism was no longer the preserve of liberation movements or a transnational counterculture, but instead that of a growing number of largely undemocratic newly independent states in Africa, Asia and Latin America that hoped to steer the United Nations towards a Third World agenda that emphasised self-determination, economic sovereignty, and the rights of the state, rather than a Western agenda focused on spreading liberal values, particularly the universal human rights of the individual.[67] When the shah hosted the 1968 UN International Conference on Human Rights in Tehran, he joined a chorus of Third World leaders who argued that individual civil and political rights were meaningless in the absence of national self-determination and economic sovereignty.[68] Pahlavism was mapped on to this Third World discourse of human rights when the shah argued, anachronistically, that human rights had in fact emanated from Iran, not the West, as it was Cyrus the Great who had issued the world's first charter of human rights after his conquest of Babylon in 539 BC.[69] The same argument was made by the shah's twin sister, Princess Ashraf, at the 1975 World Conference for the International Women's Year in Mexico City, which she had helped to plan as chair of its consultative committee. Western feminists like Betty Friedan had applauded the progress in women's rights in Pahlavi Iran, including the right to vote in 1963 under the White Revolution and greater equality and protection when it came to divorce under the 1967 Family Protection Law.[70] They watched on with dismay, however, when Princess Ashraf led the chorus of Third World representatives in Mexico City who declared that state-led modernisation

---

66 For a survey of the history of 'Third Worldism' see Malley, R., *The Call from Algeria: Third Worldism, Revolution, and the Turn to Islam*, Berkeley 1996; Prashad, V., *The Darker Nations: A People's History of the Third World*, New York 2007.

67 See Simpson, B. R., 'Self-Determination, Human Rights, and the End of Empire', in *Humanity: An International Journal of Human Rights, Humanitarianism, and Development*, vol. 4, no. 2, 2013, pp. 239–260.

68 Burke, R., 'From Individual Rights to National Development: The First UN International Conference on Human Rights, Tehran, 1968', in *Journal of World History*, vol. 19, no. 3, 2008, pp. 275–296; Jensen, S. L. B., *The Making of International Human Rights: The 1960s, Decolonization, and the Reconstruction Global Values*, Cambridge 2017, pp. 174–208.

69 See Ansari, A., *The Politics of Nationalism*, pp. 175–176.

70 See Afkhami, G. R., *The Life and Times*, pp. 238–262; Vatandoust, G., 'The Status of Iranian Women During the Pahlavi Regime', in Fathi, A. (ed.), *Women and the Family in Iran*, Leiden 1985, pp. 107–130; Kashani-Sabet, F., *Conceiving Citizens: Women and the Politics of Motherhood in Iran*, New York 2011, pp. 180–185.

and development, rather than civil and political rights, represented meaningful liberation for the women of the Third World.[71]

The global politics of oil would afford the shah his most significant opportunity to project an image of himself as a Third World nationalist by leading the oil producing countries of the global South against the American and European oil companies that had controlled the production and price of oil for decades. In an effort to eclipse the memory of Mosaddeq as the champion of Iranian oil nationalisation, the shah worked with both conservative and revolutionary leaders within the Organisation of the Petroleum Exporting Countries (OPEC) to wrest control of prices and production away from the oil companies, grounding his arguments in the anti-colonial vocabulary of Third Worldism.[72] Along with Algeria, Mexico, and Venezuela, Iran co-sponsored the UN Declaration on the Establishment of a New International Economic Order (NIEO) at a special session of the UN General Assembly in 1974. Inspired in part by the success of OPEC, the NIEO marked the high-water mark of Third Worldism and represented an attempt on the part of the South to achieve economic independence and sovereignty within a global economic system dominated by the North, just as they had achieved political independence within the international society of states created and dominated by Europeans.[73] Despite the shah's rhetoric, however, Iran's oil wealth meant that it could not speak as an authentic voice for the impoverished global South. The 1973 energy crisis that sent oil prices sky-rocketing and enriched Iran and other oil producers also generated a sovereign debt crisis for much of the Third World that ultimately undermined the solidarity of the global South.[74]

Pahlavi Third Worldism was not only grounded in the shah's diplomacy, but also in a rethinking of Pahlavism by a number of intellectuals connected to the royal court, most notably Ehsan Naraqi, Seyyed Hosseyn Nasr, and Daryush

71 Burke, R., 'Competing for the Last Utopia? The NIEO, Human Rights, and the World Conference for the International Women's Year, Mexico City, June 1975', in *Humanity: An International Journal of Human Rights, Humanitarianism, and Development*, vol. 6, no. 1, 2015, pp. 47–61.
72 Dietrich, C. R. W., *Oil Revolution: Anticolonial Elites, Sovereign Rights, and the Economic Culture of Decolonization*, Cambridge 2017, pp. 158–159, 184–189, 221–222, 255–257; Sargent, D. J., *A Superpower Transformed: The Remaking of American Foreign Relations in the 1970s*, New York 2015, pp. 131–155.
73 See Berger, M. T., 'After the Third World? History, Destiny and the Fate of the Third World', in *Third World Quarterly*, vol. 25, no. 1, 2004, pp. 9–39; Gilman, N., 'The New International Economic Order: A Reintroduction', in *Humanity: An International Journal of Human Rights, Humanitarianism, and Development*, vol. 6, no. 1, 2015, pp. 1–16.
74 See Dietrich, C. R. W., *Oil Revolutions*, pp. 263–304.

Shayegan, who warned of the dangers of Westernisation and tried to steer the Pahlavi vision of Iranian nationalism away from Aryanism and towards some notion of Iranianness rooted in Islamic mysticism or Asian civilisation.[75] They sat atop state cultural and educational institutions that were created from the late 1960s onwards, often under the patronage of Empress Farah, and engaged with the debate on cultural authenticity. These institutions included the Iranian Centre for the Study of Civilisations (Markaz-e Irani-ye Motaleʿeh-ye Farhangha), headed by Shayegan, and the Imperial Iranian Academy of Philosophy (Anjomane Shahanshahi-ye Falsafeh-ye Iran), founded by Nasr. Pahlavi Third Worldism was amplified through publications connected to the court or the Rastakhiz Party and even made its way into the shah's vocabulary, who by the late 1970s was warning against 'the penetration into our society of undesirable foreign elements and the spread of moral, social and political corruption… We must not become Westoxicated'.[76] This ideological shift was apparent in the shah's decision to host the 1974 Asian Games in Tehran, a dress-rehearsal for Iran's bid to host the 1984 Olympic Games. Like the Persepolis celebrations three years earlier, the Asian Games again heralded to the world the rebirth of Iran as a modern global power, but with the important distinction that now the audience was primarily Asian, rather than Western, and Iran was projected as an Indian Ocean power, rather than as part of the Western bloc.[77]

Despite all the resources deployed to promote Pahlavism, few were convinced by the shah's co-option of the language of *gharbzadegi* and Third Worldism, when juxtaposed against the reality of burgeoning U.S. arms sales to Iran in the 1970s.[78] Moreover, the Pahlavi state's effort to construct Iranian nationalism around dubious racial ideas like the Aryan myth or vague notions of being Eastern or Asian not only rang hollow, but also ceded Iran's centuries-old Shia Muslim identity to the opposition. The shah's decision in 1976 to replace the Islamic calendar with an imperial calendar, dating from the founding of the Persian Empire by Cyrus the

75 Boroujerdi, *Iranian Intellectuals*, pp. 120–130, 136–140, 147–155.

76 As quoted in Shakibi, Z., 'The Rastakhiz Party and Pahlavism: The Beginnings of State Anti-Westernism in Iran', in *British Journal of Middle Eastern Studies*, vol. 45, no. 2, 2018, p. 260. See also Mirsepassi, A., and Faraji, M., 'De-Politcizing Westoxification: The Case of Bonyad Monthly', in *British Journal of Middle Eastern Studies*, vol. 45, no. 3, 2016, pp. 355–375.

77 See Amirtash, A., 'Iran and the Asian Games: The Largest Sports Event in the Middle East', in *Sport in Society: Cultures, Commerce, Media, Politics*, vol. 8, no. 3, 2005, pp. 449–467; Huebner, S., 'Iran and the Indian Ocean Region Project: The Great Persian Empire, Oil Wealth, and the Seventh Asian Games (1–16 September 1974)', in his *Pan-Asian Sports and the Emergence of Modern Asia, 1913–1974*, Singapore 2016, pp. 230–260.

78 See McGlinchey, S., *US Arms Policies Towards the Shah's Iran*, London 2014.

Great, meant that Iranians awoke to find themselves suddenly living in the year 2535, confirming for many the shah's insensitivity, if not outright contempt, for their faith.[79] Furthermore, the shah's claims about the moral superiority of Iran's autocratic monarchy, versus the decadence and decline of Western democracy, were unconvincing in the light of the Western mass consumerism that the Pahlavi state had fostered. For example, despite the best efforts of the state censor, Iranian popular culture of the 1970s was epitomised by the low-budget *film-fārsi* movies that titillated mass Iranian audiences with gratuitous sex and violence, at the same time that the shah was disparaging the traditional guardians of public morality, the Shia clergy, as reactionaries who stood in the way of modernity.[80]

Rather than seeing the shah as a Third World nationalist or even a Persian imperialist, his nativist opponents saw his boasting about Iran's 'Great Civilisation' as a sign of his insecurity, dependence, and Westoxification. The shah's social and economic reforms, from women's rights to economic modernisation, were not regarded as sincere attempts at improving the lot of Iranians. Rather, they were seen by his opponents as efforts to convince Westerners, particularly Americans, that Pahlavi Iran was a 'civilised' country according to the Western standard of civilisation. This contradiction was apparent in many of the cultural activities of the Pahlavi state, which undermined the state's attempt to co-opt the narrative of *gharbzadegi*. Throughout the 1970s the state sponsored a series of festivals organised by the High Council of Culture and Art to promote 'familiarisation (*āshnā'i)* and reconciliation (*āshti*) with the forgotten face of our heritage'. These included the Festival of Culture and Art, the Festival of Tus (which celebrated Ferdowsi's *Shahnameh*), the Festival of Popular Culture, and the Festival of Popular Traditions, all of which showcased and celebrated Iran's classical and folk arts.[81] The most controversial, however, was the Shiraz Arts Festival (Jashn-e Honar-e Shiraz), which is the subject of a chapter in this volume by H. E. Chehabi. The idea for this international arts festival originated with Empress Farah, who sought to introduce Iranians to arts from around the world while also showcasing the best in traditional Iranian arts to a global audience. Held annually between 1967

79 Similar criticisms were levelled at the government's decision to adopt daylight-saving time (DST) on 22 March 1977. See Movahedi, S., 'Cultural Preconceptions of Time: Can We Use Operational Time to Meddle in God's Time', in *Comparative Studies in History and Society*, vol. 27, no. 3, 1985, pp. 385–400.

80 See Atwood, B., 'When the Sun Goes Down: Sex, Desire and Cinema in 1970s Tehran', in *Asian Cinema*, vol. 27, no. 2, 2016, pp. 127–150; Partovi, P., *Popular Iranian Cinema before the Revolution: Family and Nation in* Filmfarsi, London 2017.

81 Nabavi, N., *Intellectuals and the State*, pp. 103–118.

and 1977, the Shiraz Arts Festival was intended, as Chehabi argues, to reaffirm Iran's place as 'a genuine equal among equals on an international scene dominated by Western countries'. Instead, it provided grist for the mills of the opposition narrative of *gharbzadegi.* As Chehabi points out, the annual festival is mainly remembered for the Western avant-garde performances that offended the tastes and sensibilities of Iranians, even though the festival featured a variety of art forms, many of them traditional and uncontroversial. The most notorious performance was at the 1977 festival featuring Péter Hálasz's play, *Pig, Child, Fire!* which scandalised the Shirazi audience with its depiction of nudity and sex. The 1977 festival was seized upon by the opposition, particularly Ayatollah Khomeini, as a clear demonstration of the royal family's Westoxification and their contempt for Islam and Iranian culture.

The Shiraz Arts Festival, like much of the international cultural activities of the Pahlavi state, focused on a dialogue of civilisations. This was the state's response to the narrative of *gharbzadegi*: that Iran was an equal of the West in cultural and civilisation terms and had something of value to offer the West, as well as much to learn from it. As such, the Shiraz Festival was an expression of elite cosmopolitan worldliness in an era characterised by populist nativism. As Chehabi argues, 'the appreciation of many of the festival's programmes necessitated an aesthetic sensibility and a cosmopolitan habitus that were rare even among most upper middle class, let alone middle-class Iranians.' Moreover, even for Iran's more cosmopolitan intellectuals, the idea of 'art for art's sake' amounted to collaboration with the regime's efforts to depoliticise art. The radical leftist writer Gholam Hosseyn Sa'edi branded those artists who participated in these festivals as 'pseudo-artists' (*shebh-e honarmand*) who had been co-opted by the state.[82] Just as Western governments had been criticised for participating in the Persepolis celebrations in 1971, Western artists who participated in the Shiraz Festival faced similar criticism back home for having helped to legitimise a state that tortured its own citizens. Iannis Xenakis, the Greek-French pioneer of electronic and computer music who had lost an eye fighting with the Greek resistance against the Nazis, had performed commissioned works at the festival since 1968 and at the Persepolis celebrations in 1971. In an open letter to his critics in *Le Monde* in December 1971, he wrote, 'I am not an isolationist in a world as tangled and complicated as

82 Nabavi, N., *Intellectuals and the State*, pp. 112–118. On Sa'edi see Milani, A., 'Gholamhoseyn Sa'edi,' in his *Eminent Persians: The Men and Women Who Made Modern Iran, 1941–1979, Volume Two*, Syracuse and New York 2008, pp. 878–883.

today's.' Yet, by 1976, he could no longer resist the pressure and pulled out of the festival.[83]

For the shah's critics, cultural activities such as the Shiraz Festival were not seen as a dialogue of civilisations, but as an attempt by a Westoxified Pahlavi elite to Westernise Iranians. Just as Reza Shah had imposed a Western dress code on men and women so that Iranians 'would not be made fun of', Mohammad Reza Shah intended to teach primitive Iranians to appreciate sophisticated Western art and culture.[84] Iranian modernity would only be achieved when Iranians were capable of consuming the most avant-garde Western art. As Chehabi points out, the shah himself actually had little appetite for modern art, but he ceded much of the realm of cultural policy to his consort, who had studied architecture in Paris and was intimately connected to the world of modern American and European art. Empress Farah dominated the cultural policy-making of the Pahlavi state in the 1970s. Although she was a champion of preserving Iran's cultural heritage, particularly its Islamic architecture and traditional handicrafts in the face of relentless modernisation, she also exhibited an artistic sensibility and worldliness that rejected the radicalism and parochialism of the *gharbzadegi* narrative.[85] This was evident not only in the Shiraz Arts Festival, but also in the construction of the Tehran Museum of Contemporary Art (TMOCA), which is the subject of Samine Tabatabaei's chapter.

Opened in 1977 under the direction of Empress Farah's cousin, Kamran Diba, the museum amassed an impressive collection of Western, particularly American, modern art. Opened in the same year as Paris's Centre Pompidou and modelled on New York's Guggenheim Museum, TMOCA was designed to give Iran 'agency' in a global art scene dominated by Europe and the United States. The museum not only brought to Tehran some of the most important works of Impressionist, Cubist, Expressionist, Abstract Expressionist, Pop and Minimalist art from the West, it also exhibited and promoted the work of Iran's own Saqqa-khaneh school of contemporary art, which fused modernism with traditional Iranian and Islamic art forms.[86] The museum was unabashedly designed to introduce Western

83 Gluck, R., 'The Shiraz Arts Festival: Western Avant-Garde Arts in 1970s Iran', in *Leonardo*, vol. 40, no. 1, 2007, p. 26.

84 See Chehabi, H. E., 'Staging the Emperor's New Clothes: Dress Codes and Nation-Building under Reza Shah', in *Iranian Studies*, vol. 26, no. 3–4, 1993, p. 226.

85 See Grigor, T., *Building Iran: Modernism, Architecture, and National Heritage under the Pahlavi Monarchs*, New York 2009, p. 184.

86 Keshmirshekan, H., 'Neo-Traditionalism and Modern Iranian Painting: The *Saqqa-khaneh* School in the 1960s', in *Iranian Studies*, vol. 38, no. 4, 2005, pp. 607–630.

modern art to Iranians and to support Iran's 'cultural diplomacy', in Tabatabaie's words, by promoting an image of the country as 'open to and engaged with the Western world'. Much like the Shiraz Arts Festival, the museum's explicit goal of teaching Iranians to consume avant-garde Western culture, while at the same time seeking the acknowledgement of Western cultural elites, only served to reinforce the *gharbzadegi* critique and to undermine the shah's claims to independence from the West. The Saqqa-khaneh school of art, which was iconic of the age of Aryamehr, was viewed with disdain by Iranian intellectuals as 'decorative' art that blithely ignored Iran's social and political realities.[87]

No single figure better encapsulated the tension between cosmopolitanism and nativism in the age of Aryamehr than the shah's long-serving prime minister, Amir Abbas Hoveyda, who is the subject of Chehabi's other contribution to this volume. A Francophile cosmopolitan, a freemason, a secular man of Baha'i lineage, sexually ambiguous – a man who 'consciously or unconsciously, constructed his persona along the lines of the classical European dandy' – Hoveyda seemed completely out of step and out of touch with the cultural nativism and political radicalism that gripped Iran during his premiership from 1965 to 1977. Yet, thanks to his unwavering loyalty to the shah and his political acumen in dealing with his rivals, he was the longest serving prime minister in modern Iranian history.[88] As Chehabi points out, Hoveyda's 'sycophancy' towards the shah was uncharacteristic of the traditionally independent and insolent figure of the European dandy, but in the eyes of the shah's opponents Hoveyda's obsequiousness was characteristic of the unprincipled and inauthentic Westoxified Pahlavi man. Hoveyda the Europeanised dandy nominally presided over a system that claimed the mantle of Iranian nationalism. The shah and his prime minister boasted of the renaissance of Iran's Great Civilisation, while at the same time viewing ordinary Iranians as backward and in need of cultivation and modernisation so that they might be accepted by the West as civilised, just as the highly refined and cosmopolitan Hoveyda was held in high esteem by many of the leading political and cultural figures of Europe. The shah's decision to first dismiss Hoveyda from the premiership in July 1977 and to then have him arrested in November 1978, so as to appease the tide of revolutionary fervour in Iran, was a belated admission that Pahlavism had failed to reconcile such contradictions.

87 Moussavi-Aghdam, C., 'Art History, "National Art" and Iranian Intellectuals in the 1960s', in *British Journal of Middle Eastern Studies*, vol. 41, no. 1, 2014, p. 146.
88 See Milani, A., *The Persian Sphinx*; Hoveyda, F., *The Fall of the Shah*, London 1980.

Iran and the Shock of the Global

American intervention, mass consumerism, and unprecedented economic growth had allowed the Pahlavi state to survive the twin global shocks of the Cold War and decolonisation. However, by the close of the 1970s, it was clear that the state's narrative of the 'Great Civilisation' and Pahlavi Third Worldism were inadequate for responding to the powerful *gharbzadegi* critique. Instead, an Iranian brand of revolutionary political Islam, developed by Ali Shariati and embraced by Ayatollah Khomeini, offered young Iranians a way to 'return' to an imagined authentic Islamic self, while at the same time joining the global revolutionary struggle against American imperialism. The nativism, populism and anti-imperialism inherent in this ideology allowed for a broad coalition of both leftist and Islamist political groups and individuals to join forces to topple the shah in a popular revolution in 1978–79.[89] The coming to power of political Islam in Iran would come to be seen as part of the 'shock of the global' in the 1970s.[90] Few if any contemporary observers had anticipated the revolution, let alone the Islamic Republic that it would give birth to. The Iranian Revolution was enthusiastically applauded by the European left, who saw it primarily as a decisive blow against American imperialism. They wilfully ignored the illiberalism and underestimated the impact of the Islamic trends of the opposition to the shah and were therefore surprised when Islamists came to dominate the revolution and destroy the Iranian left after seizing power.[91] In chapter eight, Claudia Castiglioni examines the case of Fred Halliday, a prominent Anglo-Irish intellectual of the New Left and scholar of the Middle East who would go on to teach International Relations at the London School of Economics (LSE). A prominent, though often dissenting, Marxist intellectual, Halliday's initial enthusiasm for the Iranian Revolution quickly turned to disillusionment after his visit to Iran in the summer of 1979, where he witnessed

89 See Aghaie, K., 'Islam and Nationalist Historiography: Competing Narratives of the Iranian Nation in the Pahlavi Period', in *Studies in Contemporary Islam*, vol. 2, no. 2, 2000, pp. 21–47; Mahdavi, M., 'The Rise of Khomeinism: Problematizing the Politics of Resistance in Pre-Revolutionary Iran', in Adib-Moghaddam, A. (ed.), *A Critical Introduction to Khomeini*, Cambridge 2014, pp. 43–68; Mirsepassi, A., *Intellectual Discourse and the Politics of Modernization*, Cambridge 2000, pp. 96–128; Rahnema, A., *An Islamic Utopian*.
90 Jalal, A., 'An Uncertain Trajectory: Islam's Contemporary Globalization, 1971–1979', in Ferguson, N., et al (eds.), *The Shock of the Global: The 1970s in Perspective*, Cambridge 2010, pp. 319–336; Saikal, A., 'Islamism, the Iranian Revolution, and the Soviet invasion of Afghanistan', in Leffler, M. P., and Westad, O. A. (eds.), *The Cambridge History of the Cold War, Volume 3: Endings*, Cambridge 2010, pp. 112–134; Westad, O. A., *The Global Cold War*, pp. 288–330.
91 See Moghadam, V. M., 'Socialism or Anti-Imperialism? The Left and Revolution in Iran', in *New Left Review*, no. 166, 1987, pp. 5–28.

the closure of the *Ayandegan* newspaper by the new revolutionary government and the attacks on leftist forces by the triumphant Islamists.[92]

Castiglioni's chapter highlights the importance of the Iranian Revolution for the intellectual history of the European left in the 1970s, who looked to the Third World at a time of profound ideological disillusionment with the Soviet and Chinese models of communism. Their initial enthusiasm for Iran's anti-imperialist revolution, followed by their surprise and disenchantment with the triumph of political Islam in Iran, hinted at even bigger global shocks that awaited the left with the fall of the Berlin Wall in 1989. We can only understand the left's 'misreading' of the Iranian Revolution, as Castiglioni puts it, if we examine their opposition to the shah in a global context. The shah's Marxist opponents, both Iranian and non-Iranian, regarded the Pahlavi regime as a manifestation of global capitalism and American imperialism. Consequently, their ideological disdain for bourgeois liberalism and their virulent anti-Americanism made them cheerleaders for Ayatollah Khomeini, until they found themselves eliminated by the same illiberal forces of political Islam that had mobilised the Iranian masses against the shah. This 'anti-imperialism of fools', in Halliday's words, only makes sense through the lens of a world-view that regards Iran as merely one front in a global struggle.[93] Castiglioni makes the important point that the left had no monopoly on misreading the Iranian Revolution. Nonetheless, what her chapter highlights is the crucial global context of a revolution that was supported and applauded by those whom Hoveyda denigrated as 'little cry-baby communists trained at the London School of Economics'.[94]

To understand any aspect of Iran's history in the age of Aryamehr – political, social, economic, intellectual, or artistic – we need to escape the boundaries of national history and examine the international and transnational threads that connected Iran to the world. As Iran's interconnectedness with the world increased, the impact of global forces on Iranian politics and society were profound. Iranians experienced decolonisation, the Cold War, and the concomitant struggle to reconcile modernity and nativism. As showcased in the chapters in this volume, the globalisation of the historiography of modern Iran continues apace. Historians of modern Iran will have much to say about the global issues that shaped the 1950s, 1960s and 1970s, such as the politics of oil, the elevation of human rights,

---

92 Halliday, F., 'Right-wingers on the rampage', *New Statesman*, 17 August 1979, p. 224; Halliday, F., 'The revolution turns to repression', *New Statesman*, 24 August 1979, p. 262.

93 Halliday, F., 'The Iranian Revolution and Its Implications', in *New Left Review*, no. 166, 1987, p. 37.

94 Quoted in Bill, J. A., *Eagle and the Lion*, p. 166.

the struggle to contain nuclear proliferation, or the emergence of political Islam, to name but a few of the major themes of twentieth-century global history. While the Pahlavi monarchy was relegated to history in 1979, the age of Aryamehr marked the return of Iran from the periphery to the centre of the global stage, whence it has never retreated.

Bibliography

Abrahamian, E., *Iran between Two Revolutions*, Princeton 1982.

Abrahamian, E., *Radical Islam: The Iranian Mojahedin*, London 1989.

Abrahamian, E., *Tortured Confessions: Prisons and Public Recantations in Modern Iran,* Berkeley 1999.

Afkhami, G. R., *The Life and Times of the Shah*, Berkeley 2009.

Aghaie, K., 'Islam and Nationalist Historiography: Competing Narratives of the Iranian Nation in the Pahlavi Period', in *Studies in Contemporary Islam*, vol. 2, no. 2, 2000, pp. 21–47.

Alvandi, R., 'Flirting with Neutrality: The Shah, Khrushchev, and the Failed 1959 Soviet-Iranian Negotiations', in *Iranian Studies*, vol. 47, no. 3, 2014, pp. 419–440.

Alvandi, R., 'Muhammad Reza Pahlavi and the Bahrain Question, 1968–1970', in *British Journal of Middle Eastern Studies*, vol. 37, no. 2, 2010, pp. 159–177.

Alvandi, R., *Nixon, Kissinger, and the Shah: The United States and Iran in the Cold War*, New York 2014.

Amini, P. M., 'A Single Party State in Iran, 1975–78: The Rastakhiz Party – the Final Attempt by the Shah to Consolidate his Political Base', in *Middle Eastern Studies*, vol. 38, no. 1, 2002, pp. 131–168.

Amirtash, A., 'Iran and the Asian Games: The Largest Sports Event in the Middle East', in *Sport in Society: Cultures, Commerce, Media, Politics*, vol. 8, no. 3, 2005, pp. 449–467.

Ansari, A., 'The Myth of the White Revolution: Mohammad Reza Shah, "Modernization" and the Consolidation of Power', in *Middle Eastern Studies*, vol. 37, no. 3, 2001, pp. 1–24

Ansari, A., *The Politics of Nationalism in Modern Iran*, Cambridge 2012.

Ansari, A., 'Taqizadeh and European Civilisation', in *Iran*: *Journal of the British Institute of Persian Studies*, vol. 65, no. 1, 2016, pp. 47–58.

Ashraf, A., and Banuazizi, A., 'Class System vi. Classes in the Pahlavi Period', in *Encyclopaedia Iranica*, available at: <http://www.iranicaonline.org/articles/class-system-vi>.

Atwood, B., 'When the Sun Goes Down: Sex, Desire and Cinema in 1970s Tehran', in *Asian Cinema*, vol. 27, no. 2, 2016, pp. 127–150.

Behrooz, M., *Rebels with a Cause: The Failure of the Left in Iran*, London 1999.

Belmonte, M. (ed.), *Foreign Relations of the United States, 1969–1976, Volume E-4, Documents on Iran and Iraq, 1969–1972*, Washington, DC 2006.

Berger, M. T., 'After the Third World? History, Destiny and the Fate of the Third World', in *Third World Quarterly*, vol. 25, no. 1, 2004, pp. 9–39.

Bill, J. A., *The Eagle and the Lion: The Tragedy of American-Iranian Relations*, New Haven 1988.

Bookmiller, R. J., *Engaging Iran: Australian and Canadian Relations with the Islamic Republic*, Dubai 2009.

Bostock, F., and Jones, G., *Planning and Power in Iran: Ebtehaj and Economic Development under the Shah*, London 1989.

Boroujerdi, M., *Iranian Intellectuals and the West: The Tormented Triumph of Natavism*, Syracuse 1996.

Burke, R., 'Competing for the Last Utopia? The NIEO, Human Rights, and the World Conference for the International Women's Year, Mexico City, June 1975', in *Humanity: An International Journal of Human Rights, Humanitarianism, and Development*, vol. 6, no. 1, 2015, pp. 47–61.

Burke, R., 'From Individual Rights to National Development: The First UN International Conference on Human Rights, Tehran, 1968', in *Journal of World History*, vol. 19, no. 3, 2008, pp. 275–296.

Castiglioni, C., 'No Longer a Client, Not Yet a Partner: The US-Iranian Alliance in the Johnson Years', in *Cold War History*, vol. 15, no. 4, 2015, pp. 491–509.

Chehabi, H. E., *Iranian Politics and Religious Modernism: The Liberation Movement of Iran under the Shah and Khomeini*, Ithaca 1990.

Chehabi, H. E., 'The Shah's Two Liberalizations: Re-Equilibration and Breakdown', in Chehabi, H. E., et al (eds.), *Iran and the Challenges of the Twenty-First Century: Essays in Honor of Mohammad-Reza Djalili*, Costa Mesa 2013, pp. 24–49.

Chehabi, H. E., 'South Africa and Iran in the Apartheid Era', in *Journal of South African Studies*, vol. 42, no. 4, 2016, pp. 687–709.

Chehabi, H. E., 'Staging the Emperor's New Clothes: Dress Codes and Nation-Building under Reza Shah', in *Iranian Studies*, vol. 26, no. 3–4, 1993, pp. 209–233.

Chehabi, H. E., and Linz, J. J. (eds.), *Sultanistic Regimes*, Baltimore 1998.

Collier, D. R., 'To Prevent a Revolution: John F. Kennedy and the Promotion of Democracy in Iran', in *Diplomacy & Statecraft*, vol. 24, no. 3, 2013, pp. 456–475.

Cullather, N., 'Development and Technopolitics', in Castigliola, F., and Hogan, M. J. (eds.), *Explaining the History of American Foreign Relations*, Third Edition, Cambridge 2016, pp. 102–118.

Dietrich, C. R. W., *Oil Revolution: Anticolonial Elites, Sovereign Rights, and the Economic Culture of Decolonization*, Cambridge 2017.

Dorman, W. A., and Farhang, M., *The U.S. Press and Iran: Foreign Policy and the Journalism of Deference*, Berkeley 1987.

Esfahani, H. S., and Pesaran, M. H., 'The Iranian Economy in the Twentieth Century: A Global Perspective', in *Iranian Studies*, vol. 42, no. 2, 2009, pp. 177–211.

Erdman, P. E., *The Crash of '79*, New York 1976.

Fath, S., *L'Iran et de Gaulle: Chronique d'un Rêve Inachevé*, Neuilly 1999.

Ferguson, N., et al (eds.), *The Shock of the Global: The 1970s in Perspective*, Cambridge 2010.

Fisher, C. T., '"Moral Purpose is the Important Thing": David Lilienthal, Iran, and the Meaning of Development in the US, 1956–63', in *The International History Review*, vol. 33, no. 3, 2011, pp. 431–451.

Fursenko, A., and Naftali, T., *Khrushchev's Cold War: The Inside Story of an American Adversary*, New York 2006.

Gasiorowski, M. J., 'The Qarani Affair and Iranian Politics', in *International Journal of Middle East Studies*, vol. 25, no.4, 1993, pp. 625–644.

Gasiorowski, M. J., *U.S. Foreign Policy and the Shah: Building a Client State in Iran*, Ithaca 1991.

Gheissari, A., *Iranian Intellectuals in the 20th Century*, Austin 1998.

Gheissari, A., and Nasr, V., *Democracy in Iran: History and the Quest for Liberty*, New York 2006.

Gilman, N., 'The New International Economic Order: A Reintroduction', in *Humanity: An International Journal of Human Rights, Humanitarianism, and Development*, vol. 6, no. 1, 2015, pp. 1–16.

Goode, J. F., 'Assisting Our Brothers, Defending Ourselves: The Iranian Intervention in Oman, 1972–75', in *Iranian Studies*, vol. 47, no. 3, 2014, pp. 441–462.

Goode, J. F., 'Reforming Iran During the Kennedy Years', in *Diplomatic History*, vol. 15, no. 1, 1991, pp. 13–29.

Gong, G. W., *The Standard of 'Civilization' in International Society*, Oxford 1984.

Gluck, R., 'The Shiraz Arts Festival: Western Avant-Garde Arts in 1970s Iran', in *Leonardo*, vol. 40, no. 1, 2007, pp. 20–28.

Grigor, T., *Building Iran: Modernism, Architecture, and National Heritage under the Pahlavi Monarchs*, New York 2009.

Hakimian, H., 'Industrialization and the Standard of Living of the Working Class in Iran, 1960–79', in *Development and Change*, vol. 19, no. 1, 1988, pp. 3–32.

Halliday, F., 'The Iranian Revolution and Its Implications', in *New Left Review*, no. 166, 1987, pp. 29–37.

Hooglund, E. J., *Land and Revolution in Iran, 1960–1980*, Austin 1982.

Hoveyda, F., *The Fall of the Shah*, London 1980.

Huebner, S., *Pan-Asian Sports and the Emergence of Modern Asia, 1913–1974*, Singapore 2016.

Jafari, P., 'Reasons to Revolt: Iranian Oil Workers in the 1970s', in *International Labour and Working-Class History*, vol. 84, 2013, pp. 195–217.

Jensen, S. L. B., *The Making of International Human Rights: The 1960s, Decolonization, and the Reconstruction Global Values*, Cambridge 2017.

Johns, A. L., 'The Johnson Administration, the Shah of Iran, and the Changing Pattern of U.S.-Iranian Relations, 1965–1967: "Tired of Being Treated like a Schoolboy"', in *Journal of Cold War Studies*, vol. 9, no. 2, 2007, pp. 64–94.

Karimi-Hakkak, A., 'Protest and Perish: A History of the Writer's Association of Iran', in *Iranian Studies*, vol. 18, no. 2–4, 1985, pp. 189–229.

Kashani-Sabet, F., *Conceiving Citizens: Women and the Politics of Motherhood in Iran*, New York 2011.

Katouzian, H., *Khalil Maleki: The Human Face of Iranian Socialism*, London 2018.

Katouzian, H., 'Khalil Maleki: The Odd Intellectual Out', in Nabavi, N. (ed.), *Intellectual Trends in Twentieth-Century Iran: A Critical Survey*, Gainesville 2003, pp. 24–52.

Katouzian, H., *The Political Economy of Modern Iran: Despotism and Pseudo-Modernism, 1926–1979*, London 1981.

Katouzian, H., 'Seyyed Hasan Taqizdeh: Three Lives in a Lifetime', in *Comparative Studies of South Asia, Africa and the Middle East*, vol. 32, no. 1, 2012, pp. 195–213.

Keddie, N. R., *Roots of Revolution: An Interpretive History of Modern Iran*, New Haven 1981.

Keshmirshekan, H., 'Neo-Traditionalism and Modern Iranian Painting: The *Saqqa-khaneh* School in the 1960s', in *Iranian Studies*, vol. 38, no. 4, 2005, pp. 607–630.

Lambton, A. K. S., *The Persian Land Reform 1962–1966*, Oxford 1969.

Latham, M. E., 'Modernization', in Porter, T. M., and Ross, D. (eds.), *The Cambridge History of Science, Volume 7: The Modern Social Sciences*, Cambridge, 2008, pp. 721–734.

Latham, M. E., *The Right Kind of Revolution: Modernization, Development, and U.S. Foreign Policy from the Cold War to the Present*, Ithaca 2011.

Leffler, M. P., *For the Soul of Mankind: The United States, the Soviet Union, and the Cold War*, New York 2008.

Mahdavi, M., 'The Rise of Khomeinism: Problematizing the Politics of Resistance in Pre-Revolutionary Iran', in Adib-Moghaddam, A. (ed.), *A Critical Introduction to Khomeini*, Cambridge 2014, pp. 43–68.

Malley, R., *The Call from Algeria: Third Worldism, Revolution, and the Turn to Islam*, Berkeley 1996.

Manela, E., *The Wilsonian Moment: Self-Determination and the International Origins of Anticolonial Nationalism*, New York 2007.

Marashi, A., *Nationalizing Iran: Culture Power, & the State, 1870–1940*, Seattle 2008.

Marashi, A., 'Paradigms of Iranian Nationalism: History, Theory, and Historiography', in Aghaie, K. S., and Marashi, A. (eds.), *Rethinking Iranian Nationalism and Modernity*, Austin 2014, pp. 3–24.

Matin-Asgari, A., *Iranian Student Opposition to the Shah*, Costa Mesa 2002.

McGlinchey, S., *US Arms Policies Towards the Shah's Iran*, London 2014.

Milani, A., *Eminent Persians: The Men and Women Who Made Modern Iran, 1941–1979, Two Volumes*, Syracuse and New York 2008.

Milani, A., *The Persian Sphinx: Amir Abbas Hoveyda and the Riddle of the Iranian Revolution*, Washington, DC 2001.

Milani, A., *The Shah*, New York 2011.

Mirsepassi, A., and Faraji, M., 'De-Politcizing Westoxification: The Case of Bonyad Monthly,' in *British Journal of Middle Eastern Studies*, vol. 45, no. 3, 2016, pp. 355–375.

Mirsepassi, A., *Intellectual Discourse and the Politics of Modernization*, Cambridge 2000.

Mirsepassi, A., *Transnationalism in Iranian Political Thought: The Life and Times of Ahmad Fardid*, Cambridge 2017.

Moghadam, V. M., 'Socialism or Anti-Imperialism? The Left and Revolution in Iran', in *New Left Review*, no. 166, 1987, pp. 5–28.

Motadel, D., 'Iran and the Aryan Myth', in Ansari, A. (ed.), *Perceptions of Iran: History, Myths and Nationalism from Medieval Persia to the Islamic Republic*, London 2014, pp. 119–145.

Moussavi-Aghdam, C., 'Art History, "National Art" and Iranian Intellectuals in the 1960s', in *British Journal of Middle Eastern Studies*, vol. 41, no. 1, 2014, pp. 132–150.

Movahedi, S., 'Cultural Preconceptions of Time: Can We Use Operational Time to Meddle in God's Time', in *Comparative Studies in History and Society*, vol. 27, no. 3, 1985, pp. 385–400.

Navabi, N., *Intellectuals and the State in Iran: Politics, Discourse, and the Dilemma of Authenticity*, Gainesville 2003.

Nasr, V., 'Politics within the Late-Pahlavi State: The Ministry of Economy and Industrial Policy, 1963–69', in *International Journal of Middle East Studies*, vol. 32, no. 1, 2000, pp. 97–122.

Nasrabadi, M., '"Women Can Do Anything Men Can Do": Gender and the Affects of Solidarity in the U.S. Iranian Student Movement, 1961–1979', in *WSQ: Women's Studies Quarterly*, vol. 42, no. 3–4, 2014, pp. 127–145.

Nemchenok, V. V., 'In Search of Stability Amid Chaos: US Policy Toward Iran, 1961–63', in *Cold War History*, vol. 10, no. 3, 2010, pp. 341–369.

Nemchenok, V. V., '"That so Fair a Thing Should Be so Frail": The Ford Foundation and the Failure of Rural Development in Iran, 1953–1964', in *Middle East Journal*, vol. 63, no. 2, 2009, pp. 261–284.

Nirumand, B., *Iran: The New Imperialism in Action*, New York 1969.

Noring, N. J. (ed.), *Foreign Relations of the United States, 1961–1963, Volume XVIII: Near East, 1962–1963*, Washington, DC 1995.

Offiler, B., *US Foreign Policy and the Modernization of Iran: Kennedy, Johnson, Nixon, and the Shah*, New York 2015.

Partovi, P., *Popular Iranian Cinema before the Revolution: Family and Nation in* Filmfarsi, London 2017.

Pesaran, M. H., 'Economy ix. In the Pahlavi Period', in *Encyclopaedia Iranica*, available at: <http://www.iranicaonline.org/articles/economy-ix>.

Popp, R., 'An Application of Modernization Theory during the Cold War? The Case of Pahlavi Iran', in *The International History Review*, vol. 30, no.1, 2008, pp. 76–98.

Popp, R., 'Benign Intervention? The Kennedy Administration's Push for Reform in Iran', in Berg, M., and Etges, A., *John F. Kennedy and the 'Thousand Days': New Perspectives on the Foreign and Domestic Policies of the Kennedy Administration*, Heidelberg 2007, pp. 197–219.

Prashad, V., *The Darker Nations: A People's History of the Third World*, New York 2007.

Rahnema, A., *An Islamic Utopian: A Political Biography of Ali Shari'ati*, London 2014.

Ramazani, R. K., *Iran's Foreign Policy 1941–1973: A Study of Foreign Policy in Modernizing Nations*, Charlottesville 1975.

Ramazani, R. K., 'Iran's Search for Regional Cooperation', in *Middle East Journal*, vol. 30, no. 2, 1976, pp. 173–186.

Sabahi, F., 'Literacy Corps', in *Encyclopaedia Iranica*, available at: <http://www.iranicaonline.org/articles/literacy-corps-1>.

Sabahi, F., *The Literacy Corps in Pahlavi Iran (1963–1979): Political, Social and Literary Implications*, Lugano 2002.

Saikal, A., 'Islamism, the Iranian Revolution, and the Soviet invasion of Afghanistan', in Leffler, M. P., and Westad, O. A. (eds.), *The Cambridge History of the Cold War, Volume 3: Endings*, Cambridge 2010, pp. 112–134.

Salehi-Isfahani, D., 'The Political Economy of Credit Subsidy in Iran, 1973–1978', in *International Journal of Middle East Studies*, vol. 21, no. 3, 1989, pp. 359–379.

Sampson, C. S., and Joyce, J. M. (eds.), *Foreign Relations of the United States, 1961–1963, Volume V: Soviet Union*, Washington, DC 1998.

Schayegh, C., 'Iran's Karaj Dam Affair: Emerging Mass Consumerism, the Politics of Promise, and the Cold War in the Third World', in *Comparative Studies in Society and History*, vol. 54, no. 3, 2012, pp. 612–643.

Sargent, D. J., *A Superpower Transformed: The Remaking of American Foreign Relations in the 1970s*, New York 2015.

Shakibi, Z., 'Pahlavism: The Ideologization of Monarchy in Iran', in *Politics, Religion & Society*, vol. 14, no. 1, 2013, pp. 114–135.

Shakibi, Z., 'The Rastakhiz Party and Pahlavism: The Beginnings of State Anti-Westernism in Iran', in *British Journal of Middle Eastern Studies*, vol. 45, no. 2, 2018, pp. 251–268.

Shannon, M. K., '"Contacts with the Opposition": American Foreign Relations, the Iranian Student Movement, and the Global Sixties', in *The Sixties*, vol. 4, no. 1, 2011, pp. 1–29.

Shannon, M. K., *Losing Hearts and Minds: American-Iranian Relations and International Education during the Cold War*, Ithaca 2017.

Siavoshi, S., *Liberal Nationalism in Iran: The Failure of a Movement*, Boulder 1990.

Simpson, B. R., 'Self-Determination, Human Rights, and the End of Empire', in *Humanity: An International Journal of Human Rights, Humanitarianism, and Development*, vol. 4, no. 2, 2013, pp. 239–260.

Slobodian, Q., *Foreign Front: Third World Politics in Sixties West Germany*, Durham 2012.

Summit, A. R., 'For a White Revolution: John F. Kennedy and the Shah of Iran', in *Middle East Journal*, vol. 58, no. 4, 2004, pp. 560–575.

Suri, J., *Power and Protest: Global Revolution and the Rise of Détente*, Cambridge, MA 2003.

Suri, J., 'The Rise and Fall of an International Counterculture, 1960–1975', in *The American Historical Review*, vol. 114, no. 1, 2009, pp. 45–68.

Vahabzadeh, P., *A Guerrilla Odyssey: Modernization, Secularism, Democracy, and the Fadai Period of National Liberation in Iran*, Syracuse 2010.

Vatandoust, G, 'The Status of Iranian Women During the Pahlavi Regime', in Fathi, A. (ed.), *Women and the Family in Iran*, Leiden 1985, pp. 107–130.

Warne, A., 'Psychoanalyzing Iran: Kennedy's Iran Task Force and the Modernization of Orientalism, 1961–3', in *The International History Review*, vol. 35, no. 2, 2013, pp. 396–422.

Westad, O. A., *The Global Cold War: Third World Interventions and the Making of Our Times*, Cambridge 2007.

Young, T. C., 'Iran in Continuing Crisis', in *Foreign Affairs*, vol. 40, no. 2, 1962, pp. 275–292.

Young, T. C., and Turner, T., *The Rise and Decline of the Zairian State*, Madison 1985.

Zia-Ebrahimi, R., *The Emergence of Iranian Nationalism: Race and the Politics of Dislocation*, New York 2016.

Zonis, M., *The Political Elite of Iran*, Princeton 1971.

1

Domesticating Cold War Economic Ideas: The Rise of Iranian Developmentalism in the 1950s and 1960s

Ramin Nassehi

The global battle of economic ideas was one of the defining elements of the Cold War. Capitalism, communism, and Third Worldism competed for the hearts and minds of peoples throughout the global South. However, the economic history of the late Pahlavi period is often written in isolation from this global ideological battle. Arguably the main reason behind this isolation is the pre-occupation of the Iranian Studies literature with exploring the economic roots of the 1979 revolution. Fixated on explaining this unique domestic event, the literature has increasingly 'turned inward', searching for those unique elements of Mohammad Reza Pahlavi's rule that perpetuated its eventual downfall. This inward looking perspective, however, misses the striking similarity that existed between the Pahlavi regime and developmentalist regimes of East Asia and Latin America in terms of economic management. The main thread connecting economic management in these regimes was the internalisation of certain global development doctrines, both by these countries' leaders and technocrats.

The shah and his economic technocrats are often conceptualised in the literature as an elite who followed no particular economic thinking and superficially engaged with different policy fads and fashions depending on their political interests or personal preferences. Moving in an opposite direction to this view, this chapter argues that from 1953 onwards Iran's economic policies and institutional development were deeply influenced by two specific rival schools of Cold War development thinking: the modernisation theory and Latin American protectionism. These ideas exerted their influence via the technocrats up to the shah. These technocrats would 'pick and choose' elements from these schools that they felt would fit Iran's economic conditions and employed them to influence the shah's economic decision-making. By addressing the role of these theories, this chapter links the economic history of pre-revolutionary Iran to the Cold War battle of ideas and, in doing so, offers a novel global perspective into this subject.

In this chapter, I focus on the 1950s and the 1960s, the period when Iranian technocrats first encountered different Cold War development doctrines. In this respect, I depart from the conventional focus in much of the literature on Pahlavi Iran which locate the roots of the revolution in the mismanagement of the 1973 oil boom and the economic turmoil of the late 1970s. Consequently, Iran's economic history in the 1950s and the 1960s is often viewed as a mere prelude to the subsequent turbulence of the 1970s. This teleological reading of economic history, through the prism of the 1979 revolution, exaggerates the uniqueness of Mohammad Reza Shah's economic rule. Distancing itself from the end point of the revolution, my study seeks to highlight the importance of a neglected factor – the economic ideology of technocrats – in driving Iran's economic trajectory in the 1950s and 1960s. While doing so, I stress the intellectual similarities and differences that existed between the Iranian technocrats and their counterparts in developmentalist regimes in East Asia and Latin America.

The chapter is organised in the following manner: the first section identifies the gap in literature that this paper aims to fill and discusses the archival sources used; the second section offers a brief review of modernisation theory and explains how this theory first made inroads into Iran in the 1950s; section three explores how and why Iranian technocrats synthesised the economic ideas of modernisation theorists with that of Latin American protectionists; section four highlights the impact of this ideological synthesis on Iran's economic development and foreign relations in the 1960s.

The Economic Historiography of Late Pahlavi Iran

A large body of literature in Iranian Studies is devoted to the study of economic development before the revolution. This literature can be divided into two categories. The first category is comprised of studies that examine the technical aspects of Iran's development plans and analyse the economic impact of these plans on aggregate income, employment, inflation and income inequality.

Studies conducted by Jahangir Amouzegar, Hassanali Mehran, Masoud Karshenas, Hashem Pesaran and Hadi Salehi-Isfahani fall into this category.[1] Almost unanimously these scholars divide the shah's economic record into two periods of 'before' and 'after' the 1973 oil boom. The first period is characterised as a period of stability, high economic growth and rapid industrialisation, while the latter is known as the period of economic instability, volatile growth and widening income inequality. However, due to its technical nature, this literature does not deeply engage with the political economy of development planning as it mostly treats the government's economic policies as 'given' and does not explore the manner in which these policies were shaped in the first place.

In contrast, there is a second category of economic studies that is concerned with the political economy of development before the revolution. The first wave of such studies, which were mainly conducted in the 1980s, analyse Iran's political economy through the Marxist lens of Dependency Theory. Relying on the core-periphery dichotomy, this theory claims that the international capitalist system blocks the economic 'catch-up' of developing countries by locking them into a dependent economic relationship with rich countries.[2] By applying this lens to their analyses, Fred Halliday and others argued that the Pahlavi state was a typical 'dependent state' that heavily relied on Western multinationals for the extraction of its oil and diversification of its economy and, as a consequence, it enjoyed little autonomy in setting its own economic policies.[3] This materialist view conceptualises the Pahlavi state as a US client state that passively absorbed US development doctrines and policy prescriptions in the 1950s and 1960s and had no economic ideology of its own. More generally, the first wave of political economy literature dismissed Iran's development model as a form of 'dependent capitalism', where foreign multinationals played a dominating role in the economy.

These dependency arguments, however, have been heavily criticised in subsequent literature for exaggerating the role and influence of foreign capital in the

1 Amouzegar, J., *Managing the Oil Wealth: OPEC's Windfalls and Pitfalls*, New York 2001; Karshenas, M., *Oil, State and Industrialisation in Iran*, Cambridge 1990; Mehran, H., *The Goals and Policies of the Central Bank of Iran 1960–1978*, Washington 2013; Esfahani, H. and Pesaran H., 'The Iranian Economy in the Twentieth Century: A Global Perspective', in *Iranian Studies*, vol. 42, no. 2, 2009, pp. 177–211.

2 Cardoso, F. H., and Faletto, E. *Dependency and Development in Latin America*, Berkeley 1979; Wallerstein, I. *Historical Capitalism: With Capitalist Civilization*, London 2011.

3 Halliday, F., *Iran: Dictatorship and Development*, New York 1979; Imam-Jomeh, I., *Petroleum-Based Accumulation and the State Form in Iran*, PhD thesis, Los Angeles 1985; Rahnema, S., 'Multinationals and Iranian Industry: 1957–1979', in *The Journal of Developing Areas*, vol. 24, no. 3, 1990, pp. 293–310.

economy. For example, Parvin Alizadeh outlines that direct foreign investment only accounted for 10% of fixed capital formation in the industrial sector in 1969.[4] This percentage later dropped to 1.5% by 1975 as the state became increasingly involved in industrialisation.[5] In addition to these economic critiques, a recent wave of revisionist historiography reveals that the Pahlavi state managed to incrementally enhance its autonomy from foreign powers, especially the United States, during the 1960s and increasingly operate as an active agent in the international economic and political order rather than a passive 'peripheral' actor.[6]

Alternatively, some scholars, most notably Homa Katouzian, have conceptualised the Pahlavi state as a rentier state that enjoyed a high degree of autonomy from foreign powers and domestic social classes due to having access to oil windfalls.[7] At the same time, this structure of power enabled the shah to centralise all the power in his own hands and rule indiscriminately. This arbitrary rule manifested itself also in economic policymaking: all the critical policies of the government had to be approved personally by the shah in the meetings of High Economic Council, where all key economic decisions were taken. The anecdotal evidence suggests that his economic decision-making was *ad hoc* and susceptible to policy fads and fashions. Correspondingly, it is regularly claimed that the shah followed no specific economic ideology and, more generally, showed no respect for economics as a discipline as he often mocked economists for their pessimism and lack of vision. In short, this argument puts the spotlight on the arbitrary nature of shah's rule to explain the economic choices of Pahlavi state in the 1960s and 1970s.[8]

This chapter dose not challenge the fact that the shah played an important role in economic policymaking, but it argues that reducing Iran's economic choices in the 1960s or even the 1970s to the agency of the shah is misleading. A comparison

---

4 Alizadeh, P., *The Process of Import-Substitution Industrialisation in Iran (1960–1978) with Particular Reference to the Case of the Motor Vehicle Industry*, Sussex 1984, p. 216. Here fixed capital formation refers to plant, machinery and equipment purchases as well as construction of commercial and industrial buildings.

5 Alizadeh, P., *The Process of Import-Substitution*, p. 216

6 Alvandi, R., *Nixon, Kissinger and the Shah: The United States and Iran in the Cold War*, New York 2014, pp. 172–181; Offiler, B., *US Foreign Policy and the Modernization of Iran: Kennedy, Johnson, Nixon and the Shah*, New York 2015, pp. 154–165; Afkhami, G., *The life and times of the Shah*, Los Angeles 2009, pp. 263–285; Milani, A., *The Shah*, New York 2011, pp. 355–405.

7 Katouzian, H., 'The Pahlavi regime in Iran', in Chehabi, H. E. and Linz, J. J. (eds.), *Sultanistic Regimes*, Baltimore 1998, pp. 182–206; Katouzian, H., *The Political Economy of Modern Iran: Despotism and Pseudo-Modernism, 1926–1979*, London 1981, pp. 234–255.

8 Razavi, H. and Vakil, F., *The Political Environment of Economic Planning in Iran, 1971–1983: From Monarchy to Islamic Republic*, Boulder 1984, pp. 61–97.

between Iran and other developing countries reveals that Pahlavi Iran's overall development model in the 1960s shared many similarities with the fastest growing economies in the Third World such as Brazil, Mexico, Taiwan and South Korea.[9] Like Iran, these countries followed a state-led industrialisation strategy that was based on protectionism. Even the economic mistakes that Iran made after the quadrupling of oil prices in 1973 were similarly made by other rapidly growing oil-rich countries of that period such as Mexico and Brazil.[10] These countries similarly decided to inject almost all of their windfall petrodollars into their domestic economies and embark on a series of massive development projects. Although they possessed no oil, South Korea and Taiwan made likewise policy mistakes following the 1973 oil boom; relying on the surplus petrodollars generated by this boom, they massively increased their foreign borrowing and started an overtly ambitious industrial drive at home.[11] The high degree of policy similarity between Iran and other rapidly growing developing countries of the 1960s and 1970s indicates the presence of a strong ideological affinity among the elite policymakers in these countries. Arguably, this ideological affinity exerted a much stronger and deeper influence on Iran's economic policymaking than the shah's arbitrary rule. This suggests that rather than just focusing on the role of shah, we should open the 'black box' of the Pahlavi state and carefully investigate the motivations and ideological commitments of top-level policymakers in order to gain a better understanding of the political economy of pre-revolutionary Iran.

There have been studies conducted on the individual technocrats who played a decisive role in the shah's regime. For instance, Frances Bostock and Geoffrey Jones focus on Abol Hassan Ebtehaj – the competent banker who almost singlehandedly built the foundations of modern economic planning in Iran.[12] Similarly, Vali Nasr explores the role played by Ali-Naqi Alikhani, the minister of economy from 1963 to 1969, in managing Iran's industrial take-off in that period.[13] Abbas Milani has also documented the rise and fall of Ebtehaj, Alikhani

9 Alizadeh, P., *The Process of Import-Substitution*, pp. 143–198.
10 Karl, T. L., *The Paradox of Plenty: Oil Booms and Petro-States*, Los Angeles 1997, pp. 189–222.
11 Sachs, J. D., and Williamson, J., 'External Debt and Macroeconomic Performance in Latin America and East Asia', in *Brookings Papers on Economic Activity*, vol. 1985, no. 2, 1985, p. 533.
12 Bostock, F. and Jones, G., *Planning and Power in Iran: Ebtehaj and Economic Development under the Shah*, London 1989.
13 Nasr, V., 'Politics within the Late-Pahlavi State: The Ministry of Economy and Industrial Policy, 1963–69', in *International Journal of Middle East Studies*, vol. 32, no. 1, 2000, pp. 97–122.

and other top-level economic policymakers of the Pahlavi regime.[14] However, the main shortcoming of such studies is that they do not investigate the ideological affinities of these individuals. This is while economic ideology constitutes the most powerful weapon of technocrats in policy battles; employing various ideas, they interpret how the economy works and, more importantly, how it should work. Therefore ideas are crucial persuasion tools for technocrats. Consequently, to fully understand the role and influence of Iranian technocrats within the Pahlavi state, it is necessary to study their economic ideology and the manner in which they used theories to influence key policy decisions. This study aims to fill that crucial gap in the Iranian Studies literature.

This chapter also contributes to the global history of modernisation theory and seeks to explore the manner in which this theory was applied to the Third World, especially in the rapidly developing economies of the 1960s and 1970s.[15] A new literature has emerged on the application of this theory in Iran, thanks to the studies conducted by Cyrus Schayegh, Roland Popp, Christopher Fisher and Victor Nemchenok.[16] Generally, these scholars show that, far from being articulated in Washington, the vision of modernisation in Iran was contested and negotiated by various national and external actors in almost every field, including infrastructure building, rural development, family planning and art and culture. This literature has not yet explored, however, the intellectual impact of modernisation theory on Iranian development planners who held senior policymaking positions. As mentioned earlier, there has been no comprehensive study conducted

14 Milani, A., *Eminent Persians: The Men and Women Who Made Modern Iran, 1941–1979*, London 2008.

15 Engerman, D. C., Gilman, N., Haefele M. H., and. Latham M. L., *Staging Growth: Modernization, Development and the Global Cold War*, Amherst 2003; Gilman, N., *Mandarins of the Future: Modernization Theory in Cold War America*, Baltimore 2007. Latham, M. L., *Modernisation as Ideology: American Social Science and 'Nation Building' in the Kennedy Era*, Chapel Hill, NC 2000; Latham, M. L., *The Right Kind of Revolution: Modernisation, Development and U.S. Foreign Policy from the Cold War to the Present*, New York 2011.

16 Schayegh, C., 'Iran's Karaj Dam Affair: Emerging Mass Consumerism, the Politics of Promise, and the Cold War in the Third World', in *Comparative Studies in Society and History*, vol. 54, no. 3, 2012, p. 642; Popp, R., 'An Application of Modernization Theory during the Cold War? The Case of Pahlavi Iran', in *The International History Review*, vol. 30, no. 1, 2008, pp. 97–98; Fisher, C. T., '"Moral Purpose is the Important Thing": David Lilienthal, Iran, and the Meaning of Development in the US, 1956–63', in *The International History Review*, vol. 33, No.3, 2011, p. 431; Nemchenok, V. V., '"That So Fair a Thing Should Be So Frail": The Ford Foundation and the Failure of Rural Development in Iran, 1953–1964', in *Middle East Journal*, vol. 63, no. 2, 2009, p. 284.

on the intellectual affinities of Iran's policymaking elite. This is in stark contrast to the historiography on economic planning in similar rapidly growing economies of that era such as South Korea and Brazil.[17] Drawing on an array of archival material, I aim to trace the intellectual evolution of Iranian technocrats and, in so doing, map out the impact of modernisation theory and other Cold War development doctrines on their economic thinking.

In terms of archival sources, this chapter draws on American and British documents as well as records from the World Bank, the International Monetary Fund, and the Central Bank of Iran. Moreover, it makes use of oral history interviews with key Iranian economic decision-makers conducted by Harvard University and the Foundation for Iranian Studies, as well as interviews conducted by the author with eight Iranian technocrats of the era, namely:

- Khodadad Farmanfarmaian: head of the Economic Bureau in the Plan Organisation (1958–1962), deputy governor of the Central Bank of Iran (1962–1968), governor of the Central Bank (1968–1970) and director of the Plan Organisation (1970–1973).
- Ali-Naqi Alikhani: minister of economy (1963–1969).
- Abdolmajid Majidi: director of the Budget Bureau in the Plan Organisation (1962–1967), minister of agricultural products and consumer affairs (1967–1968), minister of labour and social affairs (1968–1973), director of the Plan Organisation (1973–1977).
- Gholamreza Moqaddam: deputy governor of the Central Bank of Iran (1961–1963), deputy director of the Plan Organisation (1969–1973).
- Farrokh Najmabadi: deputy minister of economy (1967–1974), minister of industry and mines (1974–1977).
- Hasan-Ali Mehran: deputy minister of economy (1967–1975), governor of the Central Bank (1975–1978), minister of economy and finance (1978–1979).
- Firuz Vakil: undersecretary of informatics at the Plan Organisation (1972–1979).
- Hashem Pesaran: assistant to the vice governor of the Central Bank (1973–1974), head of the economic research department of the Central Bank (1974–1976), undersecretary in the Ministry of Education (1977–1978).

17 Haggard, S., *Pathways from the Periphery. The Politics of Growth in the Newly Industrialising Countries*, New York 1990, pp. 23–51.

Modernisation Theory and the Pahlavi Regime

Modernisation theory represented the dominant paradigm in the Cold War development thinking after the Second World War. Articulated by a vast array of American social scientists during the 1950s, this theory grew increasingly influential in Washington's policy circles so that by the 1960s it became the guiding doctrine behind US foreign policy in the Third World. Before explaining how this theory was introduced in Iran, it is helpful to provide a brief description of its intellectual tenants.

Modernisation theory was born out of the research done by a large group of American social scientists who specialised in various fields such as economics, anthropology, demography, sociology, political science and psychology. The main pioneers of this theory, namely the Harvard sociologist Talcott Parsons and the MIT economist Walt Rostow, sought to combine the insights provided by different branches of social science into an overarching theory of development that could be applied to every society. These scholars conceptualised development as an interdependent process of economic, social, cultural and political change that was universal across countries. This process entailed a transition from a 'traditional society', which was defined as rural, agricultural, kinship-based, irrational and religious, to a 'modern society', defined as urban, family-based, industrial, rational and secular. However, according to these theorists, this process had to be ignited and managed from the top by a vanguard group of 'elite modernisers' who had the necessary expertise in economics, demography, sociology and other social sciences.[18]

Since its inception, economic growth occupied a central place in modernisation theory. Walt Rostow believed that the main instigator of modernisation in societies was economic development (i.e., economic determinism). According to him, the key for igniting economic growth lay in top-down economic planning and state intervention. The rationale behind this prescription came from the burgeoning discipline of 'development economics'. As articulated by the leading scholars in this discipline, long-term economic development entailed a structural transformation from 'traditional sectors', which were subject to low-productivity and diminishing returns, to 'modern sectors', which exhibited high-productivity and increasing returns. However, this structural transformation could not take place automatically in poor countries through the forces of demand and supply due to the prevalence of market failures (i.e. 'bottlenecks' and 'rigidities'); this process,

18 Gilman, N., *Mandarins of the Future*, pp. 1–24; Latham, M. L., *Modernisation as Ideology*, pp. 1–21; Latham, M. L., 'Right Kind of Revolution', pp. 36–65.

according to the leading development economists, had to be facilitated by an elite group of technocrats through top-down planning and private sector promotion. These theories constituted the economic aspect of modernisation theory.[19]

Modernisation theory first made inroads into Iran after the 1953 coup, via the revitalisation of the Plan Organisation through foreign assistance. This institution, first established in 1949, was responsible for designing the development projects of the government. In the aftermath of the coup, the Pahlavi regime began to receive ample military aid and financial support from the United States.[20] Serving as an economic advisor to Eisenhower at the time, Walt Rostow lobbied for the provision of development aid to countries such as Iran to promote economic growth with the aim of preventing the spread of the 'Red Menace' into the Third World. However, to ensure that the aid inflows to Iran were spent on development projects, the Pahlavi state was required to improve the technical capacity of its planning institution. This need for economic planning was also felt by some policymakers inside the regime due to the rising oil revenues.[21] In response to the growing internal and external demand for economic planning, the shah asked Abol Hassan Ebtehaj, an impeccable technocrat who had been passionately advocating for fiscal discipline and planning in the government, to engage in the revitalisation of the Plan Organisation in 1954.[22] Ebtehaj, who had made his career as a senior manager at Bank Melli, was highly respected by foreign development experts for his competence. For instance, Eugene Black, then head of the World Bank, retrospectively praised him as 'an outstanding pioneer of Third World development'.[23] Likewise, the British embassy considered him as 'by far the strongest and ablest of all Persians and perhaps indeed the ablest Government Official in the Middle East'.[24] He was also celebrated as 'the symbol of incorruptibility' by many due to his financial honesty.[25]

The revitalisation of the Plan Organisation by Ebtehaj marked the emergence of a new modernising technocratic elite inside the Pahlavi regime. The Ford Foundation and World Bank assisted him in institution building; the former provided

19 Gilman, N., *Mandarins of the Future*, pp. 1–24.
20 'Financial situation in Iran', April 1957, the IMF Documents (DM/57/16).
21 Ebtehaj, Abol Hassan, *Khaterat-e Abol Hassan Ebtehaj* [Abo Hassan Ebtehaj's Memoirs] Volumes 1 and 2, Tehran 1996.
22 Milani, A., *Eminent Persians, Volume Two*, pp. 735–744.
23 Bostock, F. and Jones, G., *Planning and Power in Iran*, p. vii.
24 Bostock, F. and Jones, G., *Planning and Power in Iran*, p. 5.
25 'Seven Year Economic Plan for Iran', 1958, FO 371/133023 (File 1103).

the financial assistance while the latter supplied the technical expertise.[26] The Ford Foundation was at the time a heavy supporter of modernisation ideas and a firm advocate of economic planning in the Third World.[27] This foundation gave a grant to Ebtehaj to hire a team of advisors from the Harvard School of Government to recruit and train a new group of Iranian technocrats for the Plan Organisation. Intellectually, the Harvard School of Government was at the time home to many prominent development economists such as Edward Mason (the School's Dean and the head of Iran's team), Alexander Eckstein and John K. Galbraith.[28] Unsurprisingly, this intellectual affection for development economics influenced the recruitment process in the Plan Organisation, as revealed by Khodadad Farmanfarmaian, one of Ebtehaj's protégés who later became one of the prime architects of economic planning in Iran. A Stanford-educated economist who was made responsible for recruiting experts, Farmanfarmaian vividly recalled his personal prejudice in favour of candidates who were trained in the Anglo-Saxon school of development economics:

> It was very difficult to find Iranians who were being trained as economists and [we] were looking for economists. We weren't looking for the sort of people who were educated in the softer sciences. And in recent years, when some people accuse me of being prejudiced in favour of individuals educated in Anglo-Saxon countries, I've reasoned that from their curriculum or from the knowledge that I had about, let's say, German training or French training, those people were not the type of economists and planners that one wanted… we wanted more people who had grounding in hard theory.[29]

This remark shows how, in the spirit of the modernisation school, Iranian technocrats viewed themselves as a group of 'elite modernisers' who were going to promote economic development in their home country by application of their scientific knowledge and expertise. Eventually, through the support of the Ford Foundation and the World Bank, Ebtehaj managed to gather a young group of

---

26 'Seven Year Economic Plan for Iran', 1958, FO 371/133023 (File 1103).

27 Gilman, N., *Mandarins of the Future*, p. 46.

28 Meier, G. M., *Biography of a Subject: An Evolution of Development Economics*, Oxford 2004, pp. 207–208.

29 Khodadad Farmanfarmaian, Iranian Oral History Collection (hereafter IOHC), Harvard University, tape recording 2; Farmanfarmaian himself had written his PhD on building backward and forward linkages in Iranian oil industry, which was then a central topic in development economics. Khodadad Farmanfarmaian, July 2010, personal interview.

Iranian technocrats, who had mostly PhD degrees in economics or engineering from the Ivy League universities in the United States. These technocrats, who were negatively referred to as 'Harvard boys' by the political elite, received higher salaries than ordinary bureaucrats in other ministries.[30]

The story of the emergence of elite planners in Iran during this period is very similar to the cases of South Korea and Taiwan in the 1950s and Indonesia in the mid-1960s. In all these countries, a group of economists and engineers were sent to the United States to be trained in Ivy League universities with the financial support of the Ford or Rockefeller Foundations. The American motive behind such projects was to create a group of sympathetic elite modernisers in these countries who, upon their return, would act as agents of not only economic modernisation, but also political and cultural change. Going through training projects, these Third World technocrats came under the strong influence of modernisation theorists such as Mason, Rostow and Galbraith, who at the time enjoyed tremendous intellectual influence in American policymaking circles. But at the same time, these Asian economists were exposed to rival schools of economic thought during their trainings in the United States. As will be explained later, this exposure to intellectual diversity encouraged these economists to synthesise modernisation theory with other ideas upon their return home.[31]

In the case of Iran, the young technocrats shared many of the ideas of the modernisation theorists. Firstly, they were all 'deeply enamoured of economic growth' as described by Farmanfarmaian, and saw economic development as the panacea for Iran's social, cultural and political ills. They believed that, with economic growth, the shah's dictatorship would automatically diminish in time. As stressed by Farmanfarmaian:

> At that time he [Ebtehaj] introduced me to a basic tenet of his thought which was that once you raised the standard of living for people through deliberate economic development, all these political problems – he was referring to

30 'Seven Year Economic Plan for Iran', 1958, FO 371/133023 (File 1103).

31 Kim, B., 'The Leviathan: Economic Bureaucracy under Park', in Kim, P., and Vogel E. F., *The Park Chung Hee Era: The Transformation of South Korea*, Massachusetts 2011, pp. 200–233; Brazinsky, G. A., 'Korean Modernization: Modernization Theory and South Korean intellectuals', in Engerman, D. C., Gilman N., Haefele, M. H., and Latham, M. E. (eds.), *Staging Growth: Modernization, Development and the Global Cold War*, Amherst 2003, p. 251–275; Wade, R., *Governing the Market: Economic Theory and the Role of Government in East Asian Industrialization*, Princeton 2004, p. 195–288; Simpson, B. R., *Economists With Guns: Authoritarian Development and U.S.-Indonesian Relations, 1960–1968*, Stanford 2008, p. 1–37.

> corruption, inefficiencies, jealousies, etc. – will be wiped out from their awareness, from their conscience, from their character, if you will. And as the standard of living increased, people would become more straightforward, more cooperative, and that you would get true social, political change from the development of the country.[32]

Secondly, the technocrats prioritised industrialisation above agricultural development. This bias for industrialisation ran deep in the Plan Organisation as pointed out by Reza Niyazmand who was a member of Technical Bureau at the time: 'we were either manufacturing engineers or economists; we didn't know anything about agriculture... they even hadn't sent a single one of us to study agricultural development.'[33] Perhaps the prime reason behind this neglect of agriculture was Iran's growing oil revenues. Access to oil rents meant that Iranian policymakers did not have to rely on taxing the agricultural sector to extract funds for investment in the industrial sector, unlike their counterparts in resource-poor countries like Taiwan and South Korea.[34] So, the presence of oil revenues in a way divorced the process of industrialisation from agricultural development in Iran and reduced the incentive of policymakers for promoting agricultural productivity. To be sure, the shah did introduce a major land reform later on, but arguably the prime motive behind this reform was to crush the political power of the landed elite rather than increasing the productivity of the agricultural sector.

Thirdly, the technocrats believed that Iran's economic modernisation had to be driven by the private sector. In line with Rostow, they thought the main job of the state was to 'solve the problem of entrepreneurship in the take-off stage'. This required the state to support the emergence of a new class of 'modern' capitalists in Iran, who were willing to take risks and import new technologies from the West. It is worth mentioning that in the early 1950s, Iran had a weak modern private sector, compared to South Korea, Taiwan, Brazil and India.[35] The technocrats reasoned that the enrichment of a modern capitalist class in Iran would benefit

---

32 Khodadad Farmanfarmaian, IOHC, Harvard University, tape recording 3.

33 'Revayat-e Niyazmand az por hashiyeh-tarin tarh-e keshavarzi-ye qabl az enqelab: Se dalil-e Shah baray-e ejra-ye eslahat-e arzi' [Niyazmand on the most controversial agricultural reform of the pre-Revolutionary period: three reasons why the Shah implemented the land reform], *Tejarat-e Farda*, no. 76, November 2014.

34 Kay, C., 'Asia's and Latin America's Development in Comparative Perspective: Landlords, Peasants and Industrialization', in *Institute of Social Studies Working Paper*, no. 336, 2001, pp. 43–45.

35 Alizadeh, P., *The Process of Import-Substitution*, pp. 143–198.

the whole of society because it would push the economy through the take-off stage and generate a self-reinforcing cycle of private capital accumulation and economic growth. The following remark by Farmanfarmaian highlights the allure of this trickle-down ideology among the technocrats: 'we were firm believers in the need for growth and cited the greatest world economic authorities in the defence of the thesis that once you have growth, slowly, slowly benefits begin to trickle down to the other classes and in the long term, income distribution will improve.'[36] Similarly, Reza Niyazmand recalls: 'our job was to make people millionaires. Without millionaires the country would not develop.'[37] Therefore, like most development economists at the time, Iranian planners assumed that income inequality was necessary for the preliminary stages of development.

Finally, like Rostow, the technocrats considered economic development as a more effective tool than military development in ensuring Iran's domestic political stability. Hence, they prioritised economic development over military build-up. Importantly, however, this idea was not shared by the shah; he believed that alongside investing in development projects, Iran had to build a strong army to guarantee her national security. In other words, for the shah, rapid economic growth was not sufficient for ensuring the survival of his regime.[38]

Supported by the ideas listed above, the Plan Organisation functioned in the 1950s as a typical technocratic institution envisaged by the modernisation school. It invested heavily on infrastructure projects such as building dams, roads and ports to pave the way for private investment in industry. In these projects, the Plan Organisation consciously copied the Tennessee Valley Authority, the American institution cherished by technocratic elites across the world as a role model of top-down planning. In fact, Ebtehaj asked David Lilienthal, former head of the Tennessee Valley Authority, to consult with the Plan Organisation in its grand development projects in Khuzestan.[39] Moreover, while practising top-down economic planning, Iran followed a free trade policy as recommended by modernisation theorists.[40] This policy, which had been put in place since 1953 to serve

36 Khodadad Farmanfarmaian, IOHC, Harvard University, tape recording 2.

37 'Goftogu ba Reza Niyazmand darbareh-ye teknokrasi-ye ʿasr-e Pahlavi: revayat-e sanʿati shodan' [A discussion with Reza Niyazmand about technocracy in the Pahlavi era: the story of industrialisation], *Tejarat-e Farda*, no. 70, November 2013.

38 Offiler, B., *US Foreign Policy and Modernisation of Iran*, p. 8; In time, the issue of military development generated severe tensions between the technocrats and the shah. Bostock, F. and Jones, G., *Planning and Power in Iran*, pp. 87–147.

39 Abol Hassan Ebtehaj, IOHC, Harvard University, page 184 of the manuscript.

40 '1959 Consultations- Iran', October 1959, the IMF Documents (SM /59/66).

the economic interests of classes that had supported the coup (i.e. landlords and *bāzāris*), meant that the technocrats had to direct infrastructure investment towards sectors in which Iran had the potential to compete internationally.

Alongside directly investing in infrastructure, the Plan Organisation also tried to indirectly promote private investment in the late 1950s. The first step in implementing this strategy was to build a development bank that would specialise in giving credit subsidies to large-scale industrial firms to kick-start private investment in this sector. As before, Ebtehaj asked for the World Bank's support in institution building.[41] Black, the head of the World Bank, welcomed this project and helped Ebtehaj establish the Industrial and Mining Development Bank of Iran (IMDBI) in 1959. The rationale behind this bank was to promote 'domestic and foreign investments in private industrial enterprises in Iran'.[42] The World Bank's expectation was that under Iran's free trade regime, the IMDBI would facilitate private investment in industries in which Iran enjoyed a comparative advantage such as labour-intensive industries. Therefore, as envisaged by Rostow's model, Iran would start off by specialising in consumer goods industries and then gradually shift towards intermediate and heavy industries as the country's income per capita increased.

Distinctively, the IMDBI was established as a private enterprise, in contrast to the state-owned development banks in Brazil, South Korea, and Taiwan.[43] This factor indicated Iran's stronger commitment to private sector promotion than other rapidly growing developing countries at the time. From the beginning, both Ebtehaj and the World Bank advisors insisted on private-ownership of the IMDBI to reduce the risk of government interference in distribution of credit subsidies.[44] The idea was that governments would financially support the development bank, but at the same time, leave the allocation of loans in the hands of private owners.[45] Initially, through Black, Ebtehaj attracted two Wall Street investment banks, Lazard Frères & Co. and Chase International Investment Corporations, to invest in the IMDBI. At the same time, he engaged a group of domestic private investors.

41 Abol Hassan Ebtehaaj, IOHC, Harvard University, pages 216–221 of the manuscript.

42 'Report and recommendations of the President to the Executive Directors on a proposed loan to Industrial and Mining Development Bank of Iran', August 1959, The IBRD, Report no. P-203, p. 1.

43 Amsden, A., *The Rise of 'the Rest': Challenges to the West from Late-Industrializing Economies*, Oxford 2001, pp. 125–251.

44 Abol Hassan Ebtehaaj, IOHC, Harvard University, pages 216–227 of the manuscript.

45 Mason, E. S., and Asher, R. E., *The World Bank since Bretton Woods*, Washington 1973, pp. 335–380.

Correspondingly, the bank was set up with a dual equity structure; forty percent of its shares were owned by a group of multinationals from the United States, Britain, France, Belgium, Germany, Holland and Italy (class 'B' shares) and the rest of its equity were owned by a limited number of domestic private firms (class 'A' shares).[46]

The technocrats hoped that in time the IMDBI would facilitate the rise of a new modern industrialist class and overshadow the role of traditional classes – the bazaar, in particular – in the country's economy. Inspired by the 'traditional/modern' dichotomy of the modernisation school, they actively sought to encourage *bāzāri*s to become industrialists by offering them various financial incentives such as credit subsidies and tax breaks. In this respect, Niyazmand, a technocrat who later became the deputy minister of economy, recalls:

> We sought to turn *bāzāri*s into industrialists; that was our job… for instance, we would say to a merchant, who had been importing textile, to produce textile in Iran… we would say to Haji Barkhordar that, instead of importing TVs, produce TVs inside your country. If you don't do this, we will increase the tariff rates for TVs, then you will not make any profit… this was our tool… I had to invite importers and convince them to produce the same goods inside… we decided to choose policies that facilitated the business environment for industrialists.[47]

The shah was supportive of this social and economic transformation as he considered the bazaar to be a symbol of 'backwardness' and 'traditionalism'.[48] In line with modernisation theory, technocrats attempted to propel Iran's economy from merchant capitalism to industrial capitalism in the 1950s through infrastructure investment and the provision of credit subsidies. In short, they sought to *invent* a modern private sector that shared 'the spirit of capitalism'.

---

46 'Report and recommendations of the President to the Executive Directors on a proposed loan to Industrial and Mining Development Bank of Iran', August 1959, The IBRD, Report no. P-203.

47 'Goftogu ba Reza Niyazmand'.

48 The shah particularly shared the prevalent ideological disdain for the bazaar: 'It remains my conviction that their time is past. The Bazaar consists of a cluster of small shops. There is usually little sunshine or ventilation so that they are basically unhealthy environs. The Bazaaris are a fanatic lot, highly resistant to change because their locations afford a lucrative monopoly.' Keshavarzian, A., *Bazaar and State in Iran: the Politics of the Tehran Marketplace*, Cambridge 2007, p 133.

The Ideological Slide towards Latin American Protectionism

Economic crises often provide a strong impetus for ideological change and policy revision. As Dani Rodrik argues, such crises provide a fertile moment for new ideas to gain popularity.[49] The Pahlavi regime underwent such an ideological change after being hit by a balance of payment crisis in 1960. This intellectual revision involved a slide towards the Latin American protectionist school and Import Substitution Industrialisation (ISI).

In the late 1950s, Iran experienced a widening current account deficit due to the growing volume of imports that had been financed through the accumulation of foreign debt.[50] At the same time, the multinational oil consortium that managed Iranian oil decided to lower its sale prices in 1959 by 14 cents from $1.90 to $1.76 to protect its market share.[51] This oil price drop, together with the growing foreign debt, culminated in a foreign exchange crisis in 1960. As a result, Iran's economy was bailed out by the IMF and in return, a set of austerity policies labelled as a 'stabilisation package' were imposed on Iranian policymakers. This package included sharp reductions in fiscal spending and severe restriction on credit growth. It also involved the introduction of strict import quotas and tariff barriers for improving the foreign exchange reserves. These contractionary policies, in turn, led to declining output and rising unemployment between 1960 and 1962 and consequently triggered social unrest. This episode of unrest coincided with the election of President John F. Kennedy and the ascendency of modernisation theory in American policy circles. Rostow began to follow developments in Iran closely as deputy national security advisor to the president. During this austerity period the Plan Organisation's 'Harvard boys' became a strong point of contact for the Kennedy administration because of their economic expertise and ideological proximity to the American model.[52]

The outbreak of the crisis and the subsequent austerity period had a profound impact on the ideology of Iran's technocrats. They began to question the merits of following a free trade policy and shifted intellectually towards the Latin American protectionist school. In contrast to modernisation theorists who were firm believers in free trade and internationalism, the Latin American protectionists, headed

49 Rodrik, D., 'When Ideas Trump Interests: Preferences, Worldviews and Policy Innovations', in *National Bureau of Economic Research*, NBER Working Paper no. 19631, 2013, p. 25.
50 'Staff report and recommendations 1962 Consultations', June 1962, the IMF Documents (SM/62/64).
51 Skeet, I., *OPEC: Twenty-Five Years of Prices and Politics*, Cambridge 1988, pp. 1–7.
52 Karshenas, M., *Oil, State and Industrialisation*, pp. 131–139.

by Argentine economist Raúl Prebisch, argued that the pursuit of free trade policy was detrimental for the economic development of poor countries. According to the protectionists, exposure to international competition would hold developing countries in a 'poverty trap' by forcing them to specialise in low-value added primary sectors. To support this argument, they showed that the price of primary commodities tended to fall relative to industrial goods in the long-term (i.e. Terms of Trade Hypothesis), hence plunging commodity exporting economies into a vicious circle of debt dependency and foreign exchange crisis. Alternatively, these thinkers preached protectionism and Import Substitution Industrialisation (ISI) at the initial stages of development. According to them, developing countries first had to support their infant industries behind high tariff barriers and then gradually push those industries towards global competition through export promotion.[53]

The main intellectual hub of this school was the United Nations Economic Commission for Latin America and the Caribbean (ECLAC). Through this international institution, Prebisch and his colleague the Swedish economist Hans Singer first started to popularise their ideas internationally during the 1950s. Their main agenda was to remove the global obstacles to 'catch-up' development in the South by reforming the existing international trade regime, the General Agreement on Tariff and Trade (GATT), on two fronts. Firstly, they pressed for devising a global scheme for stabilisation of commodity prices to reduce export volatility for developing countries. In line with this goal, they also argued for the removal of agricultural subsidies in rich countries. Secondly, they demanded that rich countries provide preferential access to manufacturing exports from developing countries for a limited period of time (ten years). To be sure, the GATT system did provide ample room for developing countries to practise protectionism and support their infant industries, but according to Prebisch, protectionism had to gradually give way to export promotion. For that to happen, developing countries needed to gain preferential access to rich markets. By the early 1960s, these ideas became increasingly popular on the global level as a growing number of newly independent nations became disenchanted with the existing global trade regime. The United Nations explicitly embraced these ideas as an alternative paradigm to the modernisation doctrine, which eventually resulted in the creation of the United Nations Conference on Trade and Development (UNCTAD) in 1964.[54]

53 Meier, G. M., *Biography of a Subject*, pp. 65–67.
54 Toye, J., 'From New era to Neoliberalism: US Strategy on Trade Finance and Development in the United Nations, 1964–82', in *Forum for Development Studies*, vol. 32, no. 1, 2005, pp. 143, 151–180.

Given this global background, the Iranian technocratic elite became attracted to Prebisch's theories in the early 1960s, especially because Iran, a commodity exporting economy, had recently experienced a balance of payment crisis. The Prebisch-Singer hypothesis not only provided these technocrats with a 'mental map' through which they could interpret the 1960 crisis, but also gave them an immediate solution – import substitution – for economic recovery. Therefore, this hypothesis immediately found its way into the Pahlavi regime's developmentalist discourse.

For instance, the very first policy documents published by the Central Bank of Iran referred to the falling terms of trade for commodity prices in their analysis of 'World Economic Situations'; the 1961 annual report highlighted that 'between 1956 and 1961 the price of commodities fell by 6% while the price of industrial goods increased by 7%'.[55] Picking up this point, the shah stressed at the 1963 Tehran Economic Conference that 'raw materials were becoming cheaper each year while manufactured goods supplied by the countries buying these raw materials were becoming more expensive: thus the more advanced and industrial nations were exploiting the backward countries producing only agricultural and raw materials'.[56] Accordingly, he urged economic diversification and industrialisation through protectionism. In time, the technocrats showed more explicit appreciation for the economic ideas of Prebisch and UNCTAD. The Central Bank, for instance, championed the cause of this conference in its annual reports published between 1964 and 1968 by frequently referring to the problem of declining 'terms of trade' for developing countries.[57] As an example, the 1967 report highlighted that:

> Coupled with unfavourable terms of trade, the real purchasing power of their [developing countries] exports has diminished noticeably. Consequently, the developing countries' financial ability to increase imports, which is essential to attain a reasonable rate of growth, is also decreased thus exposing them to the problems of import capacity. Under these conditions, the implementation of the recommendations made by UNCTAD has gained greater importance than ever.[58]

55 'Annual report for 1961', March 1962, The Central Bank of Iran, p. 5.

56 'Economic planning and development', 1963, FO 371/170389 (File 1102).

57 'Annual report for 1964', March 1965, The Central Bank of Iran, 1–9; 'Annual report for 1965', March 1966, The Central Bank of Iran, pp. 1–3; 'Annual report for 1966', March 1967, The Central Bank of Iran, 5 & 13; 'Annual report for 1968', March 1969, The Central Bank of Iran, pp. 29–30 & pp. 46–49.

58 'Annual report for 1967', March 1968, The Central Bank of Iran, p. 6.

Moreover, the technocrats explicitly alluded to UNCTAD and Prebisch in their speeches. For instance, at the conference held for Commission on Asian and Far Eastern Affairs (CAFEA) of the International Chamber of Commerce in Tehran in 1964, the governor of Central Bank argued that:

> We have to bear in mind that the income gap between industrial and developing countries has been continuously widening in the recent years and this has been due to the falling price of raw materials relative to industrial goods. If uninterrupted, this trend can endanger the international peace... Dr. Prebisch points out that over 60% of developing countries are now specialised in unproductive agricultural activities. Is there any alternative for these countries to develop their economies other than industrialisation? This ratio [agriculture to industry] is 75 to 25 in Iran and the transformation of this structure is the goal that the Shah has set for Iran's economic development.[59]

It is important to stress that throughout the shift towards protectionism and import substitution, the technocrats remained committed to many tenants of modernisation theory, specifically to private sector promotion. Hence, they intellectually synthesised the ideas of the modernisation school with that of Latin American protectionism. The outcome of this synthesis was a native developmentalist discourse that preached a business-oriented import substitution policy.

Iranian Developmentalism in the 1960s

Recovering from the humiliating experience of the austerity period, the shah became determined to rapidly diversify Iran's economy away from oil by promoting industrialisation. To realise this goal, he supported the creation of new policymaking institutions and placed the management of the economy in the hands of technocrats.[60] The technocrats decided to keep the high tariff barriers that had been introduced since 1960 and to start an import substitution policy; their goal was to initially help domestic industries to develop through protectionism and then gradually push those industries towards global competition through

59 'Konferans-e CAFEA va seminar-e bankdari-ye asiya'i' [The CAFEA Conference and the Asian Banking Seminar], The Central Bank of Iran Bulletin (henceforth CBIB), No 31 (March 1964).

60 'Pul-e naft bala rafteh bud va ma balad nabudim masrafash konim' [Alikhani: The oil revenue had gone up but we didn't know how to spend it], *Radio Farda*, 4 September 2010.

export promotion.[61] At the same time, they retained their commitment to creating a modern industrialist class in Iran. Therefore, they based their import substitution strategy on promoting the domestic private sector rather than state-owned companies. This pro-business orientation is best expressed by a leading policy figure, Mehdi Samiʿi,[62] who was the governor of the Central Bank:

> It is evident that governments have announced their inability [in generating economic profits] one after another. It is said that 'governments are not good entrepreneurs'. It is true, given that, so far, our governments have not been good entrepreneurs.[63]

To encourage the emergence of modern businesses, the Ministry of Economy was established with the technical support of Plan Organisation and the Central Bank in 1963 and the shah placed Alikhani, a young Sorbonne-educated economist who had a background in private business and Iran's intelligence service, SAVAK, as the head of this ministry.[64] In terms of economic thinking, Alikhani was a firm believer in protectionism and private sector promotion like the rest of the top policy figures.[65] In fact, he had written his PhD on the role of government in fostering industrialisation. Mohammad Yeganeh, who had a strong background as an academic researcher, was also selected as the deputy minister of economy.[66] Having received a PhD in economics from the Columbia University, he had been employed as a top researcher at the United Nations Industrial Development Organisation in Vienna.[67] After supporting the creation of the Ministry of Economy, the shah gave a considerable degree of autonomy to Alikhani and Samiʿi to lead the economy out of recession.

---

61 'Iran-1963 Article XIV Consultations', October 1963, the IMF Documents (SM/63/100); 'Economic planning and development', 1963, FO 371/170389 (File 1102).
62 Milani, *Eminent Persians, Volume Two*, pp. 760–771.
63 'Sarmayeh gozari-ye sanʿati dar Iran: kholaseh-ye sokhanrani-ye aqa-ye Mehdi Samiʿi' [Industrial investment in Iran: a summary of speech given by Mehdi Samiʿi], CBIB, no. 16-1 (December 1962).
64 Nasr, V., 'Politics within the Late-Pahlavi State', p. 106–107; Milani, A., *Eminent Persians, Volume Two*, p. 56–63.
65 Alikhani, March 2013, personal interview; Moghadam, February 2012, personal interview.
66 The biography of Mohammad Yeganeh was provided at 'Sanayeʿ va maʿaden dar barnameh-ye chaharom: sokhanrani-ye jenab-e aqay-e Mohammad-e Yeganeh, moʿaven-e eqtesadi-ye vezarat-e eqtesad' [Industries and mines in the Fourth Plan: the speech given by Mohammad Yeganeh, the deputy minister of economy], CBIB, no. 84 (August 1968).
67 'Sanayeʿ va maʿaden'.

As a first step, the Ministry of Economy invited a mission from the United Nations to study Iran's industrial sector. In line with UNCTAD's ideas, this mission advised the government to start the first phase of import substitution and identified a number of consumer goods industries, such as textile, furniture, and beverages, that were suitable for this purpose.[68] Subsequently, on the back of rising oil revenues, the technocrats embarked on an impressive ISI take-off during the Third Five-Year Development that ran from 1963 to 1968. They provided private firms with tax breaks and showered them with credit subsidies via the IMDBI.[69] These measures facilitated the rise of new private industrial conglomerates that were engaged in consumer goods industries such as air conditioners, automobiles, furniture, and shoes.[70] Naturally, these new-born conglomerates had multinational partners, but as mentioned, these partners did not play a dominant role in the economy.[71] In this respect, Iranian conglomerates resembled large-scale industrial firms (chaebols) in South Korea.

During the Third Plan, Iran's economy grew by 9.8% per year, while inflation remained below 2%.[72] Manufacturing output increased by 11% annually and, in effect, urban employment in this sector expanded by 77% over the span of five years.[73] By 1968, Iran managed to develop a flourishing domestic consumer goods sector by following a pro-business industrial policy, as evident from the five-fold increase in the value of output in this sector since 1959.[74] According to Rostow's assessment, by the end of this plan, the country was at the 'point on the development ladder where the "take off" is just about finished and the nation is beginning to diffuse its resources and technology into a broad range of new industries'.[75] Accordingly, President Lyndon B. Johnson praised the shah for his effective economic leadership, mentioning that 'he did not know any country… where the leadership has been wiser or more effective. Some people talk about

68 'United Nations technical assistance in the industrialisation of Iran', CBIB, no. 13 (May-June 1964).
69 'The Economic Development of Iran, Volume III: Statistical Appendix', The IBRD, Report no. 378-IRN (October 1974).
70 'Iran Chamber of Industries and Mines', *Financial Times*, May 24, 1968.
71 Alizadeh, P., *The Process of Import-Substitution*, p. 216.
72 'The Economic Development of Iran, Volume III: Statistical Appendix', The IBRD, Report no. 378-IRN (October 1974), pp. 16 & 67.
73 'The Economic Development of Iran, Volume III: Statistical Appendix', The IBRD, Report no. 378-IRN (October 1974), p. 111.
74 Alizadeh, P., *The Process of Import-Substitution*, p. 208.
75 'Memorandum of Conversation', 13 June 1968, in Howland, N. D. (ed.), *Foreign Relations of the United States* (henceforth FRUS), *1964–1968, Volume XXII, Iran*, Washington, DC 1999, Document 298.

development. Some people do it'.[76] He even looked to translate 'Iran's experience to Vietnam'.[77]

Importantly, however, in terms of heavy and capital goods industries, Iran severely lagged behind other rapidly industrialising economies in the Third World. For instance, the share of electric and non-electric machinery in the total manufacturing value added was only 2.9% in Iran in mid-1960s, compared to 11.2% and 10.3% in India and Brazil respectively. In fact, Iran had started its import substitution in the virtual absence of any machinery industry. Thus, the country had a lot of 'catching up' to do in terms of building intermediate and capital goods industries. To fulfil this industrial ambition, the shah had already started approaching the Soviet Union from the early 1960s.[78]

Looking Eastward

When Iran embarked on import substitution industrialisation (ISI) in 1963, neither the United States nor the World Bank opposed this protectionist policy. This was because the policy was initially aimed at protecting and developing consumer goods industries, a sector in which Iran had a comparative advantage according to the World Bank.[79] The ISI policy, the first phase of which was implemented in the Third Development Plan (1963–1968), was approved by the World Bank as 'the logical first step in industrialisation policy'.[80] In addition, Iran's protectionist industrial policy was aligned with the economic interests of multinational firms, since it allowed them to conduct their business behind high tariff berries in partnership with the new born domestic conglomerates.

Importantly, however, the World Bank stressed that after finishing the Third Plan, Iran had to continue supporting industries that conformed to her comparative advantage, such as light industries and the petrochemical sector.[81] This assessment was also shared by Rostow, who continued to follow Iranian affairs as a

76 'Memorandum of Conversation', 5 December 1968, in Howland, N. D. (ed.), *FRUS, 1964–1968, Volume XXII, Iran*, Document 321.

77 'Memorandum for President Johnson's Diary', 7 June 1967, in Howland, N. D. (ed.), *FRUS 1964–1968, Volume XXII, Iran*, Document 211.

78 Alizadeh, P., *The process of Import-Substitution*, pp. 226–227.

79 'Industrialisation of Iran: The record, the problems and the prospects', The IBRD, Record no. SA-14 (May 1970), pp. 13–20.

80 'Industrialisation of Iran: The record, the problems and the prospects', The IBRD, Record no. SA-14 (May 1970), p. 25.

81 'Industrialisation of Iran: The record, the problems and the prospects', The IBRD, Record no. SA-14 (May 1970), p. 13.

senior advisor to President Johnson. Advising Samiʿi, Rostow emphasised the importance of 'getting industry to develop in such a way as to support and complement the agricultural development' and at the same time highlighted the merits of developing petrochemical industries: 'the important principle will be for Iran to reap the profits of value added to its raw materials rather than to let these profits go to processors outside Iran.'[82] In a nutshell, he urged the policymakers to only support sectors in which the country had a comparative advantage and refrain from moving towards heavy and capital-intensive sectors.

However, ignoring these prescriptions, the shah and the technocrats sought to move Iran's ISI towards intermediate and capital goods industries after finishing the Third Plan. Like most leaders in the Third World, the shah equated economic progress with establishing large infrastructure projects and heavy industries. He was particularly keen on building a steel industry to showcase Iran's advancement and growing economic independence. Unsurprisingly, the World Bank was against this project since it did not conform to the country's comparative advantage; in fact, the bank had already rejected Iran's loan request for this project on several occasions in the past on the same grounds.[83] Yet, despite this discouragement, the Pahlavi regime remained determined to move towards the development of heavy industries in its Fourth Five-Year Development Plan (1968–1972). The technocratic and political elite believed that taking the ISI model a step further would not only reduce the import needs of the industrial sector in the future, but also direct the industrialisation programme towards sectors that had high geopolitical importance.[84] Ultimately, to realise its developmental goals, the Pahlavi regime approached the Soviet Union. This move ushered in a new era of economic cooperation between Iran and the Communist bloc throughout the 1960s.

Iran and the Soviet Union had already normalised their relationship in the early 1960s.[85] Following on from this normalisation, the shah charged Alikhani, the new minister of economy, with conducting a round of economic negotiations with the communist bloc. These negotiations resulted in a series of trade deals between Iran and the Soviet Union (1964 and 1967), Poland (1965), Hungary

82 'Memorandum of Conversation', 6 June 1964, in Howland, N. D. (ed.), *FRUS 1964–1968, Volume XXII, Iran*, Document 37; 'Memorandum of Conversation', 13 June 1968, in Howland, N. D. (ed.), *FRUS 1964–1968, Volume XXII, Iran*, Document 298.

83 'Economic planning and development', 1963, FO 371/170389 (File 1102).

84 'Economy', 1966, FO 371/186690 (File 1101).

85 Alvandi, R., 'The Shah's Détente with Khrushchev: Iran's 1962 Missile Base Pledge to the Soviet Union', in *Cold War History*, vol. 14, no. 3, 2014, p. 423.

(1966), Czechoslovakia (1966), Bulgaria (1967) and Romania (1967).[86] The economic drive behind these deals was to encourage Iran's manufacturing exports.

More importantly, Alikhani entered into negotiations with the Soviets to help Iran build a domestic steel industry. Unsurprisingly, the United States and the World Bank lobbied hard against this policy. Nevertheless, Moscow and Tehran pressed ahead and reached a deal in January 1966: the Soviet Union agreed to provide the capital and technology for a steel mill in Isfahan in return for receiving piped gas from the oil fields in southern Iran.[87] The technocrats hailed this deal as a national triumph and a major step towards economic independence.[88] The development of a steel industry in Iran shares striking similarities with the case of South Korea and India. Like Iran, these countries were also discouraged by the World Bank to move into heavy industries on the grounds that these industries did not conform to their comparative advantage. However, equating steel production with economic sovereignty and geopolitical strength, these countries decided to defy the World Bank's advice and develop their own steel industries. In the case of Iran and India, this goal was realised with the financial and technical support of the Soviet Union.

Emboldened by the establishment of Isfahan's steel factory, the Iranian planners welcomed further involvement by communist countries in the construction of heavy industries. As a result, the Soviet Union signed a protocol in 1967 to help deepen Iran's ISI projects in the Fourth Development Plan.[89] In the end, by approaching the USSR and its communist allies in the 1960s, the Iranian policymakers realised their goal of building intermediate and capital goods industries during the Fourth Plan (1968–1972). In effect, the production of intermediate goods and machinery as a share of total industrial output increased from 20% in 1960 to 34% in 1972, indicating Iran's success in 'catching-up' with other rapidly growing developing economies in this respect.[90] Finally, it is important to add that the technocrats continued to support the emergence of private industrial

86 'Annual reviews for 1964 and 1965', 1965, FO 371/180780 (File 1011); 'Annual reviews for 1966 and 1967', 1967–1968, UK National Archives, Records of the Foreign and Commonwealth Office (henceforth FCO), FCO 17/351 (File EP 1/4).

87 'Annual reviews for 1964 and 1965', 1965, FO 371/180780 (File 1011); 'Annual reviews for 1966 and 1967', 1967–1968, FCO 17/351 (File EP 1/4).

88 Nasr, V., 'Politics within the Late-Pahlavi', pp. 106–107.

89 'Annual reviews for 1966 and 1967', 1967–1968, FCO 17/351 (File EP 1/4); 'Soviet Union', 1967, FCO 17/382 (File EP 6/21 Part A).

90 Alizadeh, P., *The Process of Import-Substitution*, pp. 226–227.

conglomerates via the IMDBI.[91] During the Fourth Plan, the economy grew by 11% per year and industrial output rose by 13%.[92]

However, it is important not to exaggerate the policy autonomy of technocrats such as Alikhani and Samiʿi within this period. After all, the power of these economists directly depended on the shah's support as they lacked an independent political or social base. Thus, the shah had to personally approve all the aggregate growth and investment targets. Also, planners who went against the shah's directives risked losing their position, the most famous example of which was Ebtehaj who resigned in February 1959 after a quarrel with the shah over the growing share of military expenditure in the national budget. Indeed, Ebtehaj was imprisoned for seven months after publicly criticising the shah during a visit to the United States in September 1961.[93] Samiʿi and Alikhani were also eventually dismissed due to their disagreements with the shah. However, when judged from a comparative perspective, the Iranian technocrats were no less autonomous than their counterparts in other rapidly growing economies. For instance, research done by Kim Byung-Kook shows that even in the case of South Korea, which is often hailed as an ideal type of a developmental state, the Korean technocrats had no independent source of power in the 1960s and the 1970s; their authority ultimately rested on Park Chung-Hee's personal support.[94] Similarly, Park revised the development targets that they set according to his preferences; in practice, the Korean Economic Planning Board prepared policy by working backward from Park's outlined targets.[95] There is no evidence to suggest that the Iranian planners had much less policy autonomy than their counterparts in East Asian developmental states.

In summary, thanks to the technocratic management of the economy and rising oil revenues, Iran experienced remarkable economic growth between 1960 and 1972, as evident from the drastic jump in income per capita from $168 to $366.[96]

---

91 The credit subsidies provided to the industrial sector under the Fourth Plan (1968–1972) were three times larger than under the previous plan. Again, most of these subsidies (66%) were channelled towards the private industrial conglomerates via the IMDBI. Overall, thanks to this pro-business credit policy, the private sector accounted for 55% of total investment in the manufacturing sector in the entire 1960–1978 period. 'The Economic Development of Iran, Volume III: Statistical Appendix', The IBRD, Report no. 378-IRN (October 1974).

92 'The Economic Development of Iran, Volume III: Statistical Appendix', The IBRD, Report no. 378-IRN (October 1974), p. 16.

93 Milani, A., *Eminent Persians, Volume Two*, pp. 735–744.

94 Kim, B., 'Leviathan', pp. 202 & p. 213–214.

95 Kim, B., 'Leviathan', pp. 213–214.

96 Alizadeh, P., *The Process of Import-Substitution*, p. 200. Needless to say, the rise in income per capita shows that the total GDP grew faster than the total population in this period.

Table 1 shows how Iran's growth rate in this period was higher than that of South Korea, Taiwan, Brazil or Mexico, the fastest growing economies in East Asia and Latin America. Also, in terms of manufacturing growth, Iran's performance not only surpassed Brazil and Mexico, but was even comparable to that of South Korea and Taiwan, the two well-known cases of the 'East Asian Miracle'. It is important to stress that Iran's economic take-off was not solely based on rising oil revenues, as is evident by the 9.2% annual growth figure in non-oil GDP throughout the Third and Fourth Plans.[97] Admiring this progress, the United States considered Iran as 'one of the notable success stories' of the 1960s, which was named the 'Development Decade' by the United Nations[98].

Table 1: GDP and manufacturing growth between 1960 and 1972*

Country	Iran	Brazil	Mexico	Korea	Taiwan
GDP Growth	10.6%	7.6%	6.8%	8.2%	9.1%
Manufacturing Growth	12.2%	8.4%	8.8%	16.9%	17.1%

* Data taken from World Bank Development Indicators and Karshenas, M., *Oil, State and Industrialisation*, p. 210.

However, it is crucial to stress that the fruits of Iran's rapid economic growth were very unevenly distributed. Table 2 compares the share of the poorest 40% of the population of the total income in Iran, as compared with other countries that had similar levels of income per capita. As shown in the table, Iran's income inequality approximately matched Brazil, Argentina and Mexico, which were among the most unequal countries in the world. In this respect, Iran's economic advancement was similar to that of Latin America, but different from that of East Asia where the benefits of growth were more widely shared.

The 1973 Oil Boom

Although it is not the focus of this chapter, it is important to briefly trace Iran's economic trajectory after the 1973 oil boom. The quadrupling of oil prices in

97 Pesaran, H., 'The System of Dependent Capitalism in Pre- and Post-Revolutionary Iran', in *International Journal of Middle East Studies*, vol. 14, no. 4, 1982, p. 505.
98 Popp, R., 'An Application of Modernisation Theory', p. 86.

Table 2: Share of the bottom 40% of the total income*

Iran (1973)	12.5%
Argentina (1970)	16.2%
Mexico (1973)	10.2%
Brazil (1973)	9.8%
Iraq (1973)	6.8%
South Korea (1973)	19.7%

* Data for Argentina taken from 'Iran: A country economic memorandum', The IBRD, Report No 89211 (August 1977), p. 9; data for South Korea taken from Ahn, K., 'Trends in and Determinants of Income Distribution in Korea', in *Journal of` Economic Development*, vol. 22, no. 2, 1997, p. 53; data for the rest of the countries taken from Rostow, W. W., *The World Economy: History & Prospect*, London, 1978, p. 504.

1973, which was partly instigated by the shah, coincided with the first year of the Fifth Five-Year Development Plan (1973–1977).[99] Alarmed by this windfall, the economists at the Central Bank and the Plan Organisation expressed concern about Iran's future macroeconomic stability. In contrast, the shah viewed the oil boom as a perfect opportunity to push ahead with the ongoing import substitution policy at full speed. Hence, he ordered the doubling of expenditures under the Fifth Plan, completely ignoring the advice of his planners.[100] As documented by Masoud Karshenas, Hadi Salehi Esfahani and Hashem Pesaran, this plan generated soaring inflation, widening income inequality and growing corruption, hence paving the way for the eventual downfall of the Pahlavi regime in 1979.[101]

The massive upward revision of the Fifth Plan marked the political downfall of the technocrats. This downfall, however, did not mean the complete abandonment of economic ideas that had been promulgated by the technocrats; some of these ideas, especially the ones taken from Latin American protectionist school, remained very influential. For example, the shah still followed the same policy of import substitution industrialisation after the oil boom, but on a much larger scale than approved by the technocrats. So Latin American protectionism was not abandoned, but taken to an extreme. Also, on the international front, the shah frequently relied on the 'declining terms of trade' – the central thesis of Latin

99 Razavi, H. and Vakil, F., *The Political Environment of Economic Planning*, pp. 61–97.
100 Razavi, H. and Vakil, F., *The Political Environment of Economic Planning*, pp. 61–97.
101 Karshenas, M., *Oil, State and Industrialisation*, pp. 166–207; Esfahani, H. and Pesaran H., 'The Iranian Economy', pp. 188–192.

American protectionist school and UNCTAD – to legitimise his hawkish oil policy stance in OPEC during the 1970s. He regularly mentioned in his interviews that the price of oil was still cheap relative to the price of industrial goods due to the high rate of inflation in the West.[102] As a solution, he proposed indexing the price of oil to the inflation rate in rich countries.[103] Going further, based on the popular legitimacy of the 'declining terms of trade' thesis in the Third World, the shah was one of the leaders who proposed a New International Economic Order at the United Nations in 1974, which sought to reform global commodity chains in favour of developing countries.[104] So as a leading commodity exporter in the world, Iran increasingly championed the policies promoted by Prebisch and his intellectual peers in UNCTAD during the 1970s.

In the end, it is important to add that the shah's policy response to the 1973 oil boom was in no way unique; indeed, most developmentalist leaders in the world reacted in the same way to this economic shock. For instance, in Indonesia, President Suharto marginalised the economists who, like their Iranian counterparts in the Central Bank and the Plan Organisation, advocated caution in fiscal and monetary spending.[105] Similarly, the recycling of petrodollars to the West after the boom gave an opportunity to Park Chung-Hee in South Korea to secure large-scale international loans and embark on a massive industrialisation drive at home, against the advice of economists in Korean Economic Planning Broad.[106]Park then marginalised those economists due to their opposition to his ambitious industrialisation project.[107] This similarity in policy blunders between Iran and other rapidly growing economies of that period further highlights the power and allure of developmentalist ideologies for these countries' leaders in the wake of the 1973 oil boom.

---

102 'Discussions with Shah of Iran on General Oil Questions', FCO 8/2280.
103 'Memorandum of Conversation', 16 May 1975, in Belmonte, M. L. (ed.), *FRUS 1969–1976, Volume XXVII, Iran; Iraq, 1973–1976*, Washington, DC 2012, Document 127.
104 Karshenas, M., 'Power, Ideology and Global Development: On the Origins, Evolution and Achievements of UNCTAD', in *Development and Change*, vol. 47, no. 4, 2016, p. 675.
105 Bevan, D., Collier, P., and Gunning, J., *Nigeria and Indonesia: Political Economy of Poverty, Equity, and Growth*, New York 1999, pp. 244–259.
106 Haggard, S., 'Macroeconomic policy through the first oil shock, 1970–1975', in Haggard, S., Cooper, R. N., Collins, S., Kim, C. and Ro, S., *Macroeconomic Policy and Adjustment in Korea 1970–1990*, Cambridge, MA 1994, pp. 23–49.
107 Haggard, S., 'Macroeconomic policy', pp. 23–49.

Conclusion

Iran's conventional historiography does not pay much attention to economic ideologies as a crucial factor in analysing the political economy of development before the revolution. Of course, frequent references are made to the 'developmentalist mindset' of the technocrats or the 'pseudo-modernist' vision of the shah in the literature, but these factors only receive a superficial treatment by scholars and are never considered as central in explaining the state's economic policies. Accordingly, when it comes to economic ideology, the Pahlavi regime is often conceptualised as a regime that had no affinity for any particular economic thinking. Going against this view, I have argued here that Iranian technocrats *did* have a deep affinity for certain economic ideas, notably modernisation theory and Latin American protectionism, and this affinity *did* have a major influence on the state's policies in the 1950s and 1960s. By bringing ideology in, this chapter has situated the economic history of the late Pahlavi period in the wider context of battle of ideas during the Cold War and, in so doing, opened a global perspective into Iran's political economy in the 1950s and 1960s.

As demonstrated in this chapter, the Pahlavi regime shared striking similarities with developmentalist regimes in East Asia and Latin America. Like those regimes, it had a group of economic planners who were trained at Ivy League universities with the support of the World Bank and charitable foundations in the United States. Seeing themselves as the vanguard of modernisation, these planners fetishised economic growth and industrialisation. Thanks to their effective management and stable rising oil revenues, Iran managed to achieve remarkable economic growth from 1960 to 1972, outperforming South Korea, Taiwan and Brazil. Again, similar to these countries, Iran defied the World Bank's advice and moved into heavy industries during this period. Most importantly, in the wake of the 1973 oil boom, Iran made the same policy mistakes as South Korea, Taiwan, Indonesia, Brazil and Mexico; just like the shah, political leaders in those countries embarked on ambitious development projects against the advice of their economists. This factor indicates that the shah's reaction to the 1973 oil boom was typical of a developmentalist leader.

The Iranian case further confirms the arguments put forward by David Engerman, Nils Gilman and others regarding the contested nature of exporting modernisation theory to the Third World during the Cold War.[108] Just like their counterparts

108 Engerman, D. C., 'Introduction: Modernization, International History, and the Cold War World', in Engerman, D. C., Gilman N., Haefele, M. H., and Latham, M. E., *Staging Growth: Modernization, Development and the Global Cold War*, Amherst 2003, pp. 1–25.

in South Korea, Taiwan, Indonesia, Brazil, and India, Iranian technocrats adapted and interpreted modernisation theory according to their country's economic conditions. But their adaptation of this theory was distinctive in two ways. Firstly, they were far more committed to the business promotion aspect of modernisation theory than their peers in other countries. For example, they delegated the management of Iran's largest development bank – the IMDBI – to the private sector. Secondly, they mixed modernisation theory with the ideas of the Latin American protectionist school, as they found Prebisch-Singer's 'declining terms of trade' hypothesis very relevant to Iran as a commodity-rich country. In contrast, the technocrats in South Korea, Taiwan and Indonesia, mixed modernisation theory with the Japanese development model, or in the case of India with the Soviet planning doctrine. Iran's case suggests that, when studying the commodity-rich countries of the Third World, scholars should pay special attention to the Latin American protectionist school as possibly a powerful intellectual influence, on par with American modernisation theory and Soviet development planning.

Overall, this chapter shows that the economic thinking of the Pahlavi elite was deeply influenced by the competing development ideas of their time. However, far from being passive consumers of ideas, the shah and his economic planners domesticated various Cold War development doctrines according to their needs, just like their counterparts in the developmentalist regimes of East Asia and Latin America.

Bibliography

Afkhami, G., *The Life and Times of the Shah*, Los Angeles 2009.

Ahn, K., 'Trends in and Determinants of Income Distribution in Korea', in *Journal of Economic Development*, vol. 22, no. 2, 1997, pp. 27–56.

Alizadeh, P, *The Process of Import-Substitution Industrialisation in Iran (1960–1978) with Particular Reference to the Case of the Motor Vehicle Industry*, PhD thesis, University of Sussex 1984.

Alvandi, R., *Nixon, Kissinger and the Shah: The United States and Iran in the Cold War*, New York 2014.

Alvandi, R., 'The Shah's détente with Khrushchev: Iran's 1962 Missile Base Pledge to the Soviet Union', in *Cold War History*, vol. 14. no. 3, 2014, pp. 423–444.

Amouzegar, J., *Managing the Oil Wealth: OPEC's Windfalls and Pitfalls*, New York 2001.

Amsden, A., *The Rise of 'the Rest': Challenges to the West from Late-Industrializing Economies*, Oxford 2001.

Belmonte, M. L. (ed.), *Foreign Relations of the United States 1969–1976, Volume XXVII, Iran; Iraq, 1973–1976*, Washington, DC 2012.

Bevan, D., Collier, P. and Gunning, J., *Nigeria and Indonesia: Political Economy of Poverty, Equity, and Growth*, New York 1999.

Bostock, F. and Jones, G., *Planning and Power in Iran: Ebtehaj and Economic Development under the Shah*, London 1989.

Brazinsky, G. A., 'Korean Modernization: Modernization Theory and South Korean intellectuals', in Engerman, D. C., Gilman, N., Haefele, M. H. and Latham, M. E, *Staging Growth: Modernization, Development and the Global Cold War*, Amherst 2003, pp. 251–275.

Cardoso, F. H., and Faletto, E., *Dependency and Development in Latin America*. Berkeley 1979.

Ebtehaj, A., *Khaterat-e Abodl Hassan Ebtehaj* [Abol Hassan Ebtehaj's Memoirs] Volumes one and two, Tehran 1996.

Engerman, D. C., Gilman, N., Haefele, M. H. and Latham, M. E., *Staging Growth: Modernization, Development and the Global Cold War*, Amherst 2003.

Esfahani, H. S. and Pesaran, M. H., 'The Iranian Economy in the Twentieth Century: A Global Perspective', in *Iranian Studies*, vol. 42, no. 2, 2009, pp. 177–211.

Fisher, C. T., '"Moral Purpose is the Important Thing": David Lilienthal, Iran, and the Meaning of Development in the US, 1956–63', in *The International History Review*, vol. 33. no. 3, 2011, pp. 431–451.

Gilman, N., *Mandarins of the Future: Modernization Theory in Cold War America*, Baltimore 2007.

'Goft-e Goo Ba Reza Niyazmand Dar Barey-e Technocracy-e Asr-e Pahlavi: Revayat-e Sanati Shodan' [A discussion with Reza Niyazmand about technocracy in the Pahlavi era: the story of industrialisation], *Tejarat-e Farda*, no. 70, November 2013.

Haggard, S., 'Macroeconomic policy through the first oil shock, 1970–1975', in Haggard, S., Cooper, R. N., Collins, S., Kim, C. and Ro, S., *Macroeconomic Policy and Adjustment in Korea 1970–1990*, Harvard Studies in International Development, Cambridge, MA 1994.

Haggard, S., *Pathways from the Periphery: The Politics of Growth in the Newly Industrialising Countries*, New York 1990.

Halliday, F., *Iran: Dictatorship and Development*, New York 1979.

Howland, N. D. (ed.), *Foreign Relations of the United States, 1964–1968, Volume XXII, Iran*, Washington, DC 1999.

Imam-Jomeh, I., *Petroleum-Based Accumulation and the State Form in Iran*, PhD thesis, Los Angeles 1985.

International Bank for Reconstruction and Development, 'The Economic Development of Iran, Volume III: Statistical Appendix', October 1974, Report No 378-IRN.

International Bank for Reconstruction and Development, 'Industrialisation of Iran: The record, the problems and the prospects', May 1970, Record No SA-14.

International Bank for Reconstruction and Development, 'Iran: A country economic memorandum', August 1977, Report No 89211.

International Bank for Reconstruction and Development, 'Report and recommendations of the President to the Executive Directors on a proposed loan to Industrial and Mining Development Bank of Iran', August 1959, Report No P-203.

International Monetary Fund, '1959 Consultations-Iran', October 1959, the IMF Documents (SM /59/66).

International Monetary Fund, 'Financial situation in Iran', April 1957, the IMF Documents (DM/57/16).

International Monetary Fund, 'Iran-1963 Article XIV Consultations', October 1963, the IMF Documents (SM/63/100).

International Monetary Fund, 'Staff report and recommendations-1962 Consultations', June 1962, the IMF Documents (SM/62/64).

'Iran Chamber of Industries and Mines', *Financial Times*, May 24, 1968.

Karl, T. L., *The Paradox of Plenty: Oil Booms and Petro-States*, Los Angeles 1997.

Karshenas, M., 'Power, Ideology and Global Development: On the Origins, Evolution and Achievements of UNCTAD', in *Development and Change*, vol. 47, no 4, 2016, pp. 664–685.

Karshenas, M., *Oil, State and Industrialisation in Iran*, Cambridge 1990.

Katouzian, H., 'The Pahlavi Regime in Iran', in Chehabi, H. E. and Linz, J. J. (eds.), *Sultanistic Regimes*, Baltimore 1998.

Katouzian, H., *The Political Economy of Modern Iran: Despotism and Pseudo-Modernism, 1926–1979*, London 1981.

Kay, C., 'Asia's and Latin America's Development in Comparative Perspective: Landlords, Peasants and Industrialization', in *Institute of Social Studies*, Working Paper no. 336, 2001.

Keshavarzian, A., *Bazaar and State in Iran: the Politics of the Tehran Marketplace*, Cambridge 2007.

Kim, B., 'The Leviathan: Economic Bureaucracy under Park', in Kim P. and Vogel, E. F., *The Park Chung Hee Era: The Transformation of South Korea*, Cambridge, Massachusetts 2011.

Latham, M. L., *Modernisation as Ideology: American Social Science and 'Nation Building' in the Kennedy Era*, Chapel Hill 2000.

Latham, M. L., *The Right Kind of Revolution: Modernisation, Development and U.S. Foreign Policy from the Cold War to the Present*, New York 2011.

Mason, E. S. & Robert E. A., *The World Bank since Bretton Woods*, Washington, DC 1973.

Mehran, H., *The goals and policies of the Central Bank of Iran 1960–1978*, Washington, DC 2013.

Meier, G. M., *Biography of a Subject: An Evolution of Development Economics*, Oxford 2004.

Milani, A., *Eminent Persians: The Men and Women Who Made Modern Iran, 1941–1979*, London 2008.

Milani, A., *The Shah*, New York 2011.

Nasr, V., 'Politics within the Late-Pahlavi State: The Ministry of Economy and Industrial Policy, 1963–69', in *International Journal of Middle East Studies*, vol. 32, no. 1, 2000, pp. 97–122.

Nemchenok, V. V., "'That So Fair a Thing Should Be So Frail": The Ford Foundation and the Failure of Rural Development in Iran, 1953–1964', in *Middle East Journal*, vol. 63, no. 2, 2009, pp. 261–84.

Offiler, B., *US Foreign Policy and the Modernization of Iran: Kennedy, Johnson, Nixon and the Shah*, New York 2015.

Pesaran, H., 'The System of Dependent Capitalism in Pre- and Post-Revolutionary Iran', in *International Journal of Middle East Studies*, vol. 14, Issue 4, 1982, pp. 501–522.

Popp, R., 'An Application of Modernization Theory during the Cold War? The Case of Pahlavi Iran', in *The International History Review*, vol. 30, no. 1, 2008, pp. 76–98.

'Pool-e Naft Bala Raft-eh Bood va Ma Balad Nabudim Masrafesh Konim' [Alikhani: The oil revenue had gone up but we didn't know how to spend it], *Radio Farda*, 4 September 2010.

Rahnema, S., 'Multinationals and Iranian Industry: 1957–1979', in *The Journal of Developing Areas*, vol. 24, no. 3, 1990, pp. 293–310.

Razavi, H. and Vakil, F., *The Political Environment of Economic Planning in Iran, 1971–1983, From Monarchy to Islamic Republic*, Boulder 1984.

'Revayat-e Niyazmand az Por Hashiyeh Tarin Tarh-e Keshavarzi-e Ghabl az Enghelab: Se Dalil-e Shah Baray-e Ejray-e Eslahat-e Arzi' [Niyazmand on the most controversial agricultural reform of the pre-Revolutionary period: three reasons why the Shah implemented the land reform], *Tejarat-e Farda*, no. 76, November 2014.

Rodrik, D., 'When Ideas Trump Interests: Preferences, World Views and Policy Innovations', in *National Bureau of Economic Research*, NBER Working Paper no. 19631, 2013.

Rostow, W. W., *The World Economy: History & Prospect*, London 1978.

Sachs, J. D., and Williamson, J., 'External Debt and Macroeconomic Performance in Latin America and East Asia', in *Brookings Papers on Economic Activity*, vol. 1985, no. 2, 1985, pp. 523–73.

Schayegh, C., 'Iran's Karaj Dam Affair: Emerging Mass Consumerism, the Politics of Promise, and the Cold War in the Third World', in *Comparative Studies in Society and History*, vol. 54, no. 3, 2012, pp. 612–643.

Simpson, B. R., *Economists with Guns: Authoritarian Development and U.S.-Indonesian Relations, 1960–1968*, Stanford 2008.

The Central Bank of Iran Bulletin, 'Konfrans-e CAFEA va Seminar-e Bankdari Asiyayi' [The CAFEA Conference and the Asian Banking Seminar], no. 31 (March 1964).

The Central Bank of Iran Bulletin, '*Sanaye va Ma-aden dar Barnamey-e Chaharom: Sokhanrani-e Jenab-e Aghay-e Mohammad-e Yeganeh, Moaven Eghtesadi-e Vezarat-e Eghtesad*' [Industries and mines in the Fourth Plan: the speech given by Mohammad Yeganeh, Deputy Minister of Economy], no. 84 (August 1968).

The Central Bank of Iran Bulletin, 'Sarmay-eh Gozari Sanati Dar Iran: Kholasey-e Sokhanrani-e Aghay-e Mehdi Samiee', [Industrial investment in Iran: a summary of the speech given by Mehdi Samiee], no. 16- 1 (December 1962).

The Central Bank of Iran Bulletin, 'United Nations technical assistance in the industrialisation of Iran', no. 13 (May-June 1964).

The Central Bank of Iran, 'Annual report for 1961', March 1962.

The Central Bank of Iran, 'Annual report for 1964', March 1965.

The Central Bank of Iran, 'Annual report for 1965', March 1966.

The Central Bank of Iran, 'Annual report for 1966', March 1967.

The Central Bank of Iran, 'Annual report for 1967', March 1968.

The Central Bank of Iran, 'Annual report for 1968', March 1969.

The World Bank, *World Development Indicators*, Washington, DC 2018.

Toye, J., 'From New Era to Neoliberalism: US Strategy on Trade Finance and Development in the United Nations, 1964–82', in *Forum for Development Studies*, vol. 32, no. 1, 2005, pp. 151–180.

United Nations Conference on Trade and Development, 'UNCTAD at 50: a short history', Unites Nations, New York, 2014.

UK National Archives, Records of the Foreign and Commonwealth Office.

UK National Archives, Records of the Foreign Office.

Wade, R., *Governing the Market: Economic Theory and the Role of Government in East Asian Industrialization*, Princeton 2004.

Wallerstein, I., *Historical Capitalism: With Capitalist Civilization*, London 2011.

2

The Opium of the State: Local and Global Drug Prohibition in Iran, 1941–1979

Maziyar Ghiabi

'Long live, long live opium and *shireh*
To hell, to hell with my children…
My first imam is the Afghan *shireh*.'
Luti Song in Praise of Opium (1969)[1]

With the establishment in the twentieth century of institutions of global governance, such as the League of Nations, and the adoption of international regulations by the global narcotics trade, many countries reformed their domestic narcotics policies. Iran was no exception. Narcotics, themselves a quintessential global commodity, figure prominently in the history of Iran. Opiates have had a cultural, social and economic place in the life of Iranians and contributed to the highs and lows of national history from times immemorial. Panacea painkiller, lucrative crop, poetic intoxicant and sexual inhibitor, the drug played a role in situating national policymakers, traders and smugglers within a great game of global trade

1 The last line plays with words: *shireafghān* sounds as *shirafkan*. The first refers to the Afghan opium residue, *shireh*, the second is Imam Ali's appellative *shirafkan*, 'one who can defeat a lion'. 'Song in Praise of Opium', *Encyclopaedia Iranica*, 27 April 1969, available at: <http://www.iranicaonline.org/articles/song-praise-opium>.

at a time when Western powers, spearheaded by the United States, intended to create a more moral, sober world.[2] Between 1909 and 1979 (and indeed to this very day), Iran's approach stood out in the history of drugs as one of great experimentation with few equals worldwide. Over a period of four decades between 1941 and 1979, when drug prohibition occupied a central element of domestic and international governance discourse, the vicissitudes of Iran's drugs policy were shaped by a tension between global and domestic pressures, involving geographic, social, medical, political, and cultural scripts.

The Iranian case has much to say about the global history of opium trade, although this case has been largely ignored in the scholarship on drugs. Equally, it is impossible to separate the social history of opiates from political history.[3] Both were influenced by people's changing consumption habits, transnational trafficking networks, and global conventions on drug control, as well as the surge of new ideas about 'society'. What the Iranian case suggests is that here modernisation did not manifest as a systematic derivative of the international drugs conventions; it was indigenised and re-produced through localised projects, which had no equal in the Global South, then also known as the Third World.[4]

This chapter narrates and analyses the 'abrupt reversals, sudden initiatives and equally sudden retreats' that feature in the drug politics of this period.[5] Opium smokers, medical practitioners, and police officers hence found themselves entangled in a web of events and transformations that encompassed the Pahlavi court and American federal officials, indigenous modernisers and impoverished farmers. This study of 'inconsistencies' – a tragiccomic *pièce* – provides insights into the place of Iranians and Iran in the global history of narcotics, while also revealing how the global politics of prohibition shaped and reformed opiate consumption in Iran.

The Birth of Drug Policy in Iran

For much of its history, opium was a regular feature of life in Iran. At the end of

---

2 Tyrrell, I., *Reforming the World: The Creation of America's Moral Empire*, Princeton 2010.
3 Courtwright, D. T., *Dark Paradise*, Cambridge, MA 2009, p. xi.
4 Cf. Engerman, D. C., and Unger, C. R., 'Introduction: Towards a Global History of Modernization', in *Diplomatic History*, vol. 33, no. 3, 2009. For a definition of 'Global South', see Ghiabi, M., 'Spirit and Being: Interdisciplinary Reflections on Drugs across History and Politics', in *Third World Quarterly*, vol. 39, no. 2, 2018, pp. 207–217.
5 Cronin, S., *Tribal Politics in Iran: Rural Conflict and the New State, 1921–1941*, London 2007, p. 3.

a day of fasting or before the sunrise hour in the month of Ramadan, ambulant vendors would provide water and, for those in need, opium pills by shouting in the squares and in front of the mosques, 'here is water and opium! [*āb ast va taryāk*].'[6] In northern Iran, mothers would give small bits of opium to their children before heading to the fields to do their work. Later, before sleep time, children would be given a *sharbat-e baccheh* (child's syrup), made of the poppy skin boiled with sugar, which would ensure a sound sleep.[7] The use of these sedatives, which had global equivalents in southern Italy under the name of *papagna* (papaverum), or in Britain under the corporate label of Godfrey's Cordial, contributed to the demonisation of the popular classes (workers and peasants) in the public imagination, whose opium consumption was viewed as irresponsible and not in tune with modern nursing practices.[8] Drug use among individual Iranians was captured in the novels of the modernist writer, Sadegh Hedayat, whose narrators and characters, amid existential sorrows and melancholies, partook in opium and spirit exploitation.[9] The idea of 'addiction' as a concept inescapably connected to opium use, however, had already been adopted by Iranian intellectuals and political entrepreneurs in the early days of the Constitutional Revolution at the turn of the twentieth century. Iranian constitutionalists referred to opium addiction as one of the most serious social and political ills of the country and were actively advocating a drastic 'cure' for this pathology. Opium played an important role in the metaphorical framing of late Qajar Iran as an 'ailing' country, an imagery which would last well into the middle of the twentieth century.[10] Hosseyn Kuhi Kermani, an influential intellectual of that era, reports that when the constitutionalists

---

6 Azarkhosh, J. A., *Afat-e Zendegi*, Tehran 1956 [1334], pp. 367–8. Also Neligan, A. R., *The Opium Question with Special Reference to Persia*, London 1927, p. 25.

7 Alemi, A., and Naraghi, M. M., 'The Iceberg of Opium Addiction an Epidemiological Survey of Opium Addiction in a Rural Community' in *Drug and Alcohol Dependence*, vol. 3, no. 2, 1978, p. 109; Groseclose, E. E., *Introduction to Iran*, Oxford 1947, p. 198; Neligan, A. R., *The Opium Question*, p. 16.

8 Berridge, V., and Edwards, G., *Opium and the People*, London, 1982, pp. 98–101 and 105. Berridge shows how these practices were widespread also among upper-class families, but this never became a concern in the public debate.

9 Hedayat, S., *Zendeh be Gur*, Tehran 1930; and *Buf-e Kur*, Tehran 1952.

10 Cfr. Tavakoli-Tarqi, M., 'Tajaddod-e Ruzmarreh va Ampul-e Tadvin', in *Iran nameh*, vol. 24, no. 4, 2009; see Kashani-Sabet, F., 'Hallmarks of Humanism: Hygiene and Love of Homeland in Qajar Iran', in *The American Historical Review*, vol. 105, no. 4, p. 2000. In 1947, Arthur C. Millspaugh, the American director of Iran's finances, wrote a book that included a section entitled, 'Report from the Clinic', with sub-chapters such as, 'Can Persia Save Herself?', 'Suggestions for a Prescription', 'How Shall the Doctoring be Done?'. See Millspaugh, A. C., *Americans in Persia*, Washington, DC 1946.

conquered Tehran, they waged a serious struggle against *taryāki*s (opium addicts), organising missions led by police officers and volunteers who ventured into the southern districts of Tehran to close down drug nests.[11]

The constitutionalists' engagement with the problem of opium coincided with the first international conferences on opium control. The first of these meetings took place in Shanghai in 1909, a year that can be regarded as a stepping-stone to the advent of a global prohibitionist regime. By the early twentieth century, prohibition of intoxicants had become a mantra in public debates, especially in the United States, thanks to the activities of the 'temperance movement'. Despite the stupendous revenues brought in by the drugs trade in the United States, reformers, under pressure from returning Protestant missioniries and women's associations, pushed for a strict regulation of narcotics and alcoholic drinks. This domestic shift in the United States coincided with a similar push on the international stage. In Shanghai, US officials encouraged opium-producing and opium-trading countries to introduce controls on narcotics, principally opium, at the level production and trade. The objective was to limit the flow of opium to medical use only. The conference, presided over by the American Episcopal bishop, Charles Henry Brent, included representatives from Britain, France, Germany, Japan, the Netherlands, Portugal, Russia, China, Siam, and Austria-Hungary. The only Middle Eastern country to participate in the conference was Iran.[12] These countries were either large opium producers and/or major traders in the substance.

For Iran, participation in the meeting meant joining the global diplomatic arena of modernity at a time of epochal domestic changes. Ironically, though, the Iranian envoy was Mirza Jafar Rezai, an opium trader who was rather disturbed by an appointment which could have potentially 'cut his own throat', given that opium represented Iran's major export and his principal business.[13] Iran signed the international agreement that followed the meeting in Shanghai, the 1912 Hague Opium Convention, which was later incorporated into the 1919 Treaty of Versailles. But the government in Tehran expressed reservations about the crucial Article 3a (Chapter I), which stated that 'it was undesirable to import drugs into a country

11 Shahidi, M. H., *Mavadd-e Mokhadder, Amniyat-e Ejtema'i va Rah-e Sevvom*, Tehran 2010 [1389], p. 67.

12 The Ottoman Empire was invited but refused to attend the conference, perhaps given the unsettled domestic situation. Afghanistan was not a sovereign country until 1919. See McAllister, W. B., *Drug Diplomacy in the Twentieth Century: An International History*, New York 2000, p. 28.

13 Regavim, R. B., 'The Most Sovereign of Masters: The History of Opium in Modern Iran, 1850–1955', PhD thesis, University of Pennsylvania 2012, p. 151.

where their use was illegal'.[14] This was unsurprising given that opium contributed greatly to Iran's national budget and was a key asset in the state-building process. These moralising principles on drug prohibition were nonetheless influential for Iran's domestic policies on opiates, as they legitimised norms concerning public conduct, 'sobriety', and increasing state control on the production and trade of opiates. Indeed, in the wake of the momentum produced by the constitutionalists' anti-opium campaigns, Iran was the first opium-producing country to introduce a limitation on cultivation and to restrain opium use in public.[15] On March 15, 1911, a year before the Hague Convention, Iran's Majles approved the Law of Opium Limitation, which proscribed a seven-year period for opium users to give up their habit.[16] This provision also made the government effectively accountable for the delivery of opium to the people, with the creation of a quota system (*sahmiyeh*) that required the registration of drug users through state administrative offices and the payment of taxes against the provision of opium. In other words, state intervention in the private sphere of individual behaviour, i.e., consumption, was sanctioned in this law and the right of intervention was granted to officials of the Ministry of Finance. Although this decision did not mean the end of the poppy economy, it demonstrated how the new politics engendered by the Constitutional Revolution were in tune with global trends regarding the regulation of public space and modern lifestyles. Iranian lawmakers adopted the moralistic principles enunciated at the Shanghai Conference and rapidly codified them into law. They preceded by three years the Harrison Act in the United States, which granted the US Treasury supervision over all narcotics matters and imposed a special tax on manufacturers and distributers of opiates.[17]

Whether Iranian opium prohibition was inspired by the influence of the Western powers, or whether it emerged indigenously, is a debate that is beyond the scope of this chapter, which is focused on the period between 1941 and 1979.[18] Less debatable is the fact that the effectiveness of these prohibition policies was greatly impacted by the formation of a modern state machinery in Iran, which

---

14 UNODC, 'That day in history: The Shanghai Opium Commission 1909', February 2, 2009, available at: <http://www.unodc.org/unodc/en/frontpage/this-day-in-history-the-shanghai-opium-commission-1909.html>.

15 Groseclose, E. E., *Introduction to Iran*, p. 208.

16 Qahrfarkhi, S. M., *E'tiyad dar Iran*, Tehran 2011 [1390], p. 144.

17 Musto, D., *The American Disease: Origins of Narcotic Control*, Oxford 1999, pp. 54–67.

18 Campos, I., *Home Grown: Marijuana and the Origins of Mexico's War on Drugs*, Chapel Hill 2012; Windle, J., *Suppressing Illicit Opium Production: Successful Intervention in Asia and the Middle East*, London 2016. Although from an initial look at the sources, Iranian policies on drugs precede or follow closely international drugs conventions.

Figure 1: Donkey Smoking Opium in a Suit (Small statue dating back to the late 1950s. Courtesy of Antonio Mazzitelli, former UNODC Representative in Iran.)

progressively disposed of the instruments of intrusion into the life of opium users. Prior to this, Iranian rulers had at different times ruled in favour or against the use of opium and other drugs, including wine, but at no time had they disposed of the practical means which affected the lives of multitudinous drug users.[19] The shahs themselves were known in popular narratives to be divided between those fighting against and those indulging in opium consumption. At times, the rulers would indulge in drug use so heavily as to destabilise their reign.[20] Therefore, the idea of a ruler whose mind and body was intoxicated by opium or other substances had become by the time of the Constitutional Revolution a central political theme. Reformers used the failures of past sovereigns to warn against the danger of intoxication, arguing that modernity did not have space for old pastimes and

19 Matthee, R. P., *The Pursuit of Pleasure: Drugs and Stimulants in Iranian History, 1500–1900*, Princeton 2005; Shahidi, M. H., *Mavadd-e Mokhadder*, p. 28.
20 Shahidi, M. H., *Mavadd-e Mokhadder*, pp. 28–29.

intoxication. Genealogically, opium and addiction were interpreted as the causes of and the rationale for Iran's backwardness, a *leitmotif* that can also be situated aptly in post-1979 Iran.

State Building and Popular Economy

Although Iranian authorities sought to restrain opium consumption, they were neither willing nor capable of giving up this important share of the state's income, which in some years was as high as 9% of total revenues.[21] Opium represented a major resource for the state-building project of the newly established Pahlavi dynasty. It contributed directly to the building and upgrading of the national army, leading Reza Shah to create the Opium State Monopoly in 1928 as a form of 'legislative radicalism' (other examples include: conscription, dress code, and tobacco monopoly).[22] By that time, Iran was producing 30% of the world's opium, exporting enormous, unregistered quantities to East Asia, which contributed to quelling revolts against the Japanese in occupied Manchuria.[23] As a strategic asset, however, opium never came under full control of the Iranian state; resilient farmers, including nomadic tribes, threatened by the encroachment of the state and its anti-tribal/sedentarisation policy, continued to harvest and bargain with the authorities, at times successfully, at other times contentiously. Emblematic of the contentious nature of opium politics was the *bast* (a manner of peaceful gathering or occupation in protest) performed by the people of Isfahan in the city's Telegraph Compound in 1923. In a matter of days, if not hours, this *bast* turned into a demonstration by seven thousand people against the attempts by the central government, on the advice of the American financial adviser Arthur Millspaugh, to control and tax opium production.[24] Members of the clergy participated, not least because a considerable portion of *vaqf* lands (religious endowments) in Iran's southwest were cultivated with poppy. Similar events took place across southern Iran during the 1920s.[25]

Opium, as such, constituted a vital source of capital, which made poppy growers (and their capitalist patrons, with the clergy topping the list) the wealthiest class

21 Hansen, B., 'Learning to Tax: The Political Economy of the Opium Trade in Iran, 1921–1941', in *The Journal of Economic History*, vol. 61, no. 1, 2001, p. 97.
22 Cronin, S., *Soldiers, Shahs and Subalterns in Iran: Opposition, Protest and Revolt, 1921–1941,* London 2010, p. 161.
23 Groseclose, E. E., *Introduction to Iran*, p. 212.
24 Cronin, S., 'Resisting the New State: Peasants and Pastoralists in Iran, 1921–41', in *The Journal of Peasant Studies*, vol. 32, no. 1, 2005.
25 Cronin, S., *Soldiers.*

in Iran.[26] Inevitably, this led to a contraband economy of vast proportions. This economy had few equals globally and supplied the market at its bottom and top ends, respectively petty merchants in the many ports connecting Bushehr to Vladivostok as well as elites across Eurasia. Legitimate pharmaceutical houses benefited from this trade, as they privileged Iranian opium over Turkish, Yugoslavian or Indian opium 'because of its superior quality and high morphine content'.[27] In Iran, capital accumulation over the first half of the twentieth century among a circumscribed class of landowners may well have occurred because of opium production.

Besides the international trafficking networks, the opium economy produced a social life of its own, one in which the presence of the state remained a latency well into the Pahlavi era. With the creation of the Opium Monopoly, the state required all the opium produced locally to be stocked in governmental warehouses, which were administrated by state officials. Yet, much of the opium sap never reached these locations. Even when it actually did, it did so only at face value, with quantities much inferior to the actual level of production. Concealed during the period of harvest, opium was then sold at a higher price to smugglers, who would resell abroad at even higher rates.[28]

The list of those involved in the opium economy was not restricted to landowners, cultivators and smugglers. Labourers, commission and export merchants, brokers, bazaar agents, chiefs, clerks, manipulators, packers, porters, carpenters, coppersmiths, retailers, and mendicants were all part of the chain of production. During harvest time, they were often accompanied by a motley crew of dervishes, story-tellers, musicians, owners of performing animals and a whole industry of amusement providers who were paid for their company or 'given alms by having the flat side of the opium knife scrapped on their palms'.[29] One observer of such events reported to have seen from three to five thousand strangers in a single area during the harvest season. The village mullahs, who might have blessed the event with a *salavāt* (eulogy to the prophet and his family), were given as a token of gratitude a small amount of premium opium sap. Among the 80,000 inhabitants of Isfahan, it was reported than about one quarter made their living directly or

26 MacCormack, M., and Ameri, M. K., *Memorandum on Persian Opium: Prepared for Dr. A. C. Mispaugh, Administrator General of the Finances*, London 1924, p. 11

27 Iranian opium was known as having a higher morphine (12%) value compared to the Indian, Turkish and Balkan opium. See Groseclose, E. E., *Introduction to Iran*, p. 108; Neligan, A. R., *The Opium Question*, p. 37.

28 Groseclose, E. E., *Introduction to Iran*, pp. 108–109.

29 Millspaugh, A. C., *The American Task in Persia*, London 1925, pp. 190–1.

indirectly off the opium economy.[30] Retailers (often operating as drugstores or *ʿattāris*) advertised different 'brands' of opium in their windows and cabinets with signs reading: 'Here the best Shirazi and Isfahani opium is sold!'[31] Stephanie Cronin writes that, in certain regions of the country, opium had even become a local currency.[32] When the modernising state increased its effort at controlling the opium economy, the effect was that a large number of middlemen and beneficiaries of this economy became unemployed or saw their revenues decline significantly. It is plausible to think that many of these categories joined forces with the widespread associations of smugglers which have enriched the informal economy ever since. But the risk of 'moral reputation' and 'moral isolation' compelled Iranian policymakers to cooperate with the nascent international drugs control regime.[33] For the first time in Iranian history, the crime of smuggling (*qāchāq*) was codified in new legislation. It is reported that between the late 1920s and the early 1930s, more than 10,000 traffickers were arrested per year, prompting the government to acknowledge that there were more people smoking contraband opium than government opium.[34]

Reza Shah himself was a regular user of opium, although it is said, perhaps hagiographically, that he smoked twice a day standing on his feet, as opposed to those laying on their side indulging in poetry, conversation and day-dreaming.[35] In this image one can interpret the difference between the traditional shahs of the pre-Pahlavi period, several of them known opium users, and the modernising Reza Shah, who used opium without losing his mental alertness and bodily stamina. Together with the veil, the traditional hat, nomadic life, and Sufi practice, opium smoking was seen as a habit that had no place in the making of modern Iran. Even within the practice of apothecaries, it had to be replaced by modern science and Western medicine. The shah banned the use of opium for those in the army and in the bureaucracy, although the Majles itself had a lounge in which deputies could ease their nerves and discuss issues of concern over an opium pipe.[36] It was the façade produced by a lifestyle that included opium consumption, particularly

30 Millspaugh, A. C., *The American Task*, p. 190; Neligan, A. R., *The Opium Question*, p. 37.

31 Azarkhosh, J. A., *Afat-e Zendegi*, p. 373.

32 Cronin, S., *Soldiers*, p. 191.

33 MacCormack, M., and Ameri, M. K., *Memorandum*, pp. 1–2.

34 Hansen, B., 'Learning to Tax', p. 103.

35 Alimardani, A. A., 'Mavadd-e Mokhadder va Rezhim-e Pahlavi', in *Faslnameh-ye Motaleʿat-e Tarikh*, vol. 25, p. 114.

36 McLaughlin, G., and Quinn, T., 'Drug Control in Iran: A Legal and Historical Analysis', in *Iowa Law Review*, vol. 59, 1973, p. 486; *The New York Times*, 11 February 1973.

when witnessed by Western observers, which preoccupied the shah. To demonstrate that the real concern of the government was alignment with Western models of governance, in 1928 the government passed the Opium Restriction Act, which made opium cultivation legitimate only after acquiring government certification from the State Opium Organisation. The Organisation supervised all opium exports as stipulated by the 1925 Geneva Agreement; together with the Ministry of Finance, it collected the opium residue (*sukhteh*) from public places and restricted the sale of cooked opium residue (*shireh-ye matbukh*) to smoking dens (*shirehkesh khāneh*).[37] The idea that the government was keen to purchase the residue of smoked opium contributed to the shift from traditional opium eating, as had been common in Iran since the distant past, to smoking, which was a practice emerging at the turn of twentieth century under the influence of Chinese opium culture.

It was after the fall of Reza Shah in 1941 that the prohibition of opium advanced in Iran in response to a combination of international and domestic factors. That same year, the government banned opium production in twenty-two regions, excluding Isfahan which was by far the highest opium producing region in the country. The move, meant to legitimise the new political order just as the constitutionalists had done at the beginning of the century, would have had drastic consequences were Iran not occupied by the Allied armies.[38] Allied occupation meant that local authorities could not enforce the law systematically. Indeed, the ban was a complete failure. Cultivators protested by selling their opium at very cheap prices, in order to empty their stocks, forcing the government to allow cultivation again in order to refill the national opium reservoir.[39] The resilience and tactics of the farmers demonstrated the influence these non-elites could have on policymakers. However, the consequences of their defiance were catastrophic. Cheap prices combined with the perception of opium as an essential source of pain relief and protection against illnesses, encouraged large numbers of Iranians to consume the drug. In some cases, consumers even set up small opiate factory-shops to cook and sell the opium residue.[40] *Shireh*, which was considered more detrimental and more addictive than opium because of its higher morphine content, was sought after by longer-term smokers. Because these factory-shops were frequented mostly by working-class men who smoked *shireh*, they had a stigma attached to them akin to

37 Azarkhosh, J. A., *Afat-e Zendegi*, pp. 404–405.
38 Groseclose, E. E., *Introduction to Iran*, p. 215.
39 In times of war, morphine reservoirs represent a strategic asset for their analgesic virtue.
40 Qahrfarkhi, S. M., *E'tiyad*, pp. 190–191.

brothels.[41] Interestingly enough, these places were called *dār al-ʿalāj*, the Arabic expression for 'clinic' or 'house of treatment', which hints at the inseparability of recreational and medicinal opiate use.[42] There were hundreds of these establishments in Tehran alone, spread across the landscape of the city from south to north. In one instance, a bus operated as a peripatetic smoking house on the Karaj road to avoid police raids that were aimed at closing the factory-shops or *shirehkesh-khānehs*. The driver's assistant shouted the slogan, 'we take them in dead, we return them revived' [*mordeh mibarim, zendeh miyārim*].[43] During the 1940s, the numbers of *shirehkesh-khānehs* increased dramatically, not only in Tehran but across the country (Figure 2).

Figure 2: Number of* shirehkesh-khānehs *in Iran (1940s)*

Tehran (Shemiran Municipality)	175
Zahedan	142
Hamedan	37
Markaz-e Rasht	24
Sabzevar	23
Kermanshah	23
Qazvin	21
Gonabad	19
Qom	14
Yazd	9
Ahvaz	9
Khorramabad	8
Damghan	3
Sanandaj	3
Sari	2

* Latifi Niya, M., 'Taryak va Eqdamat-e Anjoman-e Mobarezeh ba Taryak va Alkol', in *Gangineh*, vol. 2, no. 3–4, 1992, pp. 111–112.

41 Azarkhosh, J. A., *Afat-e Zendegi*, p. 404.
42 Azarkhosh, J. A., *Afat-e Zendegi*, p. 373.
43 Azarkhosh, J. A., *Afat-e Zendegi*, p. 510.

The widespread use of opium and shireh reached a climax during the Allied wartime occupation, due to the unsettling conditions in which most Iranians found themselves living. American officials stationed in Iran advised the US Army to employ foreign workers to manage the Persian Gulf supply route through Iran to the Soviet Union, since 'three out of four Iranian workers in the south are [opium] addicts'.[44] With prohibitionist discourse on the rise in the United States, the use of exotic drugs (anything but alcohol) remained associated with degenerate deviance and 'addiction'.

Chaos and Crisis ahead of Prohibition (1941–1955)

Following the Second World War, European powers could no longer challenge the American prohibitionist agenda on the global stage, which, in addition, encountered no substantial opposition from the Soviet Union.[45] Moscow had generally maintained an insular approach to international drugs policy, given that the Soviets regarded 'addiction' as a capitalist problem that did not have a place in the communist order.[46] In 1944, the United States circulated to all opium-producing countries a joint resolution of the US Congress, urging these countries to eradicate or reduce poppy cultivation and to limit their opium production to legitimate medical needs.[47] Two years later, moreover, the United States advanced its anti-narcotics agenda on the global stage with the Lake Success Protocol, which amended all previous drugs conventions signed within the framework of the League of Nations. The new protocol instituted the Commission on Narcotics Drugs, which became the main drugs policymaking institution within the United Nations. The agreement signalled the transition of international drugs control from a system based on moral principles, as it had been in the conventions earlier in the century, to one governed by legal codes and policies, following the Second World War. These international developments on narcotics control left their footprint on Iran's domestic policies.

One of the primary reasons for this international move was the seizure of opium in the United States, three-quarters of which allegedly came from Iran.[48]

44 Azarkhosh, J. A., *Afat-e Zendegi*, p. 510.

45 In fact, European power only timidly challenged the US international prohibitionist discourse in the period preceding the Second World War.

46 Kramer, J. M., 'Drug Abuse in the USSR', in Joyce, W. (ed.), *Social Change and Social Issues in the Former USSR*, London 1992, pp. 53–79.

47 Groseclose, E. E., *Introduction to Iran*, p. 216.

48 Gingeras, R., 'Poppy Politics: American Agents, Iranian Addicts and Afghan Opium,

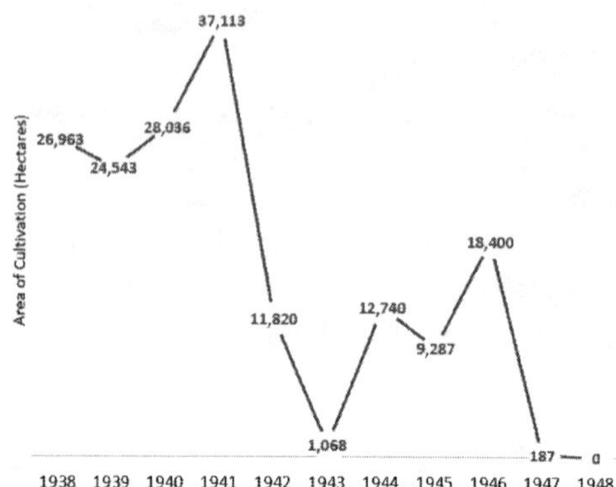

Figure 3: Area under Poppy Cultivation (1938–48) (Extrapolated from Hansen, B., 'Learning to Tax', pp. 95–113.)

A global network of opium smuggling had existed before the coming of organised criminal groups, although the Iranian authorities maintained that they had progressively eradicated poppy cultivation. The reality on the ground, however, spoke of a stupendous flow of opium from Iran, much to the chagrin of the Western powers.

Thus, by the end of the Second World War, a small number of US narcotics officials, many of whom had previously worked as intelligence officers, were helping the Pahlavi state to establish a prohibitionist regime in Tehran, which they hoped would act as a model for the rest of the region and beyond.[49] Through this collaboration, American influence in Iran increased greatly, especially within the repressive, coercive institutions of the Pahlavi state: the police, the intelligence services and the army. On their side, Iranian authorities had repeatedly played the opium card to convince Western powers, especially the United States, to provide much needed development assistance funds. The poppy represented a key asset in Iran's war-torn economy; eradicating it required the creation of alternative sources of revenues and compensation. Cooperation with US officials remained, nonetheless, ambivalent, with Iranian authorities refusing to provide statistics and information about the opium trade, legal and illegal, to the Federal Bureau of Narcotics (FBN) officials. Knowledge about the Iranian drug situation came mostly from non-governmental sources and local observers, who provided

1945–80', in *Iranian Studies*, vol. 45, no. 3, 2012, pp. 318–9.

49 Gingeras, R., 'Poppy Politics', p. 16.

at times a distorted image of the life of opium, exaggerated in its quantitative dimension.[50]

The establishment in Iran of the Society for the Fight against Alcohol and Opium, founded in 1943, helped to fill the void in statistics and monitoring of the government. Its founder, Esmaʿil Marzban (Amin al-Dowleh), a French-trained physician, had been Minister of Health during the premiership of Ahmad Qavam in 1942–1943.[51] Concerned elites and moral entrepreneurs sponsored the activities of the Society, which had local branches in many Iranian cities.[52] There, they campaigned aggressively for the prohibition of all alcoholic spirits and opiates and regularly published astonishing data on the toll of 'addiction'. In the first three years of its life, the Society distributed around eighty thousand information leaflets, participated in more than a hundred public meetings and broadcasted regularly on national radio.[53] Members of this organisation belonged almost exclusively to the elites, including members of parliament, judges, prominent public figures and their wives. Other local organisations, such as the Union of Ali's Followers (Ettehadiyeh-ye Peyrovan-e Ali), the Iranian Physicians Association, and clerical representatives joined forces with the Society on an *ad hoc* basis. Their influence operated in a discursive way towards the public, but it also affected the perception of the drug *problematique* among the authorities, including American officials in Iran. The use of statistics, for instance, was programmatically aimed at engendering a moral panic:

> [T]wo million grams of opium used daily… six million *rial*s lost every day… 5,000 suicide attempts with opium [women figuring prominently]… one thousand three hundred *shirekhāneh* operating in the country, one hundred thousand people dying every year for opium use and fifty thousand children becoming orphans.[54]

In its manifesto, the Society declared, 'it seems that the question of the effects of opium and alcohol has reached a point where the extinction of the Iranian race and generation will take place… In the name of the protection of the nation,

---

50 Collins, J., 'Regulations and Prohibitions: Anglo-American Relations and International Drug Control, 1939–1964', PhD thesis, London School of Economics 2015, p. 92.
51 Latifi Niya, M., 'Taryak va Eqdamat', p. 110–112.
52 See Becker, H. S., *Outsiders: Studies in the Sociology of Deviance*, New York 2008.
53 Qahrfarkhi, S. M., *Eʿtiyad*, p. 149.
54 Qahrfarkhi, S. M., *Eʿtiyad*, p. 149.

this committee has been created.'[55] This emphasis on Iranian nationalism tainted the public discourse on opiates and pushed Iranian lawmakers to adopt tougher measures. In other parts of the world, similar drug scares were populating people's imaginary: cocaine, opium and cannabis embodied new social evils. Of course, the scaremongering targeted specific social classes and groups, such as the poor, vagrants, or Arab, Black, Indian and Hispanic immigrants.

In Iran, opium was described as a primary impediment to labour, although it was known that workers ate opium for its tonic effect.[56] Coincidently, the government first issued a ban on the fifteen-minute break for opium smokers and then circulated a communiqué pointing out that 'workers should not use opium on their jobs'.[57] Employment of officials was conditional on their abstaining from opium, a behaviour which could cost them their job.[58] Modernisation of the national economy, which had to move conjunctly with social behaviour, encouraged the abandonment of opium in favour of other habits such as alcohol consumption. The *tariyāki* was regarded as inherently weak, as Cyrus Schayegh points out, and therefore their place in the discursive frame of the post-1941 Pahlavi state was to be condemned. The 'addict' became generally associated with lying, and was therefore unreliable in the workplace, both in urban and rural contexts.[59] By establishing a semantic dialogue based on ideological and ethical contraposition to drug addiction, the educated bourgeoisie found its nemesis in the old-fashioned opium and *shireh* smokers. At one point, the Majles, in order to impress American officials, discussed a bill which would have introduced the death penalty for those found smoking opium.[60] Largely supported by the modernising middle class, this approach attempted to connect modern Iranians to the global bourgeoisie, with its code of conduct that was at odds with the slow rhythms of opium smoking. The Iranian middle class and officials, hence, became more Catholic than the Pope in their appraisal of opium prohibition, much to the satisfaction of the US anti-narcotics officials.

On January 28, 1945, a Majles deputy from Hamadan, Hassan Ali Farmand,

55 Shahidi, M. H., *Mavad-e Mokhadder*, p. 80.

56 Cfr. Schayegh, C., *Who Is Knowledgeable Is Strong: Science, Class, and the Formation of Modern Iranian Society, 1900–1950*, Berkeley 2009, pp. 186–7. As the Egyptian *fellahin*, the Chinese dock workers and European peasants did, the latter drinking alcohol; see Courtwright, D. T., *Forces of Habit*, Cambridge, MA 2009, p. 136.

57 Groseclose, E. E., *Introduction to Iran*, p. 215; *The New York Times*, 11 February 1973.

58 Azarkhosh, J. A., *Afat-e Zendegi*, pp. 450–451.

59 Schayegh, C., *Who Is Knowledgeable*, passim. Beck, L., *Nomad: A Year in the Life of a Qashqa'i Tribesman in Iran*, Berkeley 1991, p. 401.

60 Collins, J., 'Regulations', p. 172

who had previously opposed the Opium Monopoly in 1928, introduced a bill to the Majles for the total prohibition of the cultivation of poppies and the use of opium.[61] The bill never passed into a law, but between 1941 and 1953 a number of other legislative acts were approved by the Majles: the creation of a 'coupon system' for registered drug users, as had been attempted already in 1912; the prohibition of opium cultivation in 1942–43; a ban on opium consumption in August 1946 under Prime Minister Ahmad Qavam, which lasted only ten months; and under the government of Mohammad Mosaddeq (1951–1953), an amendment banning production, purchase and sale of opium and its derivatives and the consumption of alcoholic drinks.[62] Over this period the government declared a war on coffee houses, which were either closed or had to cover up opium use in public; enforcement of laws against public intoxication (*tajāhor*) increased, enshrining a legal framing which would last into to the new millennium.

Prohibitionist rhetoric gained further momentum ahead of oil nationalisation under the premiership of Mohammad Mosaddeq. In December 1951, Abdolhosseyn Taba, a member of the Majles, amid the debates that preceded the vote on a law which would have prohibited poppy cultivation and opium production, addressed his colleagues to vote 'on this very day to prohibit poppy cultivation and not to make this matter less important than the oil nationalisation'.[63] On February 8, 1953, parliament voted unanimously to ban alcohol and opium use within six months.[64] The move, however, was largely a populist tactic to gather support (including that of the clergy) at a time when economic sanctions and international isolation were crippling the daily life of Iranians. Even government officials had very little faith in the effectiveness of the law. Asked by a journalist whether one could get a drink in Tehran six months from the entry in force of the law, a government official laughed and responded, 'Yes, and six years from now, too…'[65]

Prior to that, Mosaddeq, in agreement with the Majles, had sought a steady increase in opium production in order to compensate for the drop in state revenues from oil exports. The strategy had limited results and 'the government reported opium revenues of over 200 million *rial*s a year from 1951 to 1954, about 20

61 Groseclose, E. E., *Introduction to Iran*, p. 216.

62 Qahrfarkhi, S. M., *E'tiyad*, pp. 153–156.

63 'Mozakerat-e Majles-e Shura-ye Melli, Second Session on December 16, 1951', *Ruznameh-ye Rasmi-ye Keshvar-e Shahanshahi-ye Iran*, 23 December 1951, available at: <https://mashruteh.org/wiki/index.php>.

64 *The New York Times*, 7 May 1952.

65 *The New York Times*, 15 February 1953.

percent of the total [budget]'.[66] In 1952, Iran, together with Communist China, was accused by the United Nations of smuggling opium, following a period of poor cooperation between the country and the US-led international drug control regime.[67] Britain also attempted to delegitimise the nationalist government in Tehran, ahead of the planned August 1953 coup, by among other methods 'spreading the rumor that Mosaddeq reeked of opium and "indulged freely" in that drug'.[68] Paradoxically, while Britain and the United States were planning to topple Iran's democratically-elected prime minister, the US army was stockpiling large amounts of Iranian opium, out of fear that the 'Soviet bomb' and the outbreak of a nuclear confrontation amid the Korean War (1950–53) would bring unprecedented levels of casualties.[69] Morphine endured as the global painkiller for all social classes, while the rules of the Cold War dictated the primacy of strategic calculi over other diplomatic objectives, including that of international drug control.[70]

The Iron Law of Prohibition in Tehran

With the Anglo-American-orchestrated coup d'état that returned Mohammad Reza Shah to the peacock throne in August 1953, the United States gained far-reaching influence over Iran's domestic politics. The decision to cooperate with Washington's *in fieri* fight against narcotics, writes Ryan Gingeras, provided an essential model for future agreements, 'should America's global campaign against narcotics proceed successfully'.[71] Strategically, Iran paved the way, so to say, for the globalisation of anti-narcotics interventions.

Jahanshah Saleh, who served as minister of health under Mohammad Reza Shah in several governments between 1941 and 1961, was the promotor of the ban. He conceded that, 'Prohibition [of opium] was motivated by prestige reasons. At a time of modernization, which in most developing countries means imitation of Western models, the use of opium was considered a shameful hangover of a dark Oriental past. It did not fit with the image of an awakening, Westernizing Iran

66 Hansen, B., 'Learning to Tax', p. 109.

67 Qahrfarkhi, S. M., *E'tiyad*, p. 155. *The New York Times*, 7 May 1952.

68 Abrahamian, E., *The Coup: 1953, the CIA, and the Roots of Modern US-Iranian Relations*, New York 2013, p. 101.

69 McAllister, W. B., *Drug Diplomacy in the Twentieth Century: An International History*, New York 2000, p. 171; Collins, J., 'Regulations', p. 213.

70 Chouvy, P. A., *Opium: Uncovering the Politics of the Poppy*, Cambridge, MA 2009, p. 97.

71 Gingeras, R., 'Poppy Politics', p. 323.

that the shah was creating.'[72] But it was mostly the urbanised middle class and the modernising elites that perceived opium consumption as retrograde behaviour. In fact, the poppy had endured as a 'popular' (*mardomi*) element of life, in so far as it belonged to the *people* (*mardom*). It stood at the heart of a large economy of production and trade; it was the tonic of many labourers and peasants; the medicine for dispersed rural communities and elderly people; and the pastime and recreation of respectable adults.

In practice, though, prohibition was instrumebtal in the scrutiny of domestic politics, while aligning the monarchy with the US-led camp in the Cold War. Thus, in November 1955, Saleh pushed for the approval of the Law Prohibiting Poppy Cultivation and Opium Use, a timeframe which coincided with Iran's entry into the Baghdad Pact. In light of the embeddedness of the opium economy and culture in Iran, the legislative process encountered obstacles from a variety of social groups, such as coffee shop owners, opium traders, apothecaries, landowners in poppy cultivating regions and those who thought that the poppy was an inalienable part of Iranian culture and the backbone of its people's economy. Yet, the public discourse on drug (ab)use as a social liability and a danger to people's health trumped any economic considerations related to revenues derived from the poppy economy. This loss of revenue was also compensated for by the promise of international support for alternative development programmes, including poppy crop substitution. Reports were widespread that the number of opiate (ab)users in Iran – the term used was inevitably 'addict' – had reached two million; in areas such as Gorgan, for instance, it was said that 90% to 100% of the population were addicts.[73] Evidently, some exaggeration was at play here and which was instrumental in the engendering of a public crisis about opium, a genealogical feature that would prove long lasting.[74]

Proposing the prohibition bill in his speech to the Iranian Senate, Jahanshah Saleh first downplayed the financial value of opium in Iran's economy, then made clear that no monetary price could be set on people's health and that 'people's productivity would consequently increase by hundredfold'.[75] This argument did not convince his opponents, who requested that the bill be further discussed in the relevant committees, which were numerous since the opium question touched on legal, social, health and economic matters. However, this attempt at derailing the

72 *The New York Times*, 11 February 1973.
73 Shahidi, M. H., *Mavad-e Mokhadder*, p. 116.
74 Ghiabi, M., 'Maintaining Disorder: the Micropolitics of Drugs Policy in Iran', in *Third World Quarterly*, vol. 39, no. 2, 2018.
75 Azarkhosh, J. A., *Afat-e Zendegi*, p. 513.

bill was attacked by Senator Mehdi Malekzadeh, who with emphatic sentiment and a trembling voice, declared, 'I am a staunch supporter of this bill, I know every bit of it, there is not a single section of this bill that does not have a financial or judicial aspect, but this is a health bill and when confronted with health questions other questions have no value. This is a bill on the lives and wellbeing of people.'[76] Following the debate, the bill passed to the Majles, which approved it and added to the text an article on the prohibition of alcohol sale and procurement, much to the astonishment of the court entourage and modernist elites. Negotiations ensued to remove references to alcohol; during a meeting with the members of parliament, the shah pronounced that 'one of the significant undertakings that have been made is the outset of the fight against opium, which must be fulfilled with attention', omitting any reference to alcohol.[77] On October 30, 1955, the bill was amended to remove any references to alcohol and was approved as the 'Law on Prohibition of Poppy Cultivation and Opium Use'.[78] The law envisaged heavy penalties for producers, traffickers and consumers. If found with fifty grams of opium or one gram of heroin or cocaine in their possession, offenders could face up to ten years solitary confinement and, if they re-offended, the death sentence. For the 'addict', a six-month period of grace was conceded to kick their habit. Opium use in public places, such as cafes and hotels, could result in hefty fines and between six months to one year imprisonment, with recidivists seeing the weight of the sentence increased.[79] It was a moral onslaught accompanied with the machinery of policing, much in line with what American officials proselytised abroad, but were incapable of implementing systematically at home.

It is no coincidence that the institutionalisation of a national system of incarceration took place during these years.[80] Two years after the entry into force of the law, the government had to declare an amnesty for drug offenders because of the overcrowding of prisons. In 1958, Shahab Ferdowsi, then advisor to the Ministry of Justice, declared: 'poor people are paying the price of this policy and are used by traffickers to transport opium and other dangerous substances.'[81] The recriminations were against the international pressure on Iran to eradicate the poppy, while other countries in the Middle East, Turkey and Afghanistan, carried on with their opium industry, the product of which was smuggled into Iran.

76 Azarkhosh, J. A., *Afat-e Zendegi*, p. 514.
77 Azarkhosh, J. A., *Afat-e Zendegi*, p. 517.
78 Azarkhosh, J. A., *Afat-e Zendegi*, p. 514.
79 McLaughlin, G., and Quinn, T., 'Drug Control', p. 492.
80 See Rabi'i, N., *Tarikh-e zendan dar 'asr-e Qajar va Pahlavi*, Tehran 2011.
81 Shahidi, M. H., *Mavad-e Mokhadder*, p. 119.

Beside the heavy sentences, the prohibitionist regime of 1955 reproduced and alimented itself by funnelling the monies generating from drug confiscations (including propriety) to the anti-narcotic machinery. By the early 1960s, the government was allocating an annual $5 million budget for anti-narcotics efforts, while the United States provided around $250,000 for Iran's contribution to the regional anti-narcotics fight, including military hardware, planes, helicopters, and training.[82] Up to the late 1970s, the FBN and its successor the DEA trained groups of Iranian police officers in anti-narcotic enforcement, considering this programme 'of paramount importance and [...] part of the overall policy for attaining US Government objectives more effectively and realistically'.[83] These anti-narcotics efforts went hand in hand with the expansion of Iran's intelligence services. In 1957, Garland Williams, one of the influential FBN supervisors, arrived in Tehran to set up a narcotic squad while CIA and Mossad were helping the Iranians to establish Savak, Iran's infamous secret service.[84]

Heroin, Organised Crime and the Westoxified State

Iran preceded its American anti-narcotics patron in fighting illicit drugs. In 1956, a year after the Majles had passed the Prohibition Law, the US Congress approved the Narcotic Control Act which heavily sanctioned drug use and drug dealing.[85] Alignment in narcotics strategy resulted from the post-coup political environment, which made the Pahlavi dynasty and the Iranian state close geopolitical followers of the Eisenhower administration (1953–1961). And as long as geopolitics and international drugs control did not contradict each other, the alignment remained solidly in place. When anti-narcotics programmes clashed with geopolitical priorities, US administrations systematically privileged the latter.[86] Iranian officials

82 *The New York Times*, 2 April 1964.
83 Cited in *Efsha-ye Amperializm*, Tehran, Daneshjuyan-e Peyrov-e Khatt-e Emam, undated. This is a unsystematic collection of classified documents published by the Iranian students who took over the US Embassy in Tehran in 1979. Excerpts are available at: https://archive.org/stream/DocumentsFromTheUSEspionageDen/Documents%20from%20the%20U.S.%20Espionage%20Den%20v07_djvu.txt.
84 Valentine, D., *The Strength of the Wolf: The Secret History of America's War on Drugs*, London 2004, p. 169; Moravei K., 'Savak and the Cold War: Counter-intelligence and Foreign Intelligence (1957–68)', PhD thesis, University of Manchester 2011, pp. 276–77. See also Curtis, G., and Hooglund, E., 'Iran: A Country Study', Federal Research Division, 2009, available at: <http://www.loc.gov/rr/frd/cs/pdf/CS_Iran.pdf>.
85 Musto, D., *The American Disease*, p. 242.
86 Musto, D., *The American Disease*, p. 250.

and transnational drug traffickers were apparently aware of this willingness to compromise and played ball, as the drugs history of 1960s demonstrates.

In what seemed a global competition for tougher drugs policies in the 1960s, Iranian legislators introduced new punishments for drug offenders. Concomitant with the militarisation of the anti-narcotic machine, in 1961, a cabinet decree re-instated the death penalty for those engaging in drug trafficking. The number of sentences increased substantially after the announcement of the White Revolution in 1963 and the political repression of the June 5 revolt (*15 Khordad*) led by Ayatollah Khomeini. In his book, *Islamic Government*, Khomeini writes about the shah's approach to drugs:

> I am amazed at the way these people think. They kill people for possessing ten grams of heroin and say, 'That is the law' [...] (I am not saying it is permissible to sell heroin, but this is not the appropriate punishment. The sale of heroin must indeed be prohibited but the punishment must be in proportion to the crime.) When Islam, however, stipulates that the drinker of alcohol should receive eighty lashes, they consider it 'too harsh'. They can execute someone for possessing ten grams of heroin and the question of harshness does not even arise![87]

However, the impact of harsher punishments and prohibition went beyond the cost in human lives. With harsher punishments against opium and hashish, harder drugs became more accessible and increasingly popular. 'The harder the enforcement, the harder the drugs,' so says the 'Iron Law of Prohibition'.[88] In 1957, two years following the entry into force of prohibition, a man was hospitalised for heroin abuse after being found in Tehran's Mehran Gardens.[89] It was the first reported case of heroin 'addiction' in Iranian history and a hint at a changing drug phenomenon. In fact, heroin is more difficult to detect, easier to transport over long distances, more lucrative with higher margins of profit, and at the same time has a much stronger effect. It requires no specific space for its use and, unlike opium, does not have a strong smell, which can attract unsolicited attention. Yet heroin had no place in popular culture, neither as a medical nor a recreational

87 Khomeini, R., and Algar, H., *Islamic Government: Governance of the Jurist*, London 2002, p. 12. A change of mind occurred when Khomeini came to power. See Ghiabi, M., 'Drugs and Revolution in Iran: Islamic Devotion, Revolutionary Zeal and Republican Means', in *Iranian Studies* vol. 48, no. 2, 2015.

88 See Cowan, R., 'How the Narcs Created Crack', in *National Review*, vol. 38, 1986.

89 Qahrfarkhi, S. M., *E'tiyad*, p. 157.

product and its repercussions on the user's health were far more problematic than opium (and *shireh*). If opium had an ambiguous status within Iran's table of values and social habitus, being simultaneously medicinal, ritual and indigenous, heroin represented the intrusion of global consumption behaviours in the pursuit of pleasure and modernity into Iran. The tastes of Iranian modernisers spilled over into drug choice too.

By that time, the Pahlavi state regarded the question of 'addiction' as an epidemic that had to be isolated, as if it were cholera or the plague. Heroin, instead, instantiated a paradigmatic case of material Westoxification (*gharbzadegi*), an intrusion extraneous and alien to life in Iran, including the life of drugs. Upper-class young Iranians embraced the nascent counterculture of 1960s Europe and North America, where heroin culture was on the rise. As such, heroin use in Iran did not enter into the practice of the ordinary people, but remained an elite pastime up to the end of the Pahlavi era, given the higher price of heroin and its availability in urban areas only.[90] The words of Jalal Al-e Ahmad, without referring to heroin directly, echoed a lifestyle embodied by it. '*Gharbzadegi* is like cholera,' he writes, 'a disease that comes from without, fostered in an environment made for breeding diseases.'[91] This environment to which the Iranian author refers was that of the reformist programmes promoted by Mohammad Reza Shah over the 1960–1970s. Contributing to the changing atmosphere was the shah's White Revolution in 1963, which produced a mass exodus from villages to urban centres, especially Tehran. These developments signified an epochal change in the life of Iranians at all levels and their acquaintance with forms of sociability, consumption and recreation that differed substantially from that of rural communities. Inevitably, consumption patterns (including those pertaining to psychoactive, narcotic substances) were affected by this transformation. In cities, heroin became the new wonder drug of the century, inducing interest and curiosity for the newly urbanised communities, when compared to the obsolete practice of smoking or eating opium.[92] Women were equally attracted to this new substance. For instance, when the Imperial Gendarmerie discovered heroin in the bags of two women, Havva and Monavvar, heroin was described by them as having quasi-miraculous effects.

---

90 Central Treaty Organisation (CENTO), '*Seminar on Public Health and Medical Problems Involved in Narcotics Drug Addiction*', Tehran, April 8–12, 1972, pp. 25–26, available at: <http://pdf.usaid.gov/pdf_docs/PNABI608.pdf>.

91 Al-e Ahmad, J., and Campbell, R., *Occidentosis: A Plague from the West*, Berkley 1983, p. 166.

92 This is part of my next project which intends to look at the social life of drugs prior the Islamic Revolution of 1979.

Brought to court, Monavvar defended herself, explaining: 'Havva's son gave it to me and, since my daughter is bald [*kachal-e*]... I intended to put the drug [*dāru*] on her head.'[93] Monavvar, who perhaps overestimated the anti-oxidant benefits of opiates, was sentenced to six months prison, for believing in (or lying about) the wonderful powers of heroin.

According to government data, 'the Iranian addict population was reduced from, conservatively speaking 1,500,000 (in 1955) to 400,000 (in 1974)'.[94] Although there are no other figures for drug use for this period, the simple decrease in the number is not an exhaustive description of the drug consumption phenomenon. In the decades following the adoption of the 1955 prohibition regime, organised criminal groups found their way into the domain of Iran's drugs politics. Secret laboratories mushroomed across the country, with the northwestern area in the proximity of Tabriz and Malayer becoming a key production zone. Prohibition made the business of opiates highly profitable and persuaded groups of ordinary people who had previously little contact with the opium economy to set up morphine and heroin production lines. Police records show bakers, butchers and other unskilled workers using their workplace, house or farmhouse to produce opium derivatives, which they then sold to traffickers.[95] By using opium smuggled into Iran from Afghanistan, or morphine base coming southward from Turkey, 'heroin chemists' developed underground networks of procurement and production.[96] A contemporary commentator acknowledged that such production 'is not more complex than making a bootleg of whiskey in the United States', an analogy that recalls the early days of American prohibition and the production of moonshine. At times, heavy armed confrontations between the gendarmerie and drug traffickers occurred, especially when the latter were members of tribes or Afghan immigrants. For example, in 1957, an 11-hour shooting battle broke out between the gendarmerie (in charge of anti-narcotics) and the Kakavand Tribe, in the western city of Kermanshah, leaving 18 tribesmen dead and 45 wounded.[97] The financial bonanza of heroin trafficking had soon established international networks between Iranian drug business and the West. In particular, West Germany became a major storage depot for Iranian drug traffickers, who had interwoven close connections with the German underworld

93 *Ettela'at*, September 19, 1969.

94 Rejali, D., *Torture & Modernity: Self, Society, and State in Modern Iran*, Boulder 1994, p. 66.

95 Shahidi, M. H., *Mavad-e Mokhadder*, p. 121.

96 McLaughlin, G., and Quinn, T., 'Drug Control', p. 477.

97 *The New York Times*, 12 January 1958; *The New York Times*, 12 January 1958.

through an emerging diaspora, which facilitated the transhipment of Iranian heroin and Afghan hashish.[98]

The road to hell is paved with good intentions. The Pahlavis, however, seemed to have none in matters of drugs policy and, in fact, witnessed a great deal of narcotics trafficking at the heart of the royal court, although there is no explicit evidence that the shah himself was aware or involved in the illegal business. While FBN advisors maintained their support for Iran's opium prohibition – advocating globally in favour of Iran's 'selfless effort' – they were also well-informed about the role of the shah's family and acolytes in the narcotic trade.[99] The shah's twin sister, Princess Ashraf Pahlavi, had been allegedly involved in cases of narcotics trafficking and critics of the Pahlavi regime associated her with international criminal organisations.[100] It was reported that in 1967, while on her way out of Geneva airport, Ashraf's luggage was searched by the Swiss anti-narcotics police, who allegedly found large amounts of heroin. Because of her diplomatic immunity, she was not prosecuted, but the international media covered the event in-depth, causing a scandal. Swiss and French newspapers spread the news about the accident, although official accounts of the incident have so far remained contested, especially by supporters of the Pahlavi monarchy. Ashraf sued *Le Monde* for these allegations and eventually won her libel case, having the story retracted.[101]

In 1960, the Swiss authorities were warned of an Iranian national, Amir Hushang Davallou, a Qajar prince at the Pahlavi court who was suspected of shipping heroin into Europe. Stopped at the border, Davallou claimed diplomatic

98 McLaughlin, G., and Quinn, T., 'Drug Control', p. 518.

99 Gingeras, R., 'Istanbul Confidential: Heroin, Espionage, and Politics in Cold War Turkey, 1945–1960', in *Diplomatic History*, vol. 37, no. 4 , 2013, p. 25.

100 Ashraf Pahlavi systematically rejected the claims. Claims are made especially in General Fardust's memoires published posthumously. Fardust, H., *The Rise and Fall of the Pahlavi Dynasty*, Delhi 1995. While the materials provided by the SAVAK documentation on the regime appears to be reliable, albeit at times with lacunae, some of the claims in the above-mentioned memoires remain dubious. For methodological consideration of these sources, see 'About the Sources' in Kurzman, C., *The Unthinkable Revolution in Iran*, Cambridge, MA 2009.

101 For this purpose, she also requested support from the US Government. See: 'Telegram 64317 From the Department of State to the Embassy in Iran', April 14, 1972, and: 'Telegram 2080 From the Embassy in Iran to the Department of State', April 11, 1972, in Belmonte, M. (ed.), *Foreign Relations of the United States, 1969–1976, Volume E–4, Documents on Iran And Iraq, 1969–1972*, Washington, DC 2006, Documents 177 and 178. See Ashraf's memoire, Pahlavi, A., *Faces in a Mirror: Memoirs from Exile*, Englewood Cliffs 1980, pp. 188–191.

immunity and flew back to Tehran on the shah's plane.[102] Davallou was an intimate of the royal court, described by some as the person in charge of procuring women for the monarch. For these duties, he was popularly known as the 'Prince Pimp'.[103] Ten years later, his house in Switzerland was searched by the police and found to contain narcotics, but Davallou, who was a regular opium smoker and suffered from heart problems, was allowed to return home to Tehran.[104]

The shah's two brothers, too, were seemingly involved in the trafficking business. Prince Hamid-Reza, the shah's younger brother, is described in SAVAK records as 'having established in Takht-e Jamshid Street a headquarter, which used air companies to smuggle drugs, especially opium from outside the country into Iran, to produce heroin and then distribute it in Tehran and other cities'. Hamid-Reza's enterprise reached such fame that the best heroin in Tehran in the 1960s was known as *hero'in-e Hamid-Reza.*[105] Another one of shah's brothers, Prince Mahmud-Reza, had also been involved in the business. A *bon vivant* with a habit for opium and heroin, his relations with the shah were strained and he was forbidden from attending the royal court.[106] Since 1951, American officials had been observing the movements and affairs of Mahmud-Reza across the Mediterranean Sea and the Atlantic Ocean. The FBN discovered that Mahmud-Reza, under the *alias* Mahmoud Kawa, smuggled heroin between Tehran, Paris, New York and Detroit, but the Americans never followed up this lead and instead arrested an Armenian associate of the prince, who operated a network that included Iran's consuls in Brussels and Cairo.[107] Earlier in 1957, two American officials were found smuggling large quantities of opium into the United States. Their principal contact in Iran was General Mohammad Asad Bakhtiari.[108]

During the 1960s, American regional interests in the Middle East and the ongoing global Cold War prevented the FBN from disclosing the vast network of international heroin trafficking that operated through networks connected or close to the Pahlavi family and high-ranking state officials. The state itself remained in

102 Kuchekian-Fard. H., 'Rosva'i dar Su'is: Asnadi az darbar-e shahanshahi darbareh-ye qachaq-e mavvad-e mokhadder', in *Faslnameh-ye Tarikh-e Mo'aser-e Iran (Quarterly of Contemporary Iranian History)*, vol. 1, no. 4, 1997.

103 Buchan, J., *Days of God: The Revolution in Iran and its Consequences*, New York 2013, pp. 100–101.

104 Alimardani, A. A., *Mavad-e Mokhadder va Rezhim-e Pahlavi*, p. 119.

105 *Parvandeh-ye enferadi-ye Hamid-Reza*, 17/06/1341, cited in Alimardani, A. A., *Mavad-e Mokhadder va Rezhim-e Pahlavi*, p. 125.

106 Alimardani, A. A., *Mavad-e Mokhadder va Rezhim-e Pahlavi*, pp. 119–125.

107 Valentine, D., *The Strength*, pp. 117–119.

108 Gingeras, R., *Poppy Politics*, p. 325.

a paradoxical position: it hardened its drug laws, it militarised its drugs policy, and expanded its intelligence networks through anti-narcotic cooperation with the United States. At the same time, it coexisted with informal networks made up of private interests, at times connected to the royal court, that managed a global distribution of heroin. Iran was part of the regional machinery of American anti-narcotics strategy, particularly through intelligence sharing, yet also one of the main hubs for the trade in illegal narcotics in the region.[109] It is clear that US strategy prioritised national security and the Cold War over narcotics control.

Meanwhile, the number of people punished for drug offenses in Iran over the 1960s increased substantially. Iranian heroin seizures topped international ranking by the end of the 1960s.[110] The prison population reached unprecedented levels with administrative costs becoming a burden in budgetary allocations. The subaltern classes (e.g. impoverished rural migrants, homeless and vagrant men, petty criminals) were the primary targets of these policies. Welfare services for drug rehabilitation remained weak and the promise to uproot drugs from Iranian society sounded farcical. In 1969, however, the government overturned the 1955 opium prohibition and established a regulated system of opium distribution and poppy cultivation. This occurred, most symbolically, when the newly-elected US President Richard Nixon declared a 'War on Drugs'.

An Indigenous Model of Prohibition?

The sudden overturn of the poppy ban in Iran was met with surprise and 'sharp disappointment' around the world, particularly by the International Narcotics Control Board, the main United Nations body overseeing the execution of international drug conventions.[111] The decision appeared to run counter to Iran's long-term commitments to fight the trafficking of narcotics to the West and clashed with the radical anti-drug crusade that the government had embarked on since the 1950s. However, the re-introduction of the poppy did not signify the abandonment of law enforcement in Iran's anti-narcotics strategy. Rather this new policy can be seen as an example of the reification and prioritisation of national security in the state's approach to social issues. The rationale behind this shift suggests that the trend of greater independence and autonomy that has been observed by scholars

109 *Bulletin on Narcotics*, vol. 4, no. 4, 1960.
110 Shahidi, M. H., *Mavad-e Mokhadder*, p. 126; Fort, J., *Bulletin on Narcotics*, vol. 17, no. 4, 1965, pp. 13–19.
111 *Bulletin on Narcotics*, vol. 3, no. 5, 1970, p. 39.

in Iranian foreign and developmental policy in the late Pahlavi era can be traced to Iran's drugs policy.[112]

The move occurred for several reasons, the main being the refusal by Iran's neighbours – Turkey, Afghanistan and Pakistan – to eradicate their local production of opium, most of which passed through Iran, with a considerable part consumed by Iranians. Sandwiched between two large opium producing regions, Iran could not effectively stop the flow of drugs. In the words of former Health Minister Saleh, 'gold goes out, opium comes in', to the extent that capital flight became a serious threat to economic development due to 'payment for large quantities of contraband opium with gold' from the Iranian gold reserves.[113] There was also an intention to decrease the economic burden of the anti-narcotic efforts on poorer communities, where particular hardship was imposed on families whose breadwinner had been incarcerated for drug offences. An eightfold increase in heroin confiscation occurred between 1964 and 1966, prompting the government to reconsider the feasibility and effectiveness of the prohibition of opium in Iran.[114] The government hence granted amnesty to all those condemned for poppy cultivation under the 1955 drug law and introduced a vast medical system of drug treatment and rehabilitation.[115]

The Iranians promised their American patrons that they would renew the opium prohibition once Turkey and Afghanistan had done the same.[116] In fact, Article One of the Law on 'Permission of Poppy Cultivation and Opium Production' put this in unequivocal terms: 'From the date of this law up to when neighbouring countries will continue poppy cultivation, the Ministry for Land Reform and Rural Cooperation is permitted to undertake poppy cultivation in the regions and on to the extent determined on a yearly base by the Ministerial Committee. […] The government is responsible to stop this programme once poppy cultivation is eradicated in neighbouring countries.'[117] However, despite the Turkish ban on opium between 1969 and 1974, which was imposed under heavy American pressure on Ankara, the Iranian authorities did not stop poppy cultivation programmes.

---

112 Alvandi, R., *Nixon, Kissinger, and the Shah: The United States and Iran in the Cold War*, New York 2014.

113 *The New York Times*, 11 February 1973; Chouvy, *Opium*, p. 20.

114 Windle, *Suppressing Illicit Opium*, p. 40.

115 McLaughlin, G., and Quinn, T., 'Drug Control', pp. 497–498.

116 Chouvy, P. A., *Opium*, p. 20.

117 'Qanun-e ejazeh-ye kesht-e khashkhash va sodur-e taryak', National Assembly of Iran, March 4, 1969, available at: <http://rc.majlis.ir/fa/law/show/96304>.

The state retained a total monopoly of poppy fields, which were meant to produce a set amount of opium for the 'treatment of the addicts'. Opium use was illegal unless justified by a medical certificate.[118] A strict enforcement code was applied to farmers, peasants and employees of the state agency supervising the matter. According to the law, all personnel had a three-month period to refer to a rehabilitation centre to cure any opium dependency before being re-admitted to the workplace.[119]

Under the legendary 'coupon system', which is remembered by many elderly Iranians, vouchers were issued to registered opium users, based on the need of the patient as determined by 'pharmacology and the science of treatment'.[120] Two groups were allowed to register. The first were users over 60 years of age who would receive their ration after the approval of a physician. The other group consisted of people between the ages of 20 and 59 who manifested physical or psychological medical symptoms for which opium was prescribed, or those who could not give up their opium use, in which case the state assumed the responsibility to supply them with opium. The medical symptoms for which one could receive the coupon included headache, rheumatism, back pain, depression, arthritis, etc., and these were assessed by a governmental panel under the Ministry of Health. A daily dose of opium (between 2 and 10 grams) could be purchased from a licenced pharmacy or drug store. An ID card was then issued for the individual with a photograph, personal particulars, the daily dose of opium, and the pharmacy from which he/she could secure it.[121] Two kinds of opium were available to the public. The first was of a lower standard, which the government disposed of from seizures of illicit opium traffic from Afghanistan and to a lesser extent Pakistan, costing 6 rials per gram. The second, known for its outstanding quality and sometimes called *senātori* ('of/for Senators'), was produced in the state owned poppy farms and priced at 17½ rials per gram.[122] Once the Organisation for Opium Transactions (Sazman-e Moʿamelat-e Taryak) issued the coupons for sale, the revenues

118 'Qanun-e ejazeh', Article Three.
119 *Ettelaʿat*, April 15, 1969.
120 Article One, of 'Ayin-nameh-ye ejra'i-ye maddeh-ye 3 qanun-e kesht-e mahdud-e khashkhash va sodur-e taryak mosavvab-e Esfand-e 1348', available at: <http://rc.majlis.ir/fa/law/show/96393>. For an analysis of how this model is interpreted by religious authorities in Iran, see Ghiabi, M., et al., 'Islam and Cannabis: Legalisation and Religious Debate in Iran', *International Journal of Drug Policy*, Vol. 56, June 2018, pp. 121–127.
121 See CENTO, 'Seminar', p. 112. See Siassi, I., and Fozouni, B., 'Dilemmas of Iran's Opium Maintenance Program: An Action Research for Evaluating Goal Conflicts and Policy Changes', in *International Journal of the Addictions*, vol. 15, no. 8, 1980, pp. 1127–1140.
122 CENTO, 'Seminar', p. 114.

generated from this industry would be deposited in the Agricultural Cooperative Bank of Iran (Bank-e Taʿavoni-ye Keshavarzi-ye Iran) and re-invested in drugs policy programmes, including rehabilitation and anti-smuggling. This scheme reassured international drug controllers that opium remained strictly controlled by the state, with no leakage into the illicit trafficking networks travelling westwards.

Comfortable in the knowledge that the supply of opium was assured, the registered user could walk into to their pharmacy of choice and, at a competitive price that was intended to annihilate the illegal market, purchase the highest quality of opium available anywhere in the world. By 1972 there were about 110,000 people registered out of an estimated total population of roughly 400,000 opium users. By 1978 this figure had risen to 188,000, with 52% of those registered under the age of sixty.[123] Opium had returned, one could say, to its authentic place within Iranian culture, under the supervision of family physicians. Those who did not register could buy opium illegally from registered users, who often horded quantities in excess of their needs, which they could then re-sell. Alternatively, users could access the illicit market of Afghan and Pakistani opium, which remained in place especially in rural areas, especially in the Eastern regions. The figure of the 'patient-pusher' appeared in the narrative of opium, characterised by an intergenerational mix of elderly opium users who would register for the coupon in order to help younger users avoid the illegal market, or to make some marginal profit from reselling the coupons.[124] Moreover, having opium at home, after all, was part of the (specifically Iranian) customs of greeting hosts and a *sine qua non* in areas such as Kerman, Isfahan and Mashhad.

The illegal market did not disappear overnight. In areas in which the state had limited presence, people kept on relying on their narcotics trafficking networks. Heroin gained further popularity throughout the 1970s, with Tehran having around 20–40,000 heroin users. The expatriate community based in the capital had its encounters with heroin too. Americans, in particular, found local heroin of especially high quality. The US Embassy, to counter the rise of drug use, helped establish the first Community Development Centre providing support for American drug users seeking recovery in Tehran.[125] Because of the high demand for heroin in Tehran, the flow of opium did not stop either. Traffickers would smuggle in Turkish opium, which would be refined into heroin in local laboratories, usually

123 See Mehryar, A. H., and Moharreri, M. H., 'A Study of Authorized Opium Addiction in Shiraz City and Fars Province, Iran', in *British Journal of Addiction to Alcohol & Other Drugs*, vol. 73, no. 1, 1978.
124 Siassi, 'Dilemmas of Iran', p. 1133.
125 In *Efsha-ye Amperializm*.

Figure 4: five members of an Iranian drug trafficking band (Source: *Ettela'at*, August 29, 1969).

around Orumiyeh (then known as Rezaiyeh).[126] A joint venture between Turkish criminal organisations and Iranian traffickers enabled this industry to prosper, but not without a heavy toll. On March 10, 1969, Osman Arkul, a Turkish citizen was arrested with 31 kilograms of morphine, plus a cache of arms. Later, once the new law entered into force, a band of six Iranian men were caught *in flagrante* with more than 1 kilogram of heroin and 400 grams of morphine. They were tried and sentenced to be executed by firing squad. Another prominent case was that of a German trafficker based in Abadan. Thanks to an informant, the authorities were able to trace the hierarchy of the southwest heroin network upstream to Hermann Robert Kopp, who was found in his house with almost 1 kilogram of pure heroin and names and contacts of dealers across Iran. A year later, he was sentenced to five years in prison in front of the shocked eyes of his wife, who in reaction to the sentence's announcement attempted to throw herself from the tribunal's balcony.[127] Despite these heavy measures, the heroin industry prospered as other groups would replace those incarcerated.[128]

People living in villages, for instance, witnessed very little change after the adoption of the 1969 law or, for that matter, any previous law. Distances were great, physicians few and distribution networks weak. Women, too, had a tendency not to register, mostly due to the negative perception of female opium smokers, especially when young.[129] The public perception was that the lower

126 *Ettela'at*, June 11, 1969.
127 *Ettela'at*, August 29, 1969.
128 *Ettela'at*, June 30, 1969; *Ettela'at*, June 7, 1969.
129 Mehryar, A. H., and Moharreri, M. H., 'A Study of Authorized', p. 97.

classes mostly registered for the coupons, but this is largely due to the location of opium dispensaries, which happened to be in less wealthy areas, especially in Tehran. Thus, only a small proportion of the total population had access to the service. The facilities for treatment and rehabilitation were also insufficient. The main hospital for the treatment of drug abuse in Tehran, the Bimarestan-e Mo'tadan (Addicts' Hospital), had only 150 beds in 1970, while the lack of facilities in the rest of the country was even worse.[130] The private sector provided treatment services, including psychiatric and psychological support along the lines of American psychoanalysis, but mainly directed at the urban upper class who could afford their higher fees.[131]

The majority of registered users lived in the urban centres of the north; regions such as Kerman and Isfahan with a historical connection to opium and the poppy economy had significantly lower numbers of registered patients. This suggests that those people who had access to opium without the intermediation of the state, that is to say, through the illegal market, opted for its informal acquisition.

By the mid-1970s, addiction had come to occupy a central place in discussions on society and politics in Iran. Drugs and politics were intertwined as the royal court had firstly been accused of operating an illegal network of drug trafficking and, now, the state had become the main legal provider of narcotics to the population. Socially, the presence of drugs was also conspicuous. The International Conference of Medicine, which took place in Ramsar in 1972, was entirely dedicated to the issue of 'addiction'. Its proceedings advised the government to ban poppy cultivation or to limit it to the minimum required for essential medical needs for addicts. Moreover, the conference suggested stopping the 'coupon' system because of the risk of opium diversion to the general population and the widespread over-prescription practised by doctors.[132] None of these advices were heeded by the government and the coupon system continued until the new revolutionary regime abrogated it in 1980.

The 1969 law was not dissonant with global prohibitionist discourse. Since the 1920s, British doctors had been prescribing heroin to patients who were dependent on the substance. In 1967, the National Health Service (NHS) advised doctors to continue this practice to prevent the spread of heroin trafficking in Britain, despite increasing pressures against the practice.[133] This model allowed

130 Qahrfarkhi, S. M., *E'tiyad*, p. 163.

131 *Bulletin on Narcotics*, 1976, vol. 3 no. 3.

132 Shahid, M. H., *Mavad-e Mokhadder*, p. 129.

133 Mars, S., *The Politics of Addiction: Medical Conflict and Drug Dependence in England since the 1960s*, London 2012, p. 27.

Figure 5: Registered Opium Addicts in the first Semester of 1974*

REGIONS	Registered Drug Users
Teheran	44,000
Khorasan	18,400
Mazandaran	17,700
Gilan	17,000
Kerman	11,900
Isfahan	6,700
Yazd	2,000
Kurdistan	1,100
Sistan & Baluchistan	1,000
Persian Gulf Ports	300

* Data selected as an ad hoc sample, from Qahrfarkhi, S. M., *E'tiyad*, p. 161.

an opiate abuser to seek medical support in special clinics, housed in hospitals and under the supervision of psychiatrists. The medical community in Iran was aware of the British model and had adopted a modified version of it in the early decades of the twentieth century, under the first attempt to register *shireh* users. The fundamental difference in the 1970s was the scale of the Iranian programme, which numbered hundreds of thousands of people, compared to the British model which accounted for a mere 342 people in 1964.[134] Similarly to Britain, addiction was described in Iran as a 'disability' and not simply a 'disease', with its consequences impacting not only the individual, but also the family and society.[135] Over the 1970s the government made the National Iranian Society for Rehabilitation of the Disabled the institution responsible for the treatment and maintenance of drug users.[136] In this regard, the programme could not be regarded as a niche attempt to control a marginal population, but a vast societal endeavour with the purpose of addressing a public health issue. It paralleled the global momentum towards

134 Mars, S., *The Politics of Addiction*, p. 8.
135 Berridge, V., and Mold, A., *Concepts of Addictive Substances and Behaviours across Time and Place*, Oxford 2016, p. 73.
136 Afkhami, A. A., 'From Punishment to Harm Reduction: Resecularization of Addiction in Contemporary Iran', in Gheissari, A. (ed.), *Contemporary Iran: Economy, Society, Politics*, Oxford 2009.

'addiction treatment' that was characterised by the mushrooming of rehabilitation and welfare programmes for drug users in North America and Europe.[137]

As it had been for the 1911 drug laws and for the 1955 prohibition, lawmakers in Tehran yet again preceded their colleagues in Washington in 1969. One year after the Iranian Majles's reform of the drug law, the US Congress passed the Comprehensive Drug Abuse Prevention and Control Act, which paved the way for the creation of the Drug Enforcement Administration (DEA). In the same way that the Nixon administration approved of methadone maintenance treatment to deal with the surge in heroin addiction among Vietnam veterans, the Iranian government also sought to establish a system for controlling drug (ab)use through medical supervision. In doing so, Iran did not give up its law and order priorities. In fact, the 1969 law was soon followed by further legislation which strengthened the punishments for drug offenders. Accordingly, drug trafficking cases would be tried by military courts (*dādgāh-e nezāmi*) rather than civilian courts, with heavier penalties imposed. In fact, the sentences were draconian: any person caught producing or trafficking heroin, morphine, cocaine, or hiding more than 2 kilograms of opium or 30 grams of heroin, morphine or cocaine would be sentenced to death.[138] A CIA memorandum reported that 'Tehran has embarked on a stricter smuggling eradication program [of heroin trafficking]', with more than ninety smugglers executed between 1969 and 1971.[139] It is estimated that there were six thousand prisons spread throughout Iran in 1975, with drug offenders being the largest part of the prison population.[140] Upgrading the security sensitivity of the narcotics issue can be partly interpreted as the shah's assurance to his closest ally, the United States, of Iran's sincere pledge to stop the flow of heroin westwards. It can also be seen as coercion against those operating on a terrain that was the exclusive turf of the state, namely opium production. Perhaps, from a public diplomacy perspective, the punishments were also meant to wash off the stain caused by the allegations against the royal family's connivance with international narco-traffickers. Instead of establishing a system of regulation, with an underlying non-prohibitionist mindset, the Iranian state adopted a double form of intervention aimed ultimately at the exclusive control of the narcotic issue by the state itself, both in terms of domestic distribution and production.

137 Musto, D., *An American Disease*, pp. 245–272.
138 'Qanun-e tashdid-e mojazat', June 21, 1969, available at: <http://rc.majlis.ir/fa/law/show/96375>.
139 'Memorandum for the CIA heroin coordinator', US Department of State, July 1, 1971, available at: <http://2001–2009.state.gov/documents/organization/70647.pdf>.
140 Rejali, D., *Torture & Modernity*, p. 55.

Conclusion

The inception of a drug control machinery in Iran corresponded with the country's participation in the 1909 Shanghai Opium Conference in the midst of the Constitutional Revolution. Sponsored by the United States, the conference was the first worldwide effort to draw homogenising lines of behaviour (sobriety, temperance, order, legibility) – albeit, haphazardly – into the global body politic. Drugs prohibition emerged as an international project driven by a puritan and at times racist ideology, especially in North America and the UK, where drug policy discriminated against minorities and disenfranchised communities.[141] This new ideology overlooked the cultural trajectories of non-Western peoples and (mis) represented as barbaric their consumption of intoxicants. Opium and 'addiction' as its governmental effect were associated with a life handicapped by dependence, impotency, apathy and above all slavery. Opium, in particular, embodied an anti-modern element, a hindrance in the modernisation destiny of any country, in terms of moral decency and capitalistic productivity. Walt Rostow, the patron of modernist social sciences, who announced in his cherished *Divine Ship* that 'all people of the globe sail together, sail the same voyage, are bound to the same destination', did not quite consider it necessary to include a provision of opiates in the global vessel's travel kit.[142]

The adoption of this anti-narcotic ideology, which in a matter of decades produced apparatuses of control and punishment, went through a period of experimentation, both for the state as a governmental machinery and the people as interlocutors and experimenters of the phenomenon of drugs. In this journey, the tensions arising from the drug phenomenon were located in a global-domestic nexus, built on geographic considerations, public health, cultural trends and political economy. All these factors were equally intersected with the modernisation process that characterised the life of the Pahlavi state and which, in the field of anti-narcotics at least, was heavily altered by America's global fight against narcotics. Yet, American pressures did not always achieve the desired result; the Iranian state often adopted the modernisation impetus on its own terms, indigenising it, as in the 1969 introduction of poppy cultivation and opium distribution programmes.

Timothy Mitchell wrote that 'the essence of modern politics is not policies formed on one side of this division being applied to or shaped by the other, but the

141 Mills, J., *Cannabis Nation*, London 2009; Musto, D., *The American Disease*; Alexandre, M., *The New Jim Crow*, New York 2009.
142 Engerman, D. C., and Unger, C. R., 'Introduction', p. 375.

producing and reproducing of these lines of difference'.[143] In this regard, Mitchell's historicisation is reminiscent of Foucault's genealogical approach: it is not a 'quest for the origins of policies or values, neither is its duty to demonstrate that the past actively lives in the present'.[144] The task of genealogy, paraphrasing the French philosopher, is to record the history of unstable, incongruent and discontinuous events into a historical process that makes visible all of those discontinuities that cross state and society.[145] In the popular opium mythology, a parable emblematises all these discontinuities and tensions:

> Four public officials, connoisseurs of opium (*taryāk-shenās*) and professional opium users (*herfe'i*), would go every morning to the Office of the Treasury (*dārā'i*) to test the quality of the state opium, before attaching the government banderole to those opium cakes up to standard for national distribution. With the revolution in 1979 and the closure of the Opium Office, all four of them died due to hangover for the lack of opium (*khomāri*). Thus was abruptly closed a local chapter of global narcotic history.[146]

Bibliography

Abrahamian, E., *The Coup: 1953, the CIA, and the Roots of Modern US-Iranian Relations*, New York 2013.

Afkhami, A. A., 'From Punishment to Harm Reduction: Resecularization of Addiction in Contemporary Iran', in Gheissari, A., *Contemporary Iran: economy, society, politics*, Oxford, Oxford University Press 2009, pp. 194–210.

Afsha-ye Emperializm, Tehran, Daneshjuyan-e Peyrou-ye Khatt-e Emam, undated, available at: <https://archive.org/stream/DocumentsFromTheUSEspionageDen/Documents%20from%20the%20U.S.%20Espionage%20Den%20v07_djvu.txt>.

Al-e Ahmad, J. and Campbell, R., *Occidentosis: A Plague from the West*, Berkeley 1983.

---

143 Mitchell, T., 'Society, Economy, and the State Effect', in *The Anthropology of the State: A Reader*, Chichester 2009, p. 184.

144 Foucault, M., *Language, Counter-Memory, Practice: Selected Essays and Interviews*, Ithaca 1980, p. 146.

145 Foucault, M., *Language*, pp. 150–4, 162.

146 An apocryphal tale commonly narrated by long-term opium smokers across Iran. Referred to the author during fieldwork research carried out between 2012 and 2016.

Alemi, A., and Naraghi, M. M., 'The Iceberg of Opium Addiction: an Epidemiological Survey of Opium Addiction in a Rural Community', in *Drug and Alcohol Dependence*, vol. 3, no. 2, 1978, pp. 107–112.

Alexandre, M., *The New Jim Crow*, New York 2009.

Alimardani, A. A., 'Mavad-e Mokhadder va Rejim-e Pahlavi', in *Faslnameh-ye Motale'at-e Tarikh*, vol. 25, 2009, pp. 112–147.

Alvandi, R., *Nixon, Kissinger, and the Shah: The United States and Iran in the Cold War*, New York 2014.

'Ayin-nameh-ye Ejra'i-ye Madde-ye 3 Qanun-e Kesht-e Mahdud-e Khashkhash va Sodur-e Taryak Mosavvab-e Esfand-e 1348', available at: <http://rc.majlis.ir/fa/law/show/96393>.

Azarkhosh, J. A., *Afat-e Zendegi*, Teheran 1956 [1334].

Beck, L., *Nomad: A Year in the Life of a Qashqa'i Tribesman in Iran*, Berkley 1991.

Belmonte, M. (ed.), *Foreign Relations of the United States, 1969–1976, Volume E–4, Documents on Iran And Iraq, 1969–1972*, Washington, DC 2006.

Berridge, V., and Mold, A., *Concepts of Addictive Substances and Behaviours across Time and Place*, Oxford 2016.

Berridge, V. and Edwards, G., *Opium and the People*, London 1982,

Buchan, J., *Days of God: The Revolution in Iran and its Consequences*, New York 2013.

Bulletin on Narcotics, vol. 3, no. 3 (1976).

Bulletin on Narcotics, vol. 3, no. 5 (1970).

Bulletin on Narcotics, vol. 4, no. 4 (1960).

Campos, I., *Home Grown: Marijuana and the Origins of Mexico's War on Drugs*, Chapel Hill 2012.

Central Treaty Organisation (CENTO), 'S*eminar on Public Health and Medical Problems Involved in Narcotics Drug Addiction',* Teheran, April 8–12, 1972, available at: <http://pdf.usaid.gov/pdf_docs/PNABI608.pdf>.

Chouvy, P. A., *Opium: Uncovering the Politics of the Poppy*, Cambridge, MA 2009.

Collins, J., 'Regulations and Prohibitions: Anglo-American Relations and International Drug Control, 1939–1964', PhD dissertation, London School of Economics 2015.

Courtwright, D. T., *Dark Paradise*, Cambridge, MA 2009.

Courtwright, D. T., *Forces of Habit*, Cambridge, MA 2009.

Cowan, R., 'How the Narcs Created Crack', in *National Review*, vol. 38, 1986, pp. 26–31.

Cronin, S., 'Resisting the New State: Peasants and Pastoralists in Iran, 1921–41', in *The Journal of Peasant Studies*, vol. 32, no. 1, 2005, pp. 1–47.

Cronin, S., *Soldiers, Shahs and Subalterns in Iran: Opposition, Protest and Revolt, 1921–1941*, London 2010.

Cronin, S., *Tribal Politics in Iran: Rural Conflict and the New State, 1921–1941*. London 2007.

Curtis, G., and Hooglund, E., 'Iran: A Country Study', Federal Research Division 2009, available at: <http://www.loc.gov/rr/frd/cs/pdf/CS_Iran.pdf>.

Encyclopaedia Iranica, 'Song in Praise of Opium', April 27, 1969, available at: <http://www.iranicaonline.org/articles/song-praise-opium>.

Engerman, D. C., and Unger, C. R., 'Introduction: Towards a global history of modernization', in *Diplomatic History*, vol. 33, no. 3, 2009, pp. 375–385.

Ettelaʿat, June 7, 1969.

Ettelaʿat, April 15, 1969.

Ettelaʿat, August 29, 1969.

Ettelaʿat, June 11, 1969.

Ettelaʿat, June 30, 1969;

Ettelaʿat, September 19, 1969.

Fardoust, H., *The Rise and Fall of the Pahlavi Dynasty*, Delhi 1995.

Fort, J., *Bulletin on Narcotics,* vol. 17, no. 4, 1965.

Foucault, M., *Language, Counter-Memory, Practice: Selected Essays and Interviews*, Ithaca 1980.

Ghiabi, M., 'Drugs and Revolution in Iran: Islamic Devotion, Revolutionary Zeal and Republican Means', in *Iranian Studies*, vol. 48, no. 2, 2015, pp. 139–163.

Ghiabi, M. 'Maintaining Disorder: the Micropolitics of Drugs Policy in Iran', in *Third World Quarterly*, vol. 39, no. 2, 2018, pp. 277–297.

Ghiabi, M., 'Spirit and Being: Interdisciplinary Reflections on Drugs across History and Politics', in *Third World Quarterly*, 39, 2 (2018), pp. 207–217.

Ghiabi, M., Maarefand, M., Bahari, H., and Alavi, Z. 'Islam and Cannabis: Legalisation and Religious Debate in Iran', in *International Journal of Drug Policy*, vol. 56, June 2018, pp. 121–127

Gingeras, R., 'Istanbul Confidential: Heroin, Espionage, and Politics in Cold War Turkey, 1945–1960', in *Diplomatic History*, vol. 37, no. 4, 2013, pp. 779–806.

Gingeras R., 'Poppy Politics: American Agents, Iranian Addicts and Afghan Opium, 1945–80', in *Iranian Studies*, vol. 45, no. 3, 2012, pp. 315–331.

Groseclose, E. E., *Introduction to Iran*, Oxford 1947.

Hansen, B., 'Learning to Tax: The Political Economy of the Opium Trade in Iran, 1921–1941', in *The Journal of Economic History*, vol. 61, no. 1, 2001, pp. 95–113.

Hedayat, S., *Buf-E Kur*, Tehran 1952.

Hedayat, S., *Zende Be Gur*, Tehran 1930.

Howard, B., *Outsiders*, New York 2008.

Kashani-Sabet, F., 'Hallmarks of Humanism: Hygiene and Love of Homeland in Qajar Iran', in *The American Historical Review*, vol. 105, no. 4, 2000, pp. 1171–1203.

Khomeini, R., and Algar, H., *Islamic Government: Governance of the Jurist*, London 2002.

Kramer, J. M., 'Drug Abuse in the USSR', in *Social Change and Social Issues in the Former USSR*, London 1992, pp. 53–79.

Kuchekian-Fard, H., 'Rosvai dar Swiss: Asnadi az Darbar-e Shahanshahi dar Bareh-ye Qachaq-e Mavvad-e Mokhadder', in *Faslnameh-ye Tarikh-e Mo'aser-e Iran (Quarterly of Contemporary Iranian History),* vol. 1, no. 4, 1997.

Kurzman, C., *The Unthinkable Revolution in Iran*, Cambridge, MA 2009.

Latifi Niya, M., 'Taryak va Eqdamat-e Anjoman-e Mobarezeh ba Taryak va Alcol', in *Gangineh*, vol. 2, no. 3–4, 1992.

MacCormack, M., and Amiri, M. K., *Memorandum on Persian Opium: Prepared for Dr. A. C. Mispaugh, Administrator General of the Finances*, London 1924.

Mars, S., *The Politics of Addiction: Medical Conflict and Drug Dependence in England since the 1960s*, London 2012.

Matthee, R. P., *The Pursuit of Pleasure: Drugs and Stimulants in Iranian History, 1500–1900*, Princeton 2005.

McAllister, W. B., *Drug Diplomacy in the Twentieth Century, An International History*, New York 2000.

McLaughlin, G., and Quinn, T., 'Drug Control in Iran: A Legal and Historical Analysis', in *Iowa Law Review*, vol. 59, 1973.

Mehryar, A. H., and Moharreri, M. H., 'A Study of Authorized Opium Addiction in Shiraz City and Fars Province, Iran', in *British Journal of Addiction to Alcohol & Other Drugs*, vol. 73, no. 1, 1978, pp. 93–102.

'Memorandum for the CIA heroin coordinator', US Department of State, July 1, 1971, available at: <http://2001–2009.state.gov/documents/organization/70647.pdf>.

Mills, J., *Cannabis Nation*, London 2009.

Millspaugh, A. C., *Americans in Persia*, Washington, DC 1946.

Millspaugh, A. C., *The American Task in Persia*, London 1925.

Mitchell, T., 'Society, Economy, and the State Effect', in *The Anthropology of the State: A Reader*, Chichester 2009, pp. 169–186.

Moravei, K., 'Savak and the Cold War: Counter-intelligence and Foreign Intelligence (1957–68)', PhD thesis, University of Manchester 2011.

Musto, D., *The American Disease: Origins of Narcotic Control*, Oxford 1999.

Neligan, A. R., *The Opium Question with Special Reference to Persia*, London 1929.

The New York Times, 15 February 1953.

The New York Times, 2 April 1964.

The New York Times, 11 February 1973

The New York Times, 12 January 1958.

The New York Times, 17 June 1953

The New York Times, 7 May 1952.

Pahlavi, A., *Faces in a Mirror: Memoirs from Exile*, Englewood Cliffs 1980.

Qahrfarkhi, S. M., *E'tiyad dar Iran*, Teheran 2011 [1390].

'Qanun-e Ejazeh-ye Kesht-e Khashkhak va Sodur-e Taryak', National Assembly of Iran, March 4, 1969, available at: <http://rc.majlis.ir/fa/law/show/96304>.

'Qanun-e Tashdid-e Mojazat', June 21, 1969, available at: <http://rc.majlis.ir/fa/law/show/96375>.

Rabi'i, N., *Tarikh-e zendan dar asr-e Qajar va Pahlavi*, Tehran 2011.

Regavim, R. B., 'The Most Sovereign of Masters: The History of Opium in Modern Iran, 1850–1955', PhD thesis, University of Pennsylvania 2012.

Rejali, D., *Torture & Modernity: Self, Society, and State in Modern Iran*, Boulder, CO 1994.

Ruzname-ye Rasmi-ye Keshvar-e Shahanshahi-ye Iran, 'Mozakerat-e Majles-e Shura-ye Melli, Second Session on December 16, 1951', December 23, 1951, available at: <https://mashruteh.org/wiki/index.php>.

Schayegh, C., *Who Is Knowledgeable Is Strong: Science, Class, and the Formation of Modern Iranian Society, 1900–1950*, Berkeley 2009.

Shahidi, M. H., *Mavad-e Mokhadder, Amniyat-e Ejtema'i va Rah-e Sevvom*, Teheran 2010 [1389].

Siassi, I. and Fozouni, B., 'Dilemmas of Iran's Opium Maintenance Program: An Action Research for Evaluating Goal Conflicts and Policy Changes', in *International Journal of the Addictions*, vol. 15, no. 8, 1980, pp. 1127–1140.

Tavakoli-Tarqi, M., 'Tajaddod-e Ruzmarreh va Ampul-e Tadvin', in *Iran nameh*, vol. 24, no. 4, 2009, pp. 421–460.

Tyrrell, I., *Reforming the World: The Creation of America's Moral Empire*, Princeton 2010.

UNODC, 'That day in history: The Shanghai Opium Commission 1909', February 2, 2009, available at: <http://www.unodc.org/unodc/en/frontpage/this-day-in-history-the-shanghai-opium-commission-1909.html>.

Valentine, D., *The Strength of the Wolf: The Secret History of America's War on Drugs*, London 2004,

Windle, J., *Suppressing Illicit Opium Production: Successful Intervention in Asia and the Middle East*, London 2016.

3

Pahlavi Iran on the Global Stage: The Shah's 1971 Persepolis Celebrations

Robert Steele

In October 1971 an impressive array of global political figures gathered at the ruins of the ancient city of Persepolis to take part in a lavish celebration, hosted by the shah of Iran, Mohammad Reza Pahlavi, marking the 2500th anniversary of the founding of the Persian Empire by Cyrus the Great. It was a grand occasion, often dismissed as over-elaborate and unnecessary. Some even point to it as the origin of the widespread popular discontent with the shah's reign that ultimately culminated in the 1979 revolution. As such, the Persepolis Celebrations have come to be remembered as a costly mistake, the grandiosity of which, as Marvin Zonis noted, would 'characterize the remainder of the Shah's rule'.[1] Other historical accounts comment on the shah's 'perilous arrogance'[2] or the event's 'squanderous indulgence',[3] and a 2016 BBC documentary on the event entitled *Decadence and Downfall* illustrates the stubborn pervasiveness of this narrative. Breaking from this tradition, this chapter puts the Celebrations in the context of the shah's rise, rather than his fall, examining the global political conditions that allowed for such an extraordinary gathering of world leaders in Iran. Viewing the Celebrations in this context presents an opportunity to explore Iran's regional and global standing during this important period of Mohammad Reza Shah's reign. It is often argued

1 Zonis, M., *Majestic Failure: The Fall of the Shah*, Chicago 1991, p. 69.
2 Azimi, F., *Quest for Democracy in Iran: A Century of Struggle Against Authoritarian Rule*, Cambridge, MA 2008, p. 290.
3 Clark, M., 'The Party', in Stevenson, M. (ed.), *Celebration at Persepolis*, Bristol 2008, p. 28.

that the shah was out of touch with the realities of his country, but this chapter will show that he was in tune, at least, with global realities. Since the 1960s, the shah had pursued a policy of making Iran the strategically dominant power in Western Asia and he sought to legitimise this position at Persepolis in 1971. The Celebrations saw the rich and powerful of the world falling over themselves to pay tribute to the shah and his vision for Iran.

The sustained media scrutiny and vociferous domestic opposition to the Celebrations give the impression that they were a resounding failure; however, they were effective in helping the shah fulfil his international ambitions. As the organisers became more aware of these potential global opportunities, the Celebrations acquired a greater significance for the Pahlavi state. For a period, the Celebrations became the most pressing issue in Iranian foreign policy and foreign ministries from around the world worked tirelessly to ensure that their interests in Iran were successfully promoted through participation in this event. The shah is often caricatured as a Western puppet in both scholarly and popular accounts, however at this point in his reign, when he was reaching the zenith of his political authority, this assessment could not be further from the truth.[4] Moreover, his evocation of Ancient Persia and the presentation of himself as a spiritual successor to Cyrus the Great often leads to the conclusion that he was an obsessive megalomaniac who was not taken particularly seriously by foreign powers.[5] In fact, the shah was keenly aware of geopolitical realities and he knew how to manipulate Iran's state ideology to his advantage.[6] One of the claims of the Pahlavi state ideology was that Iran had a historical obligation to be a dominant regional power and this sentiment was articulated at Persepolis. By examining British, Dutch and US diplomatic records and other archival material, this chapter will attempt to understand what motivated individuals and organisations to take part in the Celebrations, as well as what the shah hoped to gain from the occasion. This analysis also allows

4 See for example: Saikal, A., *The Rise and Fall of the Shah: Iran from Autocracy to Religious Rule*, Princeton 2009, p. 207; Zonis, M., *Majestic Failure*, pp. 208–213. For further discussion of the US-Iran relationship in particular, see Rubin, B., *Paved with Good Intentions: The American Experience in Iran*, Harmondsworth 1981; Bill, J. A, *The Eagle and the Lion: The Tragedy of American-Iranian Relations*, New Haven 1988.

5 See for example: Shawcross, W., *The Shah's Last Ride*, London 1989, p. 47; Buchan, J., *Days of God: The Revolution in Iran and Its Consequences*, London 2012, p. 56.

6 For work on ideology, particularly Aryanism and Pahlavism, see for example: Shakibi, Z., 'The Rastakhiz Party and Pahlavism: The Beginnings of State Anti-Westernism in Iran', in *British Journal of Middle Eastern Studies*, vol. 45, no. 2, 2018, pp. 251–268; and Shakibi, Z., 'Pahlavism: The Ideologization of Monarchy in Iran', in *Politics, Religion and Ideology*, vol. 14, no. 1, 2013, pp. 114–135.

us an opportunity to observe how Pahlavi Iran interacted with the world in the 1970s, and how the world, in turn, interacted with Pahlavi Iran.

The Origins of the Persepolis Celebrations

The idea to hold such a celebration was put forward in 1958 by the shah's cultural counsellor, Shojaeddin Shafa, to commemorate Cyrus the Great's conquest of Babylon in 539 BCE and his humane treatment of its inhabitants, as recorded on the Cyrus Cylinder. The proposal was immediately approved by the shah and a committee was formed in February 1958 to oversee the development of the project headed by Javad Bushehri, a prominent government official and the uncle of Mehdi Bushehri – future husband of Princess Ashraf – with the support of the United Nations Educational, Scientific and Cultural Organisation (UNESCO).[7] UNESCO's support was significant and suggests that from the outset the Persepolis Celebrations were intended to have a global audience. Shafa had a close affiliation with UNESCO and considered it important that these ties be nurtured in order to solidify Iran's emerging position of power in the world and the United Nations. In this context, in 1965, he spearheaded Iran's UNESCO-supported campaign to end illiteracy worldwide, hosting a congress in Tehran and giving talks in Europe.[8] It even appears that the very idea for the Persepolis Celebrations originated with UNESCO. Since 1954, UNESCO had been encouraging member states to hold commemorations of events or people of significance, and published a list of proposals annually. These lists included occasions such as the 100th birthday of Anton Chekhov (1960), the 1,000th anniversary of the founding of the city of Luxembourg (1963) and the 100th anniversary of the Emancipation Proclamation (1963).[9] From a global perspective, therefore, it could be argued that the idea to commemorate Cyrus emerged from Iran's desire to cement its position within UNESCO while marking Iran's arrival as a serious power in the international community.

UNESCO responded positively to the idea, which would celebrate 'the start of the expansion of a culture whose arts, science and literature have been central

7 *Parade at Persepolis: Celebration of the 2500th Anniversary of the Founding of the Persian Empire by Cyrus the Great*, Tehran 1971.
8 There is a file dedicated to this particular project in the Shojaeddin Shafa Papers, held at the Bibliothèque Universitaire des Langues et Civilisations in Paris.
9 'Commemoration of Anniversaries of Great Personalities and Events: The Living Past', Paris, 31 August 1962, UNESCO/MC/46.

forces in the artistic and intellectual development of both Orient and Occident'.[10] At its 1960 General Conference, UNESCO urged the world to join in the commemoration of Cyrus:

> [The General Conference] Recommends to Member States and interested non-governmental organizations that they associate themselves with the celebration of this event at the cultural level, in whatever way they deem most suitable; [and] invited the Director-General to take appropriate measures to co-operate with the Iranian authorities in this commemoration.[11]

Cultural dissemination through commemoration was well within the framework of what UNESCO was attempting to achieve at the time, and the occasion proposed by Shafa contributed to this effort. The continued support of UNESCO therefore offered legitimacy to the Celebrations while underscoring the significance of Iran in both past and present.

The Celebrations were originally due to take place in 1962, but due to financial hardships were postponed until certain financial targets could be met.[12] After further setbacks throughout the 1960s, the shah personally insisted that plans for the Celebrations should be accelerated and he chose the year 1971 for the occasion. Abdorreza Ansari, a former government minister and manager of various charitable organisations headed by Princess Ashraf, was brought in to head the organising committee in September 1970 after Busherhi left Iran to receive treatment for cancer. Shortly afterwards a new High Executive Committee was established under the auspices of the Imperial Court.[13] The Committee met once a week under the chairmanship of Minister of Court Asadollah Alam and once every two weeks at the Niavaran Palace under the shahbanu's supervision.[14] A special sub-committee was established to orchestrate international operations, headed by

10 Ibid.

11 UNESCO, 'Records of the General Conference 11th session', Resolution 4.723, Paris, 1960, p. 57.

12 Hosseyn Ala to Ali Amini, 7 January 1962, 'Pahlavi-ye dovvom va nemuneh-ye andishehha-ye bastangerayaneh: negahi be asnad-e mahramaneh-ye jashnha-ye 2500 saleh-ye shahanshahi' [The Second Pahlavi and some Elements of Archaistic Thoughts: A look to the Secret Documents Relating to the 2500th Anniversary Celebrations], *Tarikh-e Mo'aser-e Iran*, vol. 2, no. 5, 1377/1998, p. 125.

13 Ansari, A., *The Shah's Iran – Rise and Fall: Conversations with an Insider*, London 2017, p. 252.

14 Kadivar, C., '2500-Year Celebrations Revisited', in *The Iranian*, 25 January 2002, available at: <http://iranian.com/CyrusKadivar/2002/January/2500/index.html>.

Shafa.[15] At the early meetings it was clear that the primary purpose of the Celebrations was the promotion of Iranian culture, however, as international interest increased, the programme expanded and took on a more political agenda.

To emphasise the significance of the occasion on an international level, a number of 'Cyrus the Great Committees' were set up in countries around the world, typically chaired by heads of state.[16] In writing to the Iranian embassy in Washington, the renowned expert on Iranian art, Arthur Upham Pope, who had been asked by the Iranians to offer suggestions as to how the Celebrations should be carried out, argued that:

> [I]t is of outstanding importance that the presentation to the American people of this occasion should stress the fact that it is not merely an episode in Persian history, but a very great event in the history of civilization.[17]

In order to achieve this, Pope was charged with forming the American committee of which it was hoped that President John F. Kennedy and former President Dwight D. Eisenhower would serve as patrons.[18] President Charles de Gaulle was installed as chair of the French committee, King Baudouin led the Belgian committee and Generalissimo Francisco Franco acted as head of the Spanish committee.[19] By the time the Celebrations were underway in 1971, seventy such committees had been established around the world and there was even a suggestion that they could remain functioning after the event as 'Friendship Committees'.[20] Iran took these committees quite seriously and the newly appointed British ambassador to Iran, Peter Ramsbotham, recorded that he was repeatedly pressed about the vacant role of head of the British committee. The Iranians viewed this as 'illustrations of the British Government's anti-Iranian policy'.[21] Eventually, Prince Philip was

15 Shojaeddin Shafa to Hendrik Jonker, 28 January 1971, *Ministerie van Buitenlandse Zaken*, Dutch Ministry of Foreign Affairs (henceforth MinBuZa) 2.05.191/554.

16 This was the official title of international committees. See, Shafa press conference, 6 July 1971, MinBuZa 2.05.191/554.

17 Arthur Upham Pope to Amir Ebrahimi, 4 December 1960, in Gluck, J., and Siver, N. (eds.), *Surveyors of Persian Art: A Documentary Biography of Arthur Upham Pope and Phyllis Ackerman*, Costa Mesa 1996, p. 427.

18 Pope to Jay Gluck, 12 December 1960, ibid, p. 426.

19 For a list of these honorary chairs, see Shafa, S., *Facts About the Celebration of the 2500th Anniversary of the Founding of the Persian Empire by Cyrus the Great*, Tehran 1971, pp. 22–24.

20 'Cyrus Committees Forge Friendship', *Kayhan International*, 28 October 1971.

21 Ramsbotham report, 11 October 1971, UK National Archives, Records of the Foreign and Commonwealth Office (henceforth FCO) 57/322.

chosen to chair the committee because it was deemed 'the Iranians want a Royal personage to take part', thus underlining both the significance of these foreign committees to Iran and the willingness of foreign governments to acquiesce to Iran's demands.[22]

Monarchy and the Ideology of the Pahlavi State

The aims of the Celebrations were manifold, motivated by both ideological and tangible factors. The Pahlavi regime had developed a robust ideological foundation based on the strength of the monarchy and the glory of pre-Islamic Iranian civilisation, which pervaded every aspect of the Celebrations and influenced how foreign powers communicated with Iran on a political level. The shah's foreign policy was also built on a strong understanding of geopolitical realities, in which sense the Celebrations provide an excellent opportunity to observe the complex synthesis between ideology and realpolitik. The shah did not merely want to attract foreign businesses, sell Iranian products and increase the marketability of Iran to foreign tourists; he wanted to announce Iran's emergence as a regional and global power, while stressing the country's fortunes as dependent on the strength and endurance of the monarchy.

Two central aspects of the Pahlavi ideology were designed to convince the world that Iran belonged to the Western family of nations, namely the employment of the Aryan myth to place Iranians in the same race as Europeans, and the appropriation of the pre-Islamic past, which demonstrated, firstly, that Iran was not, in essence, an Islamic country, and secondly, that Iran's ancient past was at least as glorious and civilised as Europe's. The Celebrations offered the regime an opportunity to promote both these aspects of Pahlavism to a global audience. The first prong of this ideological strategy consisted of the promotion of the idea of a purely 'Iranian' race, separate from the Arabs. This idea was driven also by nationalist fervour and from the middle of the nineteenth century Iranian intellectuals, such as Akhundzadeh and Mirza Aqa Khan Kermani, saw Iran not merely as a geographical space, but also viewed Iranians as a distinctive ethnic group.[23] The Aryan myth, which was embraced by Iranian nationalists towards the end of the

22 E. M. Westwood to A.L. Mayall, 4 May 1971, FCO 57/323.

23 Motadel, D., 'Iran and the Aryan Myth', in Ansari, A. (ed.), *Perceptions of Iran: History, Myths and Nationalism from Medieval Persia to the Islamic Republic*, London 2014, p. 131. For a detailed study of the works of Akhundzadeh and Mirza Aqa Khan Kermani and their influence on Iranian nationalism, see Zia-Ebrahimi, R., *The Emergence of Iranian Nationalism: Race and the Politics of Dislocation*, New York 2016.

nineteenth century, argues that humankind can be divided into a number of distinct racial groups. The myth provides an ethnological classification according to which most Europeans belong to the same race as Iranians.[24] The adoption of the Aryan myth by the Pahlavi ideologues at the beginning of the twentieth century was driven in large part by a desire to be viewed as more closely related to the modern Europeans than to Iran's Arab neighbours.[25]

The second prong, the Pahlavi appropriation of pre-Islamic Iran, likewise had its roots in the late Qajar period and was in part influenced by the West's deference to Ancient Persia. As Mohamad Tavakoli-Targhi has written:

> Identification with heterotopic Europe served as an oppositional strategy for the disarticulation of the dominant Islamicate discourse and for the construction of a new pattern of self-identity grounded on pre-Islamic history and culture.[26]

For a global audience, the Celebrations represented an opportunity to underscore Iran's affinity with the West through its un-Arabness and its pre-Islamic past. It was hoped that Iran would be transformed in the eyes of the world from a traditional Islamic country to a modern, industrial and even secular state, far more palatable to Westerners. The Pahlavi ideologues were keen to push this shift in perception at any available opportunity. In one example of this attitude, the Dutch Foreign Ministry proposed to send a carillon to Iran as a gift for the Celebrations.[27] A prominent Dutch scholar of Iran, Hanna Kohlbrugge, was consulted about the issue and advised that it might be considered insensitive to send an essentially Christian symbol to the ruler of an Islamic country.[28] The Dutch ambassador in Tehran, Hendrik Jonker, nevertheless put the proposal directly to Court Minister Asadollah Alam, who thought it a 'splendid idea', even suggesting that it could be placed at Persepolis.[29] When Jonker relayed his ministry's fears over the

24 See Zia-Ebrahimi, R., 'Self-Orientalization and Dislocation: The Uses and Abuses of the "Aryan" Discourse in Iran', *Iranian Studies*, vol. 44, no. 4, 2013, pp. 114–135.

25 For the Pahlavi manipulation of the Aryan myth, see Adib-Moghaddam, A., *Psycho-Nationalism: Global Thought, Iranian Imaginations*, London 2018, pp. 51–56.

26 Tavakoli-Targhi, M., *Refashioning Iran: Orientalism, Occidentalism and Historiography*, Houndmill 2001, p. 37.

27 A carillon is a set of bells typically placed in the bell tower of a church. Hendrik Jonker to Ministry of Foreign Affairs, 28 January 1970, MinBuZa 2.05.191/554. Jonker even promised to find out which melodies the Iranians would like for their carillon.

28 Ministry of Foreign Affairs to Embassy in Tehran, 1 March 1970, MinBuZa 2.05.191/554.

29 Jonker to Ministry of Foreign Affairs, 6 April 1970, MinBuZa 2.05.191/554.

appropriateness of the gift, Alam urged the ambassador not to worry. After all, he responded, 'we are not real Muslims, we are Shiʿites.'[30]

In accordance with the language of Pahlavism, which glorified ancient imperial heritage, the shah spoke of the dawn of Iran's 'Great Civilisation', a term with very clear ancient connotations, which promised a future for Iran as glorious as its (ancient) past. This romantic interpretation of Iran's pre-Islamic past served, in the words of Zhand Shakibi, as 'a substitute for religion and, more importantly, clericalism, as a mechanism for inculcating a common political culture and establishing new sources of state legitimacy'.[31] One of the purposes of the Celebrations, as stated by Shafa, was to further the regime's alternative understanding of Iranian national identity, based not on Islam, but on Persian kingship.[32] Echoing this sentiment in an official publication for the Celebrations, Deputy Minister of Information Mohammad Ali Samiʿi wrote: 'The secret of Iran's unique ability to withstand the devastating forces of 2,500 years of history lies in the guidance from the throne.'[33]

Through the Celebrations, Mohammad Reza Shah was portrayed as a modern Cyrus the Great, an assertive king possessing a deep sense of morality and a spiritual relationship with his people. The connection with Cyrus was a significant aspect of the shah's ideology, especially given Cyrus' global appeal. The ancient founder of the Persian Empire had a reputation as a benevolent and generous ruler, remembered both in the Old Testament as the Lord's anointed and in the Greek literary tradition, where he is described as a 'father' who was 'gentle, and procured them [his subjects] all manner of goods'.[34] Besides his noble qualities, Cyrus was also revered simply for his ancientness. The historian David Lowenthal noted this phenomenon when he observed that: 'Being ancient makes things precious by their proximity to the dawn of time, to their earlier beginnings... the more ancient a lineage the more highly venerated it is.'[35] This reasoning was

30 Jonker to Ministry of Foreign Affairs, 20 March 1970, MinBuZa 2.05.191/554. To the ambassador's disappointment, the Ministry of Foreign Affairs decided to send the shah a concert organ instead, before changing its mind and taking to Persepolis a silver model of the famous Dutch flagship of Admiral De Ruyter, *De Zeven Provinciën*, weighing 13 kilograms.

31 Shakibi, Z.,'Pahlavism', p. 118.

32 Milani, A., *The Shah*, New York 2011, p. 324.

33 Writing in the introduction to Tarverdi, R., and Massoudi, A., *The Land of Kings*, Tehran 1971, p. 1.

34 *Isaiah* 44:24–45:8; *Chronicles* 36:22–3; *Ezra* 1 and 6:1–5; Herodotus, *The Histories*, transl. George Rawlinson, London 1997, III: 89.

35 Lowenthal, D., *The Heritage Crusade and the Spoils of History*, Cambridge 1998, p. 176.

expressed by the shah in his *Mission for my Country*, where he drew a comparison between Iran and Rome:

> Most of the readers of this book will have studied Roman history, but our empire was flourishing centuries before that of Rome, and it was in fact we who showed that it was possible to govern and administer on such a large scale.[36]

The Persian Empire was, therefore, not merely relevant in the context of Iranian history, but it also had global significance. The shah thus urged the world to associate modern Iran with the glories of its ancient past, a past as illustrious as that of Rome.

Of the four motivations for the organisation of national celebrations put forward by Elie Podeh in *The Politics of National Celebrations in the Arab Middle East*, one relates to the leader's, or the regime's, quest to strengthen, acquire, or maintain legitimacy.[37] Events such as Nicholas II's tercentenary celebration of Romanov rule in 1913 or Mussolini's bimillennial celebration of the birth of Augustus in 1937 can be explained in this context, as these rulers sought to establish their place within their particular national traditions and legitimise their own rule.[38] Through the White Revolution, a far reaching set of reforms launched in 1963, the idea that the shah was the central figure in the future successes of his country was widely promoted. This served, according to Ali Ansari, as a 'strategy for legitimation', as it framed these reforms as dependent on the monarchy:

> As the founder and guarantor of a new order for Iran, he [the shah] would consolidate his dynasty's position within the political system, which he would argue was dependent upon the constitution and consolidation of his dynasty.[39]

The 1971 Celebrations in Iran should therefore be considered in the context of

36 Pahlavi, M. R., *Mission for my Country*, London 1961, p. 19.
37 Podeh, E., *The Politics of National Celebrations in the Arab Middle East*, Cambridge 2011, p. 21.
38 See Kallis, A., 'Framing Romanità: The Celebrations for the Bimillenario Augusteo and the Augusteo-Ara Pacis Project', *Journal of Contemporary History*, vol. 46, no. 809, 2011, pp. 809–831; Wortman, R.S., *Scenarios of Power: Myth and Ceremony in Russian Monarchy*, vol. 2, Princeton 2000, pp. 439–480.
39 Ansari, A. M., 'The Myth of the White Revolution: Mohammad Reza Shah, "Modernization" and the Consolidation of Power', *Middle Eastern Studies*, vol. 37, no. 3, 2001, p. 3.

the shah's effort to establish his legitimacy and that of his dynasty. His aim was to show that Iran had always had kings, and that the glory of its past had been dependent on the strength of the monarchical institution. The Pahlavi ideologues promoted the idea that patriotism was synonymous with adoration of both monarchy as an institution generally and the Pahlavi monarchy in particular.[40] If the shah's coronation in 1967 celebrated his coming to power, then the Persepolis Celebrations established, by perpetuating the myth of 2,500 years of continuous Persian monarchy, the place of his dynasty in the annals of Iranian and global history.

In the nineteenth century the monarchs of Europe had established an informal system of monarchical co-operation in order to tackle the pressing international issues of the day.[41] The Persepolis Celebrations can be seen as an attempt to revive the Royal International phenomenon and establish an international fraternity of monarchy through which the world's remaining royals would be able more effectively to assert their relevance. With the shah at the helm, its members were brought to Persepolis to promote, with a degree of swagger, the institution of monarchy as the ideal form of governance, not just in Iran but globally. According to Michael Axworthy, the shah sought to 'assert the strength and enduring character of Iranian kingship, at a time when monarchy as an institution was menaced by republicanism and communism internationally'.[42] The twentieth century had been miserable for the monarchical institution; most of Europe's monarchies were abolished by the end of the First and Second World Wars and from the 1950s onwards a number of Commonwealth countries relinquished the British crown. In the Middle East, King Farouk of Egypt was toppled in 1952, Faisal II of Iraq lost his throne (and life) in 1958, and the monarchies of Yemen and Libya were abolished in 1962 and 1969 respectively. But when asked why the shah's recently exiled friend, King Constantine II of Greece, was in attendance at the Celebrations, an Iranian protocol officer declared: 'For us, the government is the king.'[43]

Further signs of this attitude to monarchy can be observed in the Iranians' strict

40 Vaziri, M., *Iran as Imagined Nation: The Construction of National Identity*, New York 1993, p. 198.

41 Paulmann, J., 'Searching for Royal International', in Geyer, M. H., and Paulmann, J. (eds.), *The Mechanics of Internationalism: Culture, Society, and Politics from the 1840s to the First World War*, London 2001, pp. 145–176.

42 Axworthy, M., *Revolutionary Iran: A History of the Islamic Republic*, London 2013, p. 77.

43 Quoted in McWhirter, W. A., 'The Shah's Princely Party', in *Life Magazine*, 29 October 1971, p. 26. King Constantine II left Greece in 1967 following a failed counter coup in December 1967. The monarchy was abolished by plebiscite in 1973.

adherence to the rules of protocol established in the nineteenth century, according to which kings and emperors held a loftier status than presidents and prime ministers. The chief of protocol of the shah's court, Hormoz Qarib, travelled around Europe in 1971 in order to learn the finer details of these antiquated regulations, and the British were called upon to alleviate any confusion. In a letter to Qarib, Ambassador Ramsbotham advised, 'Presidents, being Heads of State, take precedence after Monarchs but before Consorts and Crown Princes.' He continues:

> I am informed that Prince Philip takes precedence over Prince Charles. Although he is not officially called 'the Consort', Prince Philip is in fact the Consort. Assuming, therefore, that Prince Bernhard of the Netherlands has been Prince Consort longer than Prince Philip, the former takes precedence over the latter. They both, of course, take precedence over the Crown Prince of Sweden.[44]

This adherence to protocol may seem old-fashioned, perhaps even amusing, but it was important in promoting the Pahlavi monarchy as part of the global and historical monarchical tradition. By observing these accepted diplomatic practices, moreover, the shah was asserting his and Iran's sovereign equality to the crowned heads of Europe.[45] Protocol did cause some practical problems, since there was little appetite among non-royal guests for being upstaged. This was the reason for French President Georges Pompidou's late withdrawal from the event, which particularly displeased the shah.[46] For this reason, the event's organisers went to great lengths to ensure that none of the guests felt underappreciated and so the smallest details were attended to in their preparations, including guests' preferences for breakfast and even their favourite brand of cigarettes.[47]

One British diplomat commented that the Celebrations were 'proof that the Pahlavi Dynasty was frivolous; it was not serious'.[48] It is, of course, the gift of hindsight that gives such statements credibility, for at the time of the Celebrations, although foreign powers did not necessarily buy into the Pahlavi ideology, they

44 Ramsbotham to Hormuz Qarib, 28 August 1971, in 'Asnad-e mahramaneh-ye jashnha-ye 2500 saleh-ye shahanshahi', p. 141.

45 For a discussion of the formation and application of norms in international society see Gong, G. W., *The Standard of 'Civilization' in International Society*, Oxford 1984.

46 See Mann, A., 'Shah Attacks Pompidou for Missing Party', *The Daily Telegraph*, 8 October 1971.

47 'Necessary Information and Questions', MinBuZa 2.05.191/554.

48 George Middleton in an interview with Habib Ladjevardi, London, UK, 16 October 1985, Iranian Oral History Collection, Harvard University, tape 3.

did not hesitate to employ it to improve their relations with the shah. Although individuals may not have taken the ideology seriously in private, in official correspondence they were careful not to challenge it. On a state visit to Iran in 1969, for example, British Foreign Secretary Michael Stewart was given a private tour of the ruins of Persepolis, after which he commented on the wisdom of Cyrus, Darius and Xerxes. 'Your present ruler seems to possess something of the qualities of all three of these mighty kings,'[49] he observed. Of course, it is likely that the minister's statement amounted to mere flattery, but it is evidence that the state ideology had become a useful tool in negotiations with the Pahlavi regime. Furthermore, foreign governments acknowledged the importance of this ideology to the shah, a fact that can be observed in the case of the loan of the Cyrus Cylinder from the British Museum to Iran to coincide with the Persepolis Celebrations.

Anglo-Iranian Relations and the Cyrus Cylinder

As early as 1968, Iran had been contacting embassies around the world to request loans of Iranian artefacts to be exhibited in Iran during the Celebrations.[50] A request to borrow the Cyrus Cylinder was relayed through Ambassador Ramsbotham in Tehran to the British Foreign Office on 20 August 1971.[51] The Foreign Office rejected the request on the grounds that it would 'merely arouse Iranian cupidity' and 'would cause immense complications for us if we ever wanted to get it back to Britain'.[52] The importance of such a loan to the Iranians was clear; the Cylinder was the emblem of the Celebrations and served as tangible evidence of the benevolent character of Cyrus. There was even a suggestion that the Cylinder should be presented to the shah as a gift, which was rejected by the Foreign Office, since it could be interpreted as 'a consolation prize if the Islands problem cannot be solved on his [the shah's] terms'.[53] The idea that the Cylinder could be used in the context of ongoing Anglo-Iranian talks over the future of the Persian Gulf islands of Abu Musa and the Tunbs, claimed by both Iran and the British-protected emirates of Sharjah and Ras al-Khaimah, was evidence of the perceived importance of the artefact.[54]

49 Quoted in Kadivar, '2500-Year Celebrations Revisited'.
50 *Echo of Iran*, 26 August 1968.
51 Ramsbotham to Sir Denis Greenhill, 21 October 1971, FCO 17/1529.
52 Ibid; Greenhill to Ramsbotham, 15 September 1971, FCO 17/1529.
53 S. L. Egerton to A. D. Parsons, 13 September 1971, FCO 17/1529.
54 On the islands dispute see Louis, W. R., 'The British Withdrawal from the Gulf, 1967–71', in *The Journal of Imperial and Commonwealth History*, vol. 33, no. 1, 2003, pp. 83–108.

As it happened, the British Museum's Board of Trustees had already agreed to a request from the Iranian Embassy in London to allow Iran to have the Cylinder for the duration of the Celebrations.[55] As soon as Ramsbotham heard of the loan he tried to warn the British Museum against it, but by that point the Cylinder was already in Iran.[56] Richard Barnett, keeper of Western Asiatic Antiquities, had been invited to take part in the Congress of Iranology in Shiraz, held in October 1971 as part of the programme for the Celebrations, and was asked to bring the Cylinder with him, an arrangement that was approved by the Board of Trustees in July 1971.[57] Neither the Iranian Embassy in London nor the British Museum informed the Foreign Office and there was a growing concern from the Foreign Office that if Iran attempted to exert pressure on Britain to allow them to keep the Cylinder, it might result in a rather uncomfortable diplomatic incident. These worries were not unfounded and the Iranian newspaper *Kayhan* suggested that Iran 'might take the opportunity afforded by the centenary celebrations and ask the British Museum to let Iran keep the cylinder for good'.[58]

Such a request came shortly after Barnett's arrival in Iran, when he was invited to a meeting with Minister of Culture and Arts Mehrdad Pahlbod. At the meeting Pahlbod sounded him out about the possibility of extending the loan, perhaps even to a permanent arrangement, but Barnett explained that the Cylinder was required back in London for the British Museum's commemorative *Royal Persia* exhibition.[59] Another request was expected to come at the opening of Tehran's Shahyad Monument, where the Cylinder was on display in the monument's museum. Ramsbotham was concerned that the shah would put a request directly to Prince Philip at the opening, who, being put on the spot, might find it difficult to refuse. To ensure that such a request was not made, Barnett chaperoned Prince Philip for the entire event, keeping him as far away from the shah as possible.[60] The Cylinder departed Iran on the evening of 19 October, stored, as it had been when it arrived, in Barnett's sports holdall.[61] The loan had been a success, in part due to Barnett's 'tactful handling' of the situation, but more vocal calls for giving the Cylinder to

55 FCO Correspondence, 26 October 1971, FCO 17/1529.

56 Ramsbotham to Greenhill, 21 October 1971, FCO 17/1529.

57 Ibid.

58 'Cyrus' Cylinder Flown to Tehran', *Kayhan International*, 23 October 1971, p. 4.

59 Conversation with David Stronach, April 2014.

60 Ramsbotham to Greenhill, 21 October 1971, FCO 17/1529.

61 Barnett to Ramsbotham, 5 November 1971, FCO 17/1529. Barnett even took the Cylinder to Israel where he stopped off to see his son on his way back to London.

Iran were voiced when the artefact was safely back in the British Museum.[62]

Lord Hartley Shawcross, Liberal MP Jeremy Thorpe, newspaper tycoon Vere Harmsworth, Conservative MP Sir Clive Bossom, and former MP and chairman of the Iran Society, Sir Peter Agnew, all respectable British establishment figures and private guests of the shah at the Celebrations, supported the idea of a permanent loan of the Cylinder to Iran. Bossom wrote directly to Prime Minister Edward Heath urging him to acquiesce to the Iranian request for a future arrangement. 'I feel that by allowing this cylinder to be on permanent loan,' he wrote, 'it could greatly smooth the way before next year's problems arise.'[63] Shawcross, a highly respected barrister and former Attorney-General, also wrote to Heath:

> The four of us [Thorpe, Bossom, Harmsworth and himself] unanimously agreed (before we had seen the place given to the Cylinder in the Museum) that we should strongly recommend to you that the Cylinder should be presented to Iran… in view of the serious disputes which exist between Britain and Iran which will soon come to a head, we have no doubt that a decision to make the gift to Iran (and naturally the sooner the better) would immensely improve the atmosphere of our relations. I believe that our Ambassador shares this view.[64]

Britain had announced in January 1968 its intention to withdraw all of its forces from the Persian Gulf by the end of 1971, beginning 26 months of secret negotiations between Iran and Britain over Iran's claims to relinquished British territory. Having retreated from Aden under humiliating circumstances in 1963, the British were eager that the withdrawal from the Gulf would not spark a regional crisis and that Britain would retain some political influence in the region following its departure.[65] The idea that the Cylinder could become a bargaining tool during this potentially awkward withdrawal was apparently not without merit, and is reflective of the importance the Iranians attached to the Cylinder within the context of the Pahlavi state's ideology. An Icelandic member of the Congress of Iranology, held in Shiraz at the time of the Celebrations, wrote to Shafa, stating his belief

62 Shawcross to Barnett, 18 November 1971, FCO 17/1529.

63 Clive Bossom to Edward Heath, 18 October 1971, FCO 17/1529.

64 Shawcross to Heath, 20 October 1971, FCO 17/1529.

65 For Anglo-Iranian diplomacy and the Bahrain dispute, see Alvandi, R., 'Muhammad Reza Pahlavi and the Bahrain Question, 1968–1970', *British Journal of Middle Eastern Studies*, vol. 37, no. 2, 2010, pp. 159–177.

that the Cylinder was a 'holy symbol, historically, culturally and nationally' and as such should be given to Iran.[66] This 'holy symbol' clearly worried the Foreign Office. A draft report on the issue of the Cylinder contains a note scribbled in pen that 'it looks as though the Iranians may develop a campaign about this, and we will be in for a long tussle'.[67] It is precisely for this reason that Heath was forced to intervene, writing to Shawcross to urge him not to make public his opinion that the Cylinder should be given to Iran.[68]

Replicas of the Cylinder were given by Iran as gifts to the United Nations and displayed at the UN Headquarters in New York and Geneva in an effort to accentuate the message of Cyrus and the Anniversary Celebrations.[69] On 14 October, in New York, Princess Ashraf presented a replica Cylinder to UN Secretary-General U Thant, who declared that 'in creating the ancient Persian Empire twenty-five hundred years ago, Cyrus displayed the wisdom of respecting the civilizations and peoples whom he "unified" under his sway.'[70] Additional casts were made and distributed among the foreign guests who attended the festivities in Iran.[71] The Cylinder was a powerful symbol, not just of Iran's past, but its present and future, under the leadership of a progressive ruler whom, the Pahlavi state claimed, could easily be compared to the benevolent Cyrus. This symbolism was clearly understood by the British, which explains why they handled the problem of the loan with such delicacy.

The shah's presentation of himself as Cyrus's successor was generally viewed with some scepticism. His speech at the tomb of Cyrus became a particular source of mockery within Iran.[72] As William Shawcross suggested, the connection that the shah hoped to make with Cyrus was a 'complete divorce from reality'.[73] The Cylinder loan is clear evidence, however, that foreign governments were more than willing to speak to the shah in his own language and use his ideology to further their own interests. Even if the political establishment did not take the comparison to Cyrus seriously in private, in public they toed the official line. The

66 Jakob Jónsson to Shafa, undated, Shafa Papers.
67 'Cyrus the Great Clay Cylinder (Defensive)', October 1971, FCO 17/1529.
68 Heath to Shawcross, 4 November 1971, FCO 17/1529. Shawcross had apparently planned to use a speech to the Iran Society in London on 4 November to argue this.
69 Shafa, *Facts About the Celebration*, p. 30.
70 Press Release: 'Iran Presents Replica of Ancient Edict to United Nations', 14 October 1971, United Nations Archives, S-0882–0002, UN HQ/264.
71 Pahlavi, F., *An Enduring Love: My Life with the Shah*, New York 2004, p. 219.
72 See, for example, Mottahedeh, R., *The Mantle of the Prophet: Religion and Politics in Iran*, London 1987, p. 327.
73 Shawcross, *The Shah's Last Ride*, p. 47.

fact that countries from around the world familiarised themselves with and used this narrative is illustrative of the emergence of the shah as a serious presence on the international stage during this period.

Pahlavi Iran's Global Cultural Diplomacy

The national committees for the Persepolis Celebrations that were established from the early 1960s onwards typically consisted of business leaders, political figures and academics. For example, the original French committee included Minister of Culture André Malraux and Minister of Foreign Affairs Maurice Couve de Murville, alongside renowned scholars Henri Massé and Roman Ghirshman, with Jacques Jaujard, famous for preserving the Louvre's collections during the Second World War, acting as President.[74] Programmes organised by these committees were primarily cultural, yet often served a political agenda. For example, in the foreword to an edited volume on Iranian history, published on behalf of the West German Committee for the Celebrations, West German President Gustav Heinemann stressed the importance of German contributions to the field of Iranian Studies, while Chancellor Willy Brandt spoke of the work as 'an expression of our will to maintain and stimulate the traditional German-Iranian friendship'.[75] Similarly, the proceedings of a congress in New Delhi included messages from Indian President V. V. Giri, Prime Minister Indira Gandhi and Iranian Minister of Culture Mehrdad Pahlbod, who stated that India with its 'longest and sincere' relations with Iran, 'has a right and proper place to celebrate this occasion with great gusto and zeal'.[76]

The Pahlavi state was keenly aware of the utility of culture in fostering bilateral relations and promoting awareness of Iran around the world. At the opening of a 1965 exhibition in Washington, DC, entitled *Seven Thousand Years of Art in Iran*, the shah said:

> This exhibition is undoubtedly the best cultural ambassador we have ever sent to our North American friends. This messenger of culture, I am sure, will be

74 '2,500ème Anniversaire de la Fondation de l'Etat Perse par Cyrus-le-Grand: Comite Francais', undated, Shafa Papers.

75 Brandt, W., in the preface to Eilers, W. (ed.), *Festgabe Deutscher Iranisten zur 2500 Jahrfeier Irans*, Stuttgart 1971, pp. v-vii.

76 Pahlbod, M. in the foreword to Ram, M., and Rao, S.B. (eds.), *Indo-Iran: Papers presented at the Congress of Iranologists and Indiologists, New Delhi, on the occasion of the 25th millennia of the Founding of Monarchy in Iran*, New Delhi 1974.

> instrumental in establishing spiritual understanding between our two nations and in bringing us closer together.[77]

Other states were also conscious of the good publicity these events could bring. For example, in 1961 the US State Department recommended that Mrs Kennedy should fly to Paris to see the *Seven Thousand Years of Art in Iran* exhibition, arguing that:

> [T]he publicity generated would be highly favourable to us in Iran, whose orientation and destiny are of great importance to us, and in the entire Arab world, especially if the trip were presented solely in the context of Mrs Kennedy's interest in art and history, and not of the cold war.[78]

The Paris exhibition was, incidentally, organised in conjunction with the 2500th Anniversary Celebrations, which were at this point planned for 1961. In the accompanying volume to the exhibit President De Gaulle declared France 'proud' to arrange this 'human and national testimonial' in the year of the planned festivities.[79] There was some discussion about organising a Dutch exhibition to be held in 1962, however the Dutch organisers felt that it was inappropriate at this stage since the Celebrations might not even take place until later that decade.[80] Conversely, in Britain an exhibition on the *Turcoman of Iran* was listed as being organised as part of the British contribution to the Celebrations, even though it had nothing whatsoever to do with the event.[81] There are instances of the Iranian government financing exhibitions, such as one held in Montreal to coincide with the Celebrations at a cost of US$677,800.[82] In other cases the Iranians merely

77 Quoted in 'A Royal Visit to the United States', *Persian Panorama: Publication of the Imperial Embassy of Iran*, London, vol. 1, no. 3, 1965, p. 62.
78 Quoted in Sabahi, F., *The Literacy Corps in Pahlavi Iran (1963–1979): Political Social and Literary Implications*, Lugano 2002, p. 22.
79 De Gaulle, C., in the introduction to *Sept mille ans d'art en Iran*, Musée du Petit Palais, Paris 1961.
80 Dutch Ambassador H. J. Levelt to Minister of Foreign Affairs, Tehran, 13 September 1962, MinBuZa 2.05.118/14175.
81 Andrews, P., *The Turcoman of Iran*, Kendal 1971; 'List of Events in the United Kingdom and Ireland in Celebration of the 2500th Anniversary of the Founding of the Persian Empire by Cyrus the Great', 27 September 1971, FCO 17/1528.
82 Mahmud Kashfian to Ministry of Finance, 20 April 1971, *Bazm-e Ahriman: Jashnha-ye 2500 saleh-ye shahanshahi beh revayat-e asnad-e savak va darbar* [The Devil's Feast: The 2500th Anniversary Celebrations according to SAVAK and court documents], vol. 4, Tehran, 1378/1999, p. 38. Also see Mehdi Bushehri to Mehrdad Pahlbod, 21 April 1971, ibid, pp. 40–41.

offered to loan items as a contribution to these events.[83] Generally, though, it seems that exhibitions were organised by cultural institutions around the world independently of Iran and often with the support of their own governments. There was clearly considerable political capital to be gained by arranging these types of cultural activities and the Celebrations presented great opportunities to do so.

The planning of cultural events thus became the principal way in which foreign countries contributed to the Celebrations. In the United States, for example, exhibitions dedicated to Iran were held in the nation's most celebrated museums including the Metropolitan Museum of Art in New York, which displayed miniatures from Shah Tahmasp's *Shahnameh*; the Boston Museum of Fine Arts, which gave a display of Iranian dishes, tiles and textiles; Walters Art Gallery in Baltimore, which presented Iranian handicrafts; and the Philadelphia Museum of Art, which presented its collection of Iranian carpets and other Islamic art. Iranian-themed social events were arranged in cities around the country and the State of Utah declared 22 July 1971 'Iran Day'.[84] In the Netherlands a ceremony was held at the Hall of Knights in The Hague on 14 October to coincide with the main festivities in Iran. At this event the Dutch scholar Arie Kampman delivered a lecture on Cyrus the Great to six hundred guests, which included Queen Juliana, Princess Beatrix and Prince Claus, along with the Iranian ambassador and the ambassadors to the Netherlands of forty other countries. Queen Juliana was presented with a special edition of the Holland-Iran Society journal *Persica*, and a film was shown about Iran chosen by the *Maison de l'Iran*.[85] The event was an interesting blend of cultural and political activity, as well as royal ceremony. Moreover, it is a measure of the growing international influence of Iran that it was able to inspire such high-level political interest outside of the country.

Much has been written about the refusal of a number of significant world leaders to attend the Celebrations. One journalist wrote mockingly at the time, 'You just weren't important if you weren't invited; but you couldn't have been that important if you actually showed up.'[86] Some had practical reasons for not attending. German President Gustav Heinemann had intended to go, but was kept away by a 'sudden – and real – eye disease'. President Nixon had agreed to attend, but

83 Abdorreza Ansari to Hushang Ansari, 22 June 1971, ibid, p. 117.
84 'Mosahebeh-ye chap nashodeh az Shojaeddin Shafa darbareh-ye jashnha-ye dohezar o pansad saleh' [Unpublished interview with Shojaeddin Shafa about: the 2500th Anniversary Celebrations], *Rahavard*, no. 95, 2011, pp. 191–193.
85 'Report on the activities of the Working Committee of the Cyrus the Great Committee in the Netherlands: June – December 1971', pp. 1–3, MinBuZa 2.05.191/554.
86 Jenkins, L., 'Iran's Birthday Party', *Newsweek*, 25 October 1971, p. 33.

later declined due to security concerns, and Emperor Hirohito of Japan cited old age as a reason not to attend.[87] There were also domestic internal pressures guiding the decisions of leaders to accept or reject their invitations. For instance, the rulers of some regional powers, such as Mohammed Zahir Shah of Afghanistan, sent medium level representatives, for fear that their attendance would embolden the fanatics in their own countries.[88] Amidst intense criticism of the shah and the Celebrations from opposition groups such as the Confederation of Iranian Students, backed by figures such as Jean-Paul Sartre and Simone de Beauvoir, who called for a boycott of the Celebrations, some Western governments may have feared the political ramifications of attending.[89] Students at Stanford University were urged to protest against 'Iran's oil-rich butcher king' and the Committee for Free Iran, a pressure group based in Washington DC, wrote letters to Western leaders, such as Pompidou, urging them not to take part in the Celebrations.[90] This international campaign clearly had some success. Princess Beatrix, for example, heir to the Dutch throne, declined to attend the Celebrations to avoid offending her country's socialists.[91]

Only French President Pompidou publicly rejected the Celebrations, and despite the shah reassuring his replacement, Prime Minister Jacques Chaban-Delmas, that the 'great desert wind and the blue sky of Persepolis have swept away the alleged clouds between us and France', he was clearly annoyed by the rejection.[92] Behind the scenes, meanwhile, there was a degree of cajoling involved from the Iranian side. According to British records the shah sent a personal message to the Romanian president, Nicolae Ceaușescu, 'almost pleading with him to attend next year's junketings in person' and Grand Master of Ceremonies Hormoz Qarib summoned

87 Jonker report, 3 November 1971, MinBuZa 2.05.191/554; Memorandum from Henry Kissinger to President Nixon, 6 April 1971, in Belmonte, M. (ed.), *Foreign Relations of the United States, 1969–1976, Volume E-4, Iran and Iraq, 1969–1972*, Document 121; 'List of Heads of States and the Imperial Missions to whom instructions for invitation have been issued', FCO 248/1708.

88 SAVAK internal report, 12 April 1971, *Bazm-e Ahriman*, vol. 4, p. 25.

89 For the letter signed by Jean-Paul Sartre, Simone de Beauvoir and 14 British Members of Parliament, see 'A Hungry Nation Does Not Need a 2500 Year Celebration: Appeal', in *Corruption and Struggle in Iran: A Defense Publication of the Iranian Student Association in the United States*, June 1972, pp. 8–10.

90 'Shah Celebrates Monarchy while Iranians Suffer', *The Stanford Daily*, vol. 160, no. 16, 18 October 1971; the letter to Pompidou was reproduced in *Iran Free Press*, vol. 1, no. 2, October 1971, p. 8.

91 Then, according to ʿAlam, she came to Iran to apologise personally to the shah. See ʿAlam, A., *The Shah and I*, London 1991, entry for 31 August 1976, p. 504.

92 Pontaut, J. M., 'La Fête Des Fêtes', *Paris Match*, 30 October 1971, p. 63.

the Dutch ambassador to inform him 'in fairly strong terms' that Queen Juliana was expected at the Celebrations.[93] The shah's inability to persuade certain heads of state to attend, particularly Queen Elizabeth II, President Nixon and President Pompidou, was undoubtedly a disappointment and undermined to some extent the image he wished to promote, through the Celebrations, of himself as a serious figure on the international stage. However, these rejections should also be seen in the broader context of public opposition to the shah's rule in the West and did not necessarily reflect the governments' position on the shah and his regime, as evidenced by a number of the absentee heads of state visiting Iran in state visits shortly after the Celebrations, most notably President Nixon in 1972.

Notwithstanding the absence of a number of important political figures, the Celebrations inspired great interest from governments, cultural organisations, academics and businesses from around the world. Indeed, international enthusiasm for the Celebrations was such that were it not for some logistical limitations then the event might have been organised on an even grander scale. For instance, there was a discussion with both the London Symphony Orchestra and the Concertgebouw Orchestra about the possibility of performing in Iran, and a number of foreign military bands performed in Tehran at the inaugurations of the Shahyad Monument and the Aryamehr Stadium.[94] A more unusual proposal was made directly to the Dutch ambassador in Tehran, Hendrik Jonker, by The Hague Balloon Club, which wanted to fly the largest ever Dutch hot air balloon over Iran during the festivities. They claimed it would be a 'unique opportunity for your relations, for television reporters, and the photographic press to experience an ascent in the large round Dutch ship'.[95] Academics were also eager to take part. Bernard Lewis, a renowned historian of the Islamic world at the School of Oriental and African Studies in London, was 'delighted to receive an invitation', as was Laurence Elwell-Sutton, a leading scholar of Iran at the University of Edinburgh who later wrote a favourable account of his experience.[96] The retired reverend

93 R. T. Eland to C. D. S. Drace-Francis, 1 October 1970; and Drace-Francis report, 5 October 1970, FCO 248/1708. Queen Juliana was ultimately unable to go due to a pre-planned state visit to Indonesia.

94 S. Dörr to Jonker, 1 April 1970, MinBuZa 2.05.191/554; and Public Relations Office of the Military Council of the Imperial Celebrations to Head of the Central Council of the Imperial Celebrations, *Bazm-e Ahriman*, vol. 4, 13 October 1971, pp. 334–335. Participant bands included Switzerland, Romania, Jordan, Algeria, Pakistan and Kuwait.

95 J. Boesman-Voorz to Jonker, 23 January 1971, MinBuZa 2.05.191/554.

96 Lewis, B., *Notes On A Century: Reflections of a Middle East Historian*, London 2013, p. 184; Elwell-Sutton, L., '2500th Anniversary Celebrations', *Bulletin of the British Association of Orientalists*, no. 6, 1973, pp. 20–25.

Norman Sharp, who lived in Iran for most of his life and was at one point professor of Old Persian and cuneiform at the Pahlavi University in Shiraz, rejoiced at receiving his invitation 'almost at the last moment'.[97]

Pahlavi Iran as an Emerging Market

Participation in the Celebrations was driven, in part, by international competition for lucrative commercial contracts in Iran. Each foreign committee strove to make a noteworthy contribution that demonstrated their country's dedication to Iran. The Germans, as already mentioned, emphasised the importance of their contributions to Iranian Studies, whereas the British Council arranged two exhibitions to tour Iran, one of which was entitled *British Contributions to Persian Studies*.[98] Ambassador Ramsbotham later argued that it had been 'particularly important for the British Council's reputation that some special activity should be mounted last year to mark the 2500th Anniversary of the Persian Monarchy by Cyrus the Great'.[99] The Dutch were eager to stress that the ceremony they hosted at the Hall of Knights formed a 'unique contribution to the commemoration outside Iran'.[100] In Pakistan a national holiday was declared during which government offices, shops and streets were dressed with coloured lights, bunting, slogans trumpeting Pakistani-Iranian friendship, triumphal arches and giant photos of the Pahlavis.[101] It is clear that there was something to be gained from contributing to the Celebrations and the more enthusiastic and imaginative the contribution, the better.

By the late 1960s, thanks to rising oil revenues, Iran offered one of the Middle East's most lucrative prospects for global trade and investment. Gross national product (GNP) rose from \$3.8 billion in 1959/60 to \$10.6 billion in 1970/71, a growth of 181 percent.[102] With vast natural resources and its recently acquired financial clout, Iran enjoyed considerable purchasing power. Realising the potential

97 Norman Sharp to Paul Gotch, 9 October 1971, Gotch Papers, British Museum.
98 Stronach, D., 'Director's Report November 1st 1970 to October 31st 1971', *Iran*, vol. 10, 1972, p. xi. The other exhibition was of the sculptures of Henry Moore. For more details see UK National Archives, Records of the British Council (henceforth BW), BW 49/31, FAAC (72) 1, 1971.
99 Ramsbotham to Alec Douglas-Home, 25 July 1972, BW 49/31.
100 'Report on the activities of the Working Committee', p. 3, MinBuZa 2.05.191/554.
101 Nahavandi, H., *The Last Shah of Iran: Fatal Countdown of a Great Patriot Betrayed by the Free World, a Great Country Whose Fault Was Success*, transl. Reed, S., Slough 2005, p. 45; Richard Escritt to Richard Fell, 2 November 1971, FCO 17/1529.
102 Issawi, C., 'The Iranian Economy 1925–1975: Fifty Years of Economic Development', in Lencozowski, G. (ed.), *Iran Under the Pahlavis*, Stanford 1978, p. 141.

of this growing market, foreign powers scrambled for influence in Iran and the Celebrations became in some respects an elaborate business fair, with many countries competing for contracts, trade deals and political leverage. Dealing with Iran required a certain savoir-faire and success depended as much on whom one knew and how one presented oneself, as on what one could offer. As already noted, business leaders were included in the international committees and many companies launched special advertisements to show their support for the occasion.[103] Being involved with the Celebrations also brought high-level exposure which companies were naturally glad to take advantage of. A number of firms even took part 'in an honorary capacity', offering their services for free, such as the famous hairdressing salons of Carita, Alexander and Elizabeth Arden.[104] Other firms competed for lucrative contracts for the Celebrations itself. One London-based British firm, Wilton Irvine, for example, won an $864,000 contract to supply street lighting for Tehran and Shiraz.[105]

There were long-term commercial opportunities on offer for those who managed to win favour. The success of this courtship was linked to political representation at the Celebrations. For example, British and French competition to win the rights to mine copper at Kerman became 'inextricably linked with the presence or absence of President Pompidou at the celebrations' according to the British Embassy in Tehran.[106] Furthermore, directly as a result of Pompidou's snub, the shah 'cancelled all the big orders given to the French and for a number of years the French were in the doghouse'.[107] Economic interests were widely presented, in some cases publicly, as a justification for participation, despite widespread concerns in some European states over issues such as human rights. According to Ramsbotham, despite concerns over human rights, President Heinemann was ordered to attend the event 'for the sake of Germany's extensive commercial interests in Iran'.[108] Facing criticism at home over the plight of political prisoners in Iran, Heinemann argued: 'When a state maintains ties to another state, in international understanding that implies neither judgement of its form of government

103 See for example, *Iran 71: An Independent Survey on the Iranian Economy on the Occasion of the 2500th Anniversary of the Founding of the Persian Empire*, Tehran 1971.
104 'Necessary Information and Questions', p. 2, MinBuZa 2.05.191/554.
105 'Decorations', *Kayhan International*, 5 June 1971.
106 Ramsbotham report, 23 October 1971, p. 4, FCO 17/1529.
107 Denis Wright, in an interview with Habib Ladjevardi, Aylesbury, UK, 10 and 11 October 1984, Iranian Oral History Collection, Harvard University, tape 6, p. 44.
108 Ramsbotham report, 23 October 1971, p. 4, FCO 479/71.

nor the politics of that state.'[109] In an open letter to his country's young socialists, Heinemann noted Iran's regional political and economic power as a justification for his decision to take part in the festivities.[110] Similarly, a member of the Swiss delegation accompanying President Rudolf Gnägi declared that his mission was 'not very pleasant', but nonetheless necessary since 'international customs and commitments simply cannot be ignored'.[111]

In the Netherlands, the Foreign Ministry was forced to defend Iran in public in order to maintain good relations during this important period, narrowly avoiding a scandal in the process. When an Iranian carpet dealer living in the Netherlands refused an order from the Iranian ambassador to give discounts during the Celebrations, his passport was revoked and he was ordered to return to Iran 'as soon as possible'.[112] The implication in the press was that this was punishment for his disobedience and the issue was debated in the Dutch House of Representatives, with House members asking whether the ambassador overstepped the mark with his 'unacceptable behaviour'.[113] Foreign Minister Norbert Schmelzer, in defence of the ambassador, argued that 'it should not be seen as uncommon that on occasion of special events or for other reasons compatriots should be asked to lend their support to such a manifestation'.[114] Schmelzer declined to take the ambassador to task over the allegations, even when pressed by House members and journalists who were critical of the shah.

Healthy international competition in Iranian markets was beneficial to Iran and it was in the interests of foreign countries to use the opportunity to strengthen their ties with the shah. In a press conference held shortly after the Celebrations the shah said to a German reporter:

> You are exporting to us 10 times more than what you buy from us. If we stopped trade with you, you would be the losers not us. We can buy what you sell to us elsewhere.[115]

---

109 'Heinemann rechtfertigt seine Persien-Reise', *Frankfurter Allgemeine Zeitung*, 18 August 1971.

110 Ibid.

111 'Zwitserland: feestje in Perzië is niet leuk', *Nieuwe Leidsche Courant*, 13 October 1971, p. 9.

112 'Intimidatie van "Nederlandse" Pers: Opponent van Sjah krijgt geen pas', *Trouw*, 12 October 1971.

113 'Kamerleden laken gedrag Perzische ambassadeur', *Volkskrant*, 13 October 1971.

114 Norbert Schmelzer, 'Reply', 27 October 1971, Aanhangsel tot het Verslag van de Handelingen der Tweede Kamer, Zitting 1971–1972, p. 479.

115 'We Stand on Our Own Feet Monarch Tells World Press', *Kayhan International*, 23 October 1971, p. 7.

The shah's message was loud and clear: you need us more than we need you. This position encouraged competition and with it a good measure of blandishment. A commemorative edition of *Anglo-Iranian Trade* was published by British Industrial Publicity Overseas, with the rather long-winded title: 'British Industry Salutes Their Imperial Majesties Mohammad Reza Pahlavi Aryamehr Shah and the Shahbanu Farah of Iran and Their Nation on the Historic Occasion of the 2500th Anniversary of the Founding of the Persian Empire by Cyrus the Great: Long Live His Imperial Majesty the Shahanshah Aryamehr!'[116] One British diplomat was struck by the 'outrageous flattery' that was the norm during this period and the Celebrations witnessed expressions of admiration for the shah that bordered on extreme sycophancy.[117] The Apadana reliefs at Persepolis depict representatives from each quarter of the Persian Empire waiting to pay homage to their emperor, and to a certain degree the Celebrations were a twentieth century manifestation of this ancient practice.

The realisation that attendance would be viewed as homage to the shah was most likely a factor in the British decision not to send Queen Elizabeth II to attend the Celebrations. Appearing to be submissive to the shah, particularly at a time when Britain was making an inglorious retreat from the Persian Gulf, was not palatable to the British. Denis Wright, who served as Britain's ambassador in Tehran until 1971, recalled that he wondered, 'why should we, having all this abuse hurled at us in the press, bring our Queen out just to please the Shah?'[118] Despite this symbolic gesture of disapproval, Britain was careful not to politicise the rejection, informing the shah that as a general rule 'the Queen does not go on international jamborees'.[119] Moreover, to soften the blow when, against the advice of the Foreign Office, the shah's second choice, Prince Charles, declined his invitation as well, the Queen was encouraged to write a personal letter to the shah since it was conjectured that he would 'regard refusal as a personal slight'.[120] In this handwritten letter the Queen wrote that she was 'deeply conscious of the disappointment' caused.[121] There was clearly some concern over the implications of the Queen's rejection for British interests in Iran.

Ultimately, the Queen was represented by Prince Philip and Princess Anne,

116 *Anglo-Iranian Trade*, vol. 4, no. 4, London 1971.
117 O'Regan, J., *From Empire to Commonwealth*, London 1994, p. 169.
118 Wright, Iranian Oral History Collection, Harvard University, tape 4, pp. 6–7.
119 Ramsbotham in an interview with Habib Ladjevardi, London, UK, 18 October 1985, Iranian Oral History Collection, Harvard University, tape 1, p. 23.
120 Wright telegram, 9 January 1971, FCO 57/323.
121 Queen Elizabeth II to the shah, January 1971, FCO 57/323.

who received a three-year-old Pahlavan stallion and two Caspian horses as gifts from the shah. However, in yet another potential slight to the shah, European laws regarding livestock imports made it impossible to immediately take the horses to Britain. Ramsbotham wrote frantically to a number of organisations in Britain in order to find a solution:

> I am concerned at this situation which could easily go sour… once having made his [the shah's] gesture and the gift having been accepted he could now take offence if it had to be rejected for reasons which he would not regard as insuperable in his own country.[122]

A solution to the problem was eventually found, but Ramsbotham's anxiety was revealing. The Celebrations were intended to announce Iran's arrival on the international scene. The efforts of the European powers to avoid causing offence suggests that this message was clearly understood. This was driven by practical considerations related to political and commercial interests. If Britain lost out on a contract, then Germany or another competitor would take its place, and thus it was in each government's interest to maintain positive relations with the shah.

The Tent City at Persepolis

Besides the development of commercial interests, there was a deeper motivation for inviting the world's leaders to Iran. In 1943, Stalin, Roosevelt and Churchill had held a wartime Allied conference in Tehran to discuss the opening of a second front in Europe. Not only was the young Mohammad Reza Shah not invited to take part in the discussions, he was not even informed of the meeting until the last moment.[123] By 1971, the shah had emerged from this insignificance and now leaders from around the world flocked to Iran to pay tribute to him. The Celebrations represented a coming of age, as the shah had finally discovered his identity and his place in the world. During his speeches throughout the festivities, the shah was eager to stress his role as a serious global leader. He spoke of international 'understanding and friendship' and of 'loving unity with the Iranian nation', and at the parade on 15 October he said:

---

122 Ramsbotham telegram, 27 October 1971, FCO 57/323.

123 Milani, *The Shah*, p. 101. During these visits to Iran, the shah was upset that Churchill in particular did not observe official protocol and pay a visit to the monarch. 'He didn't even bother to come and call on me at my residence,' said the shah, 'although I was King of the host country.' See Karanjia, R. K., *The Mind of a Monarch*, London 1977, p. 69.

> It is my ardent wish that the great cause of understanding and friendship which has brought together in one place the distinguished representatives of so many countries and nations of the world may inspire all the people on earth to pursue the way that leads to real prosperity and human society.[124]

The period of Cold War superpower détente had begun just two years earlier, so when the shah spoke about peace and goodwill he was aware that this language was in keeping with geopolitical realities. During this Cold War lull, it was possible to carve out a new direction for Iran, one in which the shah acted as a unifier. Diplomatic dialogue was promoted at the Celebrations, with time set-aside during the days at Persepolis for informal meetings and discussions. South African State President Jacobus Fouché, for example, was invited to the Indonesian tent for cocktails, and similar informal meetings were held in his own tent with, among others, King Moshoeshoe II of Lesotho.[125]

Those attending the event were made aware of the political ramifications of their visit. In his briefing for US Vice-President Spiro Agnew ahead of his visit as the representative of President Nixon, Henry Kissinger wrote:

> Your visit to Iran is essentially an expression of our respect and friendship for the Shah. The 25th Centenary Celebrations are a symbolic assertion that Iran, under the leadership of the Shah, is assuming the full promise of its ancient heritage. Your participation in these events is intended to identify the United States with these accomplishments and the Shah's leadership.[126]

The relationship between Iran and the United States developed during this period in such a way that Iran was no longer a subservient country, but a partner, a twist of fortunes that the shah certainly appreciated. In this context, Agnew was given a list of issues to discuss with the shah at the Celebrations. The escalating tension between India and Pakistan over the situation in East Pakistan, Kissinger advised Agnew, was 'the subject at the top of our priority list'.[127] Agnew was to set out the

124 'The Shahanshah's speech at the banquet on 14 October 1971', pp. 17–19, MinBuZa 2.05.191/554; 'Shahanshah's message at the Grand Parade, 15 October 1971', p. 21.
125 H. A. Hoogendoorn to Dutch Minister of Foreign Affairs, 21 October 1971, MinBuZa 2.05.191/554.
126 Memorandum Kissinger to Agnew, 9 October 1971, *Foreign Relations of the United States, 1969–1976, Volume E-4, Iran and Iraq, 1969–1972*, Document 148.
127 Ibid.

American position on the issue and inform the shah of Nixon's appreciation for anything that he 'might be able to do along these lines'.[128]

In order to underline his credentials as a global statesman, the shah did indeed attempt to mediate talks between India and Pakistan during the Celebrations. Outside of Iran such a meeting with President Nikolai Podgorny of the Soviet Union, Yahya Khan and V. V. Giri in one place would have been impossible. This substantiated, according to Ramsbotham, 'the Shah's claim to be an independent world leader'.[129] For Pakistan the meeting was considered a relative success, with the Soviets assuring them of their commitment to the preservation of Pakistan's territorial integrity.[130] For his efforts the shah received little more than a stern warning from Podgorny not to supply weapons to Pakistan, which in fact Iran was doing covertly.[131] Seemingly undeterred by his failure to conclude peace talks, the shah pledged to do 'all in our power' to avert military confrontation, 'even if our preliminary efforts do not prove as fruitful as we would like them to be'.[132]

The shah also sought to use the Celebrations to further strengthen ties with communist China, with which the United States was cultivating an opening. From 13 until 19 April 1971 Princess Ashraf visited China for a meeting with Premier Chou En-lai. During a toast at a banquet in her honour, she raised a glass to Chairman Mao, and said: 'Personal contact such as ours here today, inevitably leads to dialogue… I know that, through this unpretentious visit, we already have taken the first step in that direction.'[133] Later that month, Princess Fatemeh also visited, accompanied by Leila Hoveyda, the wife of Prime Minister Amir Abbas Hoveyda. Fatemeh's visit coincided with the May Day celebrations and affirmed, according to the *Peking Review*, 'the atmosphere of friendship between the people of China and Iran'.[134] This effort contributed to the formal establishment of diplomatic relations between the two countries, signed on 16 August 1971.[135] The Chinese had

128 Ibid.
129 Ramsbotham report, 23 October 1971, FCO 17/1529.
130 Sisson, R., and Rose, L., *War and Secession: Pakistan, India, and the Creation of Bangladesh*, Oxford 1990, fn. 4, p. 307.
131 Alvandi, R., *Nixon, Kissinger, and the Shah: The United States and Iran in the Cold War*, New York 2014, p. 61.
132 'Shahanshah's interview', p. 11, MinBuZa 2.05.191/554.
133 'Princess Ashraf Pahlavi of Iran Visits China', *Peking Review*, vol. 14, no. 17, 23 April 1971, p 4. For her memoir of the trip, see Pahlavi, A., *Faces in a Mirror: Memoirs from Exile*, Englewood Cliffs 1980, pp. 178–180.
134 'Princess Fatemeh Pahlavi in Peking', *Peking Review*, vol. 14, no. 19, 7 May 1971, p. 30.
135 Mohajer, P., 'Chinese-Iranian Relations v. Diplomatic and Commercial Relations, 1949–90', *Encyclopaedia Iranica*, vol. 5, no. 4, 1991, pp. 438–441, available at: <http://www.iranicaonline.org/articles/chinese-iranian-v>; Halliday, F., *Iran: Dictatorship*

intended to send vice-chairman of the Standing Committee of the National People's Congress, Kuo Mo-jo, to the Celebrations as China's representative, but he fell ill on the way, so China's ambassador to Pakistan, Chang Tung, was sent in his place. On 15 October, Chang Tung presented a letter from Chou En-lai, which read:

> China's Special Envoy Kuo Mo-jo has been invited to pay a friendly visit to your country. We believe that with the joint effort of our two sides the relations between China and Iran based on the principles of mutual respect for sovereignty and territorial integrity, mutual benefit, and peaceful coexistence will develop continuously, and the friendly contacts, and mutual understanding between the two peoples will be 'further strengthened'.[136]

In September 1972, just months after Nixon's historic visit, Empress Farah and Prime Minister Hoveyda led an Iranian delegation to China in order to further develop relations. Speaking on that occasion, Premier Chou En-lai noted China's presence at the Celebrations as an example of the growing friendship between the two countries.[137] The shah's diplomacy with China demonstrated that he was keen to look to Asia as well as the West in his efforts to increase Iran's global influence.

The participation of South Africa's President Fouché was also significant, particularly since his invitation was viewed in Apartheid South Africa as a contrast to the general tone of international isolation that the country experienced at this time.[138] Meanwhile, the departure of the British from the Persian Gulf had presented Iran with an opportunity to take a leading role in regional politics, too. The emirs of each of the seven Trucial States attended, as did the emir of Bahrain, whose involvement as an independent head of state allowed the shah to draw a line under his country's claims to the territory. On 16 October, during the Celebrations, Iran established diplomatic relations with Qatar, underlining the shah's intention to play a significant part in the integration of the former British

---

and Development, Harmondsworth 1979, p. 263. For text of the agreement, see 'Joint Communique on Establishment of Diplomatic Relations between China and Iran', *Peking Review*, vol. 14, no. 34, 20 August 1971, p. 4.

136 'Iran's 2,500th Anniversary of Persian Empire Greeted', *Peking Review*, vol. 14, no. 43, 22 October 1971, pp. 3–4.

137 Taheri, A., 'Ties as Old as the Silk Road: Empress, Chou Pledge Expanded Co-Operation', *Kayhan International*, 23 September 1972, p. 1.

138 Chehabi, H. E., 'South Africa and Iran in the Apartheid Era', *Journal of Southern African Studies*, vol. 42, no. 4, 2016, p. 694.

protectorates into the international community.[139] Not every state, however, was invited to Persepolis. Israel, with which Iran had a *de facto* relationship, was not officially invited so as to avoid both an Arab boycott and offending Iranian public opinion. However, Israeli scholars were secretly housed in a motel on the outskirts of Shiraz so that they could attend the Congress of Iranology.[140] Additionally, former Prime Minister David Ben-Gurion contributed a chapter on Cyrus the Great to the first volume of *Acta Iranica*, which was established in order to publish the proceedings of this congress.[141]

Despite the diplomatic successes of the Celebrations, they helped to inspire a new era of opposition to the shah's rule abroad. Abbas Milani referred to the Celebrations as a 'propaganda bonanza' for the Confederation of Iranian Students.[142] For those who sympathised with the cause of the Iranian student opposition overseas, the Celebrations provided a convenient opportunity to attack the shah's regime. *Washington Post* reporter Jonathan Randal, for example, later claimed that his derogatory reporting on the event was his way of 'pissing on the Shah's party'.[143] Jonker, the Dutch ambassador, claimed that reports in the Western press had been 'juvenile' and lacking 'profound objective analysis'.[144] The shah was personally clearly frustrated by the media criticism, but although such reports presented a negative portrait of the shah's Iran, this did not deter most attendees and did not affect their relations with Iran. To the extent that the Celebrations showcased Iran's pre-eminence, strengthened existing relationships, and developed new ones, Persepolis was a diplomatic success for the shah, regardless of the criticism from sections of the international media.

---

139 Shafa, S., *Gahnameh-ye Panjah Sal-e Shahanshahi-ye Pahlavi* [Chronology of Fifty Years of the Pahlavi Monarchy], vol. 5, Tehran 1355/1976, p. 2058.
140 Richard Frye in an interview with Shahla Haeri, Cambridge, MA, 3, 10 and 24 October 1984, Iranian Oral History Collection, Harvard University, tape 3, p. 35.
141 Ben-Gurion, D., 'Cyrus, King of Persia', in *Acta Iranica,* vol. 1, Duchesne-Guillemin, J. (ed.), Tehran; Leiden 1974, pp. 127–134.
142 Milani, *The Shah*, p. 372.
143 Cooper, A. S., *The Fall of Heaven: The Pahlavis and the Final Days of Imperial Iran,* New York 2016, p. 171. For an overview of the media coverage in the United States, see Dorman, W. A. and Farhang, M., *The U.S. Press and Iran: Foreign Policy and the Journalism of Deference*, Berkeley 1987, pp. 116–121.
144 Jonker, H., '2500 year celebration Persian Monarchy', 3 November 1971, MinBuZa 2.05.191/554.

Conclusion

The 1971 Persepolis Celebrations did not receive positive press at the time and still today, many accounts by historians and journalists adopt a disdainful tone. In 1971, *Newsweek* dismissed the Celebrations as 'a mixture of pomp and pomposity, of regal splendour and petty carping', and as recently as 2012, James Buchan wrote that they 'introduced an element of the fantastical into the Pahlavi style, as if some toy principality had gained a half-million-man army'.[145] At a conference shortly after the Celebrations, Elwell-Sutton spoke of a general misunderstanding of the occasion. He said:

> In view of the discourteous tone of the bulk of the reports sent home by some foreign journalists – rivalled only by their discourteous behaviour on the spot – it may perhaps be worth while to attempt an objective analysis of this imposing and undoubtedly expensive operation.[146]

This objective analysis has been lacking and the positive effects of the Celebrations are often lost within a narrative that refers to the occasion simply as a party, while the Islamic Republic continues to demonise them as *bazm-e ahriman*, the devil's feast. This is 'not good faith', Houchang Nahavandi observes, 'but it is good warfare'.[147]

The Celebrations have become such a crucial part of the Pahlavi court's characterisation as pompous and out-of-touch with reality that they are generally considered as merely illustrative of the perceived decadence of the court and the megalomania of the shah himself. But the evidence presented in this chapter has demonstrated that beyond the pomp and ceremony, the Celebrations largely achieved their international objectives. Despite the opposition to the event from sections of the foreign media, there was an unprecedented level of interest from global business, political and cultural figures to participate. The Celebrations announced to the world the re-emergence of Iran as a fully-fledged and independent power, free from the shackles of foreign imperialism that had overshadowed its modern history up to that point. This was the narrative that the Celebrations sought to project and on the whole they did so successfully. At the centre of this political theatre was Mohammad Reza Shah, who took his place on the international stage, presenting himself as not only the locus of Iranian nationalism

145 Jenkins, 'Iran's Birthday Party', p. 33; Buchan, *Days of God*, p. 56.
146 Elwell-Sutton, '2500th Anniversary Celebrations', p. 24.
147 Nahavandi, *The Last Shah of Iran*, p. 47.

but also a major political figure of the global 1970s. The shah had evolved from an uncertain, even timid, young monarch into a strong leader, convinced of his own destiny, becoming in the words of Ramsbotham, 'an oriental de Gaulle, but without the latter's saving grace of irony and humour'.[148]

The Cyrus Cylinder too became a powerful symbol of this Iranian renaissance and for many Iranians it took on an iconic significance which it retains to this day. In her Nobel Prize lecture in 2003, Shirin Ebadi referred to herself as a descendant of Cyrus the Great and to the Cylinder as one of the most important documents in the history of human rights.[149] In a publication coinciding with the Cylinder's tour of the United States in 2013, in words that might have been uttered by Mohammad Reza Shah, Ali Razi, chairman of the private US-based Farhang Foundation, wrote of Cyrus's 'humanitarian values of freedom for all people'.[150] The Cylinder travelled to Iran again in 2010 for a highly publicised and politically charged exhibition. Iranian President Mahmoud Ahmadinejad visited the artefact at the National Museum of Tehran, and in a ceremony referred to Cyrus as 'King of the World'.[151] Hence, the Celebrations in 1971 helped to transform the Cylinder into a relic of considerable national and global importance, framed in the context of the Pahlavi nationalist ideology. The success of this message can be observed in the reverence in which the Cylinder is still held today.

On reflection, one might conclude that the Celebrations represented a turning point in the shah's reign, the high point of a Shakespearean tragedy that would ultimately culminate in a great downfall. The Celebrations also offer a unique opportunity to investigate the peak of the shah's international standing, when heads of state from around the world flocked to Persepolis to pay tribute to him. Opportunities were observed, both political and economic, and the shah was eager to accentuate and promote the image of Iran as a land of peace and possibilities. There has been a tendency for critics to focus on refusals by some heads of state to participate in the Celebrations as evidence that they were not taken particularly seriously. However, the evidence presented here suggests that not only did foreign countries participate willingly, even eagerly, but their support was fundamental in

---

148 Ramsbotham report, 11 October 1971, p. 4, FCO 57/323.

149 Ebadi, S., *Nobel Lecture*, 10 December 2003, available at: <http://www.nobelprize.org/nobel_prizes/peace/laureates/2003/ebadi-lecture-e.html >.

150 Razi, A.C., in the foreword to Daryaee, T. (ed.), *Cyrus the Great*, Santa Monica 2013, p. xi.

151 Black, I., and Dehghan, S. K., 'Iran Lays Claim to British Museum's Cyrus Cylinder', *The Guardian*, 15 September 2010, available at: <http://www.theguardian.com/world/2010/sep/15/iran-cyrus-cylinderbritish-museum>.

achieving the principal goals of the Celebrations, and helped to cement the central position of the shah on the international stage.

Bibliography

Primary Material

Bazm-e Ahriman: Jashnha-ye 2500 saleh-ye shahanshahi beh revayat-e asnad-e savak va darbar [The Devil's Feast: The 2500th Anniversary Celebrations according to SAVAK and court documents], vol. 4, Tehran, 1378/1999.

Belmonte, M. (ed.), *Foreign Relations of the United States, 1969–1976, Volume E-4, Iran and Iraq, 1969–1972*, Washington, DC 2006, available at: <http://history.state.gov/historicaldocuments/frus1969–76ve04>.

Nationaal Archief, The Hague –

2.05.191/554, Stukken beteffende het vieren van het 2500-jarig bestaan van de monarchie van Iran in oktober 1971, 1966–1972.

2.05.118/14175, Iran; memoranda over het organiseren van de tetoonstelling Rondom het Kind, ter gelegenheid van het 2500-jarig bestaan van Iran, 1961–1963.

2.02.28.3882, Aanhangsel tot het Verslag van de Handelingen der Tweede Kamer, Zitting 1971–1972.

National Archives, Kew –

BW 49/31, British Council, Representative's Annual Reports, 1970–1973.

FCO 57/322, Visit of Duke of Edinburgh to Iran for 2500th Anniversary of Iranian Monarchy, October 1971, 1970–1971.

FCO 57/323, Visit of Duke of Edinburgh to Iran for 2500th Anniversary of Iranian Monarchy, Including Details of Gifts Given by Shah, October 1971.

FCO 17/1528, 2,500th Anniversary of Monarchy of Monarchy of Iran Celebrations in Persepolis and Tehran, 1971.

FCO 17/1529, 2,500th Anniversary of Monarchy of Monarchy of Iran Celebrations in Persepolis and Tehran: Loan of the Cyrus Liberation Tablet by the British Museum to Iran for the Celebrations Honouring the Foundation of the Persian Empire by Cyrus the Great, 1971–1972.

'Pahlavi-ye dovvom va nemuneh-ye andishehha-ye bastangerayaneh: negahi be asnad-e mahramaneh-ye jashnha-ye 2500 saleh-ye shahanshahi' [The Second Pahlavi and some Elements of Archaistic Thoughts: A look to the Secret Documents Relating to the 2500th Anniversary Celebrations], *Tarikh-e moʿaser-e Iran*, vol. 2, no. 5, 1377/1998, pp. 122–188.

Paul Gotch Papers, British Museum, London.
Shojaeddin Shafa Papers, Bibliothèque Universitaire des Langues et Civilisations, Paris.
UNESCO Archives, Paris.
United Nations Archives, New York.

Newspapers and Journals

Kayhan International
Echo of Iran
The Guardian
The Daily Telegraph
Life Magazine
Newsweek
The Stanford Daily
Paris Match
Frankfurter Allgemeine Zeitung
Nieuwe Leidsche Courant
Trouw
Volkskrant
Peking Review

Oral Histories

George Middleton in an interview with Habib Ladjevardi, London, UK, 16 October 1985, Iranian Oral History Collection, Harvard University.
Peter Ramsbotham in an interview with Habib Ladjevardi, London, UK, 18 October 1985, Iranian Oral History Collection, Harvard University.
Denis Wright, in an interview with Habib Ladjevardi, Aylesbury, UK, 10 and 11 October 1984, Iranian Oral History Collection, Harvard University.
Richard Frye in an interview with Shahla Haeri, Cambridge, MA, 3, 10 and 24 October 1984, Iranian Oral History Collection, Harvard University.

Books and Articles

Adib-Moghaddam, A., *Psycho-nationalism: Global Thought, Iranian Imaginations,* London 2018.
Alam, A., *The Shah and I*, London 1991.

Alvandi, R., 'Muhammad Reza Pahlavi and the Bahrain Question, 1968–1970', *British Journal of Middle Eastern Studies*, 37/2 (2010), pp. 159–177.

Alvandi, R., *Nixon, Kissinger, and the Shah: The United States and Iran in the Cold War*, New York 2014.

Andrews, P., *The Turcoman of Iran*, Kendal 1971.

Anglo-Iranian Trade, vol. 4, no. 4, London 1971.

Ansari, A., *The Shah's Iran – Rise and Fall: Conversations with an Insider*, London 2017.

Ansari, A. M., 'The Myth of the White Revolution: Mohammad Reza Shah, 'Modernization' and the Consolidation of Power', in *Middle Eastern Studies*, vol. 37, no. 3, 2001, pp. 1–24.

Ansari, A. M., *The Politics of Nationalism in Modern Iran*, Cambridge 2012.

Axworthy, M., *Revolutionary Iran: A History of the Islamic Republic*, London 2013.

Azimi, F., *Quest for Democracy in Iran: A Century of Struggle Against Authoritarian Rule,* Cambridge, MA 2008.

Ben-Gurion, D., 'Cyrus, King of Persia', in *Acta Iranica,* vol. 1, Jacques Duchesne-Guillemin (ed.), Tehran; Leiden 1974, pp. 127–134.

Bill, J. A., *The Eagle and the Lion: The Tragedy of American-Iranian Relations*, New Haven 1988.

Buchan, J., *Days of God: The Revolution in Iran and Its Consequences*, London 2012.

Chehabi, H. E., 'South Africa and Iran in the Apartheid Era', in *Journal of Southern African Studies*, vol. 42, no. 4, 2016, pp. 687–709.

Cooper, A.S ., *The Fall of Heaven: The Pahlavis and the Final Days of Imperial Iran,* New York 2016.

Corruption and Struggle in Iran: A Defense Publication of the Iranian Student Association in the United States, June 1972.

Daryaee, T. (ed.), *Cyrus the Great*, Santa Monica 2013.

Dorman, W. A., and Farhang, M., *The U.S. Press and Iran: Foreign Policy and the Journalism of Deference*, Berkeley 1987.

Ebadi, S., *Nobel Lecture*, 10 December 2003, available at: <http://www.nobelprize.org/nobel_prizes/peace/laureates/2003/ebadi-lecture-e.html >.

Eilers, W. (ed.), *Festgabe Deutscher Iranisten zur 2500 Jahrfeier Irans*, Stuttgart 1971.

Elwell-Sutton, L., '2500th Anniversary Celebrations', in *Bulletin of the British Association of Orientalists*', no. 6, 1973, pp. 20–25.

Gluck, J. and Siver, N. (eds.), *Surveyors of Persian Art: A Documentary Biography of Arthur Upham Pope and Phyllis Ackerman*, Costa Mesa, CA 1996.

Gong, G. W., *The Standard of 'Civilization' in International Society*, Oxford 1984.

Herodotus, *The Histories*, transl. George Rawlinson, London 1997.

Iran Free Press, 1:2, October 1971.

Issawi, C., 'The Iranian Economy 1925–1975: Fifty Years of Economic Development', in George Lencozowski (ed.), *Iran Under the Pahlavis,* Stanford, California 1978, pp. 129–166.

Kadivar, C., '2500-Year Celebrations Revisited', *The Iranian,* 25 January 2002, available at: <http://iranian.com/CyrusKadivar/2002/January/2500/index.html>.

Kallis, A., 'Framing Romanità: The Celebrations for the Bimillenario Augusteo and the Augusteo-Ara Pacis Project', in *Journal of Contemporary History*, vol. 46, no. 809, 2011, pp. 809–831.

Karanjia, R. K., *The Mind of a Monarch*, London 1977.

Katouzian, H., *Sadeq Hedayat: The Life and Legend of an Iranian Writer*, London 2002.

Lewis, B., *Notes On A Century: Reflections of a Middle East Historian*, London 2013.

Louis, W. R., 'The British Withdrawal from the Gulf, 1967–71', in *The Journal of Imperial and Commonwealth History*, vol. 33, no. 1, 2003, pp. 83–108.

Lowenthal, D., *The Heritage Crusade and the Spoils of History*, Cambridge 1998.

Milani, A., *The Shah*, New York 2011.

Mohajer, P., 'Chinese-Iranian Relations v. Diplomatic and Commercial Relations, 1949–90', *Encyclopaedia Iranica*, vol. 5, no. 4, 1991, pp. 438–441, available at: <http://www.iranicaonline.org/articles/chinese-iranian-v>.

'Mosahebeh-ye chap nashodeh-i az Shojaeddin Shafa darbareh-ye: jashnha-ye dohezar o pansad saleh' [Unpublished Interview with Shojaʿeddin Shafa about: the 2500th Anniversary Celebrations], *Rahavard*, no. 95, 2011, pp. 180–193.

Motadel, D., 'Iran and the Aryan Myth', in Ansari, Ali (ed.), *Perceptions of Iran: History, Myths and Nationalism from Medieval Persia to the Islamic Republic*, London 2014, pp. 119–145.

Mottahedeh, R., *The Mantle of the Prophet: Religion and Politics in Iran*, London 1987.

Nahavandi, H., *The Last Shah of Iran: Fatal Countdown of a Great Patriot Betrayed by the Free World, a Great Country Whose Fault Was Success*, transl. Reed, S., Slough 2005.

O'Regan, J., *From Empire to Commonwealth*, London 1994.

Pahlavi, A., *Faces in a Mirror: Memoirs from Exile*, Englewood Cliffs 1980.

Pahlavi, F., *An Enduring Love: My Life with the Shah*, New York 2004.

Pahlavi, M. R., *Mission for my Country*, London 1961.

Parade at Persepolis: Celebration of the 2500th Anniversary of the Founding of the Persian Empire by Cyrus the Great, Tehran 1971.

Paulmann, J., 'Searching for "Royal International"', in Geyer, M. H., and Paulmann, J. (eds.), *The Mechanics of Internationalism: Culture, Society, and Politics from the 1840s to the First World War*, London 2001, pp. 145–176.

Persian Panorama: Publication of the Imperial Embassy of Iran, London, vol. 1, no. 3, 1965.

Podeh, E., *The Politics of National Celebrations in the Arab Middle East*, Cambridge 2011.

Ram, M. and Rao, S. B. (eds.), *Indo-Iran: Papers presented at the Congress of Iranologists and Indiologists, New Delhi, on the occasion of the 25th millennia of the Founding of Monarchy in Iran*, New Delhi 1974.

Rubin, B., *Paved with Good Intentions: The American Experience in Iran*, Harmondsworth 1981.

Sabahi, F., *The Literacy Corps in Pahlavi Iran (1963–1979): Political Social and Literary Implications*, Lugano 2002.

Saikal, A., *The Rise and Fall of the Shah: Iran from Autocracy to Religious Rule*, Princeton 2009.

Sept mille ans d'art en Iran, Musée du Petit Palais, Paris 1961.

Shafa, S., *Facts About the Celebration of the 2500th Anniversary of the Founding of the Persian Empire by Cyrus the Great*, Tehran 1971.

Shafa, S., *Gahnameh-ye Panjah Sal-e Shahanshahi-ye Pahlavi* [Chronology of Fifty Years of the Pahlavi Monarchy], vol. 5, Tehran 1355/1976.

Shakibi, Z., 'Pahlavism: The Ideologization of Monarchy in Iran', in *Politics, Religion and Ideology*, vol. 14, no. 1, 2013, pp. 114–135.

Shakibi, Z., 'The Rastakhiz Party and Pahlavism: The Beginnings of State Anti-Westernism in Iran', in *British Journal of Middle Eastern Studies*, vol. 45, no. 2, 2018, pp. 251–268.

Shawcross, W., *The Shah's Last Ride*, London 1989.

Sisson, R. and Rose, L., *War and Secession: Pakistan, India, and the Creation of Bangladesh*, Oxford 1990.

Stevenson, M. (ed.), *Celebration at Persepolis*, Bristol 2008.

Stronach, D., 'Director's Report November 1st 1970 to October 31st 1971', in *Iran*, vol. 10, 1972, p. xi.

Tarverdi, R. and Massoudi, A. (eds.), *The Land of Kings*, Tehran 1971.

Tavakoli-Targhi, M., *Refashioning Iran: Orientalism, Occidentalism and Historiography*, Houndmill 2001.

Vaziri, M., *Iran as Imagined Nation: The Construction of National Identity*, New York 1993.

Wortman, R.S., *Scenarios of Power: Myth and Ceremony in Russian Monarchy*, vol. 2, Princeton 2000, pp. 439–480.

Zia-Ebrahimi, R., *The Emergence of Iranian Nationalism: Race and the Politics of Dislocation*, New York 2016.

Zia-Ebrahimi, R., 'Self-Orientalization and Dislocation: The Uses and Abuses of the "Aryan" Discourse in Iran', *Iranian Studies*, vol. 44, no. 4, 2013, pp. 114–135, DOI: 10.1080/21567689.2012.751911.

Zonis, M., *Majestic Failure: The Fall of the Shah*. Chicago 1991.

4

A Cosmopolitan Dandy: Amir Abbas Hoveyda[1]

H. E. Chehabi

> My whole doctrine lies in a single phrase: Hurrah for bagatelles!
>
> Valle-Inclán, *Winter Sonata*

It is ironic that at a time when the quest for authenticity became a major pre-occupation for many Iranians, within the ruling elite and even more among the opposition, the Iranian government was headed by a man who embodied cosmo-politanism as few other Iranians did. Amir Abbas Hoveyda, prime minister for over twelve years between 1965 and 1977,[2] was, in the words of his biographer, Abbas Milani, 'the first true cosmopolitan – equally at home in Beirut and Rome, or Tehran and Paris – to reach the pinnacles of power in Iran'.[3] For years Hoveyda

1 I would like to thank Paul Horowitz for helping with the photos, Mohammad Batmanglij for sending me the photo of Amir Abbas Hoveyda, and the National Portrait Gallery in London for permission to reproduce the painting of Joseph Chamberlain. I am also grateful to Manouchehr Eskandari-Qajar for his careful reading of the manuscript of this chapter.

2 This chapter eschews discussion of Hoveyda's role in the politics of that era, which has been very ably analysed by Fakhreddin Azimi in Azimi, F., *The Quest for Democracy in Iran: A Century of Struggle against Authoritarian Rule*, Cambridge, MA 2008, pp. 184–204. For a general overview of that period see Ashraf, A., 'From the White Revolution to the Islamic Revolution', in Rahnema, S., and Behdad, S. (eds.), *Iran after the Revolution: Crisis of an Islamic State*, London 1995.

3 Milani, A., *The Persian Sphinx: Amir Abbas Hoveyda and the Riddle of the Iranian Revolution*, Washington, DC 2000, p. 175.

had been dismissed as the archetypical servant of the Shah's autocratic regime at its height, a man who played the constitutionally prescribed role of prime minister while himself admitting that he took orders from the ruler; a figure more remembered for his trademark pipe, orchid, and cane than his policies and accomplishments.[4] Then, in 2000, Milani's biography revealed a much more complex personality: a polyglot intellectual, a polished cosmopolitan, a man who could have enriched himself like so many other state officials, but did not; an enigmatic personality in whom the highest ideals coincided with a political career that was inconsistent with these ideals.

Amir Abbas Hoveyda was born in 1919 in Tehran. His mother was related to the Qajar dynasty,[5] while his more middle-class father, titled Eyn al-Molk, was a career diplomat who served in the Levant and in what later became Saudi Arabia. After attending school in Beirut and university in Brussels, Hoveyda returned to Iran in 1942, and upon finishing his military service joined the state administration, serving successively in the ministry of foreign affairs, the National Iranian Oil Company, the ministry of finance, and finally as prime minister. His tenure as prime minister coincided with the most autocratic phase of Mohammad Reza Shah's reign, when the ruler dropped all pretence of letting the prime minister govern the country. Ultimately, as the opposition movement against the regime gathered momentum, the Shah saw fit to make a scapegoat out of his loyal servant and had Hoveyda arrested in November 1978. In the chaos that followed the revolution's triumph in February 1979, Hoveyda could have escaped from prison, but instead he surrendered to the new authorities, who, having subjected him to much humiliation in the course of a mock trial presided over by Sadeq Khalkhali (who would later come to be known as the 'hanging judge'), had him executed on 28 March 1979.

In this chapter, I offer an interpretation of Hoveyda's cosmopolitanism that may shed some light on the 'riddle' of his character. To this end, I would like to propose that Hoveyda, consciously or unconsciously, constructed his persona along the lines of the classical European dandy.[6]

---

4 As exemplified by a two-volume biography published in Iran: Moʿtazed, Kh., *Hoveyda: Siyasatmadar-e pip, ʿasa, gol-e orkideh*, Tehran 1378/1999.

5 Her maternal grandmother had been a sister of Naser al-Din Shah. Barjesteh van Waalwijk van Doorn, L.A.F., 'Genealogy of the Qajar Qovanlou Family; a First Draft', in *Qajar Studies*, no. 11–12, 2011, p. 254.

6 I am not alone in qualifying Hoveyda as a 'dandy'. Milani wrote, without elaborating, that as a young man in Beirut and Europe Hoveyda 'was something of a dandy. In pictures from the period, he is always sharply dressed, sometimes in a bow tie, occasionally with a

Dandyism Defined

In the technical sense in which I use the term, 'dandyism' does not merely refer to a propensity for sartorial meticulousness bordering on effeminacy, but denotes a social phenomenon that appeared first in Regency England and later in France under the Restoration and the July monarchy.[7] In this context, the connection between the two countries was established by the *ur*-dandy, George ('Beau') Brummell (1778–1840), who had to leave his native England at the height of his career in 1816 and found refuge in France, where he ended up serving as the British consul in Caen.[8]

The attributes of dandyism were first defined formally in 1844 by the French writer Jules-Amédée Barbey d'Aurevilly (1808–1889), who based his conceptualisation on the figure of Brummell.[9] The most basic characteristic of the dandy is that he is both a conformist and a rebel, in the sense that dandyism, while respecting conventionalities, 'plays' with these modes of living, and '[w]hile admitting their power, it suffers from and revenges itself upon them, and pleads them as an excuse against themselves'.[10] The dandy is thus a liminal figure in Victor Turner's sense of an entity that is 'neither here nor there' and 'betwixt and between the positions assigned and arrayed by law, custom, convention, and ceremonial'.[11] Dandyism, then, is an attitude to life, an attitude theorised most famously by Charles Baudelaire,[12] whom Hoveyda 'could easily quote'.[13]

An originally English phenomenon that was realised in France, dandyism also

---

dapper chapeau on his head'. (Milani, *The Persian Sphinx*, p. 68). A decade later, Hoshang Merchant, an Indian poet who had lived in Tehran during the revolution, averred that 'a dandy once, [Hoveyda] apologised in court about his appearance'. See Merchant, H., *The Man Who Would Be Queen: Autobiographical Fictions*, New Delhi 2011, p. 73.

7 For England, see Moers, E., *The Dandy: Brummell to Beerbohm*, Lincoln, NE 1978; for France, Boulenger, J., *Sous Louis-Philippe: Les dandys*, Paris 1932.

8 The literature on Brummell is vast. I have used Connely, W., *The Reign of Beau Brummel*, New York 1940; and Kelly, I., *Beau Brummell: The Ultimate Man of Style*, New York 2006.

9 His essay is indeed titled '*Du dandysme et George Brummell*'. For an English translation see Barbey d'Aurevilly, J.-A., *Dandyism*, transl. Ainslie, D., New York 1988.

10 Barbey d'Aurevilly, *Dandyism*, p. 23.

11 Turner, V., *The Ritual Process: Structure and Anti-Structure*, Ithaca, NY 1977, p. 95.

12 In his essay 'Le Dandy', part IX of his 'Le peintre de la vie moderne'. Here I shall quote from the English translation: Baudelaire, Ch., 'The Painter of Modern Life', in *The Painter of Modern Life and Other Essays*, transl. and ed. Mayne, J., New York 1986. For an attempt at Freudian analysis, see Chervet B., 'Dandysme et confection de fétiche ou comment habiller un vide', in *Revue Française de Psychanalyse*, vol. 58, no. 22, 1994. For a miscellany of useful information on the phenomenon, see: www.dandyism.net.

13 Milani, *The Persian Sphinx*, p. 61.

has an elective affinity with cosmopolitanism.[14] About Brummell's successor as reigning dandy of London, Count d'Orsay, who straddled 'worlds of time and place and class',[15] his biographer wrote that 'by the oddest four-cornered mingling of nations and classes, of legitimacy and illegitimacy, of temperaments romantic and phlegmatic', he was 'Franco-Germano-Italo-Flemish'.[16] Similarly, Oscar Wilde was an Irishman who blossomed in England, met with great acclaim on the lecture circuit in the United States, and died in France.

In the late nineteenth and early twentieth centuries, dandyism became a literary phenomenon all across Europe,[17] generating characters as varied as Joris-Karl Huysman's Duc des Esseintes,[18] Ramón del Valle-Inclán's Marqués de Bradomín, Marcel Proust's Baron de Charlus, Richard [von] Schaukal's Andreas von Balthesser, and in popular literature Sir Arthur Conan Doyle's Sherlock Holmes and the latter's French nemesis, Maurice Leblanc's Arsène Lupin. One of the last dandies in literature was André Malraux's Baron de Clapique, a figure with whom Hoveyda identified.[19]

Oscar Wilde's quote that life imitates art and not vice versa is by now a commonplace, and it is therefore not farfetched to surmise that Hoveyda found in classical French dandyism the models of a behaviour and habitus that some of his more prosaic compatriots found so bewildering.[20] For example, how can his

14 One recent study argues that the dandy is emblematic of 'transcultural modernity'. See Peng, H., *Dandyism and Transcultural Modernity: The Dandy, the Flâneur, and the Translator in 1930s Shanghai, Tokyo, and Paris*, London 2010, especially pp. 5–10.
15 Connely, W., *Count d'Orsay: The Dandy of Dandies*, London 1952, p. 147.
16 Connely, *Count d'Orsay*, p. 12.
17 See Lemaire, M., *Le dandysme de Baudelaire à Mallarmé*, Montreal 1978; Gnüg, H., *Kult der Kälte: Der klassische Dandy im Spiegel der Weltliteratur*, Stuttgart 1988; and Feldman, J.R., *Gender on the Divide: the Dandy in Modernist Literature*, Ithaca, NY 1993.
18 Huysmans, J. -K., *À Rebours*, Paris 1978. This novel is available in English in several translations of which I will use the latest: Huysmans, J. -K., *Against Nature (À Rebours)*, transl. Mauldon, M., Oxford 1998. For a discussion of the hero's ambiguous relationship to dandyism, see Schoolfield, G. C., *A Baedeker of Decadence: Charting a Literary Fashion, 1884–1927*, New Haven 2003, pp. 6–7.
19 Hoveyda's brother Fereydoun repeatedly pointed out this affinity to Milani; see *The Persian Sphinx*, p. 353 n52. Curiously enough the literature on dandyism has so far overlooked the figure of Clapique, although a connection is hinted at in Delbourg-Delphis, M., *Masculin Singulier*, Paris 1985, p. 95.
20 The Muslim Middle East has its own analogue to the European dandiacal tradition, but I have no evidence that Hoveyda was aware of it. See Ghazi, M.F., 'Un groupe social: "Les raffinés" (zurafa')', in *Studia Islamica*, no. 11, 1959. For a study of *fin-de-siècle* dandyism in Cairo, see Mestyan, A. and Volait, M., 'Affairisme dynastique et danydisme au Caire vers 1900: Le Club des Princes et la formation d'un quartier du divertissement rue 'Imad al-Din', in *Annales islamologiques*, no. 50, 2016. I have discussed some contemporary manifestations

recollection that, as he was travelling to Europe by boat, the smell of *bifteck frites* on deck made him feel as though he was already in France,[21] not remind one of the memorable passage in Huysman's À *Rebours* where des Esseintes, before crossing the English Channel, eats at a restaurant near the Gare St. Lazare in Paris and finds that his roast beef has provided him with such a foretaste of England that he no longer needs to undertake the trip, having already experienced the sensation of being there?[22]

With this analogy in mind, in the following sections I explore Hoveyda's dandysim, considering in turn his liminality in the context of Iranian society and the various dimensions of his dandiacal habitus.

Hoveyda's Liminality

Historically, many dandies had their family roots not in the mainstream of high society. Brummell was the grandson of a man 'alternately referred to as a confectioner, a treasury porter, an army tailor, a steward or (most likely) a valet'.[23] In politics, the classic example of this social marginality at birth was Benjamin Disraeli, who overcame what was at the time recognised as the social handicap of his Genoese Jewish roots to lead the British Empire.[24]

Hoveyda fits this pattern. His grandfather was known as Mohammad Reza Qannad, i.e., Mohammad Reza the confectioner. This grandfather was also a Baha'i, and raised his son as a Baha'i,[25] but Eyn al-Molk distanced himself from the community after the death in 1921 of its second leader, Abd al-Baha, when the latter's grandson and successor, Shoghi Effendi, reorganised the community in a manner that put it squarely outside the realm of Islam. Hoveyda was fourteen when his father died, and he never sought membership in the Baha'i community, having been much closer to his Muslim mother. Still, conventional wisdom in Iran to this day holds that Hoveyda was a Baha'i, notwithstanding the Baha'i faith's disinclination to allow its members to hold political office. This persistent

of indigenous Iranian dandyism in Chehabi, H. E., 'The Imam as Dandy: The Case of Musa Sadr', *Harvard Middle Eastern and Islamic Review*, vol. 3, no. 1–2, 1996.

21 Hoveyda, A. A., 'Yad-e ayyam-e tahsil dar Orupa', in *Donya*, no. 23, 1346/1967, p. 337.

22 Huysmans, *Against Nature*, pp. 111–114.

23 Moers, *The Dandy*, p. 24.

24 For an analysis of Disraeli's dandyhood, see Moers, *The Dandy*, pp. 84–104; and Coblence, F., 'Disraëli: du style dandy en politique', in *Critique*, no. 405–406, 1981.

25 From a Baha'i publication quoted in Alamuti, M., *Iran dar 'asr-e Pahlavi*, vol. 12, London 1992, p. 237.

misperception stems from the fact that in a traditional patriarchal society religious identity is ascriptive rather than a matter of personal choice (as it is among Baha'is), and, what is more, it is transmitted by the father. Hoveyda was profoundly indifferent to organised religion, but being a non-religious person (or a religious outsider) is not advisable for a politician in a society in which devotion runs deep, and just as Disraeli could not have become prime minister had he not converted to Christianity,[26] Amir Abbas Hoveyda had to act the part of the Twelver Shi'ite muslim that the prime minister had to be under the 1906 constitution. He dutifully went on the pilgrimage to Mecca, and took pains not to help Iran's Baha'is in any way: it was under his watch that the community (which could not claim tax-exempt status for its properties because it was not recognised by the state as a religious community) was struck with confiscatory taxes.[27] Nonetheless, a certain religious marginality remained in both cases, the 'betwixt-and-between' state theorised by Turner.

Hoveyda's paternal Baha'i ancestry was perhaps not unrelated to his cosmopolitanism, for the Baha'i faith preaches world government, a universal language, and the unity of all religions,[28] ideas which possibly informed his upbringing – at least indirectly. A diplomat by profession, Eyn al-Molk translated a number of French and Arabic books into Persian, displaying a curiosity for other cultures and an affinity for languages that he passed on to his son.[29]

If a cosmopolitan is a person 'who is multilingual, multicultural, at home in different milieus and who has wide interests across cultural and national boundaries',[30] Amir Abbas Hoveyda fits the description as few Iranians do. He grew up in cosmopolitan Beirut,[31] where East and West, Islam and Christendom, Arab and Latin culture met, and where the duality of European and Ottoman influence 'insured a certain political and social openness that remained

26 Even in our own time Tony Blair had to await the end of his tenure as prime minister before he felt free to convert to Roman Catholicism.

27 Alamuti, *Iran dar 'asr-e Pahlavi*, vol. 12, pp. 232–236.

28 Warburg, M., *Citizens of the World: A History and Sociology of the Baha'is From a Globalisation Perspective*, Leiden 2006.

29 Hoveyda, A. A., 'Yad az ayyam-e javani', in *Donya*, no. 22, 1966, pp. 336 and 338.

30 See Zubaida, S., 'Cosmopolitanism and the Middle East', in Meijer, R. (ed.), *Cosmopolitanism, Identity and Authenticity in the Middle East*, London 1999, p. 15. See also Zubaida, S., 'Cosmopolitans, Nationalists and Fundamentalists in the Modern Middle East', in his book *Beyond Islam: A New Understanding of the Middle East*, London 2001, pp. 131–155.

31 Hoveyda's younger brother, a diplomat and francophone man of letters, captured the atmosphere in which they grew up in a book. Hoveyda, F., *Les nuits féodales: Tribulations d'un Persan au Moyen-Orient*, Paris 1982.

characteristic of the city in modern times'.[32] Beirut's educational institutions attracted many Iranians, and after graduation many of these individuals rose to positions of prominence not only in Iran,[33] but in the wider Middle East as well.[34] Hoveyda attended the French lycée run by the Mission Laïque, an organisation established as a counterweight to the religious missions that were also dispensing French-language instruction throughout the world. Form an early age, therefore, he was fluent in French, Arabic, and Persian; later in life he learned English as well as some German and Italian. He loved his school, admired its pedagogical methods,[35] and seems to have come away with a particular affinity for France and the French language, the language of Voltaire and the Enlightenment and as such carrier of values that the post-modern European can afford to scoff at but that continue to resonate with free-thinking, cosmopolitan Middle Easterners.[36]

In 1938 he left Beirut for Europe, the land that had 'nourished [his] mind for the twelve years that [he] had spent on the benches of a French school'. But the Europe he found was dying, consumed by rancour, arrogance, and a lack of mutual understanding,[37] a pathology easily decipherable as a cosmopolitan's lament at the rise of nationalism. He enrolled at the Université Libre de Bruxelles, and witnessed the German occupation of Belgium in the spring of 1940. France's acceptance of defeat in late June 1940 affected him deeply:

> France! Land of freedom and sanctuary of refugees! You capitulate? You stop fighting? That evening your misfortunes made me weep together with all my French friends. Because I have always loved you, dear France, and my thoughts have always flown in your direction. You have been brought to your knees, but for me your name will always evoke the most beautiful landscapes and cities… Rousseau! Voltaire! Robespierre! Saint-Just! Hugo! Gambetta!

---

32 Fawaz, L., 'Foreign Presence and Reception of Ottoman Rule in Beirut', in Hanssen, J., Philipp, Th., and Weber, S. (eds.), *The Empire in the City: Arab Provincial Capitals in the Late Ottoman Empire*, Würzburg 2002, p. 93.
33 See Chehabi, H. E., '"The Paris of the Middle East": Iranians in Cosmopolitan Beirut', in Chehabi, H. E., Jafari, P., and Jafroudi, M. (eds.), *Iran in the Middle East: Transnational Encounters and Social History*, London 2015.
34 Vejdani, F., 'The Iranians of AUB and Middle Class Formation in the Early Twentieth-Century Middle East', *British Journal of Middle Eastern Studies*, vol. 43, no. 4, 2016.
35 Hoveyda, 'Yad az ayyam-e javani', p. 332.
36 For the role of French in disseminating Enlightenment values see Fumaroli, M., *When the World Spoke French*, transl. Howard, R., New York 2001.
37 Hoveyda, 'Yad-e ayyam-e tahsil dar Orupa', pp. 336 and 337.

> Weep from within your graves... France! ... As someone who loves you, will never despair of you, for you are steadfast and eternal.[38]

He graduated in 1941 with a *licence* (BA) in political science, having written his thesis on the Romanian author Panait Istrati, a cosmopolitan leftist who wrote in both Romanian and French and whose political activism spanned many countries.[39]

Reading Hoveyda's reminiscences, one senses a curiosity about the world which was not typical for Iranians of his generation.[40] He loved to travel so as to explore new lands, new cultures, new cuisines. He recalls the excitement of the traveller's first encounter with a new city: 'I wonder whether you feel the way I felt when you enter an unknown city about which you have read a lot?' In Paris, he competed with his like-minded friend from his Beirut days, Hamid Rahnama, at guessing the names of streets before they entered them, and recalling the events that had taken place there as well as the historical figures who had played a role in these events.[41] On another occasion, he spent two months wandering the streets by himself, admiring the city's 'ubiquitous poetic beauty'.[42] In these lines Hoveyda reveals himself as a consummate *flâneur*, a 'man of leisure who went into the street in search of some satisfaction of his overdeveloped sensibilities',[43] a social type to whom Baudelaire ascribes a cosmopolitan susceptivity: 'For the perfect *flâneur*, for the passionate spectator, it is an immense joy to... be away from home and yet to feel oneself everywhere at home.'[44] To 'feel everywhere at home' is of course the mark of a cosmopolitan.[45]

About his first visit to Brussels, he writes that 'it is always interesting carefully to study the details of the map of a city one does not know'.[46] His evaluation of

38 Hoveyda, A. A., 'Yaddashtha-ye zaman-e jang', *Donya*, no. 21, 1344/1965, p. 47.
39 On this author see Raydon, É., *Panaït Istrati, vagabond de génie*, Paris 1968; Jutrin-Klener, M., *Panaït Istrati: un chardon déraciné: écrivain français, conteur roumain*, Paris 1970.
40 I owe this insight to the late Reza Sheikholeslami.
41 Hoveyda, 'Yad-e ayyam-e tahsil dar Orupa', pp. 340 and 342.
42 Hoveyda, 'Yaddashtha-ye zaman-e jang', p. 50.
43 Shaya, G., 'The *Flâneur*, the *Badaud*, and the Making of a Mass Public in France, circa 1860–1910', in *The American Historical Review*, vol. 109, no. 1, 2004, p. 47.
44 Baudelaire, 'The Painter of Modern Life', p. 9. For a discussion of Baudelaire's concept see Tester K. (ed.), *The Flâneur*, London 1994, passim.
45 For the relationship between *flânerie* and cosmopolitanism, see van Leeuwen, B., 'If we are *flâneurs*, can we be cosmopolitans?', *Urban Studies*, 2017, available at: <https://doi.org/10.1177/0042098017724120>.
46 Hoveyda, 'Yad-e ayyam-e tahsil dar Orupa', p. 346.

the food he was served in London is worthy of any Frenchman, although he took pains to adapt to England,[47] conforming to the cosmopolitan ethos of doing as the Romans when in Rome. Finally, his depiction of Belgium, a cold and provincial country full of coarse parvenus,[48] echoes Baudelaire's malicious tirades against the Belgians.[49] When he eventually returns to Iran by train in the middle of the war, he is captivated by the beauty of Austria, and wishes he had more money so that he could spend a few months in Linz.[50]

In sum, Hoveyda was a Francophile cosmopolitan who was a prime minister of Iran at a time when America was dominant and cosmopolitanism on the wane throughout the Middle East.[51] These trends added to Hoveyda's marginality in an Iranian society in which increasing numbers of people were pining for 'authenticity'.[52] The Shah appreciated Hoveyda's cosmopolitan Francophilia and occasionally carried out conversations with him in French, but even within the narrow confines of the ruler's camarilla cosmopolitanism had its enemies: Amir Asadollah Alam, the Shah's closest confidant and scion of a long-established feudal family that had ruled over parts of eastern Iran for centuries before Reza Shah's centralising reforms,[53] impugned Hoveyda's patriotism when, in a July 1976 diary entry, he blamed Hoveyda for Tehran's unsatisfactory infrastructure, concluding that 'a cosmopolitan cannot develop the homeland'.[54] Ehsan Naraqi, one of the key non-oppositional intellectual advocates of nativism in late-Pahlavi Iran, put it thus: '[Hoveyda] did not know the people of Iran at all, and I always called him the Beiruti kid [*bacheh Beyruti*].'[55]

---

47 Hoveyda, 'Yad-e ayyam-e tahsil dar Orupa', pp. 342–344.

48 Hoveyda, 'Yad-e ayyam-e tahsil dar Orupa', pp. 345–346.

49 Baudelaire, Ch., *La Belgique déshabillé*. For an analysis of Baudelaire's Belgophobia in light of his dandyism, see Kempf, R., 'Du Belge comme contredandy', in his *Dandies: Baudelaire et Cie* , Paris 1977, pp. 105–118.

50 Hoveyda, 'Yaddashtha-ye zaman-e jang', p. 59.

51 Zubaida, 'Cosmopolitanism and the Middle East', pp. 26–30.

52 Nabavi, N. 'The Discourse of "Authentic Culture" in Iran in the 1960s and 1970s', in Nabavi, N. (ed.), *Intellectual Trends in Twentieth-Century Iran*, Gainesville, FL 2003.

53 See Mojtahed-Zadeh, P., *The Amir of the Borderlands and Eastern Iranian Borders*, London 1995.

54 *'Jahan-vatan keh nemitavanad vatan ra abad konad.'* Alikhani, A. N. (ed.), *Yaddashtha-ye 'Alam*, vol. 6, 1355–1356, Bethesda, MD 2008, p. 179. The study of Iranian politics under the shah is in its infancy, political life in the 1960s and 1970s having consisted mostly of behind-the-scenes manoeuvring of cliques and personalities. See Nasr, V., 'Politics Within the Late-Pahlavi State: The Ministry of Economy and Industrial Policy, 1963–69', *International Journal of Middle East Studies*, vol. 32, no. 1, February 2000, pp. 97–122.

55 Rasulipur, M., 'Sakhtar-e artesh va Savak va nakar amadi-ye rezhim-e Pahlavi az zaban-e Doktor Ehsan-e Naraqi', *Tarikh-e mo'aser-e Iran*, vol. 6, no. 24, 2002, p. 221.

It is congruent with a universalist frame of mind for Hoveyda to have become a freemason, another affiliation that Iran's ascendant nativists held against him. In 1960, he joined the Forughi Lodge, which at that time was presided over by his mentor Abdollah Entezam.[56] While it is safe to assume that Hoveyda's desire to get ahead in life was a major motivation for seeking initiation into the international fraternity, it is not unreasonable to speculate that there may have been other, more principled, motivations as well. Masonic lodges were one of the very few venues in Iran where Iranians and foreigners, Muslims and non-Muslims (except, ironically, Baha'is, who were barred from membership both by their own religious authorities and by the highest instances of Iranian freemasonry) interacted regularly and on an equal, *fraternal*, footing, something that must have appealed to a man so indifferent to primordial loyalties of either the ethnic or religious variety. Moreover, the Forughi lodge was founded under the auspices of French masonry,[57] which, in comparison with Anglo-Saxon masonry, is less permeated with religion if not defiantly secular. Both the Mission Laïque and the Free University of Brussels, institutions that shaped Hoveyda's worldview, are adamantly *laïque*, the latter a stronghold of masonry. Hoveyda was a close friend of the prominent French politician Edgar Faure, the most prominent mason among the Gaullists and a man whose political roots lay in the Parti radical-socialiste, a party that, as the old boutade goes, is neither radical nor socialist, but fiercely anticlerical and attached to *laïcité*. This would seem to indicate that Hoveyda's membership in the order had little to do with subservience to Britain, the power with which common Iranian prejudice associates masons,[58] and more with a commitment to French-style secularism that he could of course not reveal openly as prime minister of a country whose constitution proclaimed Twelver Shi'ism to be the state religion. In fact, the former French president Valéry Giscard d'Estaing writes in his memoirs that at a dinner given by Hoveyda in his honour he felt as though he was in Montparnasse, and that Hoveyda had the bearing of a *Radical*.[59]

Finally, there is a temporal dimension to dandyism's liminality. As a social phenomenon, dandyism blossoms in periods of uncertainty. Baudelaire makes the intriguing observation that:

---

56 Milani, *The Persian Sphinx*, p. 115.

57 *Encyclopaedia Iranica*, s.v. 'Freemasonry III. In the Pahlavi Period', p. 216.

58 Chehabi, H. E., 'The Paranoid Style in Iranian Historiography', in Atabaki, T. (ed.), *Iran in the 20th Century: Historiography and Political Culture*, London 2009.

59 Giscard d'Estaing, V., *Le pouvoir et la vie, tome 1*, Paris 1988, p. 103.

> [d]andyism appears above all in periods of transition, when Democracy is not yet all-powerful, and aristocracy is just beginning to totter and fall. In the disorder of these times, certain men who are socially, politically, and financially ill at ease, but are all rich in native energy, may conceive the idea of establishing a new kind of aristocracy, all the more difficult to shatter as it will be based on the most precious, the most enduring faculties, and on the divine gifts which work and money are unable to bestow. Dandyism is the last spark of heroism amid decadence.[60]

The twelve years of Amir Abbas Hoveyda's premiership were precisely such a period of transition in Iranian history, for it was in the interval between the White and the Islamic revolutions that the social background of Iran's political elite changed.[61] The White revolution of 1963 broke the power of the old landed elite but did not inaugurate mass participation in politics; in fact, far from becoming more liberal, the shah's regime became more despotic as the 1960s advanced. Mass participation, although in a more ochlocratic than democratic mode, came with the revolution of 1978/79. Here, too, the monarchy's last major prime minister fits the dandiacal paradigm: his mannerisms were a 'last spark of heroism amid decadence'.

Let us now turn to the various aspects of Hoveyda's dandiacal persona.

Hoveyda's Dandiacal Habitus

The most immediately recognisable trait of the dandy is his meticulous attention to appearance. According to Thomas Carlyle, 'A Dandy is a Clothes-wearing Man, a Man whose trade, office, and existence consists in the wearing of Clothes. … [S]o that as others dress to live, he lives to dress.'[62] But Carlyle disliked dandyism intensely, and exaggerated its vestimentary aspect. Baudelaire was more nuanced:

> Dandyism does not… consist, as many thoughtless people seem to believe, in an immoderate taste for the toilet and material elegance. For the perfect dandy these things are no more than symbols of his aristocratic superiority of mind.

60 Baudelaire, 'The Painter of Modern Life', p. 28. Of course Baudelaire uses 'democracy' in its Tocquevillian sense of status equality.

61 See *Encyclopaedia Iranica*, s.v. 'Class System VI: Classes in the Pahlavi Period', pp. 678–679, for data on how this was reflected among members of parliament.

62 Carlyle, Th., 'The Dandiacal Body', in *Sartor Resartus: The Life and Opinions of Herr Teufelsdröckh in Three Books*, Berkeley 2000, p. 200.

> Furthermore to his eyes, which are in love with *distinction* above all things, the perfection of his toilet will consist in absolute simplicity.[63]

Hoveyda had dressed with certain panache in his youth, as remembered by his former fellow student and life-long friend, Renée Demont: 'there was a flair even in the way he wore the school's uniform.'[64] As prime minister, he had his suits made by the shah's Italian tailor, but remained discreet about this, lest he offend the sovereign.[65] The seemingly paradoxical taste for both distinction and simplicity that characterises the dandy's sartorial tastes manifested itself in Hoveyda's choice of wearing plain white shirts – but not any old white shirts: every time the prime minister travelled to Europe, he brought back a dozen Lanvin white shirts.[66] This echoes the habits of Brummell, who had made 'shirts and their scrupulous whiteness desiderata of gentlemanly fashion'.[67]

Hoveyda will forever be remembered for his cane, orchid boutonniere, and pipe – in fact, *Towfiq*, Tehran's satirical weekly, called him *sadr-e aʿzam(-e) ʿasaʾi*, the 'walking-stick prime minister'. At least two of these accoutrements have dandiacal associations. For instance, Brummel 'saw beauty and value in walking-sticks and collected them'.[68] The most famous dandy of *fin-de-siècle* France (and inspiration for both Huysman's des Esseintes and Proust's Charlus), the Comte Robert de Montesquiou-Fézensac, was so identified with canes that they figure prominently in his many portraits, most famously in a portrait done by Jean Boldini (and note the white shirt too) (Fig. 1).[69]

Hoveyda is said to have owned 150 walking sticks,[70] but there seems to be no consensus as to whether he needed one to maintain his balance after he sustained injuries in a car accident in 1964 or whether his use of them was an affectation.[71]

63 Baudelaire, 'The Painter of Modern Life', p. 27. Emphasis in the original.
64 Quoted in Milani, *The Persian Sphinx*, p. 61.
65 Milani, *The Persian Sphinx*, p. 22.
66 Milani, *The Persian Sphinx*, p. 68.
67 Kelly, *Beau Brummell*, p. 99.
68 Connely, *The Reign*, p. 56.
69 On the occasion of the unveiling of Boldini's painting, Montesquiou, a poetaster whose esteem for his own symbolist poetry was shared by few of his contemporaries, eulogised his cane in verse: *Robert de Montesquiou considère la canne / Qui lui vient de Louis Quinze et d'Edmond de Goncourt / L'instrument tient du luth et de la sabarcane / L'harmonie y murmure et le sarcasme y court.* For further reading on the background of Montesquiou's love of canes, see Adamy, P., 'La canne de M. de Goncourt ou les stratégies de Montesquiou devant l'immortalité', available at: www.freres-goncourt.fr/montesquiou/montesquiou.htm.
70 Alamuti, *Iran dar ʿasr-e Pahlavi*, vol. 12, p. 126.
71 Milani, *The Persian Sphinx*, p. 23.

Figure 1: Robert de Montesquiou by Giovanni Boldini, Musée d'Orsay, Paris.

The association of dandyism with boutonnières is well established; one recalls Oscar Wilde's often quoted observation: 'A really well-made buttonhole is the only link between Art and Nature.'[72] The flower most used for adorning a man's lapel is the carnation, which Hoveyda did indeed use until he met his future wife, Laila Emami, who had introduced the cultivation of orchids to Iran; henceforth she supplied him with a daily orchid, which was said always to match his tie.[73]

The orchid's appeal to the dandy is obvious. For des Esseintes, orchids were 'flowers of high lineage… delicate and charming and quiveringly sensitive to cold, exotic flowers exiled in Paris to the warmth of glass palaces, princesses of the vegetable kingdom, living a segregated life, having no longer anything in common with the plants of the street or the flora of the middle classes'.[74] A telling antecedent is also provided by the British politician Joseph Chamberlain (1836–1914),

72 Wilde, O., 'Phrases and Philosophies for the Use of the Young', in Ellmann R. (ed.), *The Artist as Critic: Critical Writings of Oscar Wilde*, Chicago 1982, p. 433. In British English 'buttonhole' means both the opening in a jacket's lapel and the flower therein.

73 Milani, *The Persian Sphinx*, pp. 22 and 210.

74 Huysmans, *Against Nature*, p. 72.

Figure 2: Hoveyda with pipe and orchid, Abbas Milani, private collection.

Figure 3: Joseph Chamberlain, National Portrait Gallery, London.

who belonged to a Birmingham industrialist family, attended neither Eton nor Oxbridge, and was a Unitarian rather than a member of the Church of England to boot.[75] His marginality to Britain's ruling class may help to explain his dandiacal propensities: 'Mr. Chamberlain's orchid has been almost as constant companion as his eye-glass. Day after day in the House of Commons, he wears one in his coat – an exquisite speck of colour in a sombre scene.'[76]

Finally, there is the pipe. In Baudelaire's most famous collection of poems, the *Fleurs du Mal*, we find this enigmatic sonnet:[77]

I am a writer's pipe; you see
In looking at my dusky face,
Complexion of the Kaffir race,

75 He never became prime minister, but his son, Neville, headed the British government from 1937 to 1940.

76 Mackintosh, A., *Joseph Chamberlain: An Honest Biography*, London 1906, p. 384. For his religious affiliation, see pp. 385–386.

77 I thank my dear friend Manoutchehr Eskandari-Qajar for drawing my attention to this poem.

My master makes good use of me.
When he is full of grief and gloom
I smoke as if I were a shack
With supper stewing in the back
To feed the ploughman coming home
I cradle and enwrap his soul
Within the blue and moving net
That from my fiery mouth uncoils
And is a healing balm that rolls
To charm his weary heart, and let
His spirit rest from heavy toils.[78]

This poem may have appealed to Hoveyda in a way we will never know, but then, analogous to that other nicotian object of bewilderment, i.e., Freud's notorious cigar, one cannot *a priori* dismiss the possibility that Hoveyda's pipe was just that: a pipe.

Hoveyda's obsessive care for personal hygiene – he is said to have devoted two hours to it in the morning[79] – was also in the best tradition of dandyism: let us not forget that Brummell astonished Europeans by bathing every day and 'every part of his body'.[80] Even in his later exile in Caen, when he lived in increasingly reduced circumstances, he devoted two hours every day to washing himself, enough to lead one observer to surmise that he would gain a 'reputation for sanctity in a Mahomedan country'.[81] Hoveyda's 'Mahomedan' tormentors had different notions of sanctity, however, and left him to wallow in filth as he awaited his trial, so much so that when he appeared before his 'judges', he felt compelled to apologise for the way he was dressed, adding 'what I wear is all I have'.[82] In the

78 *Je suis la pipe d'un auteur; / On voit, à contempler ma mine / D'Abyssinienne ou de Cafrine / Que mon maître est un grand fumeur / Quand il est comblé de douleur, / Je fume comme la chaumine / Où se prépare la cuisine / Pour un retour du laboureur. / J'enlace et je berce son âme / Dans le réseau mobile et bleu / Qui monte de ma bouche en feu, / Et je roule un puissant dictame / Qui charme son cœur et guérit / De ses fatigues son esprit.* Baudelaire, Ch., *The Flowers of Evil*, transl. McGowan, J., Oxford 1993, pp. 136–139. For a discussion of this poem see Burt, E.S., 'Materiality and Autobiography in Baudelaire's "La Pipe"', *MLN*, no. 116, 2001.
79 Milani, *The Persian Sphinx*, p. 209. But note that *do sa'at* (two hours) can also connote an excessive amount of time in colloquial Persian.
80 Kelly, *Beau Brummell*, p. 95.
81 Connely, *The Reign*, p. 210. Regarding the Western perception of exemplary Muslim cleanliness see Conner, P., 'On the Bath: Western Experience of the Hammam', *Renaissance and Modern Studies*, vol. 31, no. 1, 1987.
82 Milani, *The Persian Sphinx*, p. 312.

end he was even disparaged for taking off his clothes before going to sleep in his bed.[83]

The title of a French book on dandyism, *Masculin singulier*, points to the third key feature of dandyism: whatever his sexual orientation, the dandy is not a family man.[84] Brummell, Barbey tells us, 'was not what the world calls a libertine', for 'to love… is always to depend' and the dandy values few things more than his independence. Thus 'the king of fashion had no mistress'.[85] In his youth, Hoveyda boasted, he had never fallen in love,[86] which dovetails with Baudelaire's observation that 'the dandy does not… regard love as a special target to be aimed at'.[87] Hoveyda did not mind solitude – in fact he cherished it: 'I like to be withdrawn, to be alone in my little house with my books and a few records that I like.'[88] Baudelaire would have sympathised: '[t]he true hero has fun all by himself.'[89] But as Sherlock Holmes discovered in 'A Scandal in Bohemia', even a confirmed bachelor can fall for a woman once in his life, and so it was with Hoveyda and his beloved Laila Emami, who seems to have come to appreciate his love fully only after he was gone.[90]

A fourth aspect of dandyism is 'the joy of astonishing others, and the proud satisfaction of never oneself being astonished'.[91] The dandy constantly produces the 'unexpected, that which could not logically be anticipated by those accustomed to the yoke of rules'.[92] Hoveyda's 'controlled eccentricity' shows him to have been a conformist rebel who enjoyed startling others by doing the unexpected, like driving to work himself in an Iranian-made Peykan car while occasionally picking up passengers on the way, or joking 'in the vulgar tongue of the street', and dancing 'suggestively at parties'.[93] What could have astonished his intellectual circle of friends more than his becoming a pillar of the Shah's regime?

83 Khalkhali, S., *Khaterat-e Ayat Allah Khalkhali: az ayyam-e talabagi ta dowran-e hakem-e shar'-e dadgahha-ye enqelab-e eslami*, Tehran 1379/2000, p. 393.
84 See footnote 19.
85 Barbey d'Aurevilly, *Dandyism*, pp. 47–48. This does not mean that Brummell was celibate – in fact he died of syphilis. Kelly, *Beau Brummell*, pp. 306–312.
86 Hoveyda, 'Yaddashtha-ye zaman-e jang', p. 34.
87 Baudelaire, 'The Painter of Modern Life', p. 27.
88 Hoveyda, 'Yad az ayyam-e javani', p. 331.
89 *Mon cœur mis à nu*, p. 16. My own translation.
90 Milani, *The Persian Sphinx*, p. 219. They were married in 1966 and divorced in 1971, but remained close friends.
91 Baudelaire, 'The Painter of Modern Life', p. 28. For an elaboration, see Carassus, E., *Le Mythe du dandy*, Paris 1971, chapter 13, 'Impassibilité', pp. 135–144.
92 Barbey d'Aurevilly, *Dandyism*, p. 33.
93 Milani, *The Persian Sphinx*, pp. 214–215.

Conclusion

The dandy is disrespectful but obedient, but ultimately Hoveyda was only obedient – unless one were to take his obsequious fawning before the shah *au second degré*, for which assumption there is no evidence. In Hoveyda one finds none of the insolence, none of the ironical distance from those who hold power that characterise the true dandy. Instead one sees an abject sycophancy vis-à-vis the shah that is incompatible with the dandy's ethos which is characterised above all by proud independence. At the end of the day, Hoveyda was more, to indulge in an Anglo-Arabic neologism, *mutadandi* than dandy. But then, is it not also the case that 'in matters of grave importance, style, not sincerity, is the vital thing'?[94]

As the unquestioning servant of a despot, Hoveyda made too many compromises to elicit our admiration as a politician or as an intellectual. But whatever his multifarious shortcomings, he was, both intellectually and morally, head and shoulders above the *canaille* who presumed to sit in judgment over him after his fall. In the end, as he refrained from fleeing the country while he could, and instead tried to gather materials for a rational defence of his record in office, he proved one last time how little he understood Iranians, for he simply could not conceive of the depths of utter baseness to which the likes of Sadeq Khalkhali, his henchmen, and his mentors, would sink.[95]

Hoveyda's French friends remembered his love of their country and mobilised to save him. Edgar Faure offered to be his defence council, and when he went on trial, six former French prime ministers signed a telegram to the authorities requesting that Hoveyda be judged in 'conformity with humanitarian principles of equity and justice that are common to us and to Islam'.[96] President Valéry Giscard d'Estaing sent a personal note to Ayatollah Khomeini asking that his life be spared.[97] Their solicitude was probably taken as further proof that Hoveyda was not a true patriot, for in his memoirs Khalkhali concocts an absurd story to the effect that Iran's then foreign minister Ebrahim Yazdi connived with 'Jews,

94 Wilde, O., *The Importance of Being Earnest*, New York 1965, p. 92.

95 The sheer vulgarity of Khalkhali is well captured in Naipaul, V.S., 'Iran: The Twin Revolutions', in *Among the Believers: An Islamic Journey*, New York 1981, pp. 55–56.

96 Kémoularia, C. de, *Une vie à tire-d'aile: mémoires*, Paris 2007, pp. 193–194. In September 1978, the author, a high official of the French state, urged Hoveyda to leave Iran and offered to host him in his country house, but Hoveyda refused, arguing that he had worked with a team and did not want to abandon it to save his skin (p. 192).

97 Giscard d'Estaing, V., *Le pouvoir et la vie, tome 3, Choisir*, Paris 2006, p. 202. Giscard d'Estaing believes that in response Khomeini sent a hand-written note to the Iranian prime minister asking him to see to it that Hoveyda's life be spared, but that the head of the tribunal received news of the ayatollah's decision too late.

Baha'is, Freemasons, the Israelis, and the French' to fly Hoveyda's corpse to France, whence it was taken to Israel, where at the order of Prime Minister Menachem Begin it was buried with full military honours in the Jewish cemetery of Hebron.[98]

Remembering the cruel treatment of Hoveyda by his tormentors in the early days of the Islamic Republic can serve as an antidote to the sentimental populism that still infuses much scholarly writing on the Islamic revolution, which all too often extols 'the people' and attributes the calamities that have befallen metropolitan Iranians as a result of the revolution to later deviations from the freedom-loving path initially chosen by the 'masses'. In fact, Hoveyda's fate shows that *ressentiment*, philistinism, and xenophobia, values and attitudes diametrically opposed to the cultured cosmopolitanism he embodied, are consubstantial with the Islamic Republic. As Sami Zubaida has pointed out, 'cosmopolitanism is abhorred by nationalists, fascists, and Stalinists.'[99] To this cheery list one can safely add most Iranian Islamists.

Bibliography

Adamy, P., 'La canne de M. de Goncourt ou les stratégies de Montesquiou devant l'immortalité', available at: <www.freres-goncourt.fr/montesquiou/montesquiou.htm>.

Alamuti, M., *Iran dar 'asr-e Pahlavi*, vol. 12, London 1992.

Alikhani, A. N. (ed.), *Yaddashtha-ye 'Alam*, vol. 6, 1355–1356, Bethesda, MD 2008.

Ashraf, A., 'From the White Revolution to the Islamic Revolution', in Rahnema, S., and Behdad, S. (eds.), *Iran after the Revolution: Crisis of an Islamic State*, London 1995, pp. 21–44.

Azimi, F., *The Quest for Democracy in Iran: A Century of Struggle against Authoritarian Rule*, Cambridge, MA 2008.

Barbey d'Aurevilly, J. A., *Dandyism*, transl. Ainslie, D., New York 1988.

Barjesteh van Waalwijk van Doorn, L.A.F., 'Genealogy of the Qajar Qovanlou Family; a First Draft', in *Qajar Studies*, no. 11–12, 2011, pp. 197–259.

98 Khalkhali, *Khaterat*, pp. 387–388. Jews, Baha'is, and Freemasons are of course the usual suspects of Iranians' conspiratorial imaginary. See Chehabi, 'The Paranoid Style in Iranian Historiography', passim.

99 Zubaida, 'Cosmopolitanism and the Middle East', p. 26.

Baudelaire, Ch., *The Painter of Modern Life and Other Essays*, transl. and ed. Mayne, J., New York 1986.

Baudelaire, Ch., *The Flowers of Evil*, transl. McGowan, J., Oxford 1993.

Boulenger, J., *Sous Louis-Philippe: Les dandys*, Paris 1932.

Burt, E.S., 'Materiality and Autobiography in Baudelaire's "La Pipe"', *MLN*, no. 116, 2001, pp. 941–963.

Carassus, E., *Le Mythe du dandy*, Paris 1971.

Carlyle, Th., *Sartor Resartus: The Life and Opinions of Herr Teufelsdröckh in Three Books*, Berkeley 2000.

Chehabi, H. E., 'The Imam as Dandy: The Case of Musa Sadr', *Harvard Middle Eastern and Islamic Review*, vol. 3, no. 1–2, 1996, pp. 20–41.

Chehabi, H. E., 'The Paranoid Style in Iranian Historiography', in Atabaki, T. (ed.), *Iran in the 20th Century: Historiography and Political Culture*, London 2009, pp. 162–164.

Chehabi, H. E., '"The Paris of the Middle East": Iranians in Cosmopolitan Beirut', in Chehabi, H.E., Jafari, P., and Jafroudi, M. (eds.), *Iran in the Middle East: Transnational Encounters and Social History*, London 2015, pp. 120–134.

Chervet B., 'Dandysme et confection de fétiche ou comment habiller un vide', in *Revue Française de Psychanalyse*, vol. 58, no. 22, 1994, pp. 401–414.

Coblence, F., 'Disraëli: du style dandy en politique', in *Critique*, no. 405–406, 1981, pp. 276–299.

Connely, W., *Count d'Orsay: The Dandy of Dandies*, London 1952.

Connely, W., *The Reign of Beau Brummel*, New York 1940.

Conner, P., 'On the Bath: Western Experience of the Hammam', *Renaissance and Modern Studies* vol. 31, no. 1, 1987, pp. 34–42.

Delbourg-Delphis, M., *Masculin Singulier*, Paris 1985.

Ellmann R. (ed.), *The Artist as Critic: Critical Writings of Oscar Wilde*, Chicago 1982.

Fawaz, L., 'Foreign Presence and Reception of Ottoman Rule in Beirut', in Hanssen, J., Philipp, Th., and Weber, S. (eds.), *The Empire in the City: Arab Provincial Capitals in the Late Ottoman Empire*, Würzburg 2002, pp. 93–104.

Feldman, J.R., *Gender on the Divide: the Dandy in Modernist Literature*, Ithaca, NY 1993.

Fumaroli, M., *When the World Spoke French*, transl. Howard, R., New York 2001.

Ghazi, M.F., 'Un groupe social: "Les raffinés" (zurafa)', in *Studia Islamica*, no. 11, 1959, pp. 39–71.

Giscard d'Estaing, V., *Le pouvoir et la vie, tome 1*, Paris 1988.

Giscard d'Estaing, V., *Le pouvoir et la vie, tome 3*, *Choisir*, Paris 2006.

Gnüg, H., *Kult der Kälte: Der klassische Dandy im Spiegel der Weltliteratur*, Stuttgart 1988.

Hoveyda, A. A., 'Yaddashtha-ye zaman-e jang', *Donya*, no. 21, 1344/1965, pp. 31–36.

Hoveyda, A. A., 'Yad az ayyam-e javani', in *Donya*, no. 22, 1345/1966, pp. 328–338

Hoveyda, A. A., 'Yad-e ayyam-e tahsil dar Orupa', in *Donya*, no. 23, 1346/1967, 336–346.

Hoveyda, F., *Les nuits féodales: Tribulations d'un Persan au Moyen-Orient*, Paris 1982.

Huysmans, J. K., *Against Nature (A Rebours)*, transl. Mauldon, M., Oxford 1998.

Jutrin-Klener, M., *Panaït Istrati: un chardon déraciné: écrivain français, conteur roumain*, Paris 1970.

Kelly, I., *Beau Brummell: The Ultimate Man of Style*, New York 2006.

Kémoularia, C. de, *Une vie à tire-d'aile: mémoires*, Paris 2007.

Kempf, R., *Dandies: Baudelaire et Cie*, Paris 1977.

Khalkhali, S., *Khaterat-e Ayat Allah Khalkhali: az ayyam-e talabagi ta dowran-e hakem-e shar'-e dadgahha-ye enqelab-e eslami*, Tehran 1379/2000.

Leeuwen, B., 'If we are *flâneurs*, can we be cosmopolitans?', *Urban Studies*, 2017), available at: <https://doi.org/10.1177/0042098017724120>.

Lemaire, M., *Le dandysme de Baudelaire à Mallarmé*, Montreal 1978.

Mackintosh, A., *Joseph Chamberlain: An Honest Biography*, London 1906.

Merchant, H., *The Man Who Would Be Queen: Autobiographical Fictions*, New Delhi 2011.

Mestyan, A. and Volait, M., 'Affairisme dynastique et danydisme au Caire vers 1900: Le Club des Princes et la formation d'un quartier du divertissement rue 'Imad al-Din', in *Annales islamologiques*, no. 50, 2016, pp. 55–106.

Milani, A., *The Persian Sphinx: Amir Abbas Hoveyda and the Riddle of the Iranian Revolution*, Washington, DC 2000.

Moers, E., *The Dandy: Brummell to Beerbohm*, Lincoln, NE 1978.

Mojtahed-Zadeh, P., *The Amir of the Borderlands and Eastern Iranian Borders*, London 1995.

Mo'tazed, Kh., *Hoveyda: Siyasatmadar-e pip, 'asa, gol-e orkideh*, Tehran 1378/1999.

Nabavi, N. 'The Discourse of "Authentic Culture" in Iran in the 1960s and 1970s', in Nabavi, N. (ed.), *Intellectual Trends in Twentieth-Century Iran*, Gainesville, FL 2003.

Naipaul, V.S., 'Iran: The Twin Revolutions', in *Among the Believers: An Islamic Journey*, New York 1981.

Nasr, V., 'Politics Within the Late-Pahlavi State: The Ministry of Economy and Industrial Policy, 1963-69', in *International Journal of Middle East Studies*, volume 32, no. 1, February 2000, pp. 97–22.

Peng, H., *Dandyism and Transcultural Modernity: The Dandy, the Flâneur, and the Translator in 1930s Shanghai, Tokyo, and Paris*, London 2010.

Rasulipur, M., 'Sakhtar-e artesh va Savak va nakar amadi-ye rezhim-e Pahlavi az zaban-e Doktor Ehsan-e Naraqi', *Tarikh-e mo'aser-e Iran*, vol. 6, no. 24, 2002, pp. 195–244.

Raydon, É., *Panaït Istrati, vagabond de génie*, Paris 1968.

Schoolfield, G. C., *A Baedeker of Decadence: Charting a Literary Fashion, 1884–1927*, New Haven 2003.

Shaya, G., 'The *Flâneur*, the *Badaud*, and the Making of a Mass Public in France, circa 1860–1910', in *The American Historical Review*, vol. 109, no. 1, 2004, pp. 41–77.

Tester K. (ed.), *The Flâneur*, London 1994.

Turner, V., *The Ritual Process: Structure and Anti-Structure*, Ithaca, NY 1977.

Vejdani, F., 'The Iranians of AUB and Middle Class Formation in the Early Twentieth-Century Middle East', in *British Journal of Middle Eastern Studies*, vol. 43, no. 4, 2016, pp. 486–506.

Warburg, M., *Citizens of the World: A History and Sociology of the Baha'is From a Globalisation Perspective*, Leiden 2006.

Wilde, O., *The Importance of Being Earnest*, New York 1965.

Zubaida, S., 'Cosmopolitanism and the Middle East', in Meijer, R. (ed.), *Cosmopolitanism, Identity and Authenticity in the Middle East*, London 1999, pp. 15–33.

Zubaida, S., 'Cosmopolitans, Nationalists and Fundamentalists in the Modern Middle East', in *Beyond Islam: A New Understanding of the Middle East*, London 2001, pp. 131–155.

5

The Shiraz Festival and its Place in Iran's Revolutionary Mythology[1]

H. E. Chehabi

The Shiraz-Persepolis Festival of Art, Jashn-e Honar-e Shiraz – Takht-e Jamshid, was an international performing arts festival held every summer between 1967 and 1977 in the southern Iranian city of Shiraz and at other sites in the city's vicinity. Its organisers intended it to be an occasion for Iranian artists to expand their horizons and for non-Iranian visitors to get acquainted with the cultural heritage of Iran. For those in the Iranian leadership who did not share the organisers' artistic and aesthetic sensibilities or were indifferent to cultural endeavours, the festival was still a welcome opportunity for Iran to claim its place among the world's nations.

For radical leftist opponents of the shah, however, the event symbolised the regime's warped sense of priorities and contempt for common people, while Islamists perceived it to be a token of the regime's endemic disdain for Islam and its subservience to the West. Even a few traditional royalists believe that the festival's avant-garde programmes were partly responsible for many Iranians' alienation from the regime, contributing to its final overthrow. The common denominator of these criticisms is that the festival was a culturally inappropriate extravaganza that benefited only a small coterie of rich cronies of the Pahlavis. Its purported cultural inappropriateness is at times illustrated with nuggets of information that

1 I owe very special thanks to Dariush Shayegan and Farideh Zandieh, who hosted me in Shiraz in the summer of 1970 for two unforgettable weeks at the festival. Subsequently, I attended the festival in 1971 and 1973.

are simply untrue.[2] This chapter aims at providing a dispassionate analysis of the Shiraz Festival so as to explain how it came to occupy such a prominent place in the imaginary of Iranians.

Origin and Organisation of the Festival

One common misperception of the festival is that its origin had something to do with the shah. Iran's ruler does not seem to have cared much for art, reflecting, perhaps, his upbringing in an austere military household. In fact, the festival originated in the circle around the shah's consort, Shahbanu (Empress) Farah, who is a genuine art-lover and studied architecture for two years in Paris before marrying the shah.[3]

For most of Mohammad Reza Shah's rule (1941–1979), the cultural activities of the state were the bailiwick of Mehrdad Pahlbod, *né* Ezzatollah Minbashian, who was married to one of the shah's sisters, Princess Shams Pahlavi.[4] In 1951, he became head of the fine arts administration (Edareh-ye Koll-e Honarha-ye Ziba) within the ministry of education, and when the arts were separated from education to create a ministry of culture and arts (Vezarat-e Farhang va Honar), he became its incumbent and held the portfolio until 1978. With the founding of National Iranian Radio and Television (NIRT) in 1966,[5] a new impetus was given to the nation's cultural life. Its director, Reza Qotbi, gathered creative spirits around him, including people who had earlier taken critical or even oppositional stances. As a result, NIRT developed a dynamism that contrasted favourably with the more staid ministry of culture. Qotbi is a cousin of Empress Farah, and, as she wrote in her first autobiography, 'ever since her marriage, my mother ha[d] lived in the same house as her brother, who had an only son, and we were brought up together

---

2 The former Queen of Jordan, for instance, writes in her memoirs that 'a French theater company staged the musical *Hair*, which had shocked Western audiences at the time because of its nudity'. Queen Noor, *Leap of Faith: Memoirs of an Unexpected Life*, New York 2003, p. 40. This musical was never performed at Shiraz.

3 Farah, Shahbanou of Iran, *My Thousand and One Days: an Autobiography*, transl. Harcourt, F., London 1978, pp. 16–35.

4 Pahlbod was the scion of a family long prominent in Iranian official culture; his grandfather, Salar Moazzaz, was director of the first Iranian conservatory. See Mir Ali Naqi, S. A. R., 'Musiqi-ye irani va asnad-e tarikhi-ye mo'aser 2: Asnad-e madreseh-ye muzik: 1301–1303', in *Ganjineh-ye asnad*, no. 2, 1992. Pahlbod's brother, General Fathollah Minbashian, was the shah's *aide-de-camp* and was for four years commander of the Iranian army.

5 The state radio broadcasting service, Radio Iran, went on the air in 1940, while a private TV channel operated in Tehran and Abadan between 1958 and 1966.

rather like brother and sister.'[6] Iran's state-sponsored official cultural life thus became a field of activity in which the distaff and the sword sides of the imperial family acted side-by-side, with the former more interested in conventional art forms and the latter interested in recent developments and Iran's neglected folk traditions in addition to conventional art forms.[7] In Qotbi's version of the story, one day, as he was visiting Farah, she told him:

> For some there is the possibility to go to Europe and attend art festivals and get acquainted with the latest artistic developments in the world. But not everybody has this possibility, and we must make it possible for everybody to get acquainted with world artistic developments by holding a festival ourselves. Moreover, Iranian art should not only be admired by a few orientalists; our culture and art must be known by Iran's young generation and the people of the entire world.[8]

In 1966, soon after the founding of NIRT, Qotbi asked Farrokh Ghaffari, a film-maker who had a history of run-ins with state censorship,[9] to be his deputy for cultural affairs, and Ghaffari accepted. When the decision to have a festival was taken, it was decided that it should not be held in Tehran so as to contribute to the development of cultural life in the provinces. Three cities were considered: Kashan, Isfahan, and Shiraz. The first had the advantage of being close to Tehran, but it lacked infrastructure for productions and festival goers. Isfahan could hardly cope with the many tourists that visited it in the summer, so the choice fell on Shiraz.[10] According to the official version, Shiraz and Persepolis were chosen because they were located in Fars, a province whose buildings had been for 2,500 years a living museum of Iranian architecture through which the eternal spirit of the nation was revealed, and because the excellence of its school of painting, its poets, and the existence of a school of dancing in the past. All of these factors,

6 Farah, *My Thousand and One Days*, p. 11.
7 In fact, the ministry of culture organised its own annual Festival of Culture and Art (Jashn-e Farhang va Honar) from 1347/1968 to 1356/1977, which, unlike the Shiraz Festival, had a domestic agenda of (re)acquainting Iranians with their nation's cultural heritage. See Sattari, J., *Dar bidowlati-ye farhang: Negahi beh barkhi fa'aliyatha-ye farhangi va honari dar bazpasin salha-ye nezam-e pishin*, Tehran 1379/2000, pp. 178–179, 201–218.
8 'Gozareshi az nakhostin jashn-e honar-e Shiraz Takht-e Jamshid', in Gorgin, I. (ed.), *Sevvomin jashn-e honar*, Tehran n.d., [p. 6] (This volume is not paginated).
9 His feature film on the poor south of Tehran, *Jonub-e Shahr*, had fallen victim to state censorship in 1958. See Jahanbegloo, R., *Iran va moderniteh*, Tehran 1379/2000, p. 171.
10 Ghaffari, personal telephone interview, 16 August 2004.

it was averred, made Shiraz and Persepolis with their good weather, transparent skies, pure wine, and hospitable people the most appropriate place for holding the festival.[11] The theme of the festival was to be the meeting of East and West, something like the long-established and very successful Baalbeck International Festival in Lebanon,[12] which was founded in 1955 but was suspended on account of the civil war in 1975.

The first meeting of the Shiraz Festival commission took place on 14 Esfand 1345 (5 March 1967) in the presence of Farah. To administer the festival, an Organisation of the Shiraz Art Festival (Sazeman-e Jashn-e Honar-e Shiraz) was established under the direction of the empress herself. A board of trustees comprising 31 members was formed. The composition of this body, which included more high state officials (many of them representing institutions that contributed financially to the festival) than cultural figures, remained almost unchanged until the end.[13] This board met once a year, but on the whole did not play much of a role in shaping the festival.[14] The board of trustees chose a board of directors, whose president was Mehdi Bushehri, the husband of the shah's twin sister, Princess Ashraf Pahlavi, while Reza Qotbi became the general director:[15] the sword and distaff sides were balanced, with more influence for the latter. Bushehri was director of the Maison de l'Iran on the Champs Elysées in Paris, and helped the festival by establishing and maintaining cordial contacts

11 'Gozareshi az nakhostin jashn-e honar', [pp. 6 and 8].

12 Tohme, A., 'Le Festival de Baalbek au cerrefour des paradoxes libanais d'avant guerre', in Sader H., Scheffler, Th., and Neuwirth A. (eds.), *Baalbek: Image and Monument 1898–1998*, Stuttgart 1998.

13 Khorramzadeh Esfahani, S., *Te'atr-e Iran dar gozar-e zaman 3: Kargah-e namayesh az aghaz ta payan* (1348–1357), Tehran 1387/2008, pp. 104–105. State officials included the prime minister, the minister of the imperial court, the minister of foreign affairs, the minister of culture, the minister of information, the minister of the economy, the head of the National Iranian Oil Company, the director of the plan organisation, the head of SAVAK, the governor-general of Fars, the director of the national tourist organisation, the commander of the Third Army. Cultural figures included the soprano Monir Vakili, the American orientalist Arthur Upham Pope, Fereydun Hoveyda (brother of the prime minister, respected film scholar, and longtime Iranian ambassador to the United Nations), Khojasteh Kia (theatre scholar), Farrokh Ghaffari, Bijan Saffari, the chancellor of Pahlavi University (Shiraz's anglophone university), and the director of the Pahlavi Library. Members of the imperial family included Prince Shahram Pahlavi-Nia (Princess Ashraf's eldest son), and Mehdi Bushehri (Princess Ashraf's husband) in addition to Mehrdad Pahlbod, whose brother, General Minbashian, was also a member.

14 Ghaffari, telephone interview.

15 *Jashn-e honar-e Shiraz beh revayat-e asnad-e savak*, Tehran: Markaz-e barrasi-ye asnad-e tarikhi-ye vezarat-e ettela'at, 1381/2002, pp. 4–15.

with European artists and critics.[16] There were three committees, one each for music, theatre, and film.

Programming

The second half of the 1960s saw the birth of numerous international festivals around the globe, but most of these were located in Europe and North America.[17] The Shiraz Festival was thus a means to put Iran on the map, yet another step in the perennial quest to make Iran, a country that had never been formally colonised, a genuine equal among equals on an international scene dominated by Western countries. The aim was to attract foreign artists and art critics to Iran so that they could engage in cultural exchange with Iranians. However, from the outset, the programmes of the festival were characterised by a certain asymmetry: while most (but not all) Western programmes represented the latest trends and belonged to the avant-garde, non-Western arts were mostly (but not exclusively) traditional. The organisers were aware of this asymmetry and justified it (postmodernism not having been invented yet) by Third World artists' hitherto insufficient opportunities for developing modern art forms.[18] The organisers consciously aimed at something different from the Baalbeck festival, which, in their view, was conventional and averse to risks in its Western productions and informed by eighteenth- and nineteenth-century views of the Orient in its choice of non-Western programmes.[19]

The programmes of the Shiraz Festival can be fit into four categories: theatre, music, traditional performance arts, and film.[20] Iranian plays were selected by a committee; when the Iranian director Arby Ovanessian joined the committee in 1968, he soon became the most influential member.[21] The international programming, arguably the most controversial component of the festival, owed a lot to the Festival Mondial du Théâtre Universitaire, founded in 1963 in Nancy by Jack

16 Ghaffari, telephone interview.

17 See Wallon, E., 'Le festival international: Un système relationnel', in Dulphy, A., Frank, R., Matard-Bonucci, M. A., and Ory, P. (eds.), *Les relations culturelles internationales au XXe siècle: De la diplomatie culturelle à l'acculturation*, Brussels 2010, pp. 310–312.

18 Sattari, *Dar bidowlati-ye farhang*, p. 190, quoting Ghaffari.

19 Ghaffari, telephone interview.

20 For a full list of programmes see Afshar Ghotbi, Sh. in collaboration with Ovanessian, A., 'Shiraz-Persepolis Festival of Arts (1967–1977): Detailed Catalogue of Events', available at: <https://www.academia.edu/35600387/SHIRAZ_ARTS_FESTIVAL_-_Detailed_Catalogue_of_Events>.

21 Khorramzadeh Esfahani, *Te'atr-e Iran*, p. 123.

Lang. This event was known among theatre lovers for its atmosphere: spontaneity, invention, youthful exuberance.[22] It made theatre history by purposefully introducing East European plays and directors (notably Jerzy Grotowski) as well as avant-garde American companies (such as Bread and Puppet) to West European audiences. Many of the leading organisers of the Shiraz Festival being francophone, they drew inspiration from it. In the following sections, a brief account of all eleven editions of the festival will be given, so as to illustrate the breadth of the programming and engage with the oft-repeated allegation that it was culturally inappropriate.

The first festival opened with a concert by the recently formed Chamber Orchestra of the National Iranian Radio and Television, which performed works by Pergolesi, Geminiani, Marcello, Bach, and the Iranian composer Morteza Hannaneh.[23] At another concert, this orchestra, which had been created as a counterpart to the ministry of culture's Tehran Symphony Orchestra, accompanied the violinist Yehudi Menuhin. Classical Persian music was performed on four nights at Hafeziyeh (the mausoleum of the poet Hafiz), whose grounds had been decorated with hundreds of candles by the architect Keyvan Khosravani[24] (All subsequent festivals featured this arrangement at Hafeziyeh). Where the festival was daring was in its revival of *ta'zieh*, the traditional Iranian passion play.[25] This popular art form had been outlawed under Reza Shah, and while under his son the ban was not strictly enforced, performances were confined to inconspicuous provincial settings, so much so that many feared for its survival as an art form.[26] Ghaffari, the film maker Bahram Beyzai, the theatre director Parviz Sayyad, and the theatre scholar Khojasteh Kia all called for the staging of *ta'zieh*,[27] a call that was supported by the influential scholar of Islam, Seyyed Hossein Nasr. It seems that Savak, the Iranian secret service, opposed the revival of passion plays, arguing

22 Looseley, D., 'The World Theatre Festival, Nancy, 1963–1988: a Critique and Retrospective', in *New Theatre Quarterly*, vol. 6, no. 22, 1999, p. 142.
23 On the latter, see Zahedi, T., *Beh rahbari-ye Morteza Hannaneh*, Tehran 1369/1990.
24 Keyvan Khosravani, personal interview, 5 July 2004, Paris. Khosravani also designed some of the empress's state robes, using traditional handicraft materials.
25 The literature on *ta'zieh* is vast. For a useful collection of articles see Chelkowski, P.J. (ed.), *Ta'zieh: Ritual and Drama in Iran*, New York 1979. See also Floor, W., *The History of Theater in Iran*, Washington 2005, pp. 124–212.
26 While *ta'zieh* obviously has a religious foundation, the clergy have always viewed it with ambivalence, which makes its inclusion in the festival less incongruous than it might seem. For instance, in the passion plays women's parts are played by men, which goes against the *shari'a*'s prohibition of cross-dressing.
27 Ghaffari, telephone conversation.

that they had been outlawed by Reza Shah and that repealing this ban would fan religious fervour.[28] Subsequently *ta'zieh* plays were staged almost every year at the festival,[29] in the later years at the Hosseyniyeh-ye Moshir, a major Qajar-era building dedicated to the cult of Imam Hosseyn.[30] The first festival also included the first attempt to stage *naqqāli*, the traditional story-telling art of Iran,[31] in a non-traditional setting.

The second festival in 1968 was overshadowed by an earthquake in Khorasan, as a result of which the festival began one day later than planned and no official opening ceremonies were held. Later, the NIRT Chamber Orchestra performed Paul Hindemith's *Trauermusik* in memory of the victims. Although classical music was given its due with a recital by the pianist Arthur Rubinstein, Western avant-garde music was also heard for the first time at this festival. *Nuits*, a piece for twelve mixed voices by the Romanian-born Greco-French composer Iannis Xenakis (1922–2001) that had been premièred at the Royan Festival in France a few weeks earlier, was performed, but the composer dedicated it to 'those who struggle for human freedom',[32] a reference to the opponents of the shah's regime meant, probably, to assuage Xenakis's critics in Europe. The Western press, which had started taking notice of the festival, mentioned above all Persian classical music, with which very few people in the West were familiar at the time.

The second festival is chiefly remembered today for two ground-breaking productions of innovative Iranian plays. Abbas Na'lbandian was a newspaper vendor who had written a surreal play called *Pazhuheshi Zharf va Setorg va Now dar Sangvarehha-ye Dowreh-ye Bist o Panjom-e Zaminshenasi ya Chehardahom Bistom, Farqi Nemikonad* (*A Deep, Big and New Research Concerning Fossils of the 25th Geologic period, or 14th, 20th, There is No Difference*) that he had no hope of seeing performed until it caught the eye of the director Arby Ovanessian, who successfully staged it.[33] The other was Bijan Mofid's *Shahr-e Qesseh* (*The*

28 Vali Nasr, personal communication, 10 August 2004.

29 Beeman, W. O., 'A Full Arena: The Development and Meaning of Popular Performance Traditions in Iran', in Bonine, M. E. and Keddie, N. R. (eds.), *Modern Iran: The Dialectics of Continuity and Change*, Albany, NY 1981, p. 366.

30 The Shiraz Festival organisation published a small guide to its artistic treasures. Homayuni, S., *Hoseyniyeh-ye Moshir*, Tehran 2535[1355]/1976.

31 On *naqqāli*, see Page, M. E., 'Professional Storytelling in Iran: Transmission and Practice', in *Iranian Studies*, vol. 12, no. 3–4, 1979, pp. 195–215; and Floor, *History*, pp. 85–106.

32 *Panjomin jashn-e honar-e Shiraz Takht-e Jamshid*, Tehran [1972]. This catalogue has no pagination.

33 This play is discussed at length in Kapuscinski, G., 'Persian Theatre in the 1960s', PhD dissertation, Columbia University 1982.

City of Fairy Tales), an allegorical satire that used elements of traditional folklore, for which Mofid also composed the music.[34] *Pazhuheshi...* and *Shahr-e Qesseh* were the first Iranian plays to be reviewed by foreign media, and favourably so.[35]

The third festival had percussion music as its main theme, and was opened at Persepolis with a performance of Balinese Gamelan. The world-renowned Ensemble des Percussions de Strasbourg performed the world première of Xenakis's *Persephassa*, a joint commission of the festival and the French state broadcaster ORTF.[36] The American jazz percussionist Max Roach performed with his quintet and later jammed with the Iranian *tonbak* (goblet drum) player Hosseyn Tehrani.[37] The theme of the meeting of West and East again surfaced when *Et Exspecto Resurrectionem Mortuorum* by Olivier Messiaen, a composer deeply influenced by Gamelan and Indian music,[38] was performed at Persepolis under the baton of Bruno Maderna.[39] The continuities between East and West were also explored with the ingenious idea of juxtaposing on two evenings dulcimers from five musical traditions: the Iranian, Tajik, and Kashmiri varieties of the *santur*, plus the Chinese *yang chin* and the Romanian *tambal* (cimbalom).

34 Khorramzadeh Esfahani, *Te'atr-e Iran*, pp. 124–131.

35 Afshar, M., 'Festival of Arts Shiraz-Persepolis: Or You better believe in as many as six impossible things before breakfast', p. 26. This is a paper commissioned by the Asia Society for a symposium on the Shiraz Festival held in New York City on 5 October 2013, and can be found at: https://www.academia.edu/12568899/Festival_of_Arts_Shiraz-Persepolis_1967–1977_updated_May_2015_.

36 Harley, J., *Xenakis: His Life in Music*, New York 2004, p. 64–66. In his programme notes, Xenakis wrote that *Persephassa* was the archaic form of *Persephone*, whose etymology may be related to Pars [Persia]. He added that according to a Greek myth Perseus was the ancestor of the Achaemenians, which might be an evidence of the passage of the ancient Persians who, coming from Europe, crossed the Bosphorus and also established themselves in the Aegean. *Sevvomin jashn-e honar*, preantepenultimate page. Whether Xenakis believed this fanciful story or whether he only wished to flatter Pahlavi nationalism's desire to associate Iranians with Europeans rather than with their Semitic neighbours is of course impossible to tell.

37 *Jashn-e honar-e Shiraz*, pp. 167–168.

38 On Messiaen's fascination with and use of Asian music, see Griffiths, P., *Olivier Messiaen and the Music of Time*, Ithaca, NY 1985, pp. 49, 113, and 191.

39 Commissioned by André Malraux to commemorate France's war dead, this is one of Messiaen's most accessible compositions. According to the composer, he surrounded himself with pictures of Mexican step pyramids, of temples and statues of ancient Egypt, and of Romanesque and Gothic churches while composing it, and its instrumentation destined it for vast spaces. Halbreich, H., *Olivier Messiaen*, Paris 1980, pp. 422–423. This made Persepolis a particularly felicitous setting for its performance. See also Harper, W. H., 'Olivier Messiaen's Et exspecto resurrectionem mortuorum', PhD thesis, University of Rochester, Eastman School of Music 1986.

It was at the fourth festival, in 1970, that the festival's predilection for Western avant-garde theatre began, and many productions first seen at Nancy were henceforth invited to Iran. The festival was opened with an Iranian production, *Vis and Ramin*, a stage adaptation of the eleventh-century romance of the same name.[40] Other productions included Grotowski's staging of Calderón de la Barca's *The Constant Prince*, Victor García's production of Jean Genet's *Les Bonnes*, and performances by the American Bread and Puppet Theatre and the Belgian Théâtre Laboratoire Vicinal. All of these productions had received high acclaim in Europe and the United States, but many included lots of exposed skin, which was probably the origin of the festival's association with immorality in the minds of traditionalist Iranians. There were a number of Iranian fringe productions, including Slavomir Mrozek's *Striptease* and Samuel Becket's *Waiting for Godot*.

The fifth festival, in 1971, preceded the nationwide celebrations of the 2,500th anniversary of the Iranian monarchy, whose kitschy extravagance contributed much to the unpopularity of the Pahlavi regime (and which had no organic connection to the Shiraz Festival). The festival began with the world première of yet another specially commissioned production by Xenakis, the multimedia *Polytope de Persépolis*.[41] 'The public was able to move about inside six listening areas each of which was surrounded by eight loudspeakers reconstituting eight different channels of electro-acoustical music.'[42] During this spectacle local Shiraz children bore torches on the mountains adjacent to Persepolis, while laser beams were focused on the royal Achaemenian tombs overlooking the ruins. The laser beams fused with the light-string of children, symbolising the unity of Iranian history embodied by Persepolis.[43] This production met some criticism from people for whom the fires and torches served as a reminder of Alexander of Macedon's burning down of Persepolis in 330 BC,[44] but such criticism notwithstanding, *Polytope de Persépolis* was, rebranded as *Son et Lumière*, performed again on 14 October, Empress Farah's birthday, as part of the 2,500 year celebration of the

40 For an English translation, see Gorgani, F., *Vis and Ramin*, transl. Davis, D., New York 2008.

41 Prior to embarking on this project, Xenakis had been asked to contribute an installation of sound and light to the Iranian Pavilion of the 1970 World Exposition in Osaka. Harley, *Xenakis*, pp. 66–67.

42 Phillips, N., 'Iannis Xenakis: Persepolis plus Remixes Vol. 1', available at: <http://www.citypages.com/databank/23/1135/article10685.asp>.

43 See also Gluck, R., 'The Shiraz Arts Festival: Western Avant-Garde Arts in 1970s Iran', in *Leonardo*, vol. 40, no. 1, 2007, p. 22.

44 Fleuret, J., 'L'anti-son et lumière: 2300 ans après Alexandre un un grec embrase Persépolis, mais dans un grand feu de joie', in *Le Nouvel Observateur*, 3 September 1971.

Persian Empire at the conclusion of the gala dinner offered by Iran's sovereigns to their foreign guests.[45] *Polytope de Persépolis* was deemed such an artistic success that the Paris Festival d'Automne commissioned Xenakis to create a *Polytope de Cluny* for the Roman baths in the heart of the Quartier Latin, which turned out to be a major success.[46]

The ruins of the ancient Persian capital were also the backdrop for a production that, of all the plays staged at the Shiraz Festival, arguably made the biggest and most lasting impression on theatre critics: Peter Brook's monumental *Orghast*.[47] In 1970 the English film and theatre director had established the Centre International de Recherche Théâtrale in Paris as a multicultural theatrical research and production company composed of actors, dancers, musicians and other performers from around the world. This assembly travelled widely in the Middle East and Africa for three years in the early 1970s to explore the common stories, the recognisable shorthands, the instant abstractions, the shared outlines of story and character with which an international group could work, and *Orghast* was their first public performance at an international event.

An experimental play based on the myth of Prometheus, *Orghast* mostly used an invented language by the same name created by the English poet Ted Hughes,[48] in addition to Avestan and ancient Greek. It was performed in two parts, with the first part performed around dusk at Persepolis, and the second part at dawn at Naqsh-e Rostam, a site that contains the monumental tombs of a number of Achaemenian kings as well as some Sassanian rock reliefs.[49] It created quite a stir around the world. In Spain, for instance, the eminent dramaturg and director Ricard Salvat i Ferré, while calling Brook's participation in the Shiraz Festival 'scandalous', praised Brook's innovative ideas and regretted that he could not attend an event that was by definition 'unrepeatable'.[50]

Also present at the fifth festival was Bruno Maderna, who had dedicated his

---

45 See also Robert Steele's chapter in this volume.

46 For details see Harley, *Xenakis*, pp. 68–70.

47 On this event see Smith, A. C. H., *Orghast at Persepolis, an account of the experiment in theatre directed by Peter Brook and written by Ted Hughes*, London 1972.

48 Bate, J., *Ted Hughes: The Unauthorised Life*, London 2015, pp. 307–308.

49 The entire area was swarming with soldiers in preparation for the 2,500th anniversary celebrations, and one of these at one point refused to allow Brook access to an important site, whereupon Brook took umbrage for not having been recognised by the conscript. Farah, *My Thousand and One Days*, p. 78.

50 Salvat, R., '¿Existe un nuevo lenguaje teatral? Consideraciones a propósito de "Orghast I y II", de Ted Hughes y Peter Brook', reprinted in his book *El teatro de los años 70*, Barcelona 1974, pp. 56–62.

Ausstrahlungen, first performed at this festival, to the shahbanu.[51] In the realm of theatre, Jérôme Savary's *Zartan, the Unloved Brother of Tarzan* provided some exposed skin.[52]

The highlights of the sixth festival in 1972 were a major retrospective of the works of the German composer Karlheinz Stockhausen and *KA MOUNTain AND GUARDenia TERRACE: a story about a family and some people changing*, a *very* long (it lasted seven days) dramatic production by the American director Robert Wilson.[53] Stockhausen left an indelible impression, and his name became emblematic of the festival itself. The reason is that the city of Shiraz in its entirety was suffused with his sounds, perhaps to escape the charge of elitism. After a performance of *Hymnen* at Persepolis, various concerts took place in the city of Shiraz, including a dawn-to-evening performance of *Aus den sieben Tagen* in central Shiraz. On the last evening of the festival, the gates of Delgosha Park were opened to the public, and 8,000 people flocked in, including a great many young people, some of whom lost no time climbing on top of amplifier scaffolding and were brought down by the policemen who were guarding the five groups of musicians. The atmosphere was tense and the musicians were nervous, but Stockhausen predicted that his music would have a calming effect, and he was right: nothing untoward happened that night.[54] Except that the entire city now knew that the nation's money was being spent on something few people recognised as music.[55] As for Robert Wilson's production, he himself had this to say about it:

> At that time I was interested in a kind of living in which there was very little separation between art and life… I made my next work in Iran, … in which I worked with over five hundred people, creating a work that went on for seven days and nights continuously… [W]e worked with local people, students and people who were living in the foothills. People with no hats, people that did not know that man had been on the moon, people that had never seen a TV set… The work was written by the various people who were taking part in it. It was directed by them and eventually performed by them.[56]

51 Magnani, F., Montecchi, G., Popoli, T., and Romito, M., *Bruno Maderna documenti*, Milan 1985, p. 301. For an analysis of *Ausstrahlungen* see pp. 301–303.

52 On Savary see Godard, C., *Jérôme Savary, l'enfant de la fête*, Monaco 1996.

53 On his oeuvre see Shyer, L., *Robert Wilson and His Collaborators*, New York 1989.

54 Kurz, M., *Stockhausen: Eine Biographie*, Basel 1988, pp. 248–249.

55 Stockhausen, whose surname is difficult to pronounce for the average Iranian, came to be jocularly known as 'Ostad Kazem'. Personal communication from a Shirazi who was present: Mahmud Mojahed, Cambridge, 20 April 2009.

56 Coca, J. (ed.), *Actes, Congrés Internacional de Teatre a Catalunya 1985*, vol. 1, Barcelona 1989, p. 244. According to the catalogue of the seventh festival, the production

Other programmes included a performance of the music of John Cage, Merce Cunningham's ballet company, and an interpretation of *Rostam and Sohrab*, one of the key episodes in the *Shahnameh* (Iran's national epic) by an Indian *kathakali* dance group. Commenting on the festival in its newsletter, the critic Mahmud Enayat wrote, perhaps with a tinge of irony, that while the creative act had always been painful for artists, in the twentieth century artists wanted the public to share in their pains, and that at the Shiraz Festival the aim for the spectator was not enjoyment but satisfaction, a satisfaction that can be only be gained by understanding a work of art.[57]

According to a 'very secret' SAVAK report, the programmes of this festival, some of which were broadcast on television, elicited widespread anger. The Indian adaptation of *Rostam and Sohrab* as a 'puppet' show (*kathakali* dancers are ornately made-up) was deemed an insult to Iran's epic grandeur, and 'in every gathering and circle where this was discussed most people argued that the aim of staging the festival was to eradicate nationalist zeal and killing Iranian pride and nationality by habituating people to Western traditions'. As for Stockhausen, 'people say the Germans wanted to ridicule them'.[58]

The seventh festival, in 1973, began with a presentation of Maurice Béjart's Ballets du Vingtième Siècle, which performed a specially commissioned ballet called *Golestan*. Set to classical Persian music, it was of course a reference to the literary masterpiece of Shiraz's own Sa'di.[59] This ballet company performed two more programmes, but the central theme of the festival was modern Third World theatre, as the festival had agreed to host the Second Festival Conference of the Third World Theatre. (The first had taken place in Manila.) Companies from Cyprus, Iran, Jordan, Kazakhstan, Morocco, Nigeria, and Tunisia performed, while Malaysian *wayang kulit* (shadow play) and Korean court dances provided traditional Asian art.

For the eighth festival in 1974 Robert Wilson returned and staged *DiaLog / A Mad Man A Mad Giant A Mad Dog A Mad Urge A Mad Face*, a play first shown at the Villa Borghese in Rome a few months earlier, and which elicited protests from some spectators.[60] The Polish dramatist Tadeusz Kantor staged Stanisław

began at midnight and ended at dawn, and went on for a few days after the festival officially ended. Gorgin, I. (ed.), *Ketab-e haftomin jashn-e honar – 1352*, Tehran 1352/1973, p. 199.

57 Gorgin, *Ketab-e haftomin jashn-e honar*, p. 201.

58 *Jashn-e honar-e Shiraz*, p. 212.

59 For a recent translation see Sa'di of Shiraz, Sh. M., *The Gulistan (Rose Garden) of Sa'di*, transl. Thackston, W. M., Bethesda 2008.

60 At least according to a SAVAK report. *Jashn-e honar-e Shiraz*, p. 250.

Witkiewicz's play *Lovelies and Dowdies*, a pioneer of absurdist theatre.[61] An Iranian company produced Albert Camus's *Caligula*, and another Iranian production caused SAVAK a minor headache: in an effort to assure the survival of traditional Iranian *ruhowzi* theatre,[62] the actor and director Ali Nasirian wrote a play called *Bongah-e Teatral* (*The Theatre Company*), which was extremely popular with the audience.[63] At the last performance, Nasirian used the play's dialogue to criticise state policies to the point where the live television broadcast of the piece was cut off. The SAVAK agent covering the festival requested that Nasirian be summoned to headquarters, but higher officials wrote that summoning Nasirian was not advisable.[64] The *épater le bourgeois* factor at the festival was provided by a Brazilian capoeira troupe from Bahia that took a show first shown in Rennes and La Rochelle to Iran,[65] a show in the course of which the heads of live roosters were bitten off by the dancers.

The ninth festival in 1975 was opened in Persepolis by the Alwin Nikolais Dance Theatre and it seems to have been rather uneventful. Controversy returned with the tenth festival in 1976. In 1973, Maurice Béjart had been so taken in by classical Persian music that he invited a group of Iranian musicians to Brussels and together with them created a ballet he called *Farah*, which was premièred that same year in the Belgian capital. This ballet was now staged in Iran. According to the ever-vigilant SAVAK agents, the programmes that caused indignation in 1976 were Pier-Paolo Pasolini's film *A Thousand and One Nights*, which showed naked men and women copulating,[66] and the Japanese play *Mad Ship*, in which a woman appeared on stage totally naked. What enraged many people, was that this latter play was staged in a building, the Hosseyniyeh-ye Moshir, that was part of a religious endowment.[67] Xenakis had been invited, but declined the invitation in view of the increased criticism to which the shah's regime was subjected in the West.[68]

---

61 On Kantor see Miklaszewski, K., *Encounters with Tadeusz Kantor*, transl. Hyde, G., London 2002.

62 On which see Beeman, 'A Full Arena', pp. 370–379.

63 Purmoradian, [Q. A.] (ed.), *Hashtomin jashn-e honar-e Iran*, Tehran 1353/1994, pp. 44–51.

64 *Jashn-e honar-e Shiraz*, pp. 246–247. In the same document we read that SAVAK had objected to an Iranian play in the previous year and had asked National Iranian Radio Television to forward its script, but that NIRT had not acted on the request.

65 Lonchampt, J., 'Les nuits de Chiraz', *Le Monde*, 23 August 1974.

66 Part of this film was actually shot in Isfahan's Shah Mosque, which made it even more offensive to religiously inclined people.

67 *Jashn-e honar-e Shiraz*, p. 430.

68 See: http://www.iannis-xenakis.org/english/bio.html#1960.

The eleventh festival, in 1977, began at a time when the upheavals that would culminate in the revolution of 1979 were already underway. Its most controversial programme was Péter Hálasz's Squat Theatre company's staging of a play called *Pig, Child, Fire!* – about which more below.

The above listing of festival programmes omits most non-controversial programmes, of which there were many: a plethora of symphony orchestras and chamber ensembles presented European classical music and works by Iranian composers who worked in the Western medium.[69] The festival also pioneered the staging of Iran's regional and ethnic traditions, with musicians from places as far apart as Baluchistan and Kurdistan presenting their art to a public that had hitherto more or less been ignorant of their very existence. One of the most felicitous aspects of the festivals was the uninterrupted presence of the greatest classical musicians from India: Amjad Ali Khan, S. Balachander, Bismillah Khan, D. Chaudhuri, Ram Narayan, Lakshmi Shankar, Ravi Shankar, Shivkumar Sharma, and Vilayat Khan, all performed at Hafeziyeh and Persepolis. In addition, traditional Arab, Bhutanese, Cambodian, Chinese, Japanese, Malaysian, Senegalese, Ugandan, and Vietnamese arts were presented, providing culturally curious Iranians a respite from the focus on Europe that pervaded the country's modern middle class, which was proud of Iran's ancient past but tended to be arrogantly dismissive of the often much older cultures of other non-European peoples. In addition to music, theatre, and film, festivals also featured exhibitions and round-table discussions about the programmes, discussions that were frank and open by the standards of Iran's dictatorial regime.

As time went by, the organisers of the festival felt that the festival as an institution should sponsor activities year round. The first event was a performance by the classical Indian dancer Lakshmi Viswanathan in December 1972, followed a few weeks later by a concert of the fabled Indian *shehnai* virtuoso Bismillah Khan. Many of these events were held at Tehran's recently inaugurated City Theatre, which was administered in the beginning by the Shiraz Festival Organisation but later transferred to NIRT.

At the international level, Xenakis was approached to design a *Cité des Arts* in Shiraz and Persepolis that would be an interdisciplinary and collaborative scientific research centre for sound and visual arts, cinema, theatre, ballet, poetry, and literature. In addition to public presentations, the centre would support ongoing work by up to 40 visiting and 50 permanent artists, scientists, and staff members.

---

69 For a more complete presentation of the programmes see Mahasti Afshar, 'Festival of Arts Shiraz-Persepolis'.

In his plans, Xenakis referred to the sound arts element as a 'Centre for Studies of Mathematical and Automated Music', which would have likely resembled the Centre d'Études de Mathématique et Automatique Musicales that he had established in Paris with the support of the French ministry of culture.[70] But before the plans could be concretised, the revolution put an end to state sponsorship of cosmopolitan artistic endeavours.

Unsurprisingly, the 1978 festival was cancelled a few weeks before it was due to begin, the revolution having begun in earnest in January. In the course of the revolutionary violence the beautiful door of the Hosseyniyeh-ye Moshir was burned,[71] as was the Ariana Cinema, where the festival's films had been shown. Most leading figures of the festival left Iran for Europe or the United States. A few weeks after the triumph of the revolution, Ghaffari's house in Tehran was systematically looted.[72] The playwrights Mofid and Abbas Nalbandian remained behind. The Kargah-e Namayesh (Theatre Workshop) was occupied by revolutionary guards, considered a den of corruption, and closed down.[73] Mofid soon had to go underground for several months and eventually escaped to the United States where he died in 1984, while Nalbandian spent some time in jail, was not allowed to work when released, and committed suicide in 1989.

Criticisms of the Festival

In the West, many disparaged the Shiraz Festival as an oppressive regime's public relations scheme to gain international acceptance. Consequently, those Western artists who participated in the festival were accused of betrayal by left-leaning intellectuals:

> When a creative spirit like John Cage accepted the support of the Shah of Iran, and performed modernist spectacles a few miles from where political prisoners shrieked and died, the failure of moral imagination was not his alone.[74]

---

70 Gluck, 'The Shiraz Arts Festival', pp. 25–26.

71 *Jashn-e honar-e Shiraz*, p. 427.

72 Some of the stolen art objects later turned up in New York City, like a portrait of his ancestor Amin al-Dowleh, a major political figure and sometime prime minister in the 1910s. Ghaffari, telephone interview.

73 Zohari, I., *Yadha va budha*, Spånga 1999, p. 233.

74 Berman, M., *All That is Solid Melts Into Air: The Experience of Modernity*, New York 1988, p. 32. I thank Kouross Esmaeli for bringing this book to my attention.

Some Western artists took cognisance of the criticisms and tried to address the issue of repression while in Iran. Xenakis on two occasions spoke of the world's freedom fighters, and the American theatre group Bread and Puppet insisted on performing outside Shiraz's main prison.[75] Among Iranians, criticism of the Shiraz Festival of Art has castigated its cost, its elitism, and its immoral and anti-Islamic bent. The three are of course intimately related, but let us consider them in turn.

Nobody quite knows how much the Shiraz Festival cost. Internal documents, published recently by the Islamic Republic's Ministry of Intelligence, give the expenses of the festival organisation for 1346/1967–68 as 21 million rials ($ 300,000) and 40 million rials for 1347/1968–69, of which 20 million were contributed by the National Iranian Oil Company,[76] a figure confirmed by Ghaffari in an interview in 1974.[77] These figures do not include the commissions later paid to artists, which remain unknown to the public, but it seems that 'artists, thrilled by the opportunity to explore and innovate in a singular environment, accepted minimum fees and no extra funds for commissioned or world premieres of their work'. Most travel costs for foreign artists were taken up by governments that had bilateral treaties with Iran.[78]

The second criticism of the festival, its elitism, has some validity, although ticket prices were kept so low that middle-class art lovers could afford them. In other words, the 'elite' to which the festival allegedly catered was a socio-cultural rather than an economic elite. One has to ask the question why the Baalbeck Festival has not generated the same level of hostility. I would argue that there were three components to the anti-elite resentment the Shiraz Festival engendered among many Iranians: the country's political environment , the festival's predilection for avant-garde programming, and its provincial setting.

The eleven years of the festival (1967–1977) coincided with a deepening of repression and censorship in Iran.[79] The organisers of the festival tried to ensure a freer and more open atmosphere for the festival than prevailed in the country at large, and inside Iran publications such as *Ayandegan*, *Negin*, *Sokhan*, and *Ferdowsi* got away with criticising it and the programmes it offered. As more and more secular middle-class people became alienated from the shah's regime, the idea of a temporally bound heterotopia where critical discourse was

75 Farah, *My Thousand and One Days*, p. 80.
76 *Jashn-e honar-e Shiraz*, pp. 111–112 and 151–152.
77 Quoted in Khorramzadeh Esfahani, *Te'atr-e Iran*, p. 172.
78 Afshar, 'Festival of Arts Shiraz-Persepolis', p. 3.
79 Karimi-Hakkak, A., 'Censorship', in *Encyclopaedia Iranica*, vol. 5, Costa Mesa, 1990.

allowed struck most critical intellectuals as little more than a liberal fig-leaf for the regime,[80] especially in light of the fact that most of the festival's organisers had direct ties to the ruling family. Iranian artists who participated in the event were accused of surrendering to an officially promoted formalism at the expense of being *engagé*, committed, as it behoved an intellectual to be.[81] One might even ask whether a less tangible source of hostility may play a role as well, namely a certain philistine tendency in many committed intellectuals, resulting, perhaps, from the fact that one who dedicates his life to *one* cause can hardly lead a balanced life that includes the enjoyment of art for art's sake.[82] The following assessment of the 7th festival, read on Radio Azadi on 12 Shahrivar 1352/3 September 1973, which verges on self-parody, typifies such a politically motivated and/or expressed philistinism:

> Dear listeners,
> A few days ago the Seventh Shiraz Arts Festival was opened by Farah. As usual, the majority of those present at the opening were foreign guests, courtiers, and figures of the regime. But because of its reactionary and anti-people essence the regime does not encourage art. The organisation of an annual festival in Shiraz and its opening by Farah are a propaganda ploy of the regime. Art must not be a reflection and expression of an artist's subjective whimsy but must express the truth about the demands and needs of the masses, meaning that it must be inspired by the masses so that the innovations, metaphors, and genius of the artist may develop while [art's] technical aspects are preserved. Then this art must be given back to the people.[83]

Less politicised moderately affluent upper middle-class people were kept away not for lack of financial resources but for lack of cultural capital, for the appreciation of many of the festival's programmes necessitated an aesthetic sensibility and a cosmopolitan habitus that were rare even among most upper middle-class, let

80 Sattari, *Dar bidowlati-ye farhang*, pp 188–189.
81 See for instance Soltanpur, S., *Now'i az honar, now'i az andisheh*, S. l., 1350/1972. This tract was widely disseminated among Iranian students abroad. I thank Abbas Milani for bringing this fact to my attention.
82 See Mazlish, B., *The Revolutionary Ascetic: Evolution of a Political Type*, New York 1976.
83 *Jashn-e honar-e Shiraz*, p. 238. My translation. According to Hasan Masali, Radio Azadi was an oppositionist radio station operated by Marxist dissidents of the Mujahidin (later known as Peykar) and broadcasting from Aden. Personal communication, 13 August 2004.

alone middle-class Iranians.[84] Those who did overcome the socio-cultural barriers might enjoy the concerts of traditional Persian and classical Western art music, but were bewildered by the cacophonies of Stockhausen, whose acoustic creations would probably strike even the vast majority of German concert-goers as silly. As a result, more people remember the festival for its performances of Stockhausen than for its pioneering presentation of classical Persian art music of the highest calibre.

Finally, the location of the festival in Shiraz, intended to remedy the concentration of artistic activity in the capital, exacerbated the chasm between the organisers' vision and the artistic sensibilities of the population at large. While the people of Shiraz have a reputation for appreciating 'wine, women, and song' and being *ahl-e del* (roughly translatable as having a propensity towards appreciating *la dolce vita*),[85] most of the festival's programmes did not give them pleasure.[86] The local Shirazi elites might have welcomed being introduced to Western music through Mozart's 40th symphony or Rimsky-Korsakov's *Schéhérezade*, but they had no use for the compositions of Bruno Maderna and Krzysztof Penderecki. A comparison with the Baalbeck Festival is instructive here. The latter included concerts by Umm Kulthum and Fairuz, two of the Arab world's most popular singers, which ensured it a popularity that went at least a little bit beyond cosmopolitan Ras Beirut. Moreover, while the organisers of the festival had little consideration for the interests of the poor inhabitants of Baalbeck, a small town which they considered little more than an eyesore that impaired festival goers' ability to take in the magnificence of the Roman ruins, they did have the foresight to organise preview concerts by popular Arab musicians at very low prices in order to keep the locals from infiltrating the temple area during the festival itself.[87] One cannot help but wonder what Iranians' reaction to the festival would have been had its opening night featured a concert by, say, Googoosh. While the very thought of such a choice would probably have struck the organisers as an unspeakably vulgar sell-out, a somewhat less rarefied approach might have gained the festival greater acceptance at least among secular Iranians, arguably limiting the use that the conservative clergy could make of it as an illustration of everything that was wrong

84 I am taking 'cultural capital' and 'habitus' from Bourdieu, P., *Distinction: A Social Critique of the Judgement of Taste*, Cambridge, MA 1984.

85 Arberry, A. J., *Shiraz: Persian City of Saints and Poets*, Norman, OK 1960.

86 A Shirazi taxi driver told me that he had attended a symphony concert at the festival, adding that while he enjoyed the sound of a violin as much as anybody, having a hundred violins playing the same tune had seemed stupid to him.

87 Tohme, 'Le Festival de Baalbek', pp. 232–234.

with the shah's regime. For in the eyes of the clerics and their followers the Shiraz Festival and Googoosh were part of the *same* syndrome:[88] the desire of the shah and his foreign masters to eradicate religion from society. Which brings us to the third type of criticism levelled at the festival, the one that most contributed to it becoming a leitmotif in the revolutionary discourse.

While Shiraz may have been a tolerant place in comparison with Isfahan or Mashhad, it remained a provincial city the overwhelming majority of whose inhabitants had Muslim cultural sensibilities. Empress Farah took this into account, for instance, by going from the airport directly to the shrine of Shah Cheragh, Shiraz's major religious site,[89] every time she visited the city to open the festival.[90]

While the sound art of Stockhausen and Xenakis struck people as stupid, there was probably nothing *religiously* objectionable about it. The same could not be said of a number of the many plays, ballets, and films that featured exposed skin. The eroticism of such performances was mild by contemporary European standards, but it was obscene by Iranian standards if we apply, *mutatis mutandis*, the definition American law gives of obscenity:

> For something to be 'obscene' it must be shown that *the average person*, applying contemporary *community standards* and viewing material as a whole, would find 1) that the work appeals predominantly to 'prurient' interest; 2) that it depicts or describes sexual conduct in a patently offensive way; and 3) that it lacks serious literary, artistic, political or scientific value.[91]

Religiously motivated indignation over some of the programmes had been building up almost since the beginning, but the straw that broke the camel's back was a play by the Hungarian playwright and director Péter Hálasz called *Pig,*

88 On 2 Ramadan 1397 / 27 Mordad 2536 (1356) / 18 August 1977 a cleric by the name of Seyyed Ahmad Pishva said in his sermon at Shiraz's Masjed-e Now (New Mosque): 'The artists of our time are people like Googoosh, for whom they organise festivals. People must not attend these festivals, so that they [i.e., the regime] will be forced not to organise them.' *Jashn-e honar-e Shiraz*, p. 383.

89 Shah Cheragh is the sobriquet of Mir Seyyed Ahmad, a brother of the Eighth Imam of the Twelver Shi'ites, Imam Reza, who is buried in Mashhad. Their sister, Masumeh, is buried in Qom.

90 *Jashn-e honar-e Shiraz*, pp. 127–128, 375. According to the former governor of Fars, both the shahbanu and the shah visited the shrine *every* time they went to Shiraz. Personal communication to Ghaffari.

91 'Obscene, obscenity', *The 'Lectric Law Library*, available at: <http://www.lectlaw.com/def2/o002.htm>. Emphasis added. I thank Guive Mirfendereski for bringing this idea to my attention.

Child, Fire! The cacophonies of Stockhausen and the sensuous ballet productions of Béjart paled in comparison to the scandal caused by Hálasz's play at the end of the last festival in 1977.

The Final Offence: *Pig, Child, Fire!*

The eleventh Shiraz Festival took place in September 1977 at a time that was both politically and religiously inauspicious. In the political realm, the shah's liberalisation began in early 1977, meaning that by September the press and the regime's opponents were much freer than before to speak out. In the religious sphere, the fasting month of Ramadan began on 17 August, which was also the day the festival began. While Ramadan is a time of rejoicing and festivity in the Arab world, Iranian Shiʿite Muslims consider it a time of spiritual introspection: on the 19th, the Shiʿites' first Imam, Ali, was mortally wounded during his prayers, succumbing on the 21st. The month is therefore liturgically very significant, and not the best time for a festival. On the first of Ramadan, the day of Farah's arrival in the city, one of the city's two top clerical leaders, Sheykh Bahaeddin Mahallati, told his listeners in a sermon: 'I will pray, and you say "amen".' Then he began:

> May God damn the instigators of the Arts Festival
> [The crowd: 'Amen' etc.]
> May God damn the organisers of the Arts Festival
> May God damn the participants of the Arts Festival.

The congregational prayers were probably still going on when Farah's aeroplane touched down at the airport. She went first on the pilgrimage to Shah Cheragh, then visited a blood transfusion centre. After lunch, she visited a workers' welfare centre and a family centre, and then proceeded by helicopter to Persepolis, from where she went by car to Naqsh-e Rostam, where she opened the eleventh festival. Later that night she flew back to Shiraz, where she attended a performance of Purulia Chau, a folk dance ensemble from West Bengal.[92] Two days later, on the third day of Ramadan, the other, more radical, senior cleric of Shiraz, Seyyed Abd al-Hosseyn Dastgheyb, denounced the festival from the pulpit and called God's damnation both on those who participated in it and on the person who opened it. The next day he said in his afternoon sermon: 'The human personality is different

92 *Jashn-e honar-e Shiraz*, pp. 375–378; and Khorsand, B. (ed.), *Katalog-e yazdahomin jashn-e honar 2536*, Tehran 1977, pp. 118–122.

from animals. For instance, one can dress an ass in colourful clothes and put him on the throne and tell him to rule, but would that be right? The place of an ass is in the stables; everything has its place.'[93]

The festival went ahead, with Asian art forms dominating: Bhavai folk theatre from Gujarat, classical Indian dance by Sonal Mansingh, Japanese historical films, and any number of Iranian music and theatre groups shared the programme with a La MaMa production of *As You Like It* directed by Andrei Şerban (first seen at La Rochelle) and Tadeusz Kantor's play, *Dead Class*, performed by the Cricot 2 group and directed by the playwright himself. And then, on 24 August, Hálasz and his Squat Theatre staged *Pig, Child, Fire!*[94]

A Hungarian by birth, Hálasz had emigrated to France in the spring of 1977 before settling in the United States in the summer of that year.[95] In 1977, *Pig, Child, Fire!* was the hit of the first day of America's largest alternate theatre gathering, the New Theater Festival held at the University of Maryland. According to a *Washington Post* article:

> The incredible 'Pig, Child, Fire!' uses words, but most of them were written by Dostoyevsky and Antonin Artaud and never intended to serve as a script. Actually, they're still not part of a script. Their use is closer to that of incidental music accompanying the remarkable events occurring on stage. It's difficult to describe these events without sounding like a gibbering fool; let's just say they utilize a goat, masks, flour, a giant puppet, a noose, a knife sharpener, a dinner, an automobile, three TV screens, broken glass and several more unmentionable items. Plus the devilishly witty actors from the Squat Theater who thought all this up. The piece is in four acts, largely unrelated, and the second, 'Nous Sommes Les Mannequins', is clearly the highlight of the show – an unendingly surprising 'film noir' that occurs on two stages and videotape rather than film and combines comedy and suspense with the flair of a Hitchcock.[96]

93 *Jashn-e honar-e Shiraz*, pp. 383 and 387.

94 Khorsand, *Katalog*, pp. 62–66, 96–99, 123–139.

95 On Hálasz and his Squat Theatre see Buchmuller, E., and Koós, A., *Squat Theatre*, New York 1996; and Galasso, S., and Valentini, V., *Squat theater 1969–1981*, Soveria Mannelli [Catanzaro] 1998.

96 Shirley, D., 'Theater', *The Washington Post*, 13 June 1977, Final Edition, p. B9. The play generated a rather large literature. For a bibliography, including articles published in Iran, see Galasso and Valentini, *Squat theater 1969–1981*, pp. 186–190.

The good people of Shiraz found this play more devilish than witty, and with good reason. It was staged inside a rented car dealer's shop on a commercial street of Shiraz. The actors played with their back to the shop window, and for the spectators inside the shop the pedestrians on the pavement outside were meant to be a moving backdrop, except that the passers-by became curious and instead of briefly peeking through the window and then going on their way, as anticipated, they sat down and watched the proceedings. And these included, most famously, what the *Washington Post* article quoted above considered 'unmentionable': a man committing suicide by inserting a pistol in his rear, and the vagina of an actress shown on a television screen placed inside the shop, the camera having been placed under her skirt.[97] There was also one scene where a woman embraced a man. The morning after the first show, the police chief of Shiraz complained to the festival organisers of the congestion that had been caused and suggested replacing the passers-by with policemen in mufti and their relatives, an offer that was refused.[98] News of the strange goings-on quickly spread through the city and thence through the entire country.

At 9 PM on the 25th of August, a number of clerics and bazaar merchants went to the house of Sheykh Bahaeddin Mahallati to protest against the play. Both Tehran's evening papers, *Keyhan* and *Ettela'at*, had sharply criticised the play, and these articles were read out loud. Mahallati called upon all clerics and preachers to stop congregational prayers as of the 27th of August, asking them to send a telegram to Tehran demanding that the Shiraz Festival be ended. He was later visited by the intelligence chief of the local police and told that the festival was ending on the 26th anyway, whereupon he rescinded the order to cancel congregational prayers. On that same day of August 25th, Dastgheyb gave a sermon which, characteristically, used more expressive language and played on the negative connotations of the word 'pig' (*khuk*), an animal Muslims consider not only dirty but also ritually impure (*najes*):

> I have heard something. The Feast of the Pig. Feast of the Pig. Strange name, that. Those who attend it, male and female, are lower than pigs. They be damned. The founder [of the feast] is a swine. They be damned. Until when do they want to lead this country and its young people astray and hand them to colonialism and pervert them. What are the leaders trying to do? It is the holy

97 According to Ghaffari, however, the screen was put in such an inconspicuous spot that he never noticed it, or else he would have had it taken away. Telephone interview.

98 Ghaffari, telephone interview.

> month of Ramadan and they bring in these dancers. Those who go are asses. Shiraz used to be a city of knowledge, now they have turned it into a dance-hall. They make it impossible for us not to speak up.[99]

SAVAK then forced the festival organisers to cancel further performances, and contrary to the original plan, the production was not taken to Tehran.

The deep involvement of the imperial family in the Festival now came to haunt it as the opposition quickly seized on the matter to illustrate the regime's direct sponsorship of immorality and obscenity. On 28 September 1977, in a speech extolling the ulema to speak up, Ayatollah Ruhollah Khomeini said: 'You cannot imagine the prostitution they are propagating in Iran. They did it in Shiraz, and there are plans to repeat it in Tehran. And nobody says anything!… Among all the people they showed the sexual act itself, and nobody breathed [a protest]! When will they finally speak up?'[100]

The last British ambassador to pre-revolutionary Iran, Anthony Parsons, also alluded to the play in his memoirs:

> The Shiraz Festival of 1977 excelled itself in its insult to Iranian moral values. For example, according to an eye-witness, a play was enacted which represented, as I was told, the evils of military rule and occupation. … One scene, played on the pavement, involved a rape which was performed in full (no pretence) by a man … on a woman who had her dress ripped off by her attacker. The denouement of the play, also acted on the pavement, included a scene where one of the characters dropped his trousers and inserted a stage pistol up his backside, presumably in order to all verisimilitude to his suicide. … I remember mentioning [the play] to the Shah, adding that, if the same play had been put on, say, in the main street of Winchester, … the actors and sponsors would have found themselves in trouble. The Shah laughed indulgently.[101]

Bref, the Iranian revolution now had its own *cause célèbre*: not a queen's necklace,[102] but an empress's festival. The 'immorality' of the festival, as exemplified by the Hungarian play of 1977, became a leitmotif of all of the shah's

---

99 *Jashn-e honar-e Shiraz*, pp. 388–391.

100 [Khomeini, R.], *Sahifeh-ye nur*, vol. 1, Tehran, 1361/1983, p. 241.

101 Parsons, A., *The Pride and the Fall: Iran 1974–1979*, London 1984, pp. 54–55.

102 See Maza, S., 'The Diamond Necklace Affair, 1785–1786', in *Private Lives and Public Affairs: The Causes Célèbres of Prerevolutionary France*, Berkeley 1993, pp. 167–211.

opponents. Ten years later, an Iranian prisoner of war in Iraq told an English teacher that he had 'heard that once there was a play in Tehran, containing a rape scene and they actually carried out the rape scene on stage'.[103] Decades later, Empress Farah seems to have had second thoughts, stating that 'during the 11 years of the Shiraz Festival, there had been hundreds of programs, mostly traditional but some avant-garde. Artists were free to express themselves. There was only one questionable incident'.[104]

In light of the outpouring of religiously motivated hostility to the Shiraz Festival, it is somewhat ironic that one of the main European protagonists of the festival, the French choreographer Maurice Béjart (1927–2007), was so marked by his encounter with Iran that he started reading Henri Corbin's writings on Iranian Islam and converted to Islam. While later in life his spirituality transcended individual religions, he remained attached to both Iran and Islam, expressing admiration for Iran's profound authenticity, and saying about Islam that what touched him most about it was the one and only God who is inaccessible to human smallness, Who was not begotten and did not beget.[105]

Another European who was inspired to engage more deeply with Iranian culture as a result of his Shiraz experience was Peter Brook. After *Orghast*, his next production was a play based on *The Conference of Birds*, a mystic poem by the twelfth-century Persian Sufi poet Attar of Nishapur. Brook toured the play around rural Africa before presenting two extremely successful productions to Western audiences – one in New York City at La MaMa, and one in Paris.[106]

Long-term Effects

The organisers of the festival seemed to have believed in the autonomy of the aesthetic sphere, not realising that this approach makes sense only if embedded in a liberal political system, but is problematic in an illiberal one. They also assumed

103 Brown, I., *Khomeini's Forgotten Sons: The Story of Iran's Boy Soldiers*, London 1990, p. 80.

104 Stein D., 'For the Love of Her People: An Interview with Farah Diba about the Pahlavi Programs for Arts in Iran', in Scheiwiller, S.G. (ed.), *Performing the Iranian State: Visual Culture and Representations of Iranian Identity*, London 2013, p. 81.

105 Robert, M., *Conversations avec Maurice Béjart*, Tournai 2000, pp. 65, 113, 116, and 125. Béjart also held the United States responsible for toppling the shah's regime (p. 65), an idea quite common among royalist exiles.

106 Heilpern, J. *Conference of the Birds: The Story of Peter Brook in Africa*, London 1977. For an English translation of the original poem, see Attar, F., D., *The Conference of the Birds*, transl. Darbandi, A. and Davis, D., Harmondsworth 1984.

a certain familiarity with the West in their public, and so aimed at extending this ideal public's horizons by acquainting them with the latest developments in Western art.[107] But most Iranians were *not* familiar with Western arts and culture, and so the festival became in fact even more elitist than one would expect any festival to be, and gave fundamentalist zealots a convenient opportunity to depict *all* of Western culture as decadent and immoral.[108]

In the reaction of Muslim traditionalists against such programmes, anti-elitism and class envy mixed with moral indignation to produce religious *ressentiment*, about which Max Weber wrote:

> Resentment is a concomitant of that particular religious ethic of the disprivileged which... teaches that the unequal distribution of mundane goods is caused by the sinfulness and the illegality of the privileged, and that sooner or later God's wrath will overtake them. In this theodicy of the disprivileged, the moralistic quest serves as a device for compensating a conscious or unconscious desire for vengeance.[109]

This resentful religiosity was a potent force in the Iranian revolution and explains many of the subsequent policies of the Islamic Republic, which, for a few years, were opposed to anything that had even a hint of refinement. Islamist (and, to a lesser extent, leftist) diatribes notwithstanding, the Shiraz Festival left a mark on the cultural development of Iran that is felt to this day.[110]

It was at Hafeziyeh that Iran's concert-going public first came to appreciate classical Iranian art music.[111] A key role was played by the Centre for the Preservation and Propagation of Iranian Music (Markaz-e Hefz va Esha'eh-ye Musiqi-ye

---

107 As Empress Farah put it: 'At the very beginning, in the first years of the festival, people either laughed or were shocked. These extraordinary spectacles were so new to us. But little by little, understanding has come, people have grown accustomed to them and are intensely interested.' *My Thousand and One Days*, p. 79.

108 A good example is the polemical preface to the documents published by Iran's Ministry of Intelligence. See *Jashn-e honar-e Shiraz*, pp. 3–13.

109 Weber, M. *Economy and Society*, vol. 1, Berkeley 1978, p. 494.

110 It should be noted that two more festivals were created, one in Tus, Ferdowsi's birthplace, for Iran's epic culture, and another, in Isfahan, for popular traditions. These festivals seem to have been quite uncontroversial. On the former see Gharavi, M., 'Jashnvareh-ye Tus: jelveh'i digar a azemmat-e melli va khᵛishtangara'i-ye Iraniyan', in *Honar va mardom*, no. 156, 1354/1975.

111 Let us not forget that in the last years of Reza Shah's reign the state attempted to outlaw classical Persian music, whose teaching was discontinued at the National Conservatory in 1938 but resumed after Reza Shah's departure from Iran.

Irani) founded in 1968 under the auspices of NIRT. One of the giants of Iranian art music, Nur-Ali Borumand, who had hitherto kept aloof of state institutions, was persuaded by Qotbi to collaborate with the centre,[112] which began its teaching activities in 1972. A group of young musicians (initially six, their number grew to about twenty toward the end) who were strong technically but not proficient in the traditional subtleties of authentic Iranian music, learnt these from a number of old masters whose collaboration had been secured through Borumand. Masters and students received fixed salaries so as to be able to concentrate on their music. It soon gained international acclaim, and its musicians gave concerts both in Iran, especially at the yearly Shiraz Art Festival, and abroad.[113] The musicians trained at this centre spearheaded a revival of classical Iranian music that was briefly suppressed in the immediate aftermath of the revolution but then blossomed into a veritable renaissance in the late 1980s.

The festival also had a catalytic effect on Iranian theatre. Various state institutions had promoted theatre in Iran before the Shiraz Festival,[114] but a new dynamism was injected into it by the foundation of the Kargah-e Namayesh (Theater Workshop), an organisation sponsored by NIRT and the Shiraz Festival (and presided by another cousin of the empress, the architect Bijan Saffari) and dedicated to 'helping playwrights, actors, directors, and stage designers to exercise and experiment, independent of commonly accepted professional restrictions'.[115] Some of the artists associated with it staged innovative and daring productions at the Shiraz Festival that have been considered influential milestones to this day.[116] To give but one example, a play called *The Mute Who Was Dreamed* (based on a story of Rumi) by an Iran-based theatre company, Teatr-e Bazi, was 'one of the hottest tickets' of the Edinburgh Festival's fringe in 2002, where it was staged after a successful engagement in New York City. The background notes published on that occasion read almost like a recapitulation of the Shiraz Festival:

---

112 For a biographical sketch of Borumand, see Nettl, B., *The Radif of Persian Music: Studies of Structure and Cultural Context*, Champaign, IL 1987, pp. 142–145.

113 For details see Miller, L., *The Center for Preservation and Propagation of Iranian Music*, Salt Lake City 1977. See also Caron, N., 'La création d'un centre de musique traditionnelle iranienne', in *Studia Iranica*, vol. 2, no. 2, 1973. A student's account is contained in an interview with Hosseyn Alizadeh, *Adineh* no. 39, Azar 1368/November-December 1979.

114 See Khorramzadeh Esfahani, *Te'atr-e Iran*, pp. 31–100.

115 Gaffary, F., Ovanessian, A., and Taghian, L., 'Iran', in *The World Encyclopedia of Contemporary Theatre*, vol. 5: Asia/Pacific, London 1998, p. 205.

116 Ashur Banipal Babilla, Bizhan Mofid, Abbas Nalbandian, and Arby Ovanessian.

> The roots of Attila Pessyani's artistic inspiration can be traced to the Sixties and early Seventies when Shiraz… became a cultural Mecca attracting the avant garde of world theatre. Over more than a decade, the Shiraz Festival became an important international venue which ended with the Islamic Revolution of 1979.
>
> Pessyani spent his formative years in Shiraz witness to some of the most significant contemporary theatre innovators – from Poland's Tadeusz Kantor and Jerzy Grotowski, to Britain's Peter Brook and a then young American director, Robert Wilson. Their encounters with the traditional performance genres of *Ta'zieh*, Iran's form of passion play, and *Rouhouzi*, the Iranian style of Commedia dell'Arte, influenced many of these directors, and this tradition continues to play a part in Pessyani's work.[117]

In 1989, after the end of the Iran-Iraq War, the Islamic Republic started its own Fajr Festival in winter to celebrate the victory of the revolution, and by the late 1990s began inviting European theatre groups to perform in Iran. Conservative hardliners lost no time comparing this policy to the Shiraz Festival. But there was a difference: this time young people with no connections to the regime were eager to see the productions and crashed the gates of the City Theatre in Tehran.[118] While Chesterton's boutade that 'Many forerunners… would have felt rather ill if they had seen the things they foreran'[119] may well apply to some of the organisers of the Shiraz Festival, this festival was in some ways a forerunner of the various festivals now taking place in Iran. As for the city of Shiraz, concerts of classical Persian music are still given at Hafeziyeh on special occasions.[120]

After the Shiraz Festival, similar international festivals were established elsewhere in the greater Middle East, and it seems that the organisers have tried to avoid the problems created by the Iranian festival. Among the many festivals held in Morocco, the World Festival of Sacred Music, held every June in the conservative city of Fes, stands out for being both resolutely cosmopolitan and anchored in local sacral traditions.[121] And when Queen Noor of Jordan founded the Jerash Festival of Culture and Arts in 1981 in the Jordanian city famed for its Roman

117 See: http://www.gravitas.f9.co.uk/theatre/bazi.

118 Sattari, *Dar bidowlati-ye farhang*, pp. 186–187. The comparison with the Shiraz Festival is in *Keyhan*, 13 Bahman 1377 / 2 February 1999, p. 2.

119 Quoted in Ward, M., *Gilbert Keith Chesterton*, Harmondsworth 1958, p. 243.

120 Such as the conclusion of a trip by the President Mohammad Khatami in October 2004. See *Ettela'at* 21 Mehr 1383 / 12 October 2004, p. 1.

121 Wallon, 'Le festival international', p. 313.

remains, she was 'careful to remember lessons learned from the Shiraz Festival in Iran, which made a well-intentioned effort to showcase some of the most avant-garde European and American plays and performers but had been heavily criticised because the selections offended many people'. She expressed the hope that a balance could be struck 'between paying tribute to popular traditional Arab and Muslim art forms and introducing contemporary regional and international culture'.[122] As for the Baalbeck Festival, it was revived in 1997 and seems to have met little opposition in spite of the fact that the town is politically controlled by Hezbollah, an ally of the Islamic Republic.

Conclusion

As mentioned at the beginning, Iran's pre-revolutionary elite took pride in the fact that their country had never been formally colonised.[123] Since formal equality with the powerful nations of the West did not prevent these from sometimes treating Iranians (and other non-Westerners) with condescension, gaining genuine equality in the society of nations was always (and to some extent still is) a major *desideratum*. Full membership in the society entailed the establishment of reciprocity and symmetry in interactions with the West, and events such as the Shiraz Festival have to be seen in this light.[124] If Iranians had become familiar with Western art forms since the nineteenth century, why should the West not be familiarised with Iran's creative achievements? If Iranian art was displayed in European museums, why should an Iranian museum not showcase European art?[125] Until the late 1960s this desire to be taken seriously by the West was accompanied in official circles (and among many educated Iranians) by a feeling that, deep-down, Iranians were Europeans,[126] given their 'Aryan' heritage that allegedly distinguished them from their Semitic and Turkic neighbours.[127] By the 1970s, however, the disenchantment with Western cultural influence ('Westoxication') that many anti-regime

122 Queen Noor, *Leap of Faith*, p. 210.

123 A similar phenomenon can be observed in Thailand and Ethiopia.

124 For a different interpretation of this quest for emancipation see Mahlouji, V., 'Perspectives on the Shiraz Arts Festival: A Radical Third World Rewriting', in Daftari, F. and Diba, L.S. (eds.), *Iran Modern*, New York 2013.

125 See Samine Tabatabaei's chapter in this volume.

126 Shakibi, Zh., 'Pahlavism: The Ideologization of Monarchy in Iran', in *Politics, Religion & Ideology*, vol. 14, no. 1, 2013, p. 120.

127 For a discussion of this idea, see Motadel, D., 'Iran and the Aryan myth', in Ansari, Ali M. (ed.), *Perceptions of Iran: History, Myths and Nationalism from Medieval Persia to the Islamic Republic*, London 2014, pp. 119–145.

intellectuals had begun articulating in the 1960s crept into the official discourse of the Pahlavi state.[128] The notion that Iranians could draw on the resources of their 'Eastern spirituality' to resist the negative aspects of Western civilisation, i.e., its 'materialism', came to cohabit with the older notion that, appearances notwithstanding, Iranians and Europeans belonged to the same civilisation. In the minds of a cosmopolitan but nonetheless rooted intellectual like Dariush Shayegan, this made Iran the ideal site for a civilisational dialogue between East and West, an idea that found an institutional home in the Iranian Centre for the Studies of Civilisations of which he became the founding director. In 1977, Shayegan initiated an international symposium on the 'dialogue between civilisations' at which Empress Farah said:

> Between the Orient, which does not always master its recently acquired technical means but which has not yet lost its perception of an ultimate reality beyond appearances, and the Occident, which detains the key of technology but which is worriedly searching for the lost secret of dialog with the invisible, dialog is no longer a matter of entertainment but the condition for survival.[129]

Whether such lofty considerations animated the men and women who chose the programmes of the Shiraz Festival with its theme of 'East meets West' is debatable, however. As Farrokh Ghaffari later recalled, the organisers wanted to counter the view that *honar nazd-e iraniyān ast o bas*, a common saying, more often than not used ironically, that can be translated as 'Art belongs to Iranians alone';[130] in other words, they wanted to expand the Iranians' cultural horizons. And they succeeded: while elite Iranians had been familiar with Western culture since the nineteenth century, it was the Shiraz Festival that gave Iranians the opportunity to discover the cultural achievements of Asia and Africa. At the same time, culturally sophisticated Europeans came to appreciate Iranian music and theatre, hitherto known only to a few anthropologists or musicologists. This is a legacy that has endured, as attested by the programming of, say, the Théâtre de la Ville in Paris.

The men and women who ran the Shiraz Festival belonged to the circle around

---

128 Shakibi, Zh., 'The Rastakhiz Party and Pahlavism: the beginnings of state anti-Westernism in Iran', *British Journal of Middle Eastern Studies*, vol. 45, no. 2, 2018.

129 Quoted in Reichmann, E., 'Un dialogue est-il possible entre civilisations?', *Le Monde*, 11–12 December 1977. My translation.

130 Telephone interview.

Empress Farah, who was given leeway by the shah to shape Iran's cultural life in the 1960s and 1970s. She cultivated a more relaxed and less formal style than her husband, a proclivity that was reflected in the atmosphere that reigned at Shiraz and Persepolis. One anecdote illustrates the contrast between the autocratic formality that surrounded the shah and the empress's style. In August 1971, the Iranian consul-general in Milan attended a performance of Verdi's *Aida* in the Arena of Verona, and thought the production might well be staged at Persepolis. Hence he sent a report to the Iranian Foreign Ministry, suggesting that Empress Farah be informed of the Italian director of the Verona Opera Festival's eagerness to bring his production to Shiraz. The foreign minister, Ardeshir Zahedi, personally brought the matter to the shah's attention, and wrote a letter to Farah's *chef de cabinet* which ends with these words:

> The said report received the honour of passing the august royal threshold. The universally-to-be-obeyed royal orders have received the honour of being issued to the effect that the matter be brought to the august attention of Her Majesty, the Shahbanu of Iran.[131]

Contrast this language and the decision-making structure it expresses with the spirit of the Shiraz Festival, about which Empress Farah wrote in her first autobiography:

> [The festival] takes place in an atmosphere that is infinitely appealing. People go from some very eccentric play to a highly traditional one and afterwards discuss them for hours: some are for Grotowski, others for Peter Brook, all are ready to cross swords in defence of their own conception of theatre… It is a completely relaxed setting, people dress as they like, usually carelessly, unconcerned with elegance.
>
> At the first festival, I wore a long gown and a tiara for the opening evening but, as the days went by, in keeping with the spirit of the occasion, my style of dress became increasingly informal until, in the end, I looked almost like a hippie.[132]

131 *Jashn-e honar-e Shiraz*, pp. 172–173. In the end, Qotbi informed Farah's *chef de cabinet* that the proposal had been received too late to be included in that year's festival. See p. 199.
132 Farah, *My Thousand and One Days*, p. 80.

This is important, for it shows that the shah's regime was not as monolithic as is often assumed.[133]

Bibliography

Afshar, M., 'Festival of Arts Shiraz-Persepolis: Or You better believe in as many as six impossible things before breakfast', available at: <https://www.academia.edu/12568899/Festival_of_Arts_Shiraz-Persepolis_1967–1977_updated_May_2015_>.

Afshar Ghotbi, Sh. in collaboration with Ovanessian, A., 'Shiraz-Persepolis Festival of Arts (1967–1977): Detailed Catalogue of Events', available at: <https://www.academia.edu/35600387/SHIRAZ_ARTS_FESTIVAL_-_Detailed_Catalogue_of_Events>.

Alizadeh, H., interview with, *Adineh* no. 39, Azar 1368/November-December 1979.

Arberry, A. J., *Shiraz: Persian City of Saints and Poets*, Norman, OK 1960.

Attar, F., *The Conference of the Birds*, transl. Darbandi, A. and Davis, D., Harmondsworth 1984.

Bate, J., *Ted Hughes: The Unauthorised Life*, London 2015.

Beeman, W. O., 'A Full Arena: The Development and Meaning of Popular Performance Traditions in Iran', in Bonine, M.E. and Keddie, N.R. (eds.), *Modern Iran: The Dialectics of Continuity and Change*, Albany, NY 1981, pp. 285–305, 342–346.

Berman, M., *All That is Solid Melts Into Air: The Experience of Modernity*, New York 1988.

Bourdieu, P., *Distinction: A Social Critique of the Judgement of Taste*, Cambridge, MA 1984.

Brown, I., *Khomeini's Forgotten Sons: The Story of Iran's Boy Soldiers*, London 1990.

Buchmuller, E., and Koós, A., *Squat Theatre*, New York 1996.

Caron, N., 'La création d'un centre de musique traditionnelle iranienne', in *Studia Iranica*, vol. 2, no. 2, 1973, pp. 257–266.

Chelkowski, P. J. (ed.), *Ta'zieh: Ritual and Drama in Iran*, New York 1979.

133 A similar point is made à propos of economic decision-making by Nasr, V., 'Politics Within the Late-Pahlavi State: The Ministry of Economy and Industrial Policy, 1963–69', in *International Journal of Middle East Studies*, vol. 32, no. 1, 2000, pp. 97–122.

Coca, J. (ed.), *Actes, Congrés Internacional de Teatre a Catalunya 1985*, vol. 1, Barcelona 1989.

Farah, Shahbanou of Iran, *My Thousand and One Days: an Autobiography*, transl. Felice Harcourt, London 1978.

Fleuret, J., 'L'anti-son et lumière: 2300 ans après Alexandre un grec embrase Persépolis, mais dans un grand feu de joie', *Le Nouvel Observateur*, 3 September 1971.

Floor, W., *The History of Theater in Iran*, Washington 2005.

Gaffary, F., Ovanessian, A., and Taghian, L., 'Iran', in *The World Encyclopedia of Contemporary Theatre*, vol. 5: *Asia/Pacific*, London 1998.

Galasso, S., and Valentini, V., *Squat theater 1969–1981*, Soveria Mannelli [Catanzaro] 1998.

Gharavi, M., 'Jashnvareh-ye Tus: jelveh'i digar a azemmat-e melli va kh^{v}ishtangara'i-ye Iraniyan', in *Honar va mardom*, no. 156, 1354/1975, pp. 12–19.

Gluck, R., 'The Shiraz Arts Festival: Western Avant-Garde Arts in 1970s Iran', in *Leonardo*, vol. 40, no. 1, 2007, pp. 20–28.

Godard, C., *Jérôme Savary, l'enfant de la fête*, Monaco 1996.

Gorgani, F., *Vis and Ramin*, transl. Davis, D., New York 2008.

Gorgin, I. (ed.), *Sevvomin jashn-e honar*, Tehran n.d.

Gorgin, I. (ed.), *Ketab-e haftomin jashn-e honar – 1352*, Tehran 1352/1973.

Griffiths, P., *Olivier Messiaen and the Music of Time*, Ithaca, NY 1985.

Halbreich, H., *Olivier Messiaen*, Paris 1980.

Harley, J., *Xenakis: His Life in Music*, New York 2004.

Harper, W. H., 'Olivier Messiaen's Et exspecto resurrectionem mortuorum', PhD thesis, University of Rochester, Eastman School of Music 1986.

Heilpern, J., *Conference of the Birds: The Story of Peter Brook in Africa*, London 1977.

Homayuni, S., *Hoseyniyeh-ye Moshir*, Tehran 2535[1355]/1976.

Jahanbegloo, R., *Iran va moderniteh*, Tehran 1379/2000.

Jashn-e honar-e Shiraz beh revayat-e asnad-e savak, Tehran 1381/2002.

Kapuscinski, G. 'Persian Theatre in the 1960s', PhD thesis, Columbia University 1982.

Karimi-Hakkak, A., 'Censorship', in *Encyclopaedia Iranica*, vol. 5, Costa Mesa 1990, pp. 138–139.

[Khomeini, R.], *Sahifeh-ye nur*, vol. 1, Tehran 1361/1983.

Khorramzadeh Esfahani, S., *Te'atr-e Iran dar gozar-e zaman 3: Kargah-e namayesh az aghaz ta payan* (1348–1357), Tehran 1387/2008.

Khorsand, B. (ed.), *Katalog-e yazdahomin jashn-e honar 2536*, Tehran 1977.

Kurz, M., *Stockhausen: Eine Biographie*, Basel 1988.

Lonchampt, J., 'Les nuits de Chiraz', *Le Monde*, 23 August 1974.

Looseley, D., 'The World Theatre Festival, Nancy, 1963–1988: a Critique and Retrospective', in *New Theatre Quarterly*, vol. 6, no. 22, 1999, pp. 141–153.

Magnani, F., Montecchi, G., Popoli, T., and Romito, M., *Bruno Maderna documenti*, Milan 1985.

Mahlouji, V., 'Perspectives on the Shiraz Arts Festival: A Radical Third World Rewriting', in Daftari, F. and Diba, L.S. (eds.), *Iran Modern*, New York 2013, pp. 87–91.

Maza, S., *Private Lives and Public Affairs: The Causes Célèbres of Prerevolutionary France*, Berkeley 1993.

Mazlish, B., *The Revolutionary Ascetic: Evolution of a Political Type*, New York 1976.

Miklaszewski, K., *Encounters with Tadeusz Kantor*, transl. Hyde, G., London 2002.

Miller, L., *The Center for Preservation and Propagation of Iranian Music*, Salt Lake City 1977.

Motadel, D., 'Iran and the Aryan myth', in Ansari, Ali M. (ed.), *Perceptions of Iran: History, Myths and Nationalism from Medieval Persia to the Islamic Republic*, London 2014, pp. 119–145.

Nasr, V., 'Politics Within the Late-Pahlavi State: The Ministry of Economy and Industrial Policy, 1963–69', in *International Journal of Middle East Studies*, vol. 32, no. 1, 2000, pp. 97–122.

Nettl, B., *The Radif of Persian Music: Studies of Structure and Cultural Context*, Champaign, IL 1987.

'Obscene, obscenity', *The 'Lectric Law Library*, available at: <http://www.lectlaw.com/def2/o002.htm>.

Page, M. E., 'Professional Storytelling in Iran: Transmission and Practice', in *Iranian Studies*, vol. 12, no. 3–4, 1979, 163–194.

Panjomin jashn-e honar-e Shiraz Takht-e Jamshid, Tehran [1972].

Parsons, A., *The Pride and the Fall: Iran 1974–1979*, London 1984.

Phillips, N., 'Iannis Xenakis: Persepolis plus Remixes Vol. 1', available at: <http://www.citypages.com/databank/23/1135/article10685.asp>.

Purmoradian, [Q. -A.] (ed.), *Hashtomin jashn-e honar-e Iran*, Tehran 1353/1994.

Queen Noor, *Leap of Faith: Memoirs of an Unexpected Life*, New York 2003.

Reichmann, E., 'Un dialogue est-il possible entre civilisations?', *Le Monde*, 11–12 December 1977.

Robert, M., *Conversations avec Maurice Béjart*, Tournai 2000.

Sa'di of Shiraz, Sh. M., *The Gulistan (Rose Garden) of Sa'di*, transl. Thackston, W. M., Bethesda 2008.

Salvat, R., '¿Existe un nuevo lenguaje teatral? Consideraciones a propósito de "Orghast I y II", de Ted Hughes y Peter Brook', reprinted in *El teatro de los años 70*, Barcelona 1974.

Sattari, J., *Dar bidowlati-ye farhang: Negahi beh barkhi fa'aliyatha-ye farhangi va honari dar bazpasin salha-ye nezam-e pishin*, Tehran 1379/2000.

Shakibi, Zh., 'Pahlavism: The Ideologization of Monarchy in Iran', in *Politics, Religion & Ideology*, vol. 14, no. 1, 2013, pp. 114–135.

Shakibi, Zh., 'The Rastakhiz Party and Pahlavism: the beginnings of state anti-Westernism in Iran', in *British Journal of Middle Eastern Studies*, vol. 45, no. 2, 2018, pp. 251–268.

Shirley, D., 'Theater', *The Washington Post*, 13 June 1977.

Shyer, L., *Robert Wilson and His Collaborators*, New York 1989.

Smith, A. C. H., *Orghast at Persepolis, an account of the experiment in theatre directed by Peter Brook and written by Ted Hughes*, London 1972.

Soltanpur, S., *Now'i az honar, now'i az andisheh*, S.l. 1350/1972.

Stein, D., 'For the Love of Her People: An Interview with Farah Diba about the Pahlavi Programs for Arts in Iran', in Scheiwiller, S.G. (ed.), *Performing the Iranian State: Visual Culture and Representations of Iranian Identity*, London 2013, pp. 75–82.

Tohme, A., 'Le Festival de Baalbek au cerrefour des paradoxes libanais d'avant guerre', in Sader H., Scheffler, Th., and Neuwirth A. (eds.), *Baalbek: Image and Monument 1898–1998*, Stuttgart 1998, pp. 221–234.

Wallon, E., 'Le festival international: Un système relationnel', in Dulphy, A., Frank, R., Matard-Bonucci, M. -A., and Ory, P. (eds.), *Les relations culturelles internationales au XXe siècle: De la diplomatie culturelle à l'acculturation*, Brussels 2010, pp. 307–326.

Ward, M., *Gilbert Keith Chesterton*, Harmondsworth 1958.

Weber, M. *Economy and Society*, vol. 1, Berkeley 1978

Zahedi, T., *Beh rahbari-ye Morteza Hannaneh*, Tehran 1369/1990.

Zohari, I., *Yadha va budha*, Spånga 1999.

6

Nation Branding: The Prospect of Collecting Modern and Contemporary Art in Pahlavi Iran

Samine Tabatabaei[1]

In the early 1970s, Kamran Diba, artist, architect, cousin to Empress Farah, and future director of the Tehran Museum of Contemporary Art (TMoCA), set out to build a world-class collection of modern and contemporary Iranian art and a national museum to house it. The result was the TMoCA, which was inaugurated in October 1977. Within this innovative structure, which was a blend of Western and Persian design elements, works by European, American and Iranian modern and contemporary artists were showcased. This chapter explores the significance of this project from architectural, cultural, economic and political vantage points. I situate the building and its collections – which were heavily funded by oil revenues – within the political economy of Iran in the 1970s, and demonstrate how the TMoCA functioned as an anchor for the formation of a cosmopolitan national memory, and as an instrument of cultural diplomacy during the final decade of the Pahlavi dynasty. First, I contextualise the conditions in Iran that helped finance this project. Second, I compare the museum with similar structures in Europe and North America, shedding light on the otherwise hidden reciprocities between the art and socio-politics of Iran and the Western world. Subsequently, I explore the cultural and political significance for Iran of owning a permanent collection

1 A sincere thanks goes to Professors Roham Alvandi, Houchang Chehabi, Cyrus Schayegh and Laurie Milner for offering indispensable suggestions for improving this chapter.

that included art from Iran and the West coevally, and consider how the embrace of current trends in art functioned in the cultural diplomacy of late Pahlavi Iran. Finally, by drawing a number of parallels between the TMoCA and other prominent international museums, I suggest alternative possible roles the TMoCA might have played in the global contemporary art scene were it not for the political landslide caused by events of the 1979 revolution. Rather than merely following dominant trends in the imaginary centres of art such as New York, Diba I argue, shaped a cultural enterprise in Tehran that promoted the deterritorialisation of regional attitudes toward art and culture and the growth of Iranian cultural agency. At a time when the Cold War dominated and polarised global geopolitics, Diba offered a model of cosmopolitan coevalness.

The Design of the TMoCA

The Tehran Museum of Contemporary Art, located on North Kargar Street in the eastern corner of Laleh Park, is eclectic in its design. Built mainly of concrete – the ultimate modernist material – it takes its form from the *bādgir*, or wind towers which comprise vernacular buildings whose earthly materials, curving, organic forms, and turreted rooftops contrast with the cold materials and crisp, vertical lines associated with modernist architecture. In the TMoCA, traditional Iranian architectural elements are adapted through modern techniques and know-how. A prominent element of the museum is the rotunda, which opens onto a spiral ramp that leads visitors down and into the collections. In a reversal of the iconic upward spiral of Frank Lloyd Wright's design for the Guggenheim Museum in New York, which had opened nineteen years earlier in 1959, the curving ramp of the TMoCA is not visible from the exterior of the building, and leads downward to the vault that stores the collection, rather than upward toward the sky. The descending ramp branches off to galleries at different levels; larger gallery spaces connect through an outer corridor with windows and openings onto the park. Nine galleries offering 2,500 meters of exhibition space are housed within the 8,500-square metre complex.

When Diba submitted his plan to Empress Farah in the early 1970s, the scale and purpose of the museum corresponded with his aim of creating a local museum to house works by Iranian artists.[2] The plan he proposed departed from

2 While Diba is often solely credited for the design of the building, Nader Ardalan, another prominent architect, was also involved. See McFadden, S., 'The Museum and the Revolution', in *Art in America*, October 1981, p. 10.

the museum-as-temple and gallery-as-white cube approaches that predominated museum design in the West. Guggenheim director, Hilla von Rebay, had famously asked Wright to design the Guggenheim as a 'temple of the spirit'.[3] Such an analogy of museum and temple was not exceptional in the West: exhibition spaces and temples were often aligned in museological discourse. On the other hand, the term 'white cube' was coined by critic Brian O'Doherty for the stark, unadorned, whitewashed walls and pretense to neutrality of modern and contemporary art galleries.[4] These spaces, O'Doherty observed, were designed to seclude the viewer from the hustle and bustle of everyday life and provide a space of solitude for the quasi-religious contemplation of cultural objects. The TMoCA confers an entirely different experience. In a 2013 interview, Diba explained: 'there is a small window onto adjoining sidewalks making the fortress-like building visually accessible to the outside world. The idea was to radiate strength, but never suggest a temple.'[5] Visiting the TMoCA, with its alcoves, unexpected windows, and openings to closed off spaces, offers an experience that is one of surprise and polysensorial immersion – quite unlike that of a modernist art museum.

The Collection

During the early Pahlavi period (1925–1941), under the secularising leadership of Reza Shah Pahlavi, debates about the modern nation state were infused with references to Iran's deep past that were shored up by findings from archaeological projects and excavations at historical sites. The abundance of archaeological evidence of Iran's past and its usefulness in affirming a national identity had already prompted the establishment of the National Museum of Iran in Tehran in 1910, not long after the Constitutional Revolution of 1906.[6] In this period, Persian art of the imperial past was increasingly collected and canonised by Western museums, largely through the efforts of cultural mediators such as the Americans Phyllis Ackerman and Arthur Upham Pope.[7] In 1925 Pope was invited by the Society for National Heritage to give

3 *The Guggenheim: Frank Lloyd Wright and the Making of the Modern Museum*, New York 2009, pp. 217–218.
4 O'Doherty, B., *Inside the White Cube*, Santa Monica 1986, p. 8.
5 Diba, K., and Azimi, N., 'Interview with Kamran Diba', in Diba, L., and Daftari, F. (eds.), *Iran Modern*, New York 2013, p. 83.
6 Abdi, K., 'Nationalism, Politics, and the Development of Archaeology in Iran', in *American Journal of Archaeology*, vol. 105, no. 1, 2001, p. 54.
7 See Rizvi, K., 'Art History and the Nation: Arthur Upham Pope and the Discourse on "Persian Art" in the Early Twentieth Century', in *Muqarnas: An Annual on the Visual Culture of the Islamic World*, vol. 24, 2007, pp. 45–65.

a presentation to the Ministry of Culture on the past and future of the 'art of Iran'.[8] Pope's lecture reportedly inspired Reza Shah, who enjoyed a sense of patriotism, to further his support for the revival of Iran's glorious past through art.[9]

The artistic heritage of Iran was frequently deployed in nationalist discourse to authenticate the triangulation of 'empire, the monarchy and Aryanism'.[10] Buttressed by this discourse and the growing interest in the art and culture of Iran's past, the Pahlavi state established a panoply of museums preserving and displaying historical objects during the reign of Mohammad Reza Shah Pahlavi (r. 1941–79). According to Talinn Grigor, the following museum projects had been undertaken by 1977: Archaeological Museum, Ethnographic Museum, Shahyad-e Aryamehr Museum, Qajar Golestan Palace Museum, Museum of Decorative Arts, Tehran Carpet Museum, Museum of Contemporary Art, Safavid Chehel Sotun Palace Museum in Isfahan, Pars Museum in Shiraz, Nader Shah Mausoleum-Museum in Mashhad, Ibn Sina Museum in Hamadan, Ferdowsi Museum in Tus, and Haft Tappeh Museum in Susa.[11]

The TMoCA, the first institution in Iran devoted to contemporary art, was formed in this period. Prior to the opening of the TMoCA, interdisciplinary, avant-garde European art was displayed at the Shiraz Art Festival, held annually from 1967–1977.[12] In 1965, Diba returned to Iran from the United States, where he had earned a degree in architecture, convinced that the country needed a museum that exhibited and promoted the works of living artists. Newspaper articles from the period show that a growing number of Iranian artists and critics were expressing similar ideas. For instance, Karim Emami, a veteran journalist and translator for *Kayhan International*, called for the creation of a museum of modern art in Tehran as a means for promoting innovative art: 'The Tehran Museum of Modern Art [...] would help in the popularization of the less conventional art forms.'[13] When contemporary artists and commentators such as Emami called for a museum of modern art, they were promoting a version of Iranian culture that was dialectically

8 Rizvi, K., 'Art History and the Nation', p. 47.
9 Abdi, K., 'Nationalism, Politics, and the Development of Archaeology in Iran', p. 105.
10 Shakibi, Z., 'Pahlavism: The Ideologization of Monarchy in Iran', in *Politics, Religion & Ideology*, vol. 14, no. 1, 2013, p. 134.
11 Grigor, T., *Cultivating Modernities: The Society for National Heritage, Political Propaganda, and Public Architecture in Twentieth-Century Iran*, Cambridge 2005, pp. 381–382.
12 See Mahlouji, V., 'Perspectives on the Shiraz Arts Festival', in Daftari, F. and Diba, L.S. (eds.), *Iran Modern*, New York 2013, pp. 87–91.
13 Emami, K., *Karim Emami on Modern Iranian Culture, Literature & Art*, compiled by Yavari, H., and Emami, G., New York 2014, p. 196.

opposed to the retrogressive view of the history of Iran and the primordial over-Persianisation of national identity offered and guarded by the historically-focused museums that had been established by the state.[14]

With the establishment of the TMoCA, the formation of a permanent collection of modern and contemporary art became Diba's goal.[15] With Empress Farah's support, he was able to acquire special funding to construct the museum and to build the collection (valued at $3 billion in 2015).[16]

The permanent collection showcased Iran's cultural capital and projected an image of the country as open to and engaged with the Western world. In line with museums of modern art in the West, it focused on works from 1870 to 1980, including Impressionist, Cubist, Expressionist, Abstract Expressionist, Pop and Minimalist art from Europe and North America. Among the modern art acquisitions were works by Édouard Manet, Paul Cézanne, Henri de Toulouse-Lautrec, Georges Braque, Pablo Picasso, Henry Moore, Wassily Kandinsky, Fernand Léger, René Magritte, Alexander Calder and Alberto Giacometti. American works included Donald Judd's serial sculpture, *Untitled* (1965), Jackson Pollock's *Mural on Indian Red Ground* (1950), widely considered to be a masterpiece of twentieth-century art, Willem de Kooning's *Woman III* (1953), and portraits of Mick Jagger, Marilyn Monroe, Chairman Mao, and Empress Farah by Andy Warhol.[17] English artist Francis Bacon's 1968 triptych, *Two Figures Lying on a Bed with Attendants*, featured naked men. In addition to paintings and sculptures, a vast collection of prints was amassed. Contemporary Iranian artists represented in the TMoCA's

---

14 Maryam Ekhtiar sees the interstices of modern art after the death of Kamal al-Molk and with it the symbolic end to academic painting. She maintains, 'The 1949 opening of the Apadana gallery in Tehran, and the emergence of artists like Marcos Grigorian (born 1925) in the 1950s, signaled a commitment to the creation of a form of modern art grounded in Iran.' See Ekhtiar, M., and Sardar, M., 'Modern and Contemporary Art in Iran', in *Heilbrunn Timeline of Art History*, New York 2004, available at: <http://www.metmuseum.org/toah/hd/ciran/hd_ciran.htm>.

15 In my interview with Diba in January 2016, he mentioned several times that the TMoCA was the first museum of contemporary art in the world, and its significance should not be confined within the Middle East.

16 Mohammed, A., 'Iran and the Art of Détente', *Financial Times*, December 4, 2015.

17 In 1994, the De Kooning was exchanged with leaves from a *Shahnameh* of Shah Tahmasp or better known in the market as the Houghton *Shahnameh*. This controversial exchange raises some concern among modern and contemporary art historians as to what extent the TMoCA's post-revolutionary administration are aware of the characteristics of the collection. Admittedly, the tradeoff of the *Shahnameh*, a notable artistic production of the Safavid Empire from the sixteenth century, with De Kooning's *Women III* is difficult to justify. For more details on the tradeoff see Kaylan, M., 'Clandestine Trade', *Wall Street Journal*, December 8, 2011.

collection included Mohammad Ehsai, Faramarz Pilaram, Hosseyn Zenderudi, Mansur Qandriz, Parviz Tanavoli and Sadeq Tabrizi. Both Western and Iranian art were systematically collected and promoted, a practice that, had it continued, might have helped to establish coevalness between the two traditions.[18] Until 1979, the museum staged contemporaneity on a visual register through the production of exhibitions drawn from the permanent collection. An examination of the literature, activities and oral histories of the museum and its founders reveals that the purpose of the museum was to:

- Research, acquire, display and preserve works of art for the improvement of artistic discernment in society;
- Connect to and network with other museums of the world;
- Consistently produce international exhibitions of contemporary art;
- Lend international recognition to the contemporary art of Iran;
- Research contemporary Iranian art and its development in different parts of the world in a syncretic manner;
- Educate the Iranian populace about internationally recognised cutting edge art, through different divisions and activities of the museum such as the library, cinema, seminars, and exhibition tours.

Naming and Branding

The name of a museum defines and delimits its activities, and comes to serve as its brand. On several occasions Diba spoke of his choice of the word *contemporary* for the name of the museum, a choice that signalled a rejection of the Western order of the imagery of the Orient as, to borrow from Timothy Mitchell, 'marked by a series of fundamental absences (of movement, reason, order, meaning and so on)'.[19] *Contemporary* implies being on top of new trends, always active, dynamic and moving; a sharp contrast to the clichés of passivity, stagnancy, even regression, that pervade the Western Orientalist imaginary. Through its branding, the museum declared itself an active player in the international art scene, one that did not recognise the passive and regressive positions mapped out for the Orient in Western discourse.

18 While many museums and collections around the world own art of different cultural heritages, in terms of display and exhibition, non-Western artworks are overshadowed by the Western art.

19 Mitchel, T., 'Orientalism and the Exhibitionary Order', in Preziosi, D. (ed.), *The Art of Art History*, Oxford 1998/2009, p. 409.

The first use of the word *contemporary* in the name of an art institute occurred in 1947 with the founding of the Institute of Contemporary Arts (ICA) in London. With no permanent collection, the ICA focused on temporary exhibitions. The following year, the Boston Museum of Modern Art was renamed the Institute of Contemporary Art.[20] In 1954, the City Gallery of Contemporary Art was founded in Zagreb (it would later become the Museum of Contemporary Art).[21] Over the course of the 1960s, the term *contemporary* began to be applied to institutes in museological discourse. Peter Osborne explains:

> [It was] not until the 1960s that the term 'contemporary' became more widely used, and even then it was exceptional. Museu de contemporanea da Universidade de São Paulo (1963), Musée d'art Contemporain de Montréal (1964) and the Museum of Contemporary Art, Chicago (1967) are early instances, by which time the contemporary had been around long enough to become an object of museological attention.[22]

In these various institutes, *contemporary* is used to denote art of the present rather than as a term of periodisation. Diba's use of the term for the TMoCA suggests that he perceived the museum, like its Western counterparts, as standing on the brink of developments in modern art.[23] In the absence of a native discourse about periodisation, his use of contemporary was anachronistic: rather than following developments in art, as is the usual practice for museums, it preceded developments in Iranian art. By aligning the name of the museum to the terminology used in international museums of contemporary art, Diba signalled his ambition to introduce the discourse of contemporary art to Iran. Diba explains:

> [T]he idea was to have a parallel representation, and contemporary international art might invigorate Iranian arts. In a way, this museum would give the Iranian cultural establishment confidence. [...] This confidence and exposure no doubt played a role in paving the way for today's Iranian art.[24]

---

20 Osborne, P., *Anywhere or Not at All*, London 2013, p. 219.
21 Osborne, P., *Anywhere*, p. 397.
22 Osborne, P., *Anywhere*, p. 219.
23 In current art historical usage, the term *contemporary* designates a period that begins after WWII and continues to today; it is a classification anchored in a Western view of history that does not accommodate different historical frameworks.
24 Diba, K., and Azimi, N., 'Interview with Kamran Diba', p. 83.

By contemporary Diba meant post-WWII art.[25] He did not segregate Iranian artists from their counterparts in the West and applied the same periodisation to their work.[26] Diba emphasised that the main motivation for establishing the museum was to claim agency in contemporary art.[27] By refusing to abide by the distinction between Western and non-Western art that characterised museums in the West, Diba refused to participate in the Western ordering of the imagery world, choosing instead to tamper with the hierarchies inherent in the visual discourses of 'colonial mastery'.[28] The building of the TMoCA was coincident with the widespread emergence of a critique of cultural hegemony. During the 1960s and 1970s, the foundations of modern art were challenged by feminists, post-colonialist critics, and artists of colour. A postmodern sensibility and agentive contemporary art discourse emerged. The TMoCA heralded the institutional embodiment of this critique in the Middle East in a rebellion against the hegemony of imaginary centres of art and culture.[29]

Iranian freelance curator Tirdad Zolghadr points out that while both the TMoCA and the Centre Pompidou in Paris, which was also inaugurated in 1977, are located in the heart of their country's capitals and embody national aspirations, they differed greatly in their architectural signification and programming.[30] In the illegibility of the internal structure from the exterior, the descending staircase, and the vernacular references of the architecture, as well as in the disciplinary, non-polemical programming, Zolghadr claims, the TMoCA was a striking contrast to 'the multidisciplinary temperament, the bare-bones style – meant to promote an atmosphere of "transparency" – and the polemical tenor of the programming' of the Centre Pompidou.[31] In a period when nationalist ambitions and notions of exceptionalism were often channelled through museums

25 Diba in an interview with the author, 2016.

26 Art Historian Fereshteh Daftari, a former assistant curator at the MOMA, particularly considers the art scene before the revolution with modern nomenclature rather than contemporary. See Daftari, F., 'Redefining Modernism', in *Iran Modern*, New York 2013.

27 Diba, K., and Azimi, N., 'Interview with Kamran Diba', p. 81–82.

28 Mitchel, T., 'Orientalism and the Exhibitionary Order', p. 409.

29 In an interview with the BBC, Diba described his politics in line with the left, although he was comfortably placed in the royal family; See Kamran Diba in an interview with BBC Persian, *be 'ebarat-e digar*, March 2014.

30 To underscore the national importance of the TMoCA, Diba exhibited his own experimental work at other sites, such as *Rasht 29*, a club and a project space where international artists and luminaries would gather. This space was a precedent for many contemporary alternatives and project spaces in Tehran.

31 Zolghadr, T. 'The Recognizable Landscape: Notes on the Museum of Contemporary Art in Tehran', presented at CIMAM, December 16, 2012.

and expressed in their architecture, the TMoCA, driven by a sense of social and political necessity, offered a provocative rethinking of the relationship of contemporary art to history.

For globalist Iranian elites, an association with avant-garde art, with its intellectualism, distance from traditional cultures, and frequent self-referentiality, was a marker of cultural capital. These elites preferred non-representational art that did not necessarily engage with socio-political day-to-day issues. Kamran Diba and Empress Farah shared this view of art. In the decade leading to the revolution, a different approach to contemporary art in Iran, one that set out to depict and grapple directly with politics, was evident in the work of students from University of Tehran who conflated their political views with their practice of art.

The permanent collection embodies the implicit and explicit biases of the Pahlavi cultural elite and reflects the Pahlavi state's policies on the eve of the Revolution. Diba wanted the museum to project an image of sophisticated taste to the world, and to claim agency for Iran in art and culture. A graduate of an American university, jetsetter, and self-styled cultural mediator between Iran and the United States, Diba had his finger on the pulse of the international art scene and shared in the international promotion of contemporary American art in the 1960s and 1970s. Historian William Shawcross has explained: 'Although [the Empress] was determined to preserve Iran's past, her contemporary tastes were often too avant-garde, too cosmopolitan, for most of her countrymen.'[32] The promotion of an aesthetic autonomy by the Empress and her cousin in visual art, music and theatre in the cultural sphere was not welcomed by the shah's siblings and relatives.[33] In the early 1970s, Diba had to contend with competing interests of Mehrdad Pahlbod, the minister of art and culture and the shah's brother-in-law, who supported the establishment of a symphony orchestra, rather than a contemporary art museum.[34] Were it not for the Empress's support, special attention and financing, the TMoCA project would not have been realised.

32 Shawcross, W., *The Shah's Last Ride: Fate of an Ally*, New York 1988, pp. 58–72.
33 The prominent strand of criticism in the 1950s and 1960s was put forward by Clement Greenberg, American critic who advocated the sovereignty of art from other realms of culture, relying purely on it visually. Relying on Gotthold Ephraim Lessing's (1729–81) *Laokoon* (1766), Greenberg set the criteria of late modernist visual art, which was medium-specificity and self-referentiality, that is the work of art does not require to allude to something outside of its medium or to convey a narrative.
34 My thanks to Houchang Chehabi for drawing to my attention to the tension in cultural politics that was epitomised among the royal family.

Allegations of Pro-Americanism and Activities of Taste Making

The TMoCA intervened in the Euro-American order and reversed the Western construction of the non-Western by portraying the Occident from the Orient's point of view. This, in Diba's view, gave 'confidence' to Iranian artists to take part in what was a predominantly Western ordering, and to claim agency in the realm where they had been passive. Such strategies were clearly not conveyed to the stakeholders of the museum; tensions between official aspirations for national distinction and the collective values of the nation were mounting, and crystalised in the pre-revolutionary TMoCA.

Critics who were not aware of discipline-specific developments in the domain of art in the West wanted the museum to project authenticity in the cultural sphere in response to what came to be known as the 'onslaught of cultures' *(hojum-e farhanghā)* from foreign countries.[35] The target of this criticism was the concept of *gharbzadegi*, the 'indiscriminate borrowing from the West', or 'Westoxication' – a state of fascination with the presumably superior culture of the West to the point of losing sight of one's own cultural interstices. According to Negin Navabi, 'by the mid-1970s, the concept of authentic culture had become central to the national cultural policy'.[36] Cultural authenticity could be remediated through the maintenance and promotion of traditional art and cultural heritage, which was under the purview of the Society for National Heritage.[37]

The TMoCA was able to maintain a degree of independence from the state's emphasis on tradition and heritage because of financial and political support from the empress's foundation. Initially, in the shadow of the empress, Diba made lavish purchases for the TMoCA's collection; heated public debates on the expenditures ensued. Disagreements about the choice of artistic traditions which should be developed plagued Diba's relationship with the museum's board of directors.[38]

---

35 The visual art community's lexicon was rather incompatible with their literary counterparts. 'While most of the painters in the 1960s and 1970s were dealing with the aesthetic aspects of modern art' in order 'to consider socio-political criticism in their work, their literary peers underestimated the visual qualities of art works'. The visual artists who were dealing with intrinsic values of visuality as per late modern developments of abstraction were dually distanced from a society that was under the influence of Kamal al-Molk, founder of the academic style in Iran, and his followers, in addition to literary counterparts who sought to channel their political mission in their writings. See Moussavi-Aghdam, C., 'Art History, "National Art" and Iranian Intellectuals in the 1960s', in *British Journal of Middle Eastern Studies*, vol. 41, no. 1, 2014, p. 144.

36 Nabavi, N., 'The Discourse of "Authentic Culture" in Iran in the 1960s and 1970s', in *Intellectual Trends in Twentieth Century*, Orlando 2003, p. 96.

37 Grigor, T., *Cultivating Modernities.*

38 Hobbs, R., 'Museum Under Siege', in *Art in America*, October 1981, pp. 17–25.

Diba was quite perceptive about the latest trends in art and justified his purchases as follows:

> [T]here weren't many people who realised that the artistic pendulum had swung from Europe to America. I felt strongly about bringing American art into contact with Iran, so I became a kind of default ambassador. Many individuals involved in the cultural field back then had a traditional Beaux-Arts-style education and weren't exposed to what was happening in America or elsewhere. … I felt strongly about bringing American art into contact with both art scenes.[39]

According to art historian Layla Diba, the museum complied with the International Council of Museums (ICOM) and the United Nations Educational, Scientific, and Cultural Organization (UNESCO) regulations in its administration and policies,[40] indicating that the museum administrators were keen to project a modern, progressive image in line with international standards. Western art historians, connoisseurs and curators were brought in as consultants or appointed to positions in the museum: David Galloway was the first curator, and Donna Stein frequently gave advice to the Shahbanu Farah Cultural Foundation.[41] Other influential curators were also approached, such as Harald Szeemann, who declined because of other engagements.[42]

French art critic Pierre Restany called the museum the 'jockey club of local culture',[43] a comment that implied developing countries should focus on their own native culture and tradition. This view stemmed from the idea that developing countries were not able to consume and digest high culture. Some leftist groups in Iran considered Western cultural products to be an accoutrement of cultural imperialism and an encroachment on the cultural sovereignty of Third World countries. In the context of movements toward decolonisation, many Iranian artists and intellectuals refuted their supposed marginality in relation to such centres of culture

39 Diba, K. and Azimi, N., 'Interview with Kamran Diba', p. 82.

40 Diba, L., 'The Formation of Modern Iranian art', in *Iran Modern*, p. 55.

41 Stein, D., 'For the Love of Her People: An Interview with Farah Diba about the Pahlavi Programs for the Arts in Iran', in Scheiwiller, S. G. (ed.), *Performing Iranian State*, Anthem, London, New York 2013, p. 75.

42 Daneshvar, R., *Baghi miyan-e do khiyaban*, Paris 2010, p. 131. Harald Szeemann was among the very first globetrotting curators who shaped the profession of curating beyond the institutional museum bastions as it is perceived within the contemporary cognisance today.

43 Restany, P., 'DAZ Planners: Museo Imperiale', in *Domus*, vol. 579, February 1978, p.14.

and art as New York and Paris. Writing about the American situation in the 1970s, art historian Terry Smith offers a relevant discussion of provincialism about the relations between peripheries and centres:

> Provincialism appears primarily as an attitude of subservience to a hierarchy of externally imposed cultural values. It is not simply the product of a colonialist history; nor is it merely a function of geographic location. Most New York artists, critics, collectors, dealers, and gallery-goers are provincialist in their outlook, attitudes, and positions within the system. Members of artworlds outside of New York – on every continent, including North America – are likewise provincial, although in different ways. The projection of the New York artworld as the metropolitan center for art by every other artworld is symptomatic of the provincialism of each of them.[44]

Resistance to being perceived as provincial or subservient to the United States in the cultural domain was pervasive in the popular Iranian intellectual discourse of the late 1970s. One strand of criticism of the TMoCA was that it showed a pro-American bias in its purchases; American architect and author, John Morris Dixon, called the museum an American 'transplant'.[45] Charges of lack of transparency tarnished the TMoCA's reputation. American art historian and curator Robert Hobbs, who was working at the site during the months leading up to the 1979 revolution and sought to become Diba's successor as chief curator, referenced rumours about fuzzy transactions and missing inventory. Hobbs speculated that documents related to the purchase of De Kooning's *Woman III* went missing because employees of the Empress's bureau did not want other workers to know how much had been spent on this particular American piece.[46] In an editorial about the reopening of the TMoCA titled, 'The Museum of Contemporary Art is freed from American Monopoly',[47] the first post-revolutionary director of the museum,

44 Smith, T., 'The Provincialism Problem', in *Artforum*, vol. 12, no. 1, September 1974, p. 54.
45 Dixon, J. M., 'Cultural Transplant, Cultural Hybrid', in *Progressive Architecture*, May 1978, p. 68.
46 Hobbs, R., 'Museum Under Siege', p. 21. In an interview I conducted with Diba in 2016, he maintained that he kept all the paperwork related to his purchases.
47 'Muzeh-ye honarha-ye mo'aser az enhesar-e Emrika kharej shod', *Keyhan*, 24 Aban 1358, 15 November 1979.

Masʿud Shafiʿi-Monfared, was quoted as saying: 'we hope the museum will not regurgitate Western trash anymore.'[48]

By bringing Western art to Iran rather than promoting the export of archaeological and colonial artefacts from Iran to the West, Diba inverted the state-funded traffic of art objects of the early twentieth century. The National Iranian Oil Company provided the financing to make this happen.[49] Undoubtedly, if national oil revenues had not been directed to the TMoCA, the collection would not have been built on the same scale. This campaign of bringing cultural goods from the West to the museum expressed an aspiration among Iranian elites for cultural coevalness with the West. The selective traditions of art and the history represented by the collection underpin the importance of the collection in nation branding.

Diba acknowledged that New York's Museum of Modern Art (MOMA) was an initial inspiration for TMoCA.[50] Regarded as the 'paradigmatic Modernist museum', the institutional importance of the MOMA went far beyond the United States.[51] In addition to being an important tastemaker in the United States, MOMA also played a role in American foreign policy. Supported by the politically connected and active Rockefeller family[52] (Nelson Rockefeller was president of MOMA from 1939–40 and then again in 1946), MOMA functioned as one of the spheres through which American politics were enacted within public domains at home and abroad. During the Cold War, MOMA collected and popularised Abstract Expressionist art through exhibitions and claims of greatness. By pronouncing, sanctioning and promoting Saqqa-khaneh – a home-grown modern art movement that called for an aesthetic language rooted in Iranian identity – as a national modern style, the TMoCA played a similar role in shaping Iran's global cultural profile. Saqqa-khaneh fused formal features of Islamic, Persian and folk culture, while being devoid of any religious or traditional ethos. For the inauguration of the museum in 1977, an entire gallery was devoted to the works of Saqqa-khaneh artists. The exhibition, curated by Nahid Mahdavi, was accompanied by an impressive catalogue with an introduction by Diba and essays by Iranian literary

---

48 Abrahamian, E., *Iran between Two Revolutions*, Princeton 1982, p. 425. My thanks to Roham Alvandi for drawing to my attention the relevance of the discourse of *gharbzadegi* to the reception of TMoCA's activities.

49 McFadden, S., 'The Museum and the Revolution', p. 14.

50 Diba, K., and Azimi, N., 'Interview with Kamran Diba'.

51 Franscina, F. 'Issues and Debates: the Late 1960s as a Representative Moment', in Harris, J., et al (eds.), *Modernism in Dispute: Art Since the Forties*, New Haven 1993, p. 81.

52 Cockroft, E., 'Abstract Expressionism, Weapon of the Cold War', in *Artforum*, June 1974, p. 83.

critic Karim Emami and American author Peter Lamborn Wilson. Diba proposed that an idiosyncratic convergence existed between the ethos of Saqqa-khaneh and Western Pop artists. Saqqa-khaneh, he claimed, was 'Spiritual Pop Art' in that, like Pop Art, it looked 'at the symbols and tools of a mass consumer society as a relevant and influencing cultural force'.[53] Diba's cosmopolitan perspective led him to see Iranian art through a global, rather than local, lens.

The accusation that the TMoCA was pro-American ignored the nature of the American works that it acquired. Many of the American artists in the collection were critical of American values, something that the local critics of the TMoCA neglected to consider.[54] Jasper Johns, James Rosenquist, Robert Rauschenberg, and Andy Warhol, for example, critiqued the values of American society through their work, even as it was showcased for profit and spectacle by the same system that they exposed.

The Revolution and its Aftermath

When the forces of popular revolution swept Iran in 1978 and toppled the shah the following year, the TMoCA and its collection fell into the hands of the new revolutionary government. The mission of the museum was radically altered and its international activity plummeted. The first exhibition mounted after the transfer of authority signalled this change: it showcased works from 1920–40 by followers of Kamal al-Molk in addition to works with revolutionary themes.[55] Diba had created a museum with international aspirations, but he was unable to convince the Iranian masses of its relevance during the two short years the TMoCA existed before the revolution.

The post-revolutionary director of the TMoCA, Masʿud Shafiʿi-Monfared, declared that the museum would serve the revolution's goals in advancing the people's knowledge and would not promote American values.[56] Due to Iran's international isolation following the Tehran hostage crisis, the TMoCA lost contact

53 Kamran Diba as quoted in Balaghi, S., 'Iranian Visual Arts in "The Century of Machinery, Speed, and the Atom": Rethinking Modernity', in Balaghi, S. and Gumpert, L. (eds.), *Picturing Iran: Art, Society and Revolution*, London 2003, p. 27.

54 Andy Warhol and some other artists were seeing the enterprise merely as clients according to Bob Colacello who travelled with Warhol to Iran in 1976. See *Interview: What it Was Like to Travel Iran with Andy Warhol in 1976 as Clients According to Bob Colacello 2013*, Asia Society, available at: <http://asiasociety.org/blog/asia/interviewwhatitwastraveliranandywarhol1976>.

55 'Muzehye honarha-ye mo'aser az enhesar-e Emrika kharej shod'.

56 Ibid.

with its Western counterparts.[57] The Islamic Republic of Iran was in dispute with several Western museums about the return of loaned objects to Iran. In several cases, Western galleries delayed returning artworks because of the unstable situation in Iran. One issue was the insurance of artworks. The TMoCA's collection gathered dust and was mostly forgotten.

The political and social conditions in Iran after the revolution forced many to leave the country, including Diba, who relocated to Paris. The revolutionary transformation of Iran led to the concealment of the collection from public view and the exclusion of Iran from the global art scene. The TMoCA drifted into such obscurity that it was not mentioned by art historians Hans Belting and Claire Bishop and philosopher Peter Osborne in their discussions about museums of contemporary art around the world.[58] Iran's modern and contemporary art scenes, along with its infrastructures, notably the TMoCA, were overshadowed by the tumultuous political events of the Iranian Revolution.

A museum's permanent collection is seen by some as a living entity that needs to be maintained and curated. The original meaning of 'to curate' is to attend to something. Recently it has been understood as a synonym for the verbs to improve and, most importantly, to build upon. When TMoCA ceased collecting new works, it lost its contemporary brand. Stories of mismanagement and underuse tarnished its reputation. No longer tied to the spirit of modern and contemporary art, the museum was used for a long time as a simple exhibition space for the display of undistinguished art.

Were it not for the turbulent geopolitics of Iran, it might well have become the sole country in the Middle East with a steady and sustainable art scene and a cultural infrastructure fostered by national revenues. If its importance as a decentralising force within the thickened contemporary era had been recognised and fostered, TMoCA would now be able to play a role in healing the relationship between Iran and the West in terms of taste and intellect. In the long run, the museum's collection would have anchored education in contemporary art of both the West and Iran, and the formation of collective taste. The post-revolutionary period, with its tortuous trajectory, has proven that the museum and its permanent collection were built on solid foundations. While TMoCA stopped collecting

57 At the time of revolution there were four works of TMoCA in loan to American institutes. See McFadden, 'The Museum and the Revolution', p. 14.

58 See Belting, H., Buddensieg, A., and Araujo, E. (eds.), *The Global Art World: Audiences, Markets, and Museums*, Osfildern 2009; Bishop, C., *Radical Museology, or, What's 'Contemporary' in Museums of Contemporary Art?*, Cologne 2013; and Osborne, P., *Nowhere or Not at All: Philosophy of Contemporary Art*, London 2013.

forward, after the revolution, there have been some occasional notable exhibitions by Gerhard Richter, Mona Hatoum, Shirin Neshat, Siah Armajani in addition to group exhibitions by Arab and Iranian artists. The gap between the museum's avant-garde past and its stiflingly underused present was crystalised in the failed plan to loan some parts of the permanent collection that had not been seen outside of Iran for decades to Germany in 2016.[59] In the aftermath of the cancellation very few justifications were presented to the public. This episode demonstrates that, aside from its valuable collection, the museum is poorly administered and curated and not on par with the current highly professionalised museum administration of the international art world.

Bibliography

Abdi, K., 'Nationalism, Politics, and the Development of Archaeology in Iran', in *American Journal of Archaeology*, vol. 105, no. 1, 2001.

Abrahamian, E., *Iran between Two Revolutions*, New Jersey 1982.

Balaghi, S., and Gumpert, L., *Picturing Iran: Art, Society and Revolution*, London; New York 2003.

Belting, H., Buddensieg, A., and Araujo, E. (eds.), *The Global Art World: Audiences, Markets, and Museums*, Osfildern 2009.

Bishop, C., *Radical Museology, or, What's 'Contemporary' in Museums of Contemporary Art?*, Cologne 2013.

Cockroft, E., 'Abstract Expressionism, Weapon of the Cold War', in *Artforum*, June 1974.

Daneshvar, R., *Baghi miyan do khiyaban*, Paris 2010.

Diba, L., and Daftari, F. (eds.), *Iran Modern*, New Haven 2013.

Diba, K. BBC Persian Interview, *be 'ebarati digar*, March 2014.

Ekhtiar, M., and Sardar, M., 'Modern and Contemporary Art in Iran', in *Heilbrunn Timeline of Art History*, October 2004, available at: <http://www.metmuseum.org/toah/hd/ciran/hd_ciran.htm>.

Emami, K. *Karim Emami on Modern Iranian Culture, Literature & Art*, compiled by Yavari, H., and Emami, G., New York 2014.

Franscina, F., 'Issues and Debates: the Late 1960s as a Representative Moment', in Harris, J., et al (eds.), *Modernism in Dispute: Art Since the Forties*, New Haven 1993.

59 Nayeri, F., 'Berlin Cancels Rare Show of Modern Art from Tehran Museum', *The New York Times*, 28 December 2016.

Grigor, T., *Cultivating Modernities: The Society for National Heritage, Political Propaganda, and Public Architecture in Twentieth-Century Iran,* Cambridge 2005.

Hobbs, R., 'Museum Under Siege', in *Art in America*, October 1981, pp. 17–25.

Kaylan, M., 'Clandestine Trade', *Wall Street Journal*, 8 December 2011.

Kozloff, M., 'American Painting During the Cold War', in *Artforum*, May 1973.

McFadden, S., 'The Museum and the Revolution', in *Art in America*, October 1981.

Mitchel, T., 'Orientalism and the Exhibitionary Order', in Preziosi, D. (ed.), *The Art of Art History*, Oxford 1998/2009.

Mohammed, A., 'Iran and the Art of Détente', *Financial Times,* 4 December 2015.

Dixon, J. M., 'Cultural Transplant, Cultural Hybrid', in *Progressive Architecture*, May 1978, pp. 68–71.

Moussavi-Aghdam, C., 'Art History, "National Art" and Iranian Intellectuals in the 1960s', in *British Journal of Middle Eastern Studies*, vol. 41, no. 1, 2014.

'Muzeh-ye honarha-ye mo'aser az enhesar Emrika kharej shod', *Kayhan*, 24 Aban 1358/15 November 1979.

Nabavi, N., 'The Discourse of "Authentic Culture" in Iran in the 1960s and 1970s', in *Intellectual Trends in Twentieth Century*, Orlando 2003.

Nayeri, F., 'Berlin Cancels Rare Show of Modern Art from Tehran Museum', *The New York Times*, 28 December 2016.

O'Doherty, B., *Inside the White Cube*, Santa Monica 1986.

Osborne, P., *Nowhere or Not at All: Philosophy of Contemporary Art*, London 2013.

Rizvi, K., 'Art History and the Nation: Arthur Upham Pope and the Discourse on "Persian Art" in the Early Twentieth Century', in *Muqarnas: An Annual on the Visual Culture of the Islamic World*, vol. 24, 2007, pp. 45–65.

Shakibi, Z. 'Pahlavism: The Ideologization of Monarchy in Iran', in *Politics, Religion & Ideology*, vol. 14, no. 1, 2013.

Shawcross, W., *The Shah's Last Ride: Fate of an Ally*, New York 1988.

Smith, T., 'The Provincialism Problem', in *Artforum,* vol. 12, no. 1, September 1974.

Stein, D., 'For the Love of Her People: An Interview with Farah Diba about the Pahlavi Programs for the Arts in Iran', in Scheiwiller, S. G. (ed.), *Performing Iranian State,* London, New York 2014.

The Guggenheim: Frank Lloyd Wright and the Making of the Modern Museum, New York 2009.

Zolghadr, T., 'The Recognizable Landscape: Notes on the Museum of Contemporary Art in Tehran', presented at CIMAM, December 16, 2012.

7

'Anti-Imperialism of Fools'?[1] The European Intellectual Left and The Iranian Revolution

Claudia Castiglioni

'Any Western intellectual with some integrity cannot be indifferent to what she or he hears about Iran.'[2] These words, pronounced by French philosopher Michel Foucault in September 1978 during an encounter with Iranian writer Baqer Parham, call into question a central and so far unanswered question: how did the West European intellectuals react to one of the twentieth century's most important, non-communist, modern, and popular revolutions? This question is at the core of the present chapter, which examines the response provided by European intellectuals – academics, journalists, philosophers, and to some degree students – to the crisis and collapse of the Pahlavi monarchy and to the establishment of the Islamic Republic. This study explores, on the one hand, the ties that bound the European intelligentsia to Iran's opposition on the eve of the revolution and, on the other, the elements that most affected the (mis)reading of the Iranian revolution by some of the most influential protagonists of the European intellectual milieu, with particular attention paid to those who can be ascribed to the so-called 'New Radical Left'. The term was recently coined by intellectual historian Christoph Kalter

---

1 Title drawn from: Halliday, F., 'Iran's Stolen Revolution. Anti-Imperialism of Fools', *The Nation*, 21 March 1981.

2 Afary, J., and Anderson, K. B., *Foucault and the Iranian Revolution: Gender and the Seductions of Islamism*, Chicago 2005, pp. 185–186.

to indicate scholars, thinkers, and activists ranging from anarchists, Trotskyists, Maoists, Marxist-Leninists among others, who, between the 1950s and the 1970s, considered themselves the revolutionary left, expressed a fierce anti-imperialism stance, and took a particular interest in the Third World.[3] Despite its focus on these forces, the study will also include some leftist liberals, especially the activists and lawyers who engaged in the campaign against the human rights violations perpetrated by the Pahlavi state.

The present chapter is a contribution to the study of the relationship between Western radical leftists and the Third World in the framework of the Cold War, a field that, as recently argued by Kalter, 'opens many perspectives on comparative and entangled histories'.[4] According to Kalter, the topic's significance within the broader context of the global international history is twofold: on the one hand, the idea of the Third World offered the intellectuals under scrutiny an important point of reference for a critique of their own society. Exploring their views on the non-European issues could, therefore, contribute to a better understanding of their relation with the political and cultural climate in which they lived. On the other, the notion of Third World facilitated the political communication in and between the countries of the Western and non-Western worlds and increased the transnational circulation of ideas between the West and the rest.[5] In this sense, a study of the approach taken by European leftists vis-à-vis the Third World can shed light on the mechanisms of reciprocal perception between the centre and the periphery, on the interactions, influences, and exchanges between Western leftists and

3 Kalter, C., *The Discovery of the Third World: Decolonization and the Rise of the New Left in France, c.1950–1976*, Cambridge 2016, pp. 94–96.

4 Kalter, C., *The Discovery of the Third World*, pp. 14–15. Some recent contributions to the subject, which so far have focused almost uniquely on the French case, include: Kalter, C., *The Discovery of the Third World*; Christofferson, M. S., *French Intellectuals Against the Left. The Antitotalitarian Moment of the 1970s*, New York 2000; Davey, E., *Idealism beyond Borders: The French Revolutionary Left and the Rise of Humanitarianism, 1954–1988*, Cambridge 2015; Wolin, R., *The Wind from the East: French Intellectuals, the Cultural Revolution, and the Legacy of the 1960s*, Princeton 2010; For an earlier study on the topic see: Morosini, G., 'The European Left and the Third World', in *Contemporary Marxism*, no. 2, Winter 1980, pp. 67–80.

5 Kalter, C., 'From Global to Local and Back: The "Third World" Concept and the New Radical Left in France', in *Journal of Global History*, vol. 12, no. 1, 2017, p. 115; Kalter, C., *The Discovery of the Third World*, p. 15. For a recent and thought-provoking contribution to the conceptualisation of global intellectual history and on the importance of interpreting it as a 'double-sided history' between center and periphery see Kaviraj, S., 'Global Intellectual History: Meanings and Methods', in Moyn, S., and Sartori, A. (eds.), *Global Intellectual History*, New York 2013, p. 305 and, more broadly, the entire volume to which it contributes.

their international counterparts, and on the global projection of their revolutionary aspirations. Echoing the arguments of David Engerman with regard to the global history of modernisation,[6] Kalter has stressed the importance of addressing central concepts such as the Third World which are 'universalist in their pretensions and global in their reach' with a focus on the local contexts in which they were being used and on the figures who transformed them into powerful tools of political and social praxis.[7] A discussion on leftist intellectuals and the Iranian revolution in this chapter fits into this framework.[8]

An examination of the debate amongst the European left triggered by the Iranian Revolution allows us to assess the extent to which the radical left acknowledged the novelty of the anti-shah revolt and the establishment of an Islamic Republic, and the extent to which it interpreted this process as conforming to Marxist concepts of revolution. This debate also offers us the chance to observe the process of reciprocal influence between supporters of the revolution in Iran and abroad, especially amongst those of radical leftist orientations. As argued by many commentators, by the mid-1970s, enthusiasm for Third World revolutions had started to wane amongst the European left.[9] The surfacing of a widespread critique of the notion of the Third World as essentially Euro-centric, combined with the decline in importance of categories such as neutral and anti-colonial, as well as an acknowledgement that 'these revolutions were not the Revolution' contributed to this development.[10] In this sense the importance of investigating the Iranian case study appears all the more relevant. The Iranian revolution occurred at the intersection between the dashed hopes raised by a Third Worldist discourse of global revolution, the beginning of the end of Marxist hegemony in left-wing intellectual discourse, the increase in importance of human rights in leftist intellectual discourse, and the search for new paradigms for understanding socio-political change in the developing countries.[11]

---

6 Engerman, D. C., 'Introduction: Towards a Global History of Modernization', in *Diplomatic History*, vol. 33, no. 3, 2009, p. 377.

7 Kalter, C., 'From Global to Local and Back', p. 118.

8 So far the only study that has addressed Western left's reaction to the Iranian revolution is: Greason, D., 'Embracing Death: The Western Left and the Iranian Revolution, 1978–83', in *Economy and Society*, vol. 34, no. 1, 2005, pp. 105–140. Greason's study mostly focuses on the British and American left.

9 Kalter, C., *The Discovery of the Third World*, pp. 58–59; Christofferson, M. S., *French Intellectuals*, pp. 184–229; Davey, E., *Idealism Beyond Borders*, p. 3.

10 Rodinson, M., 'La fin de compagnons de route', *Le Nouvel Observateur*, 3 July 1978.

11 On the role of Marxism in left-wing intellectual debate see: Dworkin, D. L., *Cultural Marxism in Postwar Britain: History, the New Left, and the Origins of Cultural Studies*,

This topic has so far received only scant attention in the literature on Iran or the Cold War. Studies that examined the evolution of the European left in the context of the Cold War have so far neglected its approach to Third World issues, albeit with a few notable and recent exceptions concerning the French case.[12] The scholarship on Iranian political history has so far paid little attention to European reactions to the revolution and no attention at all to its intellectual or cultural dimension, with the sole exception of the case of Foucault.[13] Nevertheless, the issue is far from minor: dealing with the response of Western European left to the revolution means examining the ability of one of the most relevant Western political traditions to cope with a phenomenon that uniquely encompassed a utopian ambition for radical socio-political change, a concomitant use of liberal, Marxist, and Islamic discourses, as well as a quest for national independence in the framework of the Cold War.

This chapter pays particular attention to the case of the journalist and International Relations scholar Fred Halliday.[14] In addition to being one of the most influential, eclectic, prolific and engaged European intellectuals, Halliday uniquely encompassed a Marxist political education, a profound knowledge of revolutionary processes perceived and understood in their transnational dimension, and a deep familiarity with the Middle East and its political, social, and economic dynamics.[15] As it has been argued, 'Halliday never looked at the Middle East in isolation or as some self-contained region set apart from what was going on in the international system at the time.'[16] These features make his views an invaluable

Durham 1997, p. 246. For a recent contribution to the debate on the human rights movement in the 1970s see, among others: Moyn, S., *The Last Utopia: Human Rights in History*, Cambridge 2010, pp. 114–119.

12 See note 4.

13 On Western Europe and the Iranian Revolution see, among others: Halliday, F., 'An Elusive Normalization: Western Europe and the Iranian Revolution', in *Middle East Journal*, vol. 48, no 2, 1994, pp. 309–326. On the debate about Foucault's views on it see, among others, Afary, J. and Anderson, K. B., *Foucault and the Iranian Revolution*; Ghamari-Tabrizi, B., *Foucault in Iran: Islamic Revolution after the Enlightenment*, Minneapolis 2016.

14 For some biographical references on Fred Halliday see, among others: Roberts, A., 'Simon Frederick Peter Halliday, 1946–2010', in *Proceedings of the British Academy*, no. 172, 2011, pp. 143–69; Colas, A., and Lawson, G., 'Fred Halliday: achievements, ambivalences and openings', in *Millennium – Journal of International Studies*, vol. 39, no. 2, 2010, pp. 235–258.

15 On Halliday's views on revolutionary processes and their international dimension see: Halliday, F., *Revolution and World Politics The Rise and Fall of the Sixth Great Power*, Basingstoke 1999.

16 Cox, M., 'Fred Halliday, Marxism and the Cold War', in *International Affairs*, vol. 87, no. 5, 2011, p. 1110.

point of reference for understanding how the European intellectual community reacted to the Iranian revolution and to its singularity. Although concentrating mostly on Halliday and other left-leaning figures and groups, this chapter aims at framing their views in the more general (mis)reading of the revolution by European intellectuals that resulted from the impact of mainstream scholarship, from the novelty of the unfolding events, and from the stance taken by the Iranian left during the revolution.

This study has no ambition to provide a definitive assessment either of the revolution or of the policies pursued by its major protagonists. 'To evaluate the long-term import of this revolution now – is… in any serious sense, impossible,' commented Halliday in 1980. Echoing Zhou Enlai's famous remark about the Chinese revolution, Halliday wrote: 'It would be like trying to assess the course of the French revolution in 1791, of the Mexican revolution in 1915, or the Russian in the summer of 1917.'[17] More than thirty years later, Halliday's comment remains a valid and crucial point of departure for any analysis of the Iranian revolution. The goal here is to provide a fresh appraisal of a rather neglected aspect of the phenomenon and of its transnational dimension, notably the relationship and mutual influence between the European intelligentsia and the forces that formed the opposition to the shah at home and abroad, through an analysis that encompasses elements of international, social, and intellectual history.

The Rise of the New Left

The 1970s marked an important moment for the West European left and for the relationship between intellectuals and politics. The previous two decades had witnessed several changes in the leftist camp: the emergence of the first signs of discontent with Soviet political and cultural leadership within the communist parties of Western Europe, the detachment by numerous left-wing politicians and philosophers from orthodox communism, and the consequent appearance and consolidation of the so-called New Left, a term that came to describe leftist politicians, intellectuals, and theorists who wanted to open up a new theoretical-political space that would provide an alternative to both Stalinism and social democracy. The process originated from the events of 1956, most notably the Algerian War, the Hungarian uprising, and the Suez Crisis. The three crises marked the emergence of a transnational movement that shared a commitment to revolutionary politics in the Third World and a dissatisfaction with orthodox communism. The

17 Halliday, F., 'Iran, First Year of Revolution', in *MERIP Reports*, vol. 88, June 1980, p. 3.

Soviet intervention in Budapest, followed by the Prague Spring of 1968, made it evident that the Soviet Union could no longer serve as a model for the revolutionary aspirations of the European left. The episodes of 1956 and 1968 also showed that traditional institutions of the European left that continued to support pro-Soviet positions, most notably the Italian and the French communist parties, had lost their moral compass and political legitimacy. The country in which these developments had their most profound effect was France, where the deepening of long-standing critiques of communism and revolution after 1968 put intellectuals on a collision course with the socialist and communist parties. The Sino-Soviet split of the 1960s also contributed to this trend. As Moscow lost its utopian status, the appeal of Maoism and of its Great Proletarian Cultural Revolution grew rapidly among many Western socialist intellectuals, denoting to some extent the substitution of China for the Soviet Union as their reference point in the politics of the Second World.

These international developments radically altered the worldview of the European political and intellectual left, contributing to the dissemination of fresh ideas that challenged the core tenets of their traditional leftist political discourse. Between the mid-1960s and the mid-1970s these intellectual shifts, combined with the radical socio-cultural changes underway in Europe, redesigned the map and the prospects of the West European left, leading to a broad reassessment of concepts such as revolution, totalitarianism, violence, and Third Worldism.[18] As a consequence of this political and ideological renewal, an innovative, rich, and heterogeneous set of political discourses surfaced, fed by a new wave of Marxist revisionism and by the open challenge launched by socialists and social democrats to the orthodox communists' cultural and political role in the leftist political scene. In Britain, the debate only marginally affected the traditional duopoly of the country's politics, but it was pivotal in altering the country's intellectual scene and political culture.[19] In Italy and France, the growing dissent from Moscow undermined even further the position of the Italian Communist Party, the PCI, and the French Communist Party, the PCF, vis-à-vis their international sponsor, the Soviet Union. Under the banner of so-called Eurocommunism, the two parties sought to increase their independence from Moscow and contribute to the prospect of

18 On the diffusion of the anti–establishment discourse in the West European left see: Sassoon, D., *One Hundred Years of Socialism: The West European Left in the Twentieth Century*, New York 1997, p. 383; and Anderson, P., and Camiller, P., *Mapping the West European Left*, London 1994.

19 On this point see, among others: Dworkin, D. L., *Cultural Marxism*, Durham, NC 1997; and Thompson, D., *Pessimism of the Intellect? A History of New Left Review*, Monmouth 2007.

communism competing with social democracy for hegemony on the left. This experiment eventually failed as a result of irreconcilable differences between the parties involved and renewed intensification of international tensions following the Euromissile crisis and the Soviet invasion of Afghanistan.[20] Nonetheless, this failed experiment revealed the emerging consensus on the left that they needed to redefine their model of socialism and their relations with the Soviet Union. The failure of Eurocommunism to offer those who were dissatisfied with Soviet communism a viable alternative to the traditional political framework of the left only increased the sense of alienation felt by many socialist intellectuals.

The changes that affected the European left in the wake of 1956 not only transformed the political landscape of Europe, but also favoured the diffusion of new revolutionary myths throughout the continent. The idea that the proletariat was no longer the only available vehicle of radical social transformation, the general crisis of orthodox communism, the wide-spread disillusion of prominent European leftist intellectuals who had previously expressed curiosity and, to differing degrees, fascination with the Soviet model and Stalinism, and the first successes of anti-colonial insurrections in the Third World, all fed into this tendency.[21] As suggested above, Europe's New Radical Left started to identify anti-colonial nationalists and peasant guerrillas as alternatives to Marxist-type revolutionaries. Many intellectuals, especially in France, where their estrangement from the Communist Party was greater, responded to the crisis of orthodox communism and of the proletariat as a revolutionary actor 'by transferring their allegiances to Third World revolutionary movements in the expectation that these were the agents of history that would bring about a social transformation abroad and perhaps even in the metropole'.[22] The result was an infatuation by Western intellectuals, especially those who placed themselves outside the traditional parties, with these

20 On Eurocommunism see, among others: Pons, S., 'The Rise and Fall of Eurocommunism', in Leffler, M. P., and Westad, O. A. (eds.), *The Cambridge History of the Cold War*, Cambridge 2010, pp. 45–65.

21 Amongst the intellectuals who looked with interest at the Soviet political experiment, a few names are worth mentioning. They are those of E. H. Carr, George Bernard Shaw, Eric Hobsbawm and André Gide. On the earlier fascination of those who have been labeled 'fellow travellers' or '*compagnons de route*' for the Soviet Union and the communist model see, amongst others: David-Fox, M., *Showcasing the Great Experiment: Cultural Diplomacy and Western Visitors to the Soviet Union, 1921–1941*, Oxford 2012; Hollander, P., *Political Pilgrims: Western Intellectuals in Search of the Good Society*, New York 1981; Caute, D., *The Fellow-Travellers: Intellectual Friends of Communism*, New Haven 1988.

22 Christofferson, M. S., *French Intellectuals*, p. 41. On the international dimension of the British New Left, see Thompson, D., *Pessimism of the Intellect?*, pp. 31–35.

new, successful, examples of mass mobilisation, which ended up providing a 'left cover to forces potentially attracted to reactionary and decidedly anti-socialist policies'.[23] The enthusiasm for such peripheral revolutions started to decline by the mid-1970s. An awareness that the anti-imperialist nature of struggles for national liberation in the Third World was no guarantee of their socialist goals, a disenchantment with China's Maoist model, and increasing attention to issues such as human rights by important sectors of the leftist intellectual community all contributed to this declining popularity.[24] In this context the relevance of the Iranian Revolution is twofold: on the one hand, those who pinned their hopes on radical change in the Third World as a motor for worldwide revolution saw in the uprisings in Iran the prelude to a socialist revolution that would pave the way for a global transformation of the Middle East. On the other hand, those who had already renounced their initial enthusiasm for peripheral revolutions and regarded the Iranian crisis mostly through the lens of human rights, looked at the collapse of the shah's regime as the first step toward the establishment of a moderate and progressive government in Iran. As we will see, both groups' expectations were soon to be disappointed.

The global challenge launched in the 1960s to the institutional left also had a profound impact on the political landscape in Iran. The strength of Iran's communist Tudeh Party had reduced drastically since the 1953 coup against Mohammad Mosaddeq and by the 1960s the Tudeh was, in Ervand Abrahamian's words, a 'mere shadow of its former self'.[25] Among the factors that led to the decline in the Tudeh's prestige and support was the growing involvement of Iranian youth in the country's political life and the consequent elaboration of a distinctive student culture and movement. This coincided with Mohammad Reza Shah's increasing repression of any form of political opposition, which in turn radicalised this new student movement and encouraged their turn to guerrilla tactics in their fight against the Pahlavi state.[26] In the words of Maziar Behrooz: 'A reverence for the Bolshevik revolution, hallmark of the previous generation, was diluted by

23 Greason, D., 'Embracing Death', p. 107. For an overview of some of the most prominent cases of infatuation with Third World revolutions in the 1960s see, among others: Hollander, P., *Political Pilgrims*, pp. 223–277.

24 Christofferson, M. S., *French Intellectuals*, pp. 113–228; Thompson, D., *Pessimism of the Intellect?*, p. 66; Davey, E., *Idealism Beyond Borders*, p. 3.

25 Abrahamian, E., *Iran between Two Revolutions*, Princeton 1982, p. 451.

26 See: Abrahamian, E., 'The Guerrilla Movement in Iran, 1963–1977', in *MERIP Reports*, vol. 86, Mar.–Apr. 1980, pp. 3–15; and Behrooz, M., 'The Iranian Revolution and the Legacy of the Guerrilla Movement', in Cronin, S. (ed.), *Reformers and Revolutionaries in Modern Iran. New Perspectives on the Iranian Left*, London 2004, pp. 189–205.

the experience of Chinese, Cuban, Algerian and Vietnamese revolutions.'[27] The groups that made their appearance on Iran's political scene in the 1970s supported either a new form of Marxism-Leninism, with no ties to the Soviet or Chinese communist parties (as in the case of the Fadaiyan-e Khalq), or proposed a reinterpretation of Shia Islam and infused it with new political thinking in order to turn it into a viable revolutionary force (as in the case of the Mojahedin-e Khalq or MKO). The members of the MKO looked to the Palestinian movement of al-Fatah and the Algerian anti-colonial groups to draw inspiration for their struggle, while for the Fadaiyan the models were the international communist movement and the liberation movements of Latin America, Palestine and Vietnam.[28] The diffusion of such revolutionary myths and the spread of these new 'dreams of revolution' helped foster ties between Iran's youth and their increasingly politicised European counterparts, a convergence encouraged and nurtured by their common anti-Americanism and by the dramatic increase in the number of Iranian students at European universities.

For some members of this new younger generation of the Iranian opposition the process of politicisation and familiarisation with Western revolutionary models simply meant reading, copying, discussing, or distributing illegal books, which had been turned by the regime into 'subversive objects'.[29] For the majority it meant criticising the *gharbzadegi* (Westoxification) of the Pahlavi state and denouncing Mohammad Reza Shah as an 'American puppet', while at the same time engaging in an alternative emulation of Western, especially European, cultural and intellectual models. As Mehrzad Boroujerdi argues, even the most prominent critics of the Pahlavi elite's *gharbzadegi*, Jalal Al-e Ahmad, was not immune to Western influences.[30] 'To the contrary, he was inspired by many Western (primarily European) thinkers and writers' and by the problem of economic and social development addressed by European Marxist and radical thinkers.[31] Al-e Ahmad's popularity stands as an example of the pervasiveness of Western, especially leftist, ideologies, among well-read Iranian youth. In the words of Hamid Dabashi, 'the ideologues of the Islamic Revolution… attended the forceful conceptual arsenal of secular ideologies and with remarkable tenacity sought to render them operative

27 Behrooz, M., *Rebels with a Cause: The Failure of the Left in Iran*, New York 1999, p. 37.
28 Behrooz, M., *Rebels with a Cause*, p. 199.
29 Sohrabi, N., 'Books as Revolutionary Objects in Iran', *Age of Revolutions*, available at: <https://ageofrevolutions.com/2016/04/04/books-as-revolutionary-objects-in-iran/>.
30 Boroujerdi, M., *Iranian Intellectuals and the West: The Tormented Triumph of Nativism*, Syracuse 1996, p. 69.
31 Boroujerdi, M., *Iranian Intellectuals and the West*, pp. 69–71.

in viable Islamic terminologies.'[32] The attempt to reconcile Western revolutionary ideals with indigenous intellectual models remained a distinctive feature of Iranian opposition movements, both at home and abroad.[33]

Forging Global Ties

Beginning in the 1950s, a growing number of young educated Iranians moved to Western Europe, attracted by the education offered by European universities or forced into exile by the shah's repressive policies. By the end of the 1960s, 28% of Iranian students overseas were enrolled in universities in West Germany, 12% in Great Britain, 8% in Austria, and 7% in France. In the following decade the oil boom and the intensification of the campaign of political repression conducted by the shah's regime led to a further surge in the rapidly growing number of Iranian students abroad.[34] Such a conspicuous and often politically active student community established very solid connections with the European cultural and political milieu.[35] Iranian students contributed to the political re-orientation of the West European New Left, especially of its student component, and aroused considerable cultural and personal empathy for the grievances and frustrations of the Iranian opposition. In the eyes of their European counterparts, the Iranians' activism was proof that the Third World could be the source of political energy, something that many of them thought the Western working class had lost.[36] As a result, by the late 1960s Iran had become a cause célèbre, like the Vietnam War or liberation movements in Palestine and Latin America.[37]

The Confederation of Iranian Students, or CIS, offers the best case in point in this regard. The association, which was established in 1960, soon became the international voice of the Iranian opposition. Through its national branches and

32 Dabashi, H., *Theology of Discontent: The Ideological Foundation of the Islamic Republic of Iran*, New York 1993, p. 368.
33 On this point see: Arman, M., 'Iranian Intellectuals and Dependency Theory', in *Khamsin*, vol. 12, 1986, pp. 27–36.
34 Data reported in Shannon, M., '"Contacts with the Opposition": American Foreign Relations, the Iranian Student Movement, and the Global Sixties', in *The Sixties: A Journal of History, Politics and Culture*, vol. 4, no. 1, 2011, p. 4.
35 On Iran's student movement, see: Matin-Asgari, A., *Iranian Student Opposition to the Shah*, Costa Mesa, 2002; Martin, L., 'L'opposition iranienne au régime de Mohammad Reza Pahlavi en France, 1960–1979' [The Iranian opposition to the regime of Mohammed Reza Pahlavi in France], PhD diss., Institute d'Études Politiques de Paris 2008.
36 Slobodian, Q., *Foreign Front: Third World Politics in Sixties West Germany*, Durham, NC 2012, p. 4.
37 Shannon, M., 'Contacts with the Opposition', p. 5.

publications, it played a major role in exposing the autocratic nature of the government of Mohammed Reza Shah, raising awareness of the political repression enacted by the regime and its systematic use of torture, presenting the popular opposition to his rule as part of the broader anti-imperialist struggle, and contributing to the radicalisation of the attitude of European youth vis-à-vis the Iranian political situation.[38] The major student organisation in France, the National Union of French Students or UNEF, proved from the start very sympathetic to the CIS's campaigns and provided ideological as much as practical support to their activities, including hosting the Confederation's meetings in its headquarters in Paris.[39] The turning point of 1968 crucially contributed to the integration of Iranian student groups into the broader context of youth mobilisation in France. In the aftermath of the May events, comparisons between the situation in South Vietnam and Iran started appearing in the leaflets of student movements, showing that 'Third-Worldism was finding traction in the [French] student milieu'.[40] At the same time Iranian student groups began to express their solidarity with the struggle of their French fellow students against the repressive features of European bourgeois capitalist societies. Though not reaching the level of political engagement of its West German counterpart, the 'German Socialist Students Organisation' or SDS, whose experience, in the words of Halliday 'provide[d] one of the most instructive models of student movement anywhere in the world',[41] UNEF proved to be quite receptive to the demands of Iranian students and their campaign against Pahlavi rule.

The picture looks quite different if we look at the British case. Despite episodes of student protests in Britain in 1967–1968, most notably at the London School of Economics (LSE), the British student movement was undoubtedly less violent and less radical than those in continental Europe. In an unpublished study of the late 1960s, Halliday critically described it as 'the weakest of all those in the major capitalist states' and, echoing an argument previously expressed by Perry Anderson,

38 'Le "procès" de dix: un complot contre le mouvement révolutionnaire iranien', Bibliothèque de Documentation International Contemporaine (hereafter BDIC), Paris West University, Nanterre; 'Iran, terre de conquise pour l'impérialisme', *Iran Report*, October 1971, BDIC.

39 Chenal, A., *Les socialistes français et l'Iran* (1975–85), Paris 2012, p. 21.

40 Martin, L., 'L'opposition iranienne', p. 128. On the UNEF's engagement in Third World issues, see also Morder, R., 'L'Unef et le conflit du Proche-Orient, 1967–1970: positionnements internationaux et contraintes syndicales', in *Matériaux pour l'histoire de notre temps*, no. 96, 2009, pp. 49–58.

41 Halliday, F., 'Students of the World Unite', in Cockburn, A., and Blackburn, R. (ed.), *Student Power: Problems, Diagnosis, Action*, London 1969, p. 316.

blamed its weakness and, more broadly, the lesser role played by the student left in Britain when compared to France, Italy or West Germany, on the failure of the British intellectual elite to produce a critical theory of society.[42] As a result, despite joining other movements in the United States and continental Europe in protesting against the Vietnam War, British student groups appeared less engaged with the Third Worldist cause and less active in support of their Iranian colleagues.[43] In this context it was often left to Marxist and Trotskyist political organisations to increase the awareness of the public of Third World issues, including on the campaign against the Pahlavi shah.

The ties established between Iranian student groups and their West European counterparts resulted in the accentuation of the transnational dimension of the Iranian student community abroad, an aspect that, by the mid-1970s, would arguably become its most relevant feature. The global engagement of the Iranian student movement in Europe emerged clearly in the support it provided to some Third World revolutionary struggles, most notably to the separatist rebellion in the Dhofar province of Oman. The battle fought by Marxist and nationalist forces against the central government in Muscat, at the time backed by the Pahlavi state, became, in the words of Iranian student activists, a struggle against 'Iranian aggression in Oman', against 'the interests of imperialism, Zionism, and the Arab reactionary governments', and, more broadly, against the 'imperial-reactionary plot in the Gulf and in the region'.[44] The campaign in solidarity with 'all the revolutionary forces of the region' was instrumental in forging stronger relations between Iranian opposition forces at home and abroad, and prominent European Trotskyists and Marxists such as Halliday.[45]

Many of the students who emigrated to Europe in the 1960s and 1970s had already experienced some form of politicisation prior to their arrival. They were often influenced by Marxist or nationalist theories, even though their political orientation showed significant fluidity, with signs of radicalisation in the second half of the 1970s. Their political references included the usual suspects of revolutionary

42 Halliday, F., 'The Genesis and Growth of the British Student Movement', Undated manuscript circa 1969, in Folder 373: 'Student Movement', Simon Frederick Peter Halliday Papers (hereafter FHP), London School of Economics. The reference is to Anderson, P., 'Components of the National Culture', in *New Left Review*, no. 50, Jul.–Aug. 1968, pp. 3–57.
43 On this point see, among others: Ellis, S., '"A Demonstration of British Good Sense?" British Student Protest during the Vietnam', in de Groot, G. (ed.), *Student Protest: The Sixties and After*, London 1998, pp. 54–69.
44 'Halte à l'agression iranienne en Oman!' *Iran Report*, June 1974, BDIC.
45 'Halte à l'agression iranienne en Oman!' *Iran Report*, June 1974, BDIC.

literature, like Karl Marx, Ho Chi Minh, Vladimir Lenin, Frantz Fanon, Che Guevara, and Maxim Gorky, and some prominent Iranian dissidents, such as Jalal Al-e Ahmad and Samad Behrangi, whose death in 1967 inspired the creation of a committee of Iranian and French militants against the Pahlavi regime. Some of them embraced political activism only after being denied the right to return to Iran, as in the case of Ahmad Salamatian, who arrived in France as a law student in the mid-1960s. When his passport was confiscated by the Iranian authorities, he decided to get involved with the anti-shah movement. In addition to establishing the Committee for the Defense of Iranian Political Prisoners, Salamatian was instrumental in connecting French human rights lawyers such as Thierry Mignon with intellectuals and prominent figures of the Iranian opposition in Paris.

Amongst the most influential members of the Iranian student community in Europe, one name stands out: Ali Shariati.[46] Shariati arrived in Paris in 1960 on a state scholarship to study sociology and Islamic history at the Sorbonne. In Paris he immersed himself in radical political philosophy and revolutionary student organisations. While at the Sorbonne he was profoundly influenced by the works of Frantz Fanon and the French scholar of Islam, Louis Massignon, whom Shariati extensively and almost hagiographically praised in his writings.[47] In the mid-1960s, he joined the Iranian Student Confederation and the Liberation Movement of Iran.[48] An avid reader of the works of contemporary radicals, and personally involved in the causes of Algerian and Palestinian independence, Shariati was pivotal in internationalising the anti-shah political discourse, linking the Iranian opposition with some of the French branches of the most prominent revolutionary movements active in the Third World, and enriching the anti-Pahlavi discourse with new categories and new models.[49] The result was an unparalleled success in the synthesis of modern socialism with traditional Shiʿism and in the adaptation of the revolutionary theories of Marx, Fanon and others to his contemporary Iranian environment.

Students were not the only active and political influential Iranian force in West Europe: intellectuals also played a very relevant role. Thanks to their more moderate positions, far from the students' Maoist or Marxist inclinations, they managed to obtain the backing of the majority of European (especially French) public

46 On Shariati's life and contribution to the revolution, see: Rahnema, A., *An Islamic Utopian: A Political Biography of Ali Shariati*, London 2000.

47 Dabashi, H., *Theology of Discontent*, p. 107.

48 On Shariati's role in the Liberation Movement, see Chehabi, H. E., *Iranian Politics and Religious Modernism*, Ithaca, NY 1990, pp. 195–202.

49 See: 'Iran, Palestine: même combat', *Iran Report*, October 1971, BDIC.

opinion in their opposition to the shah and in their denunciation of the human rights violations perpetrated by the regime.[50] Amongst them one name stands out because of the central role he would later play in the Iranian revolution: the future president of the Islamic Republic, Abolhassan Banisadr. Banisadr's attacks against the shah's regime found an especially receptive terrain among human rights associations and activists. The French Marxist sociologist Paul Vieille had a likewise pivotal role in the intellectual education and radical politicisation of the Iranian community abroad. Back in the early 1960s, Vieille had spent some years in Iran on behalf of the United Nations Educational, Scientific and Cultural Organisation (UNESCO). During his stay he had crucially contributed to the development of a new methodology of research in social sciences based on fieldwork and, through the Institute of Social Studies and Research at the University of Tehran, had cultivated a generation of scholars including Banisadr. In 1974, Vieille and Banisadr edited a volume on the impact of oil as an instrument of American capitalism and imperialism on Iran's socio-economic landscape and on the authoritarian drift taken by the regime.[51] From the 1960s to his death in 2010, Vieille exercised a profound influence on the debate on Iranian economic, urban, and social development, both in Iran and in the West.

While students concentrated their efforts on initiatives such as sit-ins, hunger strikes, rallies, and distribution of leaflets, Iranian intellectuals penetrated the European intellectual milieu mostly through contacts within major national newspapers, petitions, personal meetings, and political lobbying of local intellectuals, by whom they started to be seen as moderate opponents to the regime. In this sense the two groups differed mostly in the vehicles used for the dissemination of ideas and in the public they targeted, rather than in the aims they pursued. Thanks to their influence and personal connections, Iranian intellectuals managed to disseminate information on the human rights violations perpetrated by the regime and, more broadly, regarding the state of political freedom in Iran. Their efforts induced prominent European intellectuals such as Jean-Paul Sartre, Simone de Beauvoir, and Claude Mauriac to engage themselves in the campaign against the shah.[52]

50 'Répression et droits de l'homme en Iran', *Iran Report*, October 1971, BDIC.

51 Vieille, P., and Banisadr, A., *Pétrole et violence, terreur blanche et répression en Iran* [Oil and Violence, White Terror and Repression in Iran], Paris 1974. They also co-authored a study of the revolution: Vieille, P., and Banisadr, A., *Quelle Révolution pour l'Iran?* [What Revolution for Iran?], Paris 1980.

52 See, for example: 'Un appel de Sartre, Jean-Paul en faveur de deux condamnés à mort en Iran', *Le Monde*, 13 May 1966; 'Enquête de maître Madeleine Lafue-Veron en Iran', *Bullettin d'information*, February 1978, BDIC.

In the 1970s, Iranian intellectuals contributed to the establishment of organisations and networks that denounced the political repression enacted by the notorious Iranian secret police, the SAVAK, and the condition of political prisoners in Iran. Among these organisations it is worth mentioning the London-based Committee Against Repression in Iran (CARI), the Iranian Political Prisoners' Defense Committee founded by Ahmad Salamatian and presided by Jean-Paul Sartre, and the French Association in Support of the Iranian People (AFASPI). All these associations were committed to the dissemination of information regarding the political repression in Iran and on the human rights violations perpetrated by the shah's regime. The Political Prisoners' Defense Committee, in particular, joined forces with other similar organisations to demand the opening of a center for the promotion of freedom of expression in Tehran and to mobilise the associations of French jurists in favour of the cause of the Iranian opposition. Their efforts bore fruit. At the beginning of 1978, French lawyer Madeleine Lafue-Veron wrote a report on the condition of political prisoners in Iran based on the data she had collected during a two-week mission she conducted in the country. The report was published in newspapers in France and throughout Europe, and her conclusions drew attention to the widespread violations of human rights in Iran's prisons.[53]

Both the student movement and the most influential Iranian intellectuals successfully engaged some of their European counterparts in the anti-shah campaign and, subsequently, played a pivotal role in shaping their reading of the revolution. As it has been argued, by the time of the collapse of the Pahlavi monarchy most of the members of the Western radical left 'knew what they knew of Iran from the substantial body of leftist literature that had circulated in the West before and during the revolution', literature mostly produced by the leftist parties in exile, the student organisations linked to them, and the associations established by their international supporters.[54] This assertion is confirmed by a report published in 1978 by the Middle East Librarians Association, according to which 'apart from a few patriotic poems and short stories, the majority of current Persian publishing in Europe has as its sole theme the overthrow of the so-called imperialist regime of the Shah, and the establishment of a Marxist-Leninist (or Islamic-Marxist, whatever that means) society in Iran'.[55]

53 'Enquête de maître Madeleine Lafue-Veron en Iran', BDIC.

54 Greason, D., 'Embracing Death', p. 122.

55 Behn, W., 'Persian Literature Published in Europe in the Sixties and Seventies', in *MELA Notes*, vol. 14, 1978, p. 5.

From an Iranian to an Islamic Revolution

'What was truly "unthinkable" was not the shah's demise but the emergence of a clerical-dominated Islamic republic.'[56] This quote from Gary Sick, the principal Iran expert in the Carter White House, aptly captures the bewilderment of many observers at the unexpected turn of events after the establishment of the Islamic Republic in April 1979. Influenced by Marxist determinism or by the allure of Third Worldism and lacking a basic understanding of Iranian socio-economic features, most analysts did not make much headway in comprehending the balance of power between the various forces struggling for the control of the new Iran and the dynamics at play in the Iranian Revolution, a revolution that would prove to be 'neither bourgeois nor proletarian, and whose slogans emphasized neither democracy nor progress'.[57]

The coexistence of elements common to other modern revolutions, most notably the massive participation of the population in the revolt and the anti-imperialist rhetoric employed by its leaders, with features clearly suggesting the unprecedented character of the uprisings, such as the part played by the clergy and, more broadly, by religion, contributed to the widespread misunderstanding with regard to the nature of the phenomenon.[58] The workers' leading role in the first phase of the revolution, in particular, fuelled the hopes of those who saw the beginnings of a socialist revolution in the general strikes and in the mass demonstrations that culminated with the collapse of the Pahlavi monarchy.[59] It also induced many analysts to look predominantly at the social dimension of the revolution, neglecting its political components and, more importantly, failing to understand the forces that were shaping the revolutionary discourse and, in so doing, the struggle for power. When the workers' demands shifted from the

56 Sick, G., *All Fall Down: America's Tragic Encounter with Iran*, New York 1985, p. 165.
57 Arjomand, S. A., *The Turban for the Crown: The Islamic Revolution in Iran*, New York 1988, p. 3.
58 On the debate regarding the nature of the Iranian events and the comparison with the modern revolutions see, among others, Skocpol, T., 'Rentier State and Shia Islam in the Iranian Revolution', in *Theory and Society*, vol. 11, no. 3, 1982, pp. 265–283; Keddie, N. R., 'Iranian Revolutions in Comparative Perspective', in *The American Historical Review*, vol. 88, no. 3, 1983, pp. 579–598.; Bakhash, S., 'Iran', in *The American Historical Review*, vol. 96, no. 5, 1991, pp. 1479–1496; Halliday, F., *Revolution and World Politics*, pp. 49–51; Panah, M., *The Islamic Republic and the World. Global Dimensions of the Iranian Revolution*, London 2007, pp. 4–15.
59 On the role of oil workers in the 1978–1979 revolution, see Jafari, P., 'Reasons to Revolt: Iranian Oil Workers in the 1970s', in *International Labor and Working-Class History*, vol. 84, Fall 2013, pp. 195–217. On workers' contribution to the overthrow of the Pahlavi regime, see: Bayat, A., *Workers and Revolution in Iran: A Third World Experience of Workers' Control*, London 1987.

economic to the political, the weakness of the leftist parties that were supposed to translate their aspirations into a plan of action, combined with the ill-fated decision of the Tudeh and of most of the Fadaiyan to collaborate with the fundamentalists in the assumption that the latters' lack of managerial skills would allow the communists to manipulate the religious forces and, eventually, to seize the power resulted in their elimination by the Islamist forces.[60]

The leftist groups, the constitutionalists, and the moderate forces that participated in the uprisings faced a similar fate. After the demise of Prime Minister Shapour Bakhtiar's government and the return of Ayatollah Ruhollah Khomeini to Iran in February 1979, tensions between the various opposition groups replaced the original struggle against the shah. Khomeini established a Council of the Islamic Revolution, composed of his most loyal supporters, to purge the network of local revolutionary committees (*komiteh*) of leftist and liberal elements. The purged committees, together with the newly created system of revolutionary tribunals, acted as a parallel government that deprived the provisional government of the moderate Mehdi Bazargan of any real power. The revolution was now shifting from an Iranian to an Islamic phenomenon.

The evolution of these events suggests two major features of the revolutionary process: on the one hand the weakness of Iranian political parties in general, especially leftist parties, in interpreting, channeling, and traducing into a political programme the discontent of a wide strata of the population; on the other, the ability of the Khomeini faction to capitalise on such weakness and steer the direction of the revolution towards its own goals. The political vacuum created around traditional parties by decades of repression deprived them of any chance to redefine their language and aims in line with the new demands of growing sectors of the populations, most notably the urban poor. The result was a revolutionary campaign that was launched mostly against foreign imperialism and political dictatorship, but lacking a clear programme for democratisation and modernisation.[61] Khomeini, for his part, borrowed many ideas, slogans, and symbols from the

60 On the Tudeh's support for Khomeini and fundamentalists, see Milani, M. M., 'Harvest of Shame: The Policy of the Tudeh Party and the Bazargan Government', in *Middle Eastern Studies*, vol. 29, no. 2, 1993, pp. 307–320. On the political turmoil of late 1978 see, among others, Abrahamian, E., *Iran between Two Revolutions*, pp. 510–529. For an account of the revolutionary events, see Axworthy, M., *Revolutionary Iran: A History of the Islamic Republic*, London 2013, pp. 112–186.

61 de Groot, J., 'The Iranian Revolution: What's Happening?', in *Marxism Today*, Feb. 1980, pp. 19–22; Moghadam, V. M., 'The Revolution and the Regime: Populism, Islam and the State in Iran', in *Social Compass*, vol. 36, no. 4, 1989, p. 418.

radical and Marxist left. He redefined religious concepts, such as *mostaz'af* (dispossessed) and *shahid* (martyr), in revolutionary terms and used them to mobilise the masses as the leader of the new revolutionary state.[62]

Such developments left many European commentators and activists who had been influenced by the anti-shah campaigns carried out by the Iranian opposition abroad, who had looked with sympathy at the earlier stages of the revolution, and who persisted in rejecting the possibility of a pro-clerical revolution, in a state of profound disorientation. Only a few among them displayed the intellectual creativity and ideological flexibility to address the misunderstanding and disorientation that resulted from the Islamic revolution. Among them was the scholar, activist, and journalist Fred Halliday.

Fred Halliday and the Iranian Revolution

'The Iranian revolution,' Halliday argued in his *Revolution and World Politics*, 'provides considerable difficulties for any general theory of the causes, international or other, of revolutions.'[63] This statement was the product of more than twenty years of reflection on the demise of the Pahlavi monarchy and the establishment of the Islamic Republic, events that never ceased to fascinate Halliday, despite the bitter disillusion they caused. Such an in-depth review of the phenomenon, his unique knowledge of the region, his Marxist background, and his first-hand experience of the early phases of the revolutionary struggle, makes this scholar an invaluable point of reference for any analysis of the European intellectual reaction to the Iranian events. A fellow of the Transnational Institute in Amsterdam and future professor of International Relations at the LSE, by 1979 Halliday had already distinguished himself as a remarkable polyglot and an avid scholar of the Middle East and of Third World revolutions. In the early 1960s, his intellectual curiosity brought him to Paris where he read Fanon and first shaped his anti-imperialist views, and subsequently, in 1965, to Iran, where he entered into contact with some members of the Iranian left. Such contacts were to consolidate in the years leading up to the Iranian revolution, fostered by their shared denouncement of the shah's dictatorial policies and, later, by their solidarity with the revolutionary movement in Oman.[64] They were also to crucially contribute to

62 Abrahamian, E., *Khomeinism: Essays on the Islamic Republic*, Berkeley 1993, pp. 22–27.
63 Halliday, F., *Revolution and World Politics*, p. 190.
64 Halliday, F., 'The Iranian Revolution and Its Implications', in *New Left Review*, vol. 166, Nov.–Dec. 1987, p. 30.

shaping Halliday's notion of the centrality of international oppression in revolutions and his belief in the intrinsically transnational nature of every revolutionary process.[65]

As an undergraduate student in Oxford he met some of the leading figures of the British New Left, including his future collaborator at *Black Dwarf* and the *New Left Review,* Tariq Ali, and his later colleague at LSE, Mary Kaldor. A few years later, while at the School of Oriental and African Studies (SOAS), he became acquainted with the theories of Bill Warren, a leading British communist, who was to strongly influence Halliday's ideas on capitalism and development.[66] In the early 1970s he joined the guerrillas in Dhofar as a reporter, supporting their struggle against the Omani state, an experience that would later inspire both his first monograph, *Arabia without Sultans* (1974), and his PhD thesis, *Aspects of South Yemen's Foreign Policy* (LSE, 1985). In those years he emerged as one of the most vocal critics of Anglo-American policies in the Persian Gulf.[67] In the second half of the decade, Halliday and his wife Maxine Molyneux travelled to Ethiopia, where they witnessed the ascendance to power of Mengistu and the unfolding of the civil war.[68] Thanks to these experiences and to his provocative publications, by the late 1970s Halliday had established himself as one of the most creative and influential leftist thinkers in Europe. As noted by the distinguished scholar of International Relations and Halliday's future colleague at LSE, Michael Cox, his interest in the Middle East was not 'that of an up-and-coming academic in search of a doctoral topic'. Rather 'it was that of an engaged revolutionary for whom research was always (or at least for a very long time) connected to a political project whose goal was nothing less than the overthrow of imperialism in the Third World'.[69]

In the years between his first visit to Iran as an undergraduate student in 1965 and the revolution in 1978–1979, Halliday continued to monitor closely the country's

65 On this point see Lawson, G., 'Halliday's Revenge: Revolutions and International Relations', in *International Affairs*, vol. 87, no. 5, 2011, pp. 1069–1070.

66 See: Halliday, F., 'Imperialism and the Middle East: Review of "Imperialism: Pioneer of Capitalism", by Bill Warren', in *MERIP Reports*, vol. 117, Sept. 1983, pp. 19–22.

67 See Halliday, F., 'Class struggle in the Arab Gulf', in *New Left Review*, vol. 58, Nov.–Dec. 1969, pp. 31–36; Halliday, F., 'Oil and Revolution in the Persian Gulf', in *Ramparts*, vol. 9, 1971, pp. 52–54; Halliday, F., 'The Americanization of the Persian Gulf', in *Ramparts*, vol. 1, no. 4, 1972, pp. 18–20.

68 Halliday and Molyneux's fieldwork resulted in the publication of *The Ethiopian Revolution*, London 1982.

69 Cox, M., 'Fred Halliday, Marxism and the Cold War', in *International Affairs*, vol. 87, no. 5, 2011, p. 1110.

political and economic development. In 1971 he published a strongly critical piece on the shah's Persepolis celebrations in the American left-wing magazine *Ramparts*.[70] On the eve of the revolution in August 1978, Halliday conveyed his concern about the economic weaknesses of Iranian capitalist development in an article that warned of 'the potential for a revolutionary overthrow of the regime'.[71]

In January 1979, as the shah's regime was crumbling, Halliday's comprehensive study of Iranian politics appeared in print under the title: *Iran: Dictatorship and Development*.[72] The book, which was written during the years 1976–1977 and whose preface predated by just a few weeks the crucial escalation of the crisis in September 1978, 'sought to identify the ways in which capitalist development had transformed Iran while, simultaneously, identifying the weaknesses, economic, social and political, of that development'.[73] In the conclusion to this first edition, Halliday argued that the regime was likely to enter a period of crisis as a result of a contraction of its oil revenues and of the consequent reduction of its chances to implement social policies able to solve the country's structural problems. Though suggesting a few initiatives that would allow the shah's rule to remain intact, including a relaxation of repressive activities and changes in economic policy and military purchases, he also contended that 'the factors against a continued retention of full political power by the Pahlavi dynasty [were] going to increase, as the economic conditions that ha[d] enabled it to survive deteriorate[d]'. He therefore predicted that it was 'quite possible that before too long the Iranian people will chase the Pahlavi dictator and his associates from power', but he also expressed skepticism that the existing parties, especially the Tudeh, would display the necessary organisational skills to seriously challenge the shah's government.[74] Even though the overthrow of capitalism through a revolution and the establishment of a socialist society remained, in Halliday's view, 'conceivable', he argued that the emergence of a coherent mass challenge to capitalism in Iran would require the left to change its strategies and conduct, most notably to overcome its internal divisions, to abandon its subservience to foreign countries, and to reduce its distance from the masses and their needs.[75] According to Halliday, one consequence of the weakness of Iran's traditional parties was that the urban

70 Halliday, F., 'The Once and Future Shah', in *Ramparts*, Nov. 1971.

71 Halliday, F., 'Iran: The Economic Contradictions', in *MERIP Reports*, vol. 69, Jul.–Aug. 1978, p.17.

72 Halliday, F., *Iran: Dictatorship and Development*, 1st ed. Harmondsworth 1979.

73 Halliday, F., 'The Iranian Revolution and its Implications', p. 30.

74 Halliday, F., *Iran: Dictatorship and Development*, p. 309 and p. 299.

75 Halliday, F., *Iran: Dictatorship and Development*, p. 307.

poor and the merchants, the two driving forces of the protests, had to 'follow the religious leaders and phrase some of [their] demands in an Islamic form for want of other alternatives'.[76]

Halliday's views would evolve rapidly as the revolution unfolded. In December 1978, a few weeks before the book's release, Halliday presented a paper on Iran's opposition forces before the British Labour Party's Middle East subcommittee. While remarking that it was 'misleading to see the opposition in Iran as essentially a religious or conservative one', and emphasising that there were 'more than enough thoroughly secular reasons for the population to want the shah to go', Halliday acknowledged the role played by religious forces in the escalation of the protests in Iran.[77] Such an assessment, though only partially capturing the growing role of Khomeini in the unfolding revolution, represented a first revision of the Marxist analysis Halliday had carried out in his book, where he had argued that 'the ayatollahs and mollahs on their own can probably not sustain or channel the popular upsurge'.[78] This shift was the first sign of Halliday's awareness of the religious connotation of the unfolding revolution. Tudeh's endorsement of the fundamentalists and its praise for Khomeini and Islam also affected this shift in Halliday's views. Tudeh's choice not only reflected the Iranian communists' strategy of supporting Shia fundamentalism as a means for mobilising the masses and eventually seizing power themselves, it also conformed to Moscow's policy of promoting non-capitalist development in countries such as Iran while paving the way for coups d'état that would push them into the Soviet orbit.[79]

In the span of a few months, the direction taken by events forced Halliday to come back to the subject in an attempt to adjust his initial reading of the Iranian situation to the rapidly evolving circumstances. In March 1979, after the collapse of the Pahlavi regime, a second edition of the book was published with an appended twelve-page 'afterword'. In this new edition, Halliday praised the upheavals that had driven the shah from power as one of 'the most epic chapters of the international revolutionary movement in this century', acknowledging that

76 Halliday, F., *Iran: Dictatorship and Development*, p. 298.
77 'Iran's opposition forces: Who are they? What do they want?' Undated, approximately December 1978, UK National Archives, Records of the Foreign Office, FO 8/3377. Halliday had expressed similar views in occasion of the International Colloquium on Iran organised by the British Labour Party in Brussels in May 1978.
78 Halliday, F., *Iran: Dictatorship and Development*, p. 299.
79 On this point, see Milani, M. M.,'Harvest of Shame', p. 310. On the policy pursued by the Iranian left during and after the revolution and on the Soviet role in it, see Zabih, S., *The Left in Contemporary Iran: Ideology, Organisation and the Soviet Connection*, London 1986.

what had taken place could not be labeled 'a socialist revolution', but also showed some caution in addressing the notion of an Islamic revolution.[80] He argued that 'it is not possible to talk in any sense of an "Islamic revolution"' as the term Islamic denoted a 'conservative' and not a 'revolutionary change' and served 'as an ideological mask to conceal the multi-class character of the opposition movement and in particular to legitimize the substantial role of the petit-bourgeoisie within it'.[81] He therefore concluded that 'the term "Islamic revolution" does not indicate what kind of change has occurred in Iran but rather obscures it'.[82]

Such 'flagrant, though by no means unusual, deficiency in understanding the religious factor' also plagued the analysis of the events carried out by many fellow leftist commentators who, almost unanimously, shared Halliday's skepticism about the clergy's intentions and ability to run a national government.[83] As would be later argued: 'It is no exaggeration to say that literally none of the expectations, predictions and prognoses of leftist circles, whether inside or outside Iran, have been confirmed by the passage of time.'[84] In this respect it is worth mentioning Nikki Keddie, prominent expert of Iranian history, who argued that '[t]he closest socioeconomic revolutionary model for Iran's experience appear[ed] to be the Marxist formula',[85] and renowned international law scholar Richard Falk, who claimed that '[h]aving created a new model of popular revolution based, for the most part, on nonviolent tactics', Iran could have provided a 'model of humane governance for a third-world country'.[86] A similar enthusiasm was voiced by Pakistani anti-imperialist analyst Eqbal Ahmad, who had helped finance Halliday's project on Iran when they were both working at the Transatlantic Institute, and who praised the revolution as a 'landmark for the future'.[87] A very positive appraisal also came from Claire Brière and Pierre Blanchet, who visited the country in late 1978 as correspondents for the French leftist newspaper *Libération.* 'For one day,' they wrote describing the

80 Halliday, F., *Iran: Dictatorship and Development*, 2nd ed. Harmondsworth 1979, p. 310 and pp. 313–314.
81 Halliday, F., *Iran, Dictatorship and Development*, 2nd ed., p. 314.
82 Halliday, F., *Iran, Dictatorship and Development*, 2nd ed., p. 315.
83 Arjomand, S. A., 'Review of "Iran: Dictatorship and Development", by Fred Halliday', in *Contemporary Sociology*, vol. 10, no. 2, 1981, p. 304.
84 Jafar, M., and Tabari, A., 'Iran: Islam and the Struggle for Socialism', in *Khamsin*, vol. 8, 1980, p. 83.
85 Keddie, N. R., 'Iranian Revolutions in Comparative Perspective', p. 591. Keddie reviewed Halliday's *Dictatorship and Development* at the request of the publisher, Penguin Books
86 *The New York Times*, 16 February 1979.
87 Ahmad, E., 'The Iranian Revolution: A Landmark for the Future', in *Race & Class*, vol. 21, no.1, 1979, p. 3.

return of Khomeini in Iran, 'the breath of the epic has swept away the concerns, the clashes-to-come, the reluctances that burden on the future of the country.'[88]

A misunderstanding of the early stages of the revolution, especially on the role played by the religious forces, along with acclaim for its popular dimension, was by no means confined to radical leftist circles. In December 1978, the American historian James Bill asserted that Iran's Shia Muslim clergy would never participate directly in the formal governmental structure.[89] A few weeks earlier French journalist Jean Daniel had argued in *Le Nouvel Observateur* that the revolution was astonishing the world thanks to 'its humanism, its unbelievable and unbreakable tenacity and, above all, its non-violence'.[90] Even more emphatic praise came from Foucault, who described the revolution as 'the insurrection of men only armed with their bare hands… The craziest and yet most modern of the revolts'.[91] Foucault did not see Khomeini's faction as one of the forces competing for power, but rather as a force representing the entire Iranian population. His views stand in clear contraposition to those of Vieille. On the eve of the revolution, the Marxist sociologist underlined the risks posed by the clergy's universalist message for the future of the country. Vieille argued that 'the denial of social classes can also contribute to the weakening of the movement as a result of the programmatic emptiness that it produces among the popular classes, beyond the immediate goal of the overthrow of the regime'.[92] The British diplomat Nicholas Browne, in a postmortem study for the Foreign Office on why the Iranian Revolution came as such a surprise to Whitehall, noted that with very few exceptions, the great majority of academics and journalists with a longstanding interest in Iran had no greater foresight and no greater success in deciphering the unfolding revolution in Iran than the Foreign and Commonwealth Office.[93]

---

88 Blanchet, P., and Brière, C., *Iran: La révolution au nom de Dieu* [The Revolution in the Name of God], Paris 1979, p. 23.
89 Bill, J. A., 'Iran and the Crisis of '78', in *Foreign Affairs*, vol. 57, no. 2, 1978, p. 336.
90 *Le Nouvel Observateur*, 23 October 1978.
91 *Corriere della Sera*, 26 November 1978.
92 Vieille, Paul, 'La révolte de l'Iran. Table ronde avec A. H. Banisadr, C. Brière, A. Chenal, A. P. Lentin, P. Vieille interrogés par E. Bolo', in *Peuples méditerranéens*, no. 5, Oct.–Dec. 1978, p. 128.
93 Browne, N. W., 'British Policy on Iran. 1974–1978', Foreign and Commonwealth Office, p. 35, available at: http://webarchive.nationalarchives.gov.uk/20120102075301/http:/centralcontent.fco.gov.uk/resources/en/pdf/pdf1/iran-document-british-policy-on-iran. The main exception mentioned in the report is that of Hamid Algar. On Algar's views on the shortcomings of a Marxist reading of the Iranian revolution, see his preface to Ali Shariati's work, Shariati, A., *Marxism and Other Western Fallacies: An Islamic Critique*, North Haledon, 1980, p. 12.

As a result of the book's controversial reception in the months that followed the demise of the Pahlavi regime, Halliday became a regular speaker at meetings and rallies organised by student movements and Marxist groups.[94] In February, Halliday was invited to a conference promoted by the left-wing political group *Liberation.* During the meeting Ron Todd, future general secretary of the Transport and General Workers Union – at the time the largest general trade union in Britain – praised the 'movement for the liberation of Iran', particularly the Iranian oil workers, whose struggle marked a victory 'not only against their internal regime, but also against foreign domination of their country'.[95]

Despite his enduring support for the anti-imperialist and anti-capitalist dimensions of the revolution, starting from the summer of 1979 Halliday began to reassess his stance on the new Islamic Republic that was emerging from the ashes of the Pahlavi regime. His trip to Iran in early August crucially contributed to his rethinking of the revolution. Halliday's visit coincided with the victory of Khomeini's faction in the election for the Assembly of Experts and the resulting accusations made by secular parties of irregularities in the vote, an increase in domestic tensions, the adoption of measures limiting political freedoms and workers' rights, and the first violent crackdown against ethnic minorities. While in Iran, Halliday witnessed the storming of the offices of the opposition daily *Ayandegan,* where an earlier attempt at closure by Khomeini had resulted in massive protests led by leftist and moderate forces. The closure of *Ayendegan* followed weeks of attacks targeting offices, newspapers, and bookshops belonging to the opposition, including the headquarters of the Fadaiyan and Mojahedin. He also observed with apprehension the rhetorical campaign launched by the Islamist forces to delegitimise the other political forces and deny their contribution to the revolution.[96] During his stay Halliday attended some political gatherings and had the chance to meet some protagonists of the revolutionary movement, intellectuals, and journalists. Among them figured Shokrallah Paknejad from the National Democratic Front, Ahmad Shamlou, the famous Marxist poet, as well as Ebrahim Yazdi and Sadeq Qotbzadeh from the Liberation Movement of Iran.[97] The visit

94 Folder 161: 'Iran', FHP.
95 Folder 161, FHP.
96 Halliday, F., 'The Khomeini Regime Seeks to Impose Islamic Orthodoxy', *In These Times*, 3–9 October 1979.
97 The interview with Shokrallah Paknejad appeared a few years later as Halliday, F., and Paknejad, S., 'We Are Living Between Two Tides', in *MERIP Reports*, vol. 104, Mar.–Apr. 1982, pp. 32–33. For details on Halliday's meetings and participation at political gatherings see: Folder 35: 'Iran notebook', FHP.

increased Halliday's awareness of the power of the Islamist forces and of the instruments they had at their disposal in their bid for absolute control of the revolution. 'Islam [is] not just a set of ideological positions,' Halliday wrote in his notebook, 'but [it] is also a set of social institutions with a social force, the *ulama*... behind it. This is important both for the revolution... and for its social implications.'[98] These reflections were accompanied by his mounting concern for the direction the country was taking.[99]

Upon his return from Iran, Halliday wrote an extended report for the *New Statesman* focusing on the violent turn of events in Iran.[100] In the report Halliday drew attention to the inadequacy of the new regime's social policies, the rapidly deteriorating position of women, and the intensification of the government's attacks on those who were labeled as 'enemies of Islam'. 'In a tragic irony, many of those who were in the forefront of the struggle against the shah,' he argued, 'are now once again on the receiving end of government repression and right-wing violence.'[101] He further wrote:

> Unwilling to guarantee basic democratic rights to the press, the opposition or the nationalities, or to implement a serious program of social change, they [Khomeini and his associates] are dragging the country towards a bloodbath, the outcome of which no one can predict.[102]

In the following months, Halliday began to refer to the Islamic Republic as a 'petty bourgeois utopia', a definition that would later be used by other leftist commentators.[103] The characterisation was intended as an attack on the clergy who, while claiming that there were no classes under Islam, were taking advantage of the revolution to win back the power they had lost under the shah. It was also intended to underline the fact that the revolution was merely incorporating the petty bourgeoisie into the state, at the expenses of an overall socialist project.[104]

98 Halliday's personal notes in Folder 35, FHP.
99 Halliday's personal notes in Folder 35, FHP.
100 Halliday, F., 'Tehran 1979: The Revolution Turns to Repression', in Halliday F. (ed.), *Nation and Religion in the Middle East*, London 2000, pp. 155–168.
101 Halliday, F., 'Tehran 1979', p. 158.
102 Halliday, F., 'Tehran 1979', p. 164
103 Halliday, F., 'Ayatollah Utopia', undated in Folder 161, FHP; Moghadam, V. M., 'The Revolution and the Regime', p. 424; Jafar, M., and Tabari, A., 'Iran: Islam and the Struggle for Socialism', p. 84.
104 Moghadam, V. M., 'Socialism or Anti-Imperialism? The Left and Revolution in Iran', in *New Left Review*, vol. 166, Nov.–Dec. 1987, p. 20.

The term 'Islamic' as applied to revolution – Halliday argued – served mostly to legitimate the substantial role of the petty bourgeoisie within it, since their social power was expressed in the first instance via their influence over the clergy.[105] At the beginning of 1980, after the resignation of Bazargan, the approval of the new constitution, and above all, the seizure of the US Embassy, Halliday still described the events of the previous year as 'a blow to American imperialism' made possible by 'a triumphant mass mobilization'.[106] At the same time, he underlined the extreme volatility of the situation and the consequent uncertainty about the future outcome of the uprising. 'Whether this will lead to a social revolution,' he observed, 'or whether new forms of dictatorship will be established, remains an open question… The very role of the Islam also involves major difficulties for the revolution.'[107] A few years later Halliday's condemnation for the Islamic Republic became explicit when he affirmed that Khomeini's anti-imperialism had not led to emancipation from capitalism, but rather the 'replacement of rule by one capitalism with another' and that any liberal government 'would have been better than the clerical tyranny he established'.[108] In 1987, in an interview that appeared in the *New Left Review*, he unequivocally acknowledged that the left had 'miscalculated about Khomeini'.[109]

In the same year, the magazine published an analysis of the revolution by Iranian-American sociologist, left-wing activist, and former member of Iranian student movement in Canada, Valentine Moghadam. In an article entitled 'Socialism or Anti-Imperialism? The Left and Revolution in Iran', Moghadam drew attention to the fact that 'many foreign scholars and activists on the left were supportive of the new Islamic Republic precisely for its anti-imperialism and its defiance of the US government and capital'.[110] Her analysis aptly encompasses the flaws in Western interpretations of the Iranian revolution and the resulting implications for the policy adopted in response to it:

> Most of the Left seemed unaware in the 1970s that the religious forces were weaving a radical-populist Islamic discourse that would prove very

105 Halliday, F., 'Theses on the Iranian Revolution', in *Race & Class*, vol. 21, no. 1, 1979, pp. 84–85.
106 Halliday, F., 'Iran, First Year', p. 4.
107 Halliday, F., 'Iran, First Year', p. 4.
108 Halliday, F., and Molyneux, M., 'Marxism, the Third World and the Middle East', in *MERIP Reports*, vol. 120, Jan., 1984, p. 21.
109 Halliday, F., 'The Iranian Revolution and Its Implications', p. 36.
110 Moghadam, V. M., 'Socialism or Anti-Imperialism?', p. 6.

> compelling – a discourse which appropriated some concepts from the Left… made use of Third Worldist categories… and populist terms… and imbued certain religious concepts with new and radical meaning… This emerging revolutionary-Islamic culture did not become a terrain of contestation as the orthodox and non-orthodox secular Left seemed unaware of its growing influence, and opted for a quite tolerant approach to the new Islamic tendencies within the opposition.[111]

Moghadam's article, published in one of the most respected and influential journals of the European left, provided a more complete formulation of the criticism emerging since the early 1980s in the West and at home of the outcome of the revolution in Iran. At the same time it voiced the widespread sentiment that, in the words of the Iranian Kurdish leader Abdul Rahman Qassemlou, 'All the peoples of Iran made the revolution, but the clergy have confiscated it.'[112]

Understanding the Left's Misunderstanding

It is possible to identify a set of factors that, although general (and generalised), can help in understanding the misreading of the revolution by European activists and intellectuals, most notably their distorted view of the role of the clergy and the confusion regarding the forces that were shaping the revolutionary discourse and, in so doing, the struggle for power. A first element worth considering is the profound influence that a Marxist discourse had on the radical left and on its international outlook. In the 1970s, despite the crisis of orthodox communism, Marxist categories still played an essential role in the radical leftist intellectual approach to Third World crises, especially to those that originated from a popular revolt against a capitalist regime supported by Western powers. The socialist interpretation of the Iranian Revolution, centred on the preeminence of class struggle over any other social cleavage and on the unsuitability of the religious forces to take the lead in post-Pahlavi Iran, was combined with and influenced by the policy pursued by the Iranian communist left and 'its catastrophic stand on liberalism'.[113] Such a stand resulted in the decision by the Tudeh Party to reject any alliance with the moderate democratic forces, most notably with the provisional government of Mehdi Bazargan, against the prospect of an Islamist turn of the revolution. During

111 Moghadam, V. M., 'Socialism or Anti-Imperialism?', p. 14.
112 *The Nation*, 21 March 1981.
113 Halliday, F., 'The Iranian Revolution and Its Implications', p. 36.

the decisive months of 1979, Tudeh constantly attacked the provisional government, accusing it of representing the liberal bourgeoisie and of not responding positively to the imperatives of social justice. Such a tactic, in the view of Tudeh's leaders and of Moscow, was supposed to immobilise Bazargan's government as a step toward seizing power and pushing Iran into the Soviet orbit. As highlighted by Mohsen Milani, the democratic aspect of the revolution was to be forfeited to protect its anti-imperialism and to favour Tudeh's seizure of power.[114]This choice, in the words of Halliday, constituted 'the central avoidable error of most of the Iranian Left'.[115] For the latter, the consequence was the marginalisation, repression, and ultimately exclusion from the political scene under the Islamic Republic.[116] For their European counterparts, Tudeh's ill-fated decision crucially contributed to the misinterpretation of the dynamics at play in the context of the post-revolutionary struggle for power, fuelling hopes for an ultimate victory of the communist forces and reinforcing the widespread neglect for the growing influence of the religious forces.[117]

A second element driving the reaction of European intellectuals to the revolution was the tendency of many within the New Radical Left to look at the Iranian revolution as a typical Third World anti-capitalist revolution, 'a symbol of the structural crisis of the world economic system'.[118] This interpretation frequently appeared in articles and pamphlets produced by the Iranian student movement and echoed the analysis of Marxist German-Iranian activist Bahman Nirumand, according to whom the combination of apparent modernisation with repression, overlaid by a cultural and economic dependence on the United States, had made Iran a model of resistance and revolution for the broader Third World.[119]

Thirdly, the Third Worldist interpretation of the revolution reflected the enthusiasm aroused by its popular (and populist) dimension.[120] As observed

114 Milani, M. M., 'Harvest of Shame', p. 308.
115 Milani, M. M., 'Harvest of Shame', p. 308.
116 On the fate of the Iranian communist left see, among others, Abrahamian, E., *Tortured Confessions: Prisons and Public Recantations in Modern Iran*, Berkeley 1999.
117 *Iran aujourd'hui*, 1981, BDIC.
118 Lentin in 'La révolte de l'Iran', p. 108.
119 Slobodian, Q., *Foreign Front*, p. 109. In 1967, Nirumand published a highly critical study of the shah's modernising policies and Iranian development: Nirumand, B., *Persien, Modell eines Entwicklungslandes oder Die Diktatur der Freien Welt* [Persia, a Model of a Developing Nation or the Dictatorship of the Free World], Reinbek 1967. The works of the Iranian-German teacher and activist had a profound influence on both Iranian and European student movements.
120 On the populist allure of the Iranian revolution, see Moghadam, V. M., 'The Revolution and the Regime', p. 423; Foucault in Guolo, R., and Pansa, P., *Taccuino Persiano* [Persian Notebook], Milano 1998, p. 45.

by one of the main theorists of revolutions, Theda Skocpol, 'What Western socialists have long dreamt of doing (without success except where war has intervened to help), the people of urban Iran did accomplish as they mobilized in an all-inclusive movement against a "corrupt", "imperialist" monarchy.'[121] Mesmerised by the sense of strength conveyed by 'the largest opposition demonstrations ever seen in human history', by the boldness of the crowds marching against the shah's army, and by the apparently non-violent nature of the protests, many commentators could not help but express sympathy for the unfolding revolution.[122]

Such enthusiasm was often combined with a widespread fascination for Shia Islam as 'militant mysticism', and the challenge it posed to the shah's cult of personality and 'imperial ideology'.[123] Many observers within the radical left portrayed Khomeini as the leader of the 'anti-imperialist religious forces' and the representative of the clergy's 'long tradition of anti-despotic struggle' that had its roots in Iran's 1906 Constitutional Revolution.[124] Such fascination for Shiʿism and for Islam's revolutionary tradition was legitimised and encouraged by the policy pursued by Tudeh vis-à-vis Khomeini's forces and, more specifically, the Party's claim of an alleged ideological harmony between Marxism and Shia fundamentalism.[125] 'Shiʿism is a revolutionary and progressive ideology which we shall never encounter blocking our road to socialism,' argued the Tudeh Party's Secretary, Nureddin Kianuri, in November 1979.[126] An attraction to Islam's moral dogmatism, a common distrust of 'bourgeois values' and liberal democracy, a shared anti-imperialist stance, and Khomeini's deliberate vagueness on the question of private property help explain Tudeh's stance.[127] In the months that followed the revolution an intense debate arose within the Iranian and international left around whether Khomeini should be considered a progressive or a conservative leader, and whether the views expressed by his supporters on issues such as women's rights could be overlooked in view of their uncompromising battle against the shah's dictatorship.[128] 'How far can Muslims and Marxists work together, from

121 Skocpol, T., 'Rentier State and Shia Islam', p. 267.

122 Halliday, F., *Revolution and World Politics*, p. 49,

123 These definitions are drawn from: *Iran Report*, October 1971, BDIC.

124 *Iran Report*, October 1971, BDIC.

125 Milani, M. M., 'Harvest of Shame', p. 311.

126 Kianuri, N., 'Tudeh's Kianuri on Embassy Takeover, Relations with Khomeini', in *MERIP Reports*, vol. 86, Mar.–Apr., 1980, p. 24.

127 Abrahamian, E., *Khomeinism*, p. 31.

128 On this point see: Halliday, F., *Dictatorship and Development*, p. 297; de Groot, J., 'The Iranian Revolution', p. 20.

the standpoint of both theory and practice,' wondered Thomas Hodgkin, 'in the continuing struggle against the institutions of capitalism and imperialism?'[129] This remark, coming from a highly influential Oxford scholar with an established reputation as an 'anti-imperialist activist', effectively illustrates the terms of such fascination. A few years earlier one of the most distinguished and influential scholars of Islam, Maxime Rodinson, had already provided an answer to this question. 'The idea that early Islam can be a stimulus for socialist change,' he had argued in his *Islam and Capitalism*, 'is, simply, utterly fantastic.'[130] Yet not many seemed to pay attention to his views in 1979, in the general euphoria in the wake of the Iranian Revolution.

A fourth factor that crucially influenced the engaged intellectuals' reading of the revolution was the preferential relationship many of them, especially human rights activists and lawyers, had developed in the 1970s with so-called 'moderate Islamists' such as Banisadr. Such ties with those perceived as progressive members of the religious opposition, exemplified by Banisadr's ties with some of the most influential figures of French network of solidarity with the Iranian opposition, resulted in the belief that the Iranian Revolution would soon take a moderate course.[131]

One final, but crucial aspect is the anti-Americanism of the European left.[132] Often presented as a facet of the broader anti-imperialist critique, anti-Americanism actually attracted wider and more heterogeneous support than the former, being shared also by European liberal leftist thinkers and scholars. The overthrow of a pillar of Washington's policy in the Persian Gulf, the attacks on Western multinationals in the country and, more broadly, a 'David versus Goliath narrative', galvanised the anti-American rhetoric of many critics of US foreign policy. The seizure of the 'Yankee Embassy' in November 1979 in particular, though not justifiable from a moral standpoint, was described by a volume written in early 1980 by Iranian dissident Chapour Haghighat and distributed by French publisher Anthropos with a preface by Paul Vieille – as 'a striking warning to the American power; a signal coming from the poor and humiliated part of the world

129 Hodgkin, T., 'The Revolutionary Tradition in Islam', in *Race & Class*, vol. 21, no. 3, 1980, p. 221.

130 Rodinson, M., *Islam and Capitalism*, New York 1973, p. 175.

131 See Banisadr and Vieille in 'La révolte de l'Iran', pp. 112–114; pp. 125–127.

132 The emphasis on the anti-imperialist dimension emerges clearly in: Behrang, S., *Iran. Le maillon faible* [Iran. The Weakest Link], Paris 1979; and Haghighat, C., *Iran: la révolution inachevée et l'ordre américain* [Iran: The Unfinished Revolution and the American Order], Paris 1980.

to the wealthy one, intended to remind the former that the Third World could not continue to accept to be subjected to its will'.[133]

The combination of these factors undermined the ability of Western (as much as Iranian) commentators, especially of leftist orientation, to fully capture the meaning and the possible implications of the Iranian revolution. As Iranian diplomat and writer Fereydoun Hoveyda put it: 'Most of the Western intellectuals abandoned their rationality in the name of History and praised the collapse of reason and justice in Iran.'[134] As noted above, the misunderstanding was by no means confined to the leftist circles. The cases of James Bill, Michel Foucault, and Jean Daniel, among others, show the almost ubiquitous confusion that accompanied the early stages of the revolution and the difficulties displayed by intellectuals, activists, and politicians when trying to make sense of the rapidly evolving events. Borrowing Stephanie Cronin's words, 'the Iranian Left was hardly alone in its inability to grasp accurately and immediately the essential character of the new Islamic state.'[135]

Conclusion

The fall of the Pahlavi regime and the establishment of the Islamic Republic not only jeopardised Western economic and strategic interests in the region; it also challenged the patterns of modern revolutions. Universal in scope, but with a strong national connotation, anti-communist, despite the great emphasis placed on social justice, fought under the banner of religion despite the professed secularism of many among its protagonists, the Iranian Revolution presented a conundrum for intellectuals, especially those of leftist orientation. While later developments would clearly reveal the authoritarian character of the new regime, the early stages of the revolution triggered hopes for a socialist victory and induced some commentators to praise the popular uprising as a successful example of anti-systemic struggle, an 'attack on the weakest link in the world capitalist system' that not only overthrew an authoritarian regime but also posed a direct challenge to American imperialist hegemony in the Middle East.[136] The trans-class participation in the uprisings, the widespread criticism of the human rights violations perpetrated by

133 Haghighat, C., *Iran: la révolution inachevée*, p. 3.

134 Hoveyda, F., 'L'Intelligentsia occidentale face à Khomeyni' [The Reaction of Western Intelligentsia to Khomeini], in *Revue des deux mondes*, January 1988, p. 65.

135 Cronin, S., 'Introduction', in Cronin, S. (ed.), *Reformers and Revolutionaries in Modern Iran. New Perspectives on the Iranian Left*, London 2004, p. 5.

136 Behrang, S., *Iran. Le maillon faible*.

the shah's regime, the influence of the Third Worldist discourse, the large role played by labour strikes in the early stages of the revolution, a general misunderstanding of Iranian religious and socio-economic features, the strong ties between Iranian and European student communities, a certain fascination for Shiʿism as an instrument of political struggle, and Tudeh's initial support to Khomeini, all help explain why many leftist academics and activists initially welcomed the events of 1979 with enthusiasm, failing to realise the complex nature of the revolution which was unfolding.[137]

In some cases the initial fascination quickly made way for a more critical appraisal of the events underway. For others, the allure of the sudden demise of one of Washington's key allies in the oil-rich Middle East, the overthrow of a regime that had embraced capitalism and anti-communism in exchange for its transformation into the gendarme of the Persian Gulf, proved more resilient than expected. Some elements help to explain this divergence: the observers' personal experiences with Iran; their connections with the Iranian community, especially with opposition groups; the reasons behind their earlier criticism of the regime; their previous knowledge of the country, and, last but not least, their attitude towards orthodox Marxism. The closer the observers were to traditional, pro-Soviet positions, the more difficulties they encountered in making sense of the events taking place in Iran. In other words, whereas it is true that very few commentators managed to escape the seductive power of the Iranian revolution and of its charismatic leader, some differences persisted in the reading of the events.

Orthodox Marxists and pro-Soviet communists were the last to recognise the authoritarian character of the revolution. For many of them acknowledging the Islamic turn taken by the Iranian events meant also taking distance from some of the founding moments of socialism, such as the French and Russian revolutions. Such a process implied a revision of the notions of class struggle, nationalism, and liberalism as theorised by Marxism. It also implied a reassessment of the narrative of modern revolutions, an admission of the strategic mistakes made by Tudeh, and a reappraisal of the dogmatism of both the Iranian left and the European communist parties.

For those who had been fascinated by the anti-imperialist, romantic, and occasionally anti-modern character of the revolution, their attention to Iranian events was too short-lived to allow them to amend their initial enthusiastic appraisals. This is the case for some commentators, such as Foucault, Blanchet, Brière, and Ahmad, of many intellectuals of Maoist or Trotskyist orientations, and for

137 On this point, see: Hoveyda, F., 'L'Intelligentsia occidentale'.

numerous members of leftist student movements and associations. For them the anti-shah protests had represented either a test of theories that had little or no connection with the Iranian context, or another attempt, after the Chinese Cultural Revolution, to advance in the Third World revolutionary ambitions that had been repeatedly crushed in the West.

Academics who had some prior knowledge of Iran, members of human rights associations, and intellectuals who had distanced themselves from the totalitarian dimension of the communist revolutionary project were quicker to reassess their initial enthusiasm for the revolution.[138] Many of them, such as Fred Halliday, Maxime Rodinson, and Paul Vieille, expressed irritation at the archaic religious dimension of the revolution and feared that a clerical dictatorship would emerge from the violence and chaos of the uprisings. For most of them, and for those who took a closer, more critical, look at the unfolding events in Iran, the hostage crisis marked a major turning point in their reading of the Iranian Revolution. That episode, together with the regime's stance on gender and social issues, the violent repression of secular and leftist forces, and the crushing of nationalist movements, forced them to reevaluate their initially sympathetic appraisal of the revolution, often drawing unsympathetic reactions from other sectors of the intellectual community. When Halliday's report on his trip to Iran was published by the *New Statesman* in August 1979 under the title, 'Islam with a Fascist Face', the pro-Soviet Iranian left and its European allies condemned him for taking such a negative position on the new government in power.[139]

Their reactions suggest the difficulties many commentators and activists faced in order to overcome the European left's fascination with Iran's anti-imperialist fight and acknowledge the authoritarian and liberticidal drift that the Islamic (and no longer Iranian) Revolution was taking. To the dismay of most observers the Iranian Revolution and its dramatic outcome proved the limited applicability of the Marxist or dependency paradigms to a new set of revolutions occurring in the Third World which, though making use of anti-imperialist and anti-communist categories, clearly occurred and developed beyond and outside such consolidated yet imperfect frameworks of analysis.

The Iranian Revolution was one of the last occasions in which the European left pinned its hopes on an experiment of revolutionary change. An appraisal

138 On the so-called 'anti-totalitarian moment' of French intellectuals, see: Christofferson, M. S., *French Intellectuals*, pp. 229–266.

139 Halliday, F., 'The Iranian Left in International Perspective', in Cronin S. (ed.), *Reformers and Revolutionaries in Modern Iran. New Perspectives on the Iranian Left*, London 2004, p. 36.

of their reaction to the Iranian Revolution has shown how Third Worldist and Marxist paradigms still persisted in the radical leftist approach to a popular uprising occurring in the non-Western world. At the same time, the Iranian experience defied socialist expectations of radical social transformation in the Third World and, more importantly, demonstrated that religion, a social practice thought by Marxism to be residual, could be a driving revolutionary force against capitalism and imperialism. In this way the Iranian Revolution contributed to the discrediting of the European left in the late 1970s. Such decline occurred against the background of the rise of radical humanitarianism, the end of Marxism hegemony in left-wing intellectual discourse, the general crisis of the notion of Third World, and the broad reassessment of the radical left's attitude towards what would come to be called the Global South.[140]

Before concluding, one question remains to be addressed: did the left, both in Iran and abroad, misunderstand the revolutionary process or was the post-shah revolutionary struggle simply lost? A quote from British socialist Phil Marfleet helps frame the issue. 'Understanding the revolution', he wrote in 1988 'is the first step towards the building of a healthy socialist current within Iran.'[141] His comment highlights the close connection that exists between the comprehension of the events of 1979 and the dramatic fate of socialism in Iran. It also draws attention to the fact that the illusions of the European radical left and the political disaster of the Iranian left had similar roots. They both resulted from an overestimation of the affinities between Shia fundamentalism and Marxism and from a failure to look beyond anti-imperialism in assessing the forces at play in the revolution.

The difficulties displayed by both the European and the Iranian left also had a crucial impact on the academic debate regarding the events of 1978–1983: against the background of the narratives produced by the (disillusioned) protagonists of the revolution, it took decades for both Iranian and Western scholars to produce a more balanced reassessment of the events beyond the myth of the stolen revolution.[142]

140 On this point see Davey, E., *Idealism Beyond Borders*, pp. 181–214; Kalter, C., *The Discovery of the Third World*, pp. 99–103; Dworkin, D. L., *Cultural Marxism*, pp. 246–261. On the rise and fall of the concept of Third World and Third Worldism see, among others, Berger, M. T., 'After the Third World? History, Destiny and the Fate of Third Worldism', in *Third World Quarterly*, vol. 25, no. 1, 2004, pp. 9–39.

141 Marshall, P., *Revolution and Counter-revolution in Iran*, London 1988, p. 8.

142 A crucial contribution to the debate came from: Behrooz, M., *Rebels with a Cause* and Cronin, S., ed. *Reformers and Revolutionaries*.

The arguments presented here suggest that the international left's misreading of Khomeini in itself cannot explain what has been frequently labeled 'the tragedy of the Iranian Left', that is its support for Islamic forces and its eventual elimination from the country's political scene at the hands of those same forces. Other elements such as the weakness that plagued Iranian traditional parties, most notably Tudeh, their limited social and political base, and the effectiveness of Khomeini's political strategy, all have to be taken into account when analysing the process. Yet the opaque anti-imperialism of the left, both in Iran and abroad, and the resulting misunderstanding of the dynamics underway contributed to its failure to influence the course of the revolution and, ultimately, to its repression by Khomeini's forces. As observed by Halliday: 'No one can argue that the Left could have predicted, or successfully resisted, the onslaught of the Islamic forces. What can be argued is that a more circumspect attitude from the start, towards forces with a reactionary social and political project… were both possible and desirable.'[143]

Bibliography

Abrahamian, E., 'The Guerrilla Movement in Iran, 1963–1977', in *MERIP Reports*, vol. 86, Mar.–Apr. 1980, pp. 3–15.

Abrahamian, E., *Iran between Two Revolutions*, Princeton 1982.

Abrahamian, E., *Khomeinism: Essays on the Islamic Republic*, Berkeley 1993.

Abrahamian, E., *Tortured Confessions. Prisons and Public Recantations in Modern Iran*, Berkeley 1999.

Afary, J., and Anderson, K. B., *Foucault and the Iranian Revolution: Gender and the Seductions of Islamism*, Chicago 2005.

Ahmad, E., 'The Iranian Revolution: A Landmark for the Future', in *Race & Class*, vol. 21, no.1, 1979, pp. 3–11.

Anderson, P., 'Components of the National Culture', in *New Left Review*, no. 50, Jul.–Aug. 1968, pp. 3–57.

Anderson, P., and Camiller, P., *Mapping the West European Left*, London 1994.

Arjomand, S. A., 'Review of *Iran: Dictatorship and Development*, by Fred Halliday', in *Contemporary Sociology*, vol. 10, no. 2, 1981, p. 304.

Arjomand, S. A., *The Turban for the Crown: The Islamic Revolution in Iran*, New York 1988.

Arman, M., 'Iranian intellectuals and dependency theory', in *Khamsin* vol. 12, 1986, pp. 27–36.

143 Halliday, F., 'The Iranian Left', p. 32.

Axworthy, M., *Revolutionary Iran: A History of the Islamic Republic*, London 2013.

Bakhash, S., 'Iran', in *The American Historical Review*, vol. 96, no. 5, 1991, pp. 1479–1496.

Bayat, A., *Workers and Revolution in Iran: A Third World Experience of Workers' Control*, London 1987.

Behn, W., 'Persian Literature Published in Europe in the Sixties and Seventies', in *MELA Notes*, vol. 14, 1978, pp. 5–7.

Behrang, S., *Iran. Le maillon faible* [Iran. The Weakest Link], Paris 1979.

Behrooz, M., 'The Iranian Revolution and the Legacy of the Guerrilla Movement', in Cronin, S. (ed.), *Reformers and Revolutionaries in Modern Iran. New Perspectives on the Iranian Left*, London 2004, pp. 189–205.

Behrooz, M., *Rebels with a Cause: The Failure of the Left in Iran*, New York 1999.

Berger , M. T., 'After the Third World? History, Destiny and the Fate of Third Worldism', in *Third World Quarterly*, vol. 25, no. 1, 2004, pp. 9–39.

Bill, J. A., 'Iran and the Crisis of '78', in *Foreign Affairs*, vol. 57, no. 2, 1978, pp. 323–342.

Blanchet P., and Brière, C., *Iran: La révolution au nom de Dieu* [The Revolution in the Name of God], Paris 1979.

Boroujerdi, M., *Iranian Intellectuals and the West: The Tormented Triumph of Nativism*, Syracuse 1996.

Browne, N. W., 'British Policy on Iran. 1974–1978', Foreign and Commonwealth Office, available at: <http://webarchive.nationalarchives.gov.uk/20120102075301/http:/centralcontent.fco.gov.uk/resources/en/pdf/pdf1/iran-document-british-policy-on-iran>.

Caute, D., *The Fellow-Travellers: Intellectual Friends of Communism*, New Haven 1988.

Chehabi, H. E., *Iranian Politics and Religious Modernism: The Liberation Movement of Iran Under the Shah and Khomeini*, London 1990.

Chenal, A., *Les socialistes français et l'Iran (1975–85)*, Paris 2012.

Christofferson, M. S., *French Intellectuals Against the Left. The Antitotalitarian Moment of the 1970s*, New York 2004.

Colas, A., and Lawson, G., 'Fred Halliday: achievements, ambivalences and openings', in *Millennium – Journal of International Studies*, vol. 39, no. 2, 2010, pp. 235–258.

Cox, M., 'Fred Halliday, Marxism and the Cold War', in *International Affairs*, vol. 87, no. 5, 2011, pp. 1107–1122.

Cronin, S., 'Introduction', in Cronin, S. (ed.), *Reformers and Revolutionaries in Modern Iran: New Perspectives on the Iranian Left*, London, 2004, pp. 1–15.

Dabashi, H., *Theology of Discontent: The Ideological Foundation of the Islamic Republic of Iran*, New York 1993.

Davey, E., *Idealism beyond Borders: The French Revolutionary Left and the Rise of Humanitarianism, 1954–1988*, Cambridge 2015.

David-Fox, M., *Showcasing the Great Experiment: Cultural Diplomacy and Western Visitors to the Soviet Union, 1921–1941*, Oxford 2012.

Dworkin, D. L., *Cultural Marxism in Postwar Britain: History, the New Left, and the Origins of Cultural Studies*, Durham 1997.

Ellis, S., '"A Demonstration of British Good Sense?" British Student Protest during the Vietnam', in de Groot, G. (ed.), *Student Protest: The Sixties and After*, London, 1998, pp. 54–69.

Ghamari-Tabrizi, B., *Foucault in Iran. Islamic Revolution after the Enlightenment*, Minneapolis 2016.

Greason, D., 'Embracing Death: The Western Left and the Iranian Revolution, 1978–83', in *Economy and Society*, vol. 34, no. 1, 2005, pp. 105–140.

de Groot, J., 'The Iranian Revolution: What's Happening?', in *Marxism Today*, Feb., 1980, pp. 19–22.

Guolo, R., and Pansa, P., *Taccuino Persiano* [Persian Notebook], Milano 1998.

Haghighat, C., *Iran: la révolution inachevée et l'ordre américain* [Iran: The Unfinished Revolution and the American Order], Paris 1980.

Halliday, F., 'The Americanization of the Persian Gulf', in *Ramparts*, vol. 1, no. 4, 1972, pp. 18–20.

Halliday, F., 'Class struggle in the Arab Gulf', in *New Left Review*, vol. 58, Nov.–Dec. 1969, pp. 31–36.

Halliday, F., 'An Elusive Normalization: Western Europe and the Iranian Revolution', in *Middle East Journal*, vol. 48, no 2, 1994, pp. 309–326.

Halliday, F., 'Imperialism and the Middle East: Review of "Imperialism: Pioneer of Capitalism", by Bill Warren', in *MERIP Reports*, vol. 117, Sept., 1983, pp. 19–22.

Halliday, F., *Iran: Dictatorship and Development*, 1st ed. Harmondsworth 1979.

Halliday, F., *Iran: Dictatorship and Development*, 2nd ed. Harmondsworth 1979.

Halliday, F., 'Iran, First Year of Revolution', in *MERIP Reports*, vol. 88, June 1980, pp. 3–5.

Halliday, F., 'Iran: The Economic Contradictions', in *MERIP Reports*, vol. 69, Jul.–Aug., 1978, pp. 9–18, 23.

Halliday, F., 'The Iranian Left in International Perspective', in Cronin, S. (ed.), *Reformers and Revolutionaries in Modern Iran. New Perspectives on the Iranian Left*, London 2004, pp. 19–36.

Halliday, F., 'The Iranian Revolution and Its Implications', in *New Left Review*, vol. 166, Nov.–Dec. 1987, pp. 29–37.

Halliday, F., 'Oil and Revolution in the Persian Gulf', in *Ramparts*, vol. 9, 1971, pp. 52–54.

Halliday, F., 'The Once and Future Shah', in *Ramparts*, Nov. 1971.

Halliday, F., *Revolution and World Politics The Rise and Fall of the Sixth Great Power*, Basingstoke 1999.

Halliday, F., 'Students of the World Unite', in Cockburn, A., and Blackburn, R. (ed.), *Student Power: Problems, Diagnosis, Action*, London 1969, pp. 287–326.

Halliday F., 'Tehran 1979: The Revolution Turns to Repression', in Halliday F. (ed.), *Nation and Religion in the Middle East*, London 2000, pp. 155–168.

Halliday, F., 'Theses on the Iranian Revolution', in *Race & Class*, vol. 21, no. 1, 1979, pp. 81–90.

Halliday, F. and Molyneux, M., *The Ethiopian Revolution*, London 1982

Halliday, F. and Molyneux, M., 'Marxism, the Third World and the Middle East', in *MERIP Reports*, vol. 120, Jan. 1984, pp. 18–21.

Halliday, F. and Paknejad, S., 'We Are Living Between Two Tides', in *MERIP Reports*, vol. 104, Mar.–Apr. 1982, pp. 32–33.

Hodgkin, T., 'The Revolutionary Tradition in Islam', in *Race & Class*, vol. 21, no. 3, 1980, pp. 221–237.

Hollander, P., *Political Pilgrims: Western Intellectuals in Search of the Good Society*, New York 1981.

Hoveyda, F., 'L'Intelligentsia occidentale face à Khomeyni' [The Reaction of Western Intelligentsia to Khomeini], in *Revue des deux mondes*, January 1988, pp. 57–69.

Jafar, M., and Tabari, A., 'Iran: Islam and the Struggle for Socialism', in *Khamsin*, vol. 8, 1980, pp. 83–104.

Jafari, P., 'Reasons to Revolt: Iranian Oil Workers in the 1970s', in *International Labor and Working-Class History*, vol. 84, Fall 2013, pp. 195–217.

Kalter, C., *The Discovery of the Third World: Decolonization and the Rise of the New Left in France, c.1950–1976*, Cambridge 2016.

Kalter, C., 'From Global to Local and Back: The "Third World" Concept and the New Radical Left in France', in *Journal of Global History*, vol. 12, no. 1, 2017, pp. 115–136.

Kaviraj, S., 'Global Intellectual History: Meanings and Methods', in Moyn S., and Sartori A. (eds.), *Global Intellectual History*, New York 2013, pp. 295–319.

Keddie, N. R., 'Iranian Revolutions in Comparative Perspective', in *The American Historical Review*, vol. 88, no. 3, 1983, pp. 579–598.

Kianuri, N., 'Tudeh's Kianuri on Embassy Takeover, Relations with Khomeini', in *MERIP Reports*, vol. 86, Mar.–Apr. 1980, pp. 24–25.

'La révolte de l'Iran. Table ronde avec A. H. Banisadr, C. Brière, A. Chenal, A. P. Lentin, P. Vieille interrogés par E. Bolo', in *Peuples méditerranéens*, no. 5, Oct.–Dec. 1978, pp. 107–128.

Lawson, G., 'Halliday's Revenge: Revolutions and International Relations', in *International Affairs*, vol. 87, no. 5, 2011, pp. 1067–1085.

Marshall, P., *Revolution and Counter-revolution in Iran*, London 1988.

Martin, L., 'L'opposition iranienne au régime de Mohammad Reza Pahlavi en France, 1960–1979' [The Iranian opposition to the regime of Mohammed Reza Pahlavi in France], PhD thesis, Institute d'Études Politiques de Paris 2008.

Matin-Asgari, A., *Iranian Student Opposition to the Shah*, Costa Mesa 2002.

Milani, M. M., 'Harvest of Shame: The Policy of the Tudeh Party and the Bazargan Government', in *Middle Eastern Studies*, vol. 29, no. 2, 1993, pp. 307–320.

Moghadam, V. M., 'The Revolution and the Regime: Populism, Islam and the State in Iran', in *Social Compass*, vol. 36, no. 4, 1989, pp. 415–450.

Moghadam, V. M., 'Socialism or Anti-Imperialism? The Left and Revolution in Iran', in *New Left Review*, vol. 166, Nov.–Dec. 1987, pp. 5–28.

Morder, R., 'L'Unef et le conflit du Proche-Orient, 1967–1970: positionnements internationaux et contraintes syndicales', in *Matériaux pour l'histoire de notre temps*, no. 96, 2009, pp. 49–58.

Morosini, G., 'The European Left and the Third World', in *Contemporary Marxism,* no. 2, Winter 1980, pp. 67–80.

Moyn, S., *The Last Utopia: Human Rights in History*, Cambridge 2010.

Moyn, S. and Sartori, A., *Global Intellectual History*, New York 2013.

Nirumand, B., *Persien, Modell eines Entwicklungslandes oder Die Diktatur der Freien Welt* [Persia, a Model of a Developing Nation or the Dictatorship of the Free World], Reinbek 1967.

Panah, M., *The Islamic Republic and the World. Global Dimensions of the Iranian Revolution*, London 2007.

Pons, S., 'The Rise and Fall of Eurocommunism', in Leffler, M. P., and Westad, O. A. (eds.), *The Cambridge History of the Cold War*, Cambridge 2010, pp. 45–65.

Rahnema, A., *An Islamic Utopian: A Political Biography of Ali Shariati*, London 2000.

Roberts, A., 'Simon Frederick Peter Halliday, 1946–2010', in *Proceedings of the British Academy*, no. 172, 2011, pp. 143–69.

Rodinson, M., *Islam and Capitalism*, New York 1973.

Sassoon, D., *One Hundred Years of Socialism: The West European Left in the Twentieth Century*, New York 1997.

Shannon, M., '"Contacts with the Opposition": American Foreign Relations, the Iranian Student Movement, and the Global Sixties', in *The Sixties: A Journal of History, Politics and Culture*, vol. 4, no. 1, 2011, pp. 1–29.

Shari'ati, A., *Marxism and Other Western Fallacies: An Islamic Critique*, North Haledon 1980.

Sick, G., *All Fall Down: America's Tragic Encounter with Iran*, New York 1985.

Skocpol, T., 'Rentier State and Shi'a Islam in the Iranian Revolution', in *Theory and Society*, vol. 11, no. 3, 1982, pp. 265–283.

Slobodian, Q., *Foreign Front: Third World Politics in Sixties West Germany*, Durham 2012.

Sohrabi, N., 'Books as Revolutionary Objects in Iran', *Age of Revolutions*, available at: <https://ageofrevolutions.com/2016/04/04/books-as-revolutionary-objects-in-iran/>.

Thompson, D., *Pessimism of the Intellect? A History of New Left Review*, Monmouth 2007.

Vieille, P., and Banisadr, A., *Pétrole et violence, terreur blanche et répression en Iran* [Oil and Violence, White Terror and Repression in Iran], Paris 1974.

Vieille, P., and Banisadr, A., *Quelle Révolution pour l'Iran?* [What Revolution for Iran?], Paris 1980.

Wolin, R., *The Wind from the East: French Intellectuals, the Cultural Revolution, and the Legacy of the 1960s*, Princeton 2010.

Zabih, S., *The Left in Contemporary Iran: Ideology, Organisation and the Soviet Connection*, London 1986.

8

Iran's Global Long 1970s: An Empire Project, Civilisational Developmentalism, and the Crisis of the Global North

Cyrus Schayegh

The second half of the 1960s witnessed considerable changes in Iran's domestic situation, its relationship with the two Cold War superpowers, and its regional position. The country enjoyed run-away economic growth from the mid-1960s and expanded state welfare; moreover, the shah played a leading role in raising oil revenues in 1973/74, extraordinarily buoying Iran's purchasing power. From the later 1960s, the country's political and financial dependence on its superpower patron from 1953, the United States, decreased.[1] Bogged down in Vietnam, Washington accepted, if not welcomed, an ascendant Iran. When Britain withdrew from the Gulf in 1971, the Nixon administration did not step in to fill the vacuum.

---

1 This held true in foreign affairs, as Roham Alvandi notes in his Introduction and has elaborated elsewhere, as Robert Steele exemplifies in his contribution to this edited volume, and as another contributor, Claudia Castiglioni, has demonstrated elsewhere recently. I am indebted to Roham Alvandi for pushing me to identify and formulate my argument in more than one round of revisions, and warmly thank Ali Ansari for comments on a second draft. And it was the case domestically, in fields as distinct as narcotics, economic policy, and culture, as Maziyar Ghiabi, Ramin Nassehi, Houchang Chehabi and Samine Tabatabaei show in the present volume. Alvandi, R., *Nixon, Kissinger, and the Shah: The United States and Iran in the Cold War*, New York 2014; Castiglioni, C., *Gli Stati Uniti e la modernizzazione iraniana*, Milan 2015; Castiglioni, C., 'No Longer a Client, Not Yet a Partner: the US-Iranian Alliance in the Johnson Years', in *Cold War History*, vol. 15, no. 4, 2015, pp. 491–509.

Rather, engaged in a policy of détente with the Soviet Union and an opening towards Communist China, and invoking the Nixon Doctrine, Washington was content with Iran becoming the Gulf's primary guarantor of security. As for Irano-Soviet relations, while they had been lukewarm from 1953 due to Iran's new patronage relationship with the United States, reaching a nadir following the 1959 US-Iranian defence agreement, they steadily improved throughout the 1960s, as did Iran's relationship with the Communist bloc more broadly. Tehran and Moscow re-established full ties in 1962 and signed an agreement for heavy industry development project in 1966. Mohammad Reza Shah Pahlavi visited Moscow in 1965, 1972, and 1974, after a first visit in 1956, and toured Eastern Europe in 1966. Last but not least, in the Middle East, progressive republican Egypt, an ideological challenger to monarchic Iran since the mid-1950s, was tied down in Yemen from 1962 and beaten by Israel in 1967, and Iraq, a long-time Soviet-backed threat to Iran, signed a border agreement with Tehran in 1975.[2]

Already in 1965, in the midst of these changes, the shah had declared he was pursuing an 'independent national policy' (*siyāsat-e mostaqel-e melli*). By the end of that decade, as a result of these changes, Iran started enjoying a 'newfound international status'.[3] 'The transition in the international system from rigid bipolarity to a more flexible and complicated multipolarity' during détente 'aid[ed] Tehran's more assertive role'.[4] Iran was nobody's 'plaything' (*bāzicheh*) but 'independent', as the shah affirmed for instance during a visit to Josip Broz Tito's Yugoslavia in 1973. His Iran was like his host's country or like the Vietnamese who had 'resisted extraordinary pressure for a long time', the shah argued, emphasising that no country fighting for its independence could be controlled.[5] He stopped worrying

2 For the shah's concern about Gamal Abd al-Nasir, see 'Memorandum of Conversation', 1 July 1958, and 'Paper prepared in the Department of State', 15 April 1959, both in Keefer, E. C. (ed.), *Foreign Relations of the United States* (hereafter *FRUS*), *1958–1960, Near East Region; Iraq; Iran; Arabian Peninsula, Volume XII*, Washington, DC 1993, Documents 175 and 242. For the early 1970s, see Alvandi, R., *Nixon*; Zanchetta, B., *The Transformation of American International Power in the 1970s*, Cambridge 2014, pp. 86–115.

3 Ansari, A., *Modern Iran since 1921*, London 2003, p. 182.

4 Ramazani, R. K., 'Emerging Patterns of Regional Relations in Iranian Foreign Policy', in *Orbis*, vol. 18, no. 4, 1975, p. 1047; an earlier diagnose was Ramazani, R. K., 'Iran's Changing Foreign Policy: A Preliminary Discussion', in *Middle East Journal*, vol. 24, no. 4, 1970, pp. 421–437. See also Johns, A., 'The Johnson Administration, the Shah of Iran, and the Changing Pattern of U.S.–Iranian Relations, 1965 – 1967: "Tired of Being Treated like a Schoolboy"', in *Journal of Cold War Studies*, vol. 9, no. 2, 2007, pp. 64–94.

5 Pahlavi, M. R., *Bayanat, Mosahebehha va Payamha-ye Alahazrat-e Homayuni Shahanshah Aryamehr az Sheshom-e Bahman 1351 ta Sheshom-e Bahman 1352*, Tehran 1973, pp. 153, 120, 121.

about ideological challenges from progressive republican regimes, which from the late 1950s to the early 1960s had pushed him to carry out socioeconomic reforms to modernise Iran while preserving his rule.[6] Instead, from the late 1960s he started positioning Iran beyond other Third World countries. Iran 'should not be compared with any Middle Eastern oil-producing country', the shah insisted.[7] And from the early 1970s he began to forecast, also when addressing Western audiences, that within a generation Iran would become a regional world power, sometimes even speaking of Iran becoming the fifth strongest power in the world.[8] The world listened – including the United States. In 1973, the US ambassador to Tehran stated: '[T]he Shah's vision is that his country's internal strength will gain for Iran recognition as the leading power in this part of the world and one that will command respect even among the great powers.'[9]

In no shape or form was this just empty talk. The shah's words had political consequences, implemented by his diplomacy. He tirelessly honed relationships with countries around the world:

> Since the 1971 celebrations of the 2500th anniversary of the establishment of the Persian imperial monarchy, the Shah has pushed energetically for worldwide recognition of Iran as a power of consequence and one able to play an important international role. This was particularly notable in 1972 when President Nixon and Willy Brandt visited Tehran; when Empress Farah visited China and the Shah himself visited Moscow; and when a host of leaders from lesser countries paid highly publicised official visits to Tehran.[10]

Indeed, the shah's diplomatic offensive was not limited to large, powerful countries and to (pro)-Western and neutral states. It included smaller, weaker international players, for instance in Africa, and socialist states such as Yugoslavia

---

6 The Iranian establishment's, and the shah's, mixed conservative-progressive moves of the late 1950s to 1960s can be seen in the wider context of non-leftist Third World developmentalisms. For such an interpretation, e.g. of Diem's South Vietnam from 1955 to 1963, see Miller, E., *Misalliance: Ngo Dinh Diem, the United States, and the Fate of South Vietnam*, Cambridge 2013.

7 Pahlavi, M. R., *Bayanat*, p. 146.

8 Pahlavi, M. R., *Bayanat*, p. 252. See also ibid., pp. 149, 153, 161; and 'Meet the press', 19 May 1975, available at: <http://search.alexanderstreet.com/view/work/2806897>.

9 'Airgram from the Embassy in Iran to the Department of State', 9 January 1973, in Belmonte, M. (ed.), *FRUS, 1969–1976, Volume XXVII, Iran; Iraq, 1973–1976*, Washington, DC 2012, Document 1.

10 Ibid.

and communist states like the GDR, North Korea, and North Vietnam.[11] Tehran opened diplomatic relations with East Berlin and Pyongyang in 1972, and with Hanoi in 1973, despite the fact that Iran's US patron of old had been at war with the Southeast Asian country since the 1960s. The United States did not resist. They were certain the shah would never go as far as turn against them – indeed, they knew he still needed them – and they in turn needed Iran as the Gulf's policeman, among other things.[12]

Another consequence of the shah's intention to make Iran a world power was geostrategic. From the early 1970s, he saw Iran as *the* regional policeman not only in the Gulf, but also with interests in the wider Middle East and beyond.[13] His 'strategic interests... extend into the Indian Ocean',[14] which he, in November 1972, officially declared Iran's 'security perimeter' (*harim-e amniyyat*).[15] He wanted to make sure that the Soviet Union and its allies and partners would not gain the upper hand in the Gulf or around that ocean. Official Iranian concerns in this regard were heightened when, from 1968, Soviet vessels began patrolling the Gulf,[16] and were intensified by the consequences of the British Empire's final demise. As Peter Ramsbotham, Britain's ambassador to Tehran from 1971 to 1974, recalled, the shah

11 Ibid., and 'Telegram from the U.S. Embassy in Iran to the Department of State', Tehran, 2 July 1973, in Belmonte, M. (ed.), *FRUS, 1969–1976, Volume XXVII*, Document 20.
12 Alvandi, R., *Nixon*. See also, for example, 'Memorandum of Conversation', 24 July 1973, in Belmonte, M. (ed.), *FRUS, 1969–1976, Volume XXVII*, Document 27. In the conversation, Kissinger asked whether Iran would be willing to join the supervisory commission in South Vietnam, being a government 'that we could count on to do an objective job'.
13 On the shah's thought on the Gulf, see for example, 'Special National Intelligence Estimate 34–70', 3 September 1970, in Belmonte, M. (ed.), *FRUS, 1969–1976, Volume E–4, Documents on Iran and Iraq, 1969–1972*, Washington, DC 2006, Document 86.
14 'Research Study Prepared in the Bureau of Intelligence and Research', 28 January 1972, in Belmonte, M. (ed.), *FRUS, 1969–1976, Volume E–4*, Document 164.
15 Ramazani, R. K., 'Patterns', p. 1060. See also, for example, 'Airgram from the Embassy in Iran to the Department of State', 9 January 1973, in Belmonte, M. (ed.), *FRUS, 1969–1976, Volume XXVII*, Document 1. Contemporary analyses include also Steinbach, U., 'Irans Rolle im Arabischen Nahen Osten und Indischen Ozean', in *Orient*, vol. 17, no. 2, 1976, pp. 88–114.
16 Ramazani, R. K., 'Patterns', p. 1061. On the shah emphasising the need to keep the Soviet role in the Indian Ocean limited, see for example, 'Research Study Prepared in the Bureau of Intelligence and Research', 28 January 1972, in Belmonte, M. (ed.), *FRUS, 1969–1976, Volume E–4*, Document 164; 'Memorandum from the President's Assistant for National Security Affairs (Kissinger) to President Nixon', 19 January 1973, in Belmonte, M. (ed.), *FRUS, 1969–1976, Volume XXVII*, Document 2. The shah was also concerned that détente in Europe may give the Soviet Union more freedom of action in the Middle East and the Indian Ocean. See Alvandi, R. *Nixon*; and for example 'Telegram From the Embassy in Iran to the Department of State', 3 July 1973, *FRUS, 1969–1976, Volume XXVII*, Document 21.

knew 'there would be a withdrawal, not so gradual either, of British influence, not only in the Gulf... but also east of Suez generally, in the Indian Ocean'.[17]

To pursue his geostrategic aims, the shah adopted various measures. Politically, among other things, he coordinated his moves with the United States and executed a 'rapprochement with Peking [that was] intended, in part, to gain diplomatic support for Iran's position in the Gulf and the Indian Ocean'.[18] More spectacular was a fast-paced military buildup, also of Iran's navy and air force, including refueling aircraft to expand Iran's oceanic reach. To facilitate force projection, Iran built a massive joint army, air, and naval base in the Iranian Indian Ocean littoral town of Chah Bahar, close to the Pakistani border. It also secured naval facilities in Mauritius in 1972, 'expressed an interest in port facilities and naval cooperation [also] with... South Africa and Australia', and invited officers from other Indian Ocean states to observe Iranian naval exercises. Last but not least, in 1973–1976 Iran sent thousands of soldiers to support the Sultan of Oman's war against leftist insurrectionists in Dhofar, and the shah threatened similar armed interventions, for instance during the 1977–78 Ogaden War in which Soviet, Cuban, and South Yemeni forces supported Ethiopia against Somalia.[19]

Neither the shah's worldwide political diplomatic offensive nor his geostrategic military push into the Gulf and the Indian Ocean amounted to old-style imperialism. He did not desire to permanently occupy or control foreign territories. As CIA director Richard Helmes reported in 1970: he 'has no major territorial ambitions; save as noted below' – a few small islands in the Gulf and petroleum rights on the Gulf's sea floor – 'he accepts – as do almost all Iranians – the country's boundaries as they were determined by wars and treaties in the 18th and 19th centuries. He has, for example, given up Iranian claims to Kuwait and Bahrain'.[20] As Iran's navy commander from 1973–76, Abbas Ramzi-Attaie, put it: 'the time of empires has passed... all of them [empires] disappeared. And the world's situation was not, and is not, such that you can go and occupy a country.'[21]

17 Peter Ramsbotham, Iranian Oral History Project [hereafter, IOHP], tape 1, pp. 8–9.
18 Ramazani, R. K., 'Patterns', p. 1061.
19 'Memorandum from the President's Assistant for National Security Affairs (Kissinger) to President Nixon', 19 January 1973, in Belmonte, M. (ed.), *FRUS, 1969–1976, Volume XXVII*, Document 2. See also Ramazani, R. K., 'Patterns', p. 1061; Ramzi-Attaie, A., IOHP, tape 2, p. 5; Hassan Toufanian, IOHP, tape 3, p. 8, Khodadad Farmanfarmaian, IOHP, tape 11, p. 3; Alam, A., *The Shah and I*, London 1991, p. 261. For Oman, see Takriti, A., *Monsoon Revolution: Republicans, Sultans, and Empires in Oman, 1965–1976*, Oxford 2013.
20 'Special National Intelligence Estimate 34–70', 3 September 1970, in Belmonte, M. (ed.), *FRUS, 1969–1976, Volume E–4*, Document 86.
21 Ramzi-Attaie, A., IOHP, tape 1, p. 16.

This, of course, was quite obvious by the 1970s. Not even the mightiest countries saw themselves as an empire, or tried to permanently occupy lands. Rather, the United States and the Soviet Union posed – indeed, had always posed – as humanity's beacons, the former foregrounding freedom, the latter justice.

But while many Americans and Soviets internalised these self-characterisations, many Cold War contemporaries judged this to be less consequential than a fundamental similarity between American and Soviet behaviour and old-style European imperialism: the will, and often the ability, to systematically and permanently influence others, if need be by force. This, many held, amounted to a new form of (neo-)imperialism, however non-territorial. Many historians agree.[22]

Iran's global diplomacy and Middle Eastern and Indian Ocean geostrategy in the 1970s, too, was more than simply the actions of a nation-state player writ large. The shah's wish for Iran to become a world power, and to lead and guide a considerable area of the globe, amounted to an imperial project – though one, to stress this again, of a non-territorial, post-European empire nature.

This imperial project was manifest in terms and titles. The shah had Westerners address him as 'His Imperial Majesty', and his foremost Persian title was *shāhanshāh*, king of kings. It was precisely as such that he presented himself and Iran, too, most memorably in the 1971 celebration of 2,500 years of Iranian imperial monarchy in Persepolis.[23] Foreign observers picked up on this self-characterisation. Some US diplomats believed the shah thought in terms of a 'modern Persian Empire [that] shall command respect from even the super powers'. Ramsbotham

22 Overviews and general arguments are McMahon, R., 'The Republic as Empire: American Foreign Policy in the "American Century"', in Sitkoff, H. (ed.), *Perspectives on Modern America*, Oxford 2001, pp. 80–100; Maier, C., *Among Empires: American Ascendancy and its Predecessors*, Cambridge, MA 2006; and Porter, B., *Empire and Superempire: Britain, America, and the World*, New Haven 2006. In his landmark study, *The Global Cold War: Third World Interventions and the Making of Our Times*, Cambridge 2006, Odd Arne Westad has dubbed the United States the empire of freedom and the Soviet Union the empire of justice, demonstrating that the Third World was a principal arena for their competition. In *Empire of the Air: Aviation and the American Ascendancy*, Cambridge, MA 2013, Jenifer van Vleck has shown how aviation underpinned the global expansion of U.S. power both soft and hard. Victoria de Grazia, *Irrestistible Empire: America's Advance through Twentieth-Century Europe*, Cambridge, MA 2005, talks of a US 'Market Empire' and studies the impact of American culture on Europe as well as the European pushback. An excellent literature overview is Kramer, P., 'Power and Connection: Imperial Histories of the United States in the World', in *American Historical Review*, vol. 116, no. 5, 2011, pp. 1348–1391.

23 In this sense, my text broaches the question of the afterlife of empires. For related works see Berger, S., and Miller, A. (eds.), *Nationalising Empires*, Budapest 2015, especially idem, 'Introduction', pp. 1–30, which, however, talks not about post-imperial echoes of empire in nationalism but about nation-empire overlaps.

commented that the shah wanted to 'build up Iran as a middle kingdom'.[24] Empire had remained part of the definition of rule in Iran in the post-Safavid (1501–1722) and Qajar (1785–1921) eras, in a world of rampant Western imperialism.[25] The notion of empire not only survived into the Pahlavi era, it was updated by the last shah for a newly globalising world from the late 1960s onwards.

The first of two arguments presented in this chapter holds that the shah's imperial project had a cultural component. The shah framed Iran's afore-noted increasing hard power in the world in terms of soft power. Put differently, studying culture helps us identify the shah's diplomatic-political and military-geostrategic offensive as not simply global or international, but as imperial.[26]

In this chapter I focus on a twin-winged cultural vehicle, and hence manifestation, of Iran's new-found imperial project: the global projection of a vision of Iran as a civilisational-developmental beacon for the world. First, Iran was not some run-of-the-mill nation-state, but constituted an age-old civilisation, *tamaddon*, and one that had always bridged West and East, bringing them together.[27] The second part concerned *tamaddon-e bozorg*. The Great Civilisation, in

24 'Airgram from the Embassy in Iran to the Department of State', 9 January 1973, in Belmonte, M. (ed.), *FRUS, 1969–1976, Volume XXVII,* Document 1; and Peter Ramsbotham, IOHP, tape 1, p. 8.

25 One of the few texts touching on Qajar Iran as an empire is Kashani-Sabet, F., *Frontier Fictions: Shaping the Iranian Nation, 1804–1946*, Princeton 1999, pp. 4, 48; however, her focus is on the importance of land in nation-state building from the nineteenth century. Amanat, A., *Pivot of the Universe: Nasir al-Din Shah and the Iranian Monarchy*, London 2008, shows that the Qajar ruler 'Aqa Muhammad Khan's ambition [r. 1785–1797] was to restore the old boundaries of the Safavid empire in the Iranian periphery. ... This plan was only partly modified under Fath Ali Shah [r. 1797–1834]. The same spirit of warfare as the basis of imperial domination remained a part of the Qajar ethos under Muhammad Shah (1834–1848) and during Nasir al-Din's [r. 1848–1896] early reign.' Ibid., p. 4. See also ibid., pp. 7–9, for key cultural facets of monarchy under the Qajars.

26 My focus on culture broadly defined is inspired by the 'new imperial history' that has reshaped the study of especially the British Empire in the last two decades. See e.g. Burton, A. (ed.), *After the Imperial Turn: Thinking With and Through the Nation*, Durham 2003; Howe, S., 'Introduction', in idem (ed.,), *The New Imperial Histories Reader*, Abingdon 2010, pp. 1–18; and Ghosh, D., 'Another Set of Imperial Turns?', in *American Historical Review*, vol. 117, no. 3, 2012, pp. 772–793.

27 Intellectual historians of Iran have focused on critics of the shah and his government. See Gheissari, A., *Iranian Intellectuals in the 20th Century*, Austin 1998, esp. pp. 74–108; Boroujerdi, M., *Iranian Intellectuals and the West*, Syracuse 1996. However, Nabavi, N., *Intellectuals and the State in Iran*, Gainesville 2003, has examined state intellectuals, too, demonstrating that 'the major preoccupation of the 1970s was the issue of authentic culture. ... In the 1960s this had been primarily an outcome of third-worldist discourse taken on by the disenchanted intellectuals. Now, the establishment participated in this debate as

English, was a combination between a mixed market-state economy, an industrious workforce, bourgeoning welfare, and some human rights, though not political democracy. This Iranian establishment definition of a syncretic, distinctly Iranian development model was introduced in the late 1960s, i.e. after almost a decade of fast growth in Iran.

Like *tamaddon-e bozorg*, *tamaddon* had solid domestic roots. It reflected the view, ubiquitous even among many Iranians neutral towards the state or critical of it, that their country was more than a regular nation-state. This belief was doubly strong because it predated the shah. From the late nineteenth century, Iranian educators and historians had described Iran as part of the (presumably 'white') civilised world. In the words of historian Farzin Vejdani:

> Iranian historians used the category of civilisation… when discussing progress and decline. Civilisation encompassed the scientific, literary, religious, and artistic accomplishments of settled, agrarian, and urban societies. Historians contrasted this urban civilisation against the presumed barbarism of nomadic and pastoral societies. Finally, they often defined civilisation as toleration toward conquered peoples, particularly when it came to religious belief.[28]

Iran's civilisation and empire were mutually constitutive.

Tamaddon, and by extension *tamaddon-e bozorg*, were much more than domestic concepts, then. Iranians believed their country had always played a role far beyond its borders. It had lost that role at the latest when Western imperialism emerged in the nineteenth century. But now, from the late 1960s, it was back: a return that many Iranians, not only the shah, saw as natural and merited given Iran's historical clout. It is in this context that the global projection of *tamaddon*

---

well', sponsoring various activities to recreate an authentic Iranian culture: ibid., p. 108. In focusing on these activities and discourses, however, Nabavi focuses on a quasi-defensive side of the cultural debate; as this text indicates, there also was an aggressive side, globally projecting Iranian civilisation. See also Shakibi, Z., 'Pahlavism: The Ideologisation of Monarchy in Iran', in *Politics, Religion, and Ideology*, vol. 14, no. 1, 2013, pp. 114–135; and Mirsepassi, A. and Faraji, M., 'De-politicising Westoxification: The Case of Bonyad Monthly', in *British Journal of Middle Eastern Studies*, vol. 45, no. 3, 2016, pp. 355–375.

28 Vejdani, F., *Making History in Iran: Education, Nationalism, and Print Culture*, Stanford 2014, p. 87, see also ibid., pp. 48, 52–54, 82–95; Ansari, A., 'Taqizadeh and European Civilisation', in *Journal of the British Institute of Persian Studies*, vol. 54, no. 1, 2016, pp. 47–58 (Taqizadeh famously advised Iranians to assume Western civilisation). See also Abbas Amanat, 'Historiography ix. Pahlavi period', in *Encyclopedia Iranica*, available at: <www.iranicaonline.org/articles/historiography-ix>.

and *tamaddon-e bozorg* was more than an exercise in civilised humanism. It was a profoundly political move: the cultural framework for an imperial project. It sought to demonstrate that the shah's afore-noted global aspirations were legitimate. A civilising guide, Iran could be trusted as a stabilising and ordering force in the world as well. Characteristically, soft assurances of the world-spanning, universalistic humanist nature of Iran's civilisation were sometimes paired with more hard-nosed references to Iran's past military glories.

The late Pahlavi state's global projection of *tamaddon* and *tamaddon-e bozorg* unfolded within two wider contexts. First, legitimising empire through civilisation and development is time-honored. European empires had done so since the nineteenth century.[29] Colonial pushback was as old, growing ever louder since World War I.[30] *Tamaddon* was a variation thereof. While rejecting the view that only Westerners can lead, empire-like, the shah recognised the usefulness *per se* of a civilisational discourse. He sought to beat Westerners at their own game. This was a variation, too, of the 'post-imperial ideology' of India and China, developed to treat deep scars inflicted by European empires.[31] The shah was criticised, to be sure, doubly when his autocratic behaviour and ceremony at court became exceedingly ostentatious,[32] and after 1979 critique gave way to ridicule. Armed with the cheap wisdom of hindsight, with the knowledge of the shah's downfall, many now termed the shah 'grandiose'.[33] But this was too facile and teleological a judgement. In the West it was racist, too, and disregarded transnational royal-imperial linkages. The shah was profoundly interested in European, especially British,

29 Bowden, B., *The Empire of Civilisation: The Evolution of an Imperial Idea*, Chicago 2009.
30 Adas, M., 'Contested Hegemony: The Great War and the Afro-Asian Assault on the Civilising Mission Ideology', in *Journal of World History*, vol. 15, no. 1, 2004, pp. 31–63.
31 See Chatterjee Miller, M., *Wronged by Empire: Post-Imperial Ideology and Foreign Policy in India and China*, Stanford 2013. There are fascinating parallels between Iran and, especially, China. Both were self-styled empires in premodern times, and in both the transition to nation-state-ness is extremely complex, and empire continues to echo. See Hung, H., 'From Qing Empire to the Chinese Nation: an Incomplete Project', in *Nations and Nationalism*, vol. 22, no. 4, 2016, pp. 660–665; Pines, Y., *The Everlasting Empire: The Political Culture of Ancient China and its Imperial Legacy*, Princeton 2012; Wang, F., *The China Order: Centralia, World Empire, and the Nature of Chinese Power*, Albany 2017.
32 See for example Holden, D., 'Shah of Shahs, Shah of Dreams: Napoleonic Vision of Iran as a New Japan', in *The New York Times*, 26 May 1974, pp. 9, 46–48.
33 See for example Ramsbotham, D., IOHP, tape 1, p. 8. Equally ridiculed were pronouncements like that of Jimmy Carter, on 31 December 1977, that Iran was 'an island of stability in one of the most troubled areas in the world'. Never mind that nobody less than the President of the United States, *looking back* to the entire 1970s, basically confirmed the shah's promotion of Iran as an ordering force – and on no less an occasion than an official state visit to Tehran.

monarchies and their imperial rituals and self-representational *savoir faire*, and European monarchs proved responsive.[34]

The second context concerns the global long 1970s. As noted earlier, international politics in this era witnessed the end of US-Soviet Cold War bipolarity and the rise of a more complex multipolarity. But much more changed in that long decade.

At this point, my second argument comes into play. Iran's civilisational-developmental discourse reflected and reacted to a sense of change that captured the world – and, more acutely, a sense of crisis that gripped Western capitalist democracies in particular – in the realms not only of international politics but also of socioeconomic development and culture. By the early 1970s the post-war growth spurt of Western economies slowed down, screeching to a halt in 1973; many perceived this not as a cyclical hick-up but as a sign that post-war economic growth was unsustainable. In consequence, post-war certainties about the sustainability of Western welfare state models were shaken, too. Moreover, the transnationally linked counter-culture, counter-establishment movements of '1968' were felt far beyond that year, into the 1970s.

The global long 1970s were also, at the same time, and in a linked fashion, a particular time for empires. It was the first hour after the sunset of European empires in the 1960s: a time when, to quote US Secretary of State Dean Acheson's famous aphorism, Britain had 'lost an Empire but not yet found a role'. Not a few people in European ex-empires, particularly Britain, saw the cultural upheaval erupting in the late 1960s as a result of empire's end. To them, that political death went hand in hand with cultural chaos, with a loss of values. It was not by chance that the shah's imperial project saw the light of day at the self-same time. This was self-evident geostrategically, for that project was predicated on the end of Britain's imperial presence in the Gulf and more broadly in the Indian Ocean. But it was true also regarding the civilisational-developmental discourse that enveloped, like a velvet glove, the iron fist of political-geostrategic aspiration. They were two inseparable parts of one single imperial project.

The parallel, linked nature of European imperial demise and Iranian imperial rebirth in the global long 1970s affects how we understand 'the global' at that

34 Ramsbotham, D., IOHP, tape 1, pp. 18–20, recounts how smitten the shah was with Queen Elizabeth and how appreciative he was when she invited him to pay her a long visit at one of her family's estates and to accompany her to the Royal Ascot horse races. Similarly, ibid., tape 1, p. 27, recounted that for the 1971 Persepolis celebrations, the Iranian head of protocol, Hormoz Gharib, consulted with the British on matters of protocol. See also Hormoz Gharib, IOHP, tape 1; and Alam, A., *Shah*, pp. 48, 377.

point. Historians have stated that the long 1970s were a pivotal, transformative period in the history of globalisation, even the (re-)start of real globalisation after the 'semi-globalisation' which spanned from the 1940s to the 1970s.[35] The case of Iran's imperial project – and perhaps, concurrently, the case of an internationally re-ascendant China – shows that this reality had an imperial component.

But this was an imperial component of a new nature. To be more precise, its civilisational and developmental content was syncretic in a new way. This reflected, and simultaneously explained the world's changing balance of political power: the death of European empires by the 1960s, soon followed by the decline of a firmly North-centric US-Soviet bipolarity, and the rise of a more inclusive, geographically more expansive, more global multipolarity. Thus, *tamaddon* did not simply ape the West, which was seen as tiresomely materialistic. Rather, while not eschewing material goods, *tamaddon* was said to be also spiritual and Oriental, picking up an old trope developed in the nineteenth century, but this time with the self-confidence of a country re-ascendant. Moreover, *tamaddon* was neither exactly Eastern nor Western, but pivotal to both, the bridge between the two: Iran was the world's centre, its navel, linking a rather tired Euro-American world in the west with a re-born Asian world in the east. As for the developmental model *tamaddon-e bozorg*, it mirrored the afore-noted American and Soviet notions that the United States and the Soviet Union, respectively, were humankind's beacons. But it tore without pity into their old self-certainties, declaring their 'isms' – capitalism as well as communism – tired, bored, and boring, and positing the need for a new form of combining state, society, and economy.

The remainder of this chapter explores, first, the global projection of *tamaddon-e bozorg* and of *tamaddon*. I then turn to the broader context of the global long 1970s and to the question of how the Iranian case allows us to expand our understanding of that period.

*

Central to the concept of *tamaddon-e bozorg*, in the words of historian Ali Ansari, there was a 'super welfare state' with a solid economic foundation.[36] That concept drew on, and extrapolated into a close future, the fact that 'the 1960s and '70s

35 Osterhammel, J., and Petersson, N., *Geschichte der Globalisierung*, Munich 2003, p. 86.
36 Ansari, A., *Iran*, p. 191.

were... an era of growing prosperity, especially as oil income began to multiply in the 1970s, trickling down partially to the urban middle and lower classes'.[37] The shah himself defined *tamaddon-e bozorg* as an economically successful welfare state in his 1977 book, *Be-su-ye tamaddon-e bozorg* (Towards the Great Civilisation). Abiding by his insistence that within a generation Iran would become a world power, the shah stated that:

> [I]f all our efforts continue as at present, and if no foreseeable situation outside our control arises, we shall construct during the next 12 years a solid industrial, agricultural, and technological substructure for the country's development and will reach the present level of progress in Western Europe. At that time our country will have a population of 45 to 50 million, i.e. comparable to the population of larger countries in Europe, and the era of the 'Great Civilisation' will have begun. ... In Iran during [that] era, there will be nothing left of such age old and destructive factors as: poverty, ignorance, illiteracy, corruption, exploitation, discrimination, and the like. The widening activities of the health service will maximise the health and fitness, up to that which research allows, for each Iranian; and the spread of education will bring the maximum mental and intellectual well-being, up to available standards. ... A highly humanitarian and democratic social order will prevail in Iran during the era of the Great Civilisation, with individual freedoms, social justice, economic democracy, decentralisation, informed public participation in all affairs, and productive national culture.[38]

Although the shah talked in the future tense – and in a utopian accent at that – he reflected an ongoing focus on Iranians' individual welfare (but not collective political) rights in texts about Iran's present 'civilisation'. A good example is *Kudak-e ʿasr-e enqelab: pishgam-e tamaddon-e bozorg* (The Child of the Revolutionary Age: the Pioneer of the Great Civilisation), a book penned in 1973 for Iran's Child Protection Agency. The 'revolutionary age' in the book's title referred to the 1963 White Revolution, a bundle of social and economic reforms including land redistribution that underli(n)ed the shah's claim, made with increasing insistence

37 Matin-Asghari, A., 'The Pahlavi Era', in Daryaee, T. (ed.), *Oxford Handbook of Iranian History*, Oxford 2012, p. 359.
38 Pahlavi, M. R., *Be-su-ye Tamaddon-e Bozorg*, Tehran 1977, pp. 265, 258, 279, quoted from Ansari, A., *Iran*, p. 191. For Iran possibly reaching the level of major Western European states like France, West Germany, and Britain within a decade, see also for example Pahlavi, M. R., *Bayanat*, p. 146.

from 1958, to lead social progress.[39] Its author, Ali Akbar Sarkash, lionised a range of measures, not only land reform but also women's suffrage, the nationalisation of forests, workers' participation in factories' profit, and the Knowledge, Health, and Development Armies that were run by conscripts of Iran's military; and he feted various protective measures benefiting children. Those children, he insisted, 'develop with the values of the revolution: the revolution's Knowledge Army, the revolution's Health Army, possessing [one's own] land [and] water, having books and [school] notebooks and [school] benches and schools and [hygienic] bathes are values that are beneficial throughout one's entire life'. Hence, they would become the leaders of the *tamaddon-e bozorg* that was ostensibly taking shape in Iran as the first decade of the White Revolution was coming to a close.[40]

The centrality of broadly conceived welfare and of a virtuous, industrious work force to Iran's present 'civilisation' was emphasised not only in Persian and not simply in Iran. These elements were projected globally, though not as 'the Great Civilisation', but more broadly as 'civilisation'. A case in point was an interview the shah gave in 1975 during a visit to the United States to a major TV news show, Meet the Press. In this half-hour long meeting with leading American journalists, Lawrence E. Spivak asked him: 'Your Majesty, in an interview last year you were reported as saying in 25 years Iran will be the fifth largest world power and that your achievements will be what you can contribute to civilisation. What is it you would like to contribute to civilisation?' The shah answered:

> [T]he wages and the revenues of every individual will be enough to cover their expenses. Many of their expenses will be sustained or subsidised by the states. Studies will be free until the end of the university level and more if necessary. [We] will provide even food for the children during their school hours. Every kind of insurances will take care of everything that could happen to them during their lives. So they will, since the moment that they will

39 See e.g. Ansari, A., 'The Myth of the White Revolution: Mohammad Reza Shah, "Modernisation", and the Consolidation of Power', in *Middle East Studies*, vol. 37, no. 3, 2001, pp. 1–24.

40 Sarkash, A., *Kudak-e Asr-e Enqelab: Pishgam-e Tamaddon-e Bozorg*, Tehran 1973, p. 5. See also Pahlavi, M. R., *Rahbari-ye Ostandaran va Farmandaran be-su-ye Dowran-e Tamaddon-e Bozorg*, Tehran 1973. Hakim-Elahi, N., *Dar rah: Tamaddon-e Bozorg az Kurosh ta Pahlavi*, Tehran 1971, too, played on those themes; but also broached the concept's universal dimension. Hakim-Elahi opened his 500-page long volume on Iran's history by claiming that, 'Iran's history in effect describes the progress of humankind and recounts the formation of the world's civilisation.' Ibid.: first page of an untitled and unnumbered foreword.

> be born until they die, they will be covered by various kind[s] of insurances or measures taken by the government or their society to provide them the most decent kind of living that is possible. … [But] they will have also to work for their happiness… .[41]

That the shah, talking of Iran's contribution to a presumed world civilisation, bypassed the country's cultural past or present and focused on its contemporary socioeconomic and quasi-moral profile had a larger context: the protracted political and cultural crises of both the US and Soviet blocs, and from 1973 the economic slowdown especially in the West. This indicated to the shah that 'all those "isms" like capitalism, socialism, communism, or anything else have become dated; they are more than [one] hundred to [one] hundred fifty years old and do not suit humanity's aspirations' any longer. On a related note, in 1973 he mused that the world 'perhaps has never [really] needed the nuclear countries [i.e. principally the United States and the Soviet Union] to the extent presently felt'.[42] This view was accompanied by indignation about the presumed moral decline of Western societies. From the late 1960s the shah, time and again, excoriated Western countries in the Western media on that account.

Such royal critique was heard not only in and by Western media. International organisations, too, were responsive to the shah, providing him with a stage from the late 1960s, a development he eagerly promoted. In 1972, the International Labour Organisation (ILO) – which had sent advisors to Iran's Workers Social Insurance Organisation from 1955 and whose most serious delegation, including five specialists, were permanently stationed in Iran from 1964 to 1968[43] – invited the shah to give a special address to its 1972 annual International Labour Conference, held in Geneva. The ILO's Secretary-General, Wilfred Jenks – whose meeting with the shah is pictured below (Fig. 1) – introduced him in glowing terms: 'You, Sire, have much to tell us of the relationship to each other in the developing world of political stability, economic growth and social justice. … [You have] a distinctive place among the architects of social policy in the twentieth century as an Emperor leading a social revolution.' The shah on his part used the occasion to posit that new syncretic socioeconomic moral developmental

41 'Meet the press', 19 May 1975.

42 Pahlavi, M. R., *Bayanat*, p. 254 (interview with *Der Spiegel*), p. 120 (interview with the Yugoslav media).

43 'Rapport au government de l'Iran sur le devéloppement des mesures de sécurité sociale. Projet de rapport final sur la mission accomplie par M. J. Paléologos', 1969, TAP 0–48–4 (box 253), International Labor Organisation Archives, Geneva.

Figure 1: Wilfred Jenks (left, pictured from behind) talking with the shah, Geneva, 1972. Courtesey of the Historical Archives of the International Labour Office (ILO), Geneva (from file 3552).

visions like Iran's may be a way forward – for the world. Invoking the term *tamaddon-e bozorg*, he affirmed that 'Iran has, fortunately, found the path to its salvation. It has rapidly progressed in the direction of Great Civilisation and is ready to give other developing countries the benefit of its experience – if they so desire, of course – to help them successfully to realise their own projects.'[44]

To the shah, the decline of the global North and especially of Western capitalist democracies, including their ability to serve as models for other countries, was connected to the quadrupling of the oil price in 1973. 'When he announced the decision to raise the price of oil at a press conference', Ansari explains, the shah stated:

> [A]s far as the industrial world is concerned… the era of extraordinary progress and income… based on cheap oil has ended. They should find new energy resources and gradually tighten their belts, and eventually all the children of wealthy families who have plenty to eat, who have cars and who act almost like terrorists, planting bombs here and there, or choosing other ways will have to… work harder.[45]

44 International Labour Organisation, *International Labour Conference: 57th Session, Geneva, 1972: Record of the Proceedings*, Geneva 1972, pp. 199, 201. See also Madjid Madjidi, IOHP, tape 6, pp. 2–5.
45 Ansari, A., *Iran*, p. 183.

Such pronouncements accentuated an extant indignation about how anti-stablishment lifestyles, strikes, and protests and *in extremis* leftist terrorism had affected Western industrial societies from the late 1960s. By contrast, the shah desired a society 'free from the blemishes of your [Western] society'. As he told an Indian interviewer in 1974: '[I]f we [Eastern nations] protect [our] inheritance… I am confident that we shall avoid the abysses into which material and materialistic civilisations have fallen.'[46]

Related views about Western societies' troubles were voiced by Iranian sociologists. Relying on contemporary Western sociologists and psychologists, Ehsan Naraqi for instance diagnosed a deep 'identity crisis' and a loss of hope especially among Western youngsters. In his view, that development resulted from long-established excessively technocratic, machine-like societal structures.[47] This morally conservative diagnosis of 'the West' may have been at least partly inspired by older views, in Iran, of (Aryan) Iranians as a force for good in the world from ancient times.[48] And it was doubly strong because it ran in parallel to Iranian non- or anti-establishment intellectuals' critiques of Western society as blatantly materialistic.[49]

The shah also insisted that 'our society will be based on very high moral, social-justice inclinations' and that Iranians' welfare gains will unfold in a 'framework of… human and personal freedom and liberty'.[50] His reference to human rights built on an older view in Iran, dating back to the 1930s, that modern human rights can be traced back to ancient Iran.[51] Often mentioned was the Cyrus Cylinder, issued by the Achaemenid Persian emperor, Cyrus the Great, after his conquest of Babylon (in today's Iraq) in 539 B.C. *Inter alia* affirming that Cyrus had bettered Babylonians' lives, it was extolled by the shah and his government as the first human rights charter in history.[52]

---

46 Pahlavi, M. R., *Bayanat*, p. 257; Pahlavi, M. R., *Selection from the Shahanshah Aryamehr's Speeches and Writings on Culture*, Tehran 1975, p. 57.

47 Naraqi, E., *Ghorbat-e gharb*, Tehran 1974, p. 10. See also Pahlavi, M. R., *Bayanat*, pp. 207, 239.

48 For example Pirniya, H., *Iran-e Bastani*, Tehran 1927 [reprinted 1983], p. 504.

49 Nabavi, N., *Intellectuals and the State in Iran*, esp. pp. 67–142.

50 'Meet the press', 19 May 1975. In response, Spivak questioned the shah on Iran's increasingly dire and criticised human rights records; the shah pushed back.

51 Thus, for example Pirniya, H., *Iran-e Bastani*, p. 507, and Khachayar, A. -A., *Le culte d'Etat chez la Nation Iranienne (démontré à travers les âges en vue de la paix)*, Paris 1936, p. 43, insisted on Achaemenid tolerance *vis-à-vis* all religions.

52 The Islamic Republic picked up that description, for instance when receiving the cylinder on loan from the British Museum in 2010. See: https://www.theguardian.com/world/2010/sep/10/cyrus-cylinder-returns-iran. For the late Pahlavi reception of Cyrus the Great, see Ansari, A., *Politics*, pp. 166–179.

This utterly ahistorical claim was made not only in Iran, but also abroad.[53] Given that the roots of this claim predated the shah, and given that its global propagation started before Iran got a bad press for human rights abuses, this narrative cannot simply be explained as a defensive response to condemnations of the Pahlavi regime in the 1970s. Rather, it was meant to inscribe Iran into the origins, history, and story of human rights, an important concept in post-World War II international politics. This is evident in the contexts in which such claims were made. As Robert Steele has shown in this volume, the claim was first made in 1958 by the shah's cultural counsellor, Shojaeddin Shafa, and involved UNESCO. The cylinder also adorned a 1967 stamp commemorating that year's United Nations Day; similar stamps were issued in later years.[54] When speaking to foreign audiences, the shah praised Cyrus's presumed pioneering role in defining and guaranteeing human rights. Addressing an international congress of Iran specialists in Shiraz in 1966, he stated that 'the history of our empire began with the liberating charter of Cyrus the Great. Perhaps for the first time in human history, liberalmindedness and respect for people's rights and beliefs were proclaimed as the basic principles of government'.[55] In a speech in India in 1968, he praised the Achaemenid ruler for having 'granted to his subjects the most complete human rights ever established to that time'.[56] The most public occasion, however, took place in Persepolis in October 1971, during the 2,500 Anniversary Celebrations of the Founding of the Persian Empire by Cyrus the Great.[57] Addressing Cyrus's tomb in front of dozens of high-ranking state representatives from around the world, the shah hailed the Achaemenid king not simply 'as the founder of the oldest Empire in the world' but also 'as the great emancipator of history, as the noble son of humanity'.[58]

53 It was enough powerful and propagated to influence also non-Iranian, popular views of the historic roots of human rights. See, for example: http://www.humanrights.com/what-are-human-rights/brief-history [accessed 1 September 2017].

54 See Siebertz, R., *Die Briefmarken Irans als Mittel politischer Bildpropaganda*, Wien 2005, p. 76; picture of a stamp from 1971 in ibid., Tafel VII, Abb. 66. The shah made related statements at anniversaries of the 1948 Declaration of Human Rights; thus, in 1963, he affirmed that 'during our long-lived history, we not only have enjoyed a humanitarian civilisation and culture, but also tried to inseminate and propagate this tradition in other areas of the world'. Pahlavi, M. R., *Selections*, p. 36.

55 'Translation of his Imperial Majesty Shahanshah Aryamehr's Speech at the Inauguration of the Iranology Congress in Shiraz (9 Shahrivar 1345)', in Aryanpur (Kashani), A. (ed.), *A Translation of the Historic Speeches of His Imperial Majesty Shahanshah Ayamehr*, Tehran 1975, p. 19.

56 Pahlavi, M. R., *Speeches and Writings on Culture*, p. 34.

57 See e.g. 'First Party of Iran's 2500-Year Celebration', *The New York Times*, 13 October 1971, p. 3.

58 Pahlavi, M. R., 'Encomium upon Cyrus the Great', in idem, *Speeches and Messages*

Like *tamaddon-e bozorg*, an imperially accented *tamaddon* was intended not only for Iranians, but for global consumption. It was built on an older view, ubiquitous in Iran, of the country as a world civilisational centre. Firoozeh Kashani-Sabet has described such views in the Qajar period.[59] In the early twentieth century, too, Iranian scholars made this claim about their country's past. Mohammad Mohammadi Malayeri opened his *Farhang-e Irani va Taʾsir-e an dar Tamaddon-e Eslam va Arab* (Iranian Culture and its Influence on Islamic and Arabic Civilisations) (1944) by stating:

> [T]here are few nations (*mellat*) like Iran whose historical timespan and widely radiant culture has endured thousands of years, and that has had a great share in the establishment and development of human civilisation. The history of the culture and civilisation of our nation, which is many thousands of years old, is still an ocean that needs to be illuminated by the effort of Iranian researchers.

Similarly, a textbook used from the late 1930s, Abdallah Razi Hamadani's *Tarikh-e Iran* (A History of Iran), taught pupils that 'the inhabitants of the age-old country of Iran have both before and after the arrival of Islam contributed crucial services to human civilisation (*tamaddon-e bashar*)'.[60] Moreover, defined as a civilisation, Iran carried distinct echoes of an empire. Successive pre- and post-Islamic dynasties such as the Achaemenids and Safavids were seen as civilisation's carrier – with an impact on the history of not only Iran but the world as a whole at that. As the well-known historian Hassan Pirniya put it, under the Achaemenids 'ancient Iran was the first world empire', *nakhostin dowlat-e jahāni*, in Pirniya's own footnoted French translation, *Empire mondial*. Similarly, Razi Hamadani highlighted

---

by his Imperial Majesty Mohammad-Reza Pahlavi Aryamehr Shahanshah of Iran on the Occasion of the Celebration of the 2500th Anniversary of the Founding of the Persian Empire, n.p., 1972, p. 1. The shah repeated this point – that 'the spiritual heritage of Cyrus the Great … [is] respect for wisdom and for human rights' – addressing the official banquet of the Persepolis festivities: Mohammad Reza Shah Pahlavi, 'Speech … at the official banquet in Persepolis', in ibid., p. 2.

59 Kashani-Sabet, F., *Frontier Fictions: Shaping the Iranian Nation, 1804–1946*, Princeton 1999.

60 Mohammadi Malayeri, M., *Farhang-e Irani va Taʾsir-e an dar Tamaddon-e Eslam va Arab*, Tehran, 1944, p. 3; and Razi Hamadani, *Tarikh-e Iran*, p. 1. See also Purdavud, I., *Farhang-e Iran-e Bastan*, Tehran 1947, p. xix. For Malayeri, see also Ashraf, A., 'Iranian Identity', in *Encyclopedia Iranica*, available at: <www.iranicaonline.org/articles/iranian-identity-iv-19th-20th-centuries>.

the *jahāngiri va jahāndāri-ye pādeshāhān-e ʿazim al-shaʾn*, the 'world conquest and sovereignty of the mighty emperors', of Iran.[61]

The shah was on very well-established domestic ground, then, when he globally projected a view of Iran as a world civilisation and of the monarchy as its driving force.[62] The shah and his government started this strategy from the 1950s.[63] A first milestone came in the early 1960s: the '7000 Years of Iranian Art' exhibition. Initially curated in Paris, it toured Western Europe in 1961–1963 and the United States in 1964–1965. Originally envisioned as the opening shot for the 2,500 years celebration of the Iranian monarchy (which was postponed to 1971), it was far larger and better visited than similar earlier exhibitions in London in 1931, Leningrad in 1935, Cairo in 1935, Paris in 1938, Washington in 1940, New York and Boston in 1950, and Rome in 1956.[64] American scholars of Iran lionised it in 1962 as 'the famous exhibition that has been in Paris and is now moving from city to city in Europe'.[65] High-level Iranian and Western administrators and art historians were involved throughout. The shah and the respective host country's head of state were the honourary patrons of each exhibition committee.[66] And the Iranian authorities imprinted their view of Iran on the exhibition. Personally inaugurating the exhibition's US tour in Washington's Smithsonian Institution in June 1964, the shah said: '[O]ur American friends, as they acquaint themselves with Iran's ancient culture and civilisation through this exhibition, will grasp the humanity and universality of Iran's culture, and will become aware that Iran has always provided a link between the various cultures of the world.' Host countries

61 Pirniya, H., *Iran-e Bastan*, Tehran 1938, vol. I, p. 2; Razi Hamadani, A., *Tarikh-e Iran*, Tehran 1938, p. 1.
62 For the related issue of the (self-assigned) place of the (Pahlavi) monarch in Iranian nationalism, see Ansari, A., *Iran*, pp. 59–72 ('dynastic nationalism'); see also Ansari, A., *Politics*, pp. 170–174.
63 See for example the shah's statement, during his reception of an honorary doctorate in law from Columbia University, New York, in 1955, that '[T]hroughout the history of human civilisation, we Iranians have contributed greatly to the world's culture and civilisation.' In Pahlavi, M. R., *Selections*, p. 4.
64 Istituto italiano per il medio ed estremo Oriente, *Mostra d'arte iranica*, Milan 1956, p. 16; Gemeinnütziger Verein Villa Hügel, *7000 Jahre Kunst in Iran*, Essen 1962, pp. 19–20.
65 Memorandum of a meeting of Iranian scholars, [Harvard University], Cambridge, MA, 3 April 1962 [present: George Miles, M. B. Smith, Charles K. Wilkinson, Richard Frye, Martin Dickson, Edward Kennedy, Mark Dresden, Hussein Nasr, Ehsan Yarshater, Amin Banani, T. Cuyler Young], in folder 25, box 11, AC164 (Department of Near Eastern Studies Collection), Mudd Manuscript Library, Princeton University, Princeton.
66 Palais des beaux arts, *Sept mille ans d'art en Iran*, Paris 1962, unnumbered opening page; Verein Villa Hügel, *7000 Jahre*, p. 9; Smithsonian Institution, *7000 Years of Iranian Art*, Washington 1964, p. 7.

endorsed this view in exhibition catalogues. In the words of French President Charles de Gaulle, 'Iran is at the crossroads of the world. In consequence, it has throughout centuries been subject to attacks, made many contacts, and exercised much influence. But its genius was to always imprint its mark on what it received, just like on what it gave.'[67]

With Iran's geostrategic star rising from the late 1960s, the global projection of Iran as a civilisation relevant and central to the world became more pronounced. Inaugurating the Pahlavi Building at the University of Chicago in 1968, the shah stated that 'we Iranians are not only proud of possessing the rich relics of a valuable culture and civilisation, but also of the fact that we have played an effective role in the production of other countries' civilisations and cultures.'[68] This universalist framing of Iran as a civilisational beacon to the world, as a bridge for all, especially between 'East' and 'West', was reflected also in the theatrics of the 1971 celebrations in Persepolis. The shah's aforementioned address to Cyrus the Great at the latter's tomb peaked in the following words:

> Today, as in thy age, Iran bears the message of liberty and the love of mankind in a troubled world and is the guardian of the most sublime human aspirations. The torch thou lit, has never died in stormy times. Today it casts its light upon this land more brightly than ever and, as in thy time, its brilliance spreads far beyond the boundaries of Iran. Cyrus! Great King, King of Kings, Noblest of the Noble, Hero of the history of Iran and the world! Rest in Peace, for we are awake, and we will always stay awake.[69]

This address brought out the imperial context of Iran as a civilisation with a world mission: it was, after all, addressed to an emperor. On other occasions, the imperial subtext became even more pronounced. In an address to the first World Congress of Iranology, held in 1966 in Tehran (and repeated 1971), the shah stated:

> We do not pay respect to the history of our civilisation and culture merely because we have no record of victories or military conquests. You know better

67 Smithsonian Institution, *7000 Years*, p. 6, and Palais des beaux arts, *Sept mille ans*, unnumbered page containing a copy of a letter by de Gaulle, Paris, October 3, 1961.
68 Pahlavi, M. R., *Selections*, p. 30; see also ibid., pp. 5, 6, 30, 34–35, and 36, for similar statements the shah made in California in 1964, Brazil in 1965, Thailand in 1968, Malaysia in 1969, and Pakistan in 1969, to choose just a few examples.
69 Pahlavi, M. R., 'Encomium', p. 3.

> than we do that, during our long history, we possessed one of the largest empires in the world, and that our history is full of victories. Yet we consider our achievements over the centuries in the development and perfection of man's civilisation and culture and in the promotion of knowledge and thought to be the main source of our pride.[70]

A last example of Iran's global projection of its *tamaddon* was a project that, while located in Iran, showcased Iran's centrality in the world: the Pardisan environmental park project, situated northwest of Tehran. Pardisan was the joint brainchild of the US land planning and landscape architecture firm Wallace McHarg Roberts and Todd (WMRT) and of the Mandala Collaborative, an Iranian architecture firm. Negotiating a feasibility study with Iran's Department of Environmental Conservation in 1972, they submitted their plan in 1975; content and language was crafted to appeal in particular to the shah and to Empress Farah. Work on the site started the same year but was stopped in late 1978, when Iran's political climate became uncertain. As Kathleen John-Alder has shown in a fascinating study, Pardisan was to its planners 'an international symbol of enlightened stewardship that would outshine all other environmental parks then in existence, … and [would] provide a platform to showcase the country's rich natural and cultural history'. Referencing 'paradise', the park combined the language of 'Persian architectural grandeur, Islamic spiritualism, and traditional customs' with the narrative of a rising movement around the world in the 1970s for nature conservation. Its underlying argument that 'the technological progress made possible by Western industrialism was no longer adequate' for modernisation paralleled the Iranian establishment's aforementioned suspicion that the Global North as a whole, and the West in particular, had passed its prime. Importantly, 'WMRT… called upon ecological theory to support [Iranian co-initiator Eskandar] Firouz' desire that Pardisan represent "the cosmos and the world" from an Iranian perspective.' Specifically, the Pardisan project put Iran at the very centre of the world-habitat. It 'conceived the world as a dynamic but integrated landscape and positioned Iran as the starting point for global diversity. Paradise, it seems… could be represented as a box matrix connected by information linkages, always leading back to Iran'.[71]

70 Pahlavi, M. R., 'Message … at the inauguration of the world congress of Iranology, Shiraz, 13th October 1971', in idem, *Speeches*, p. 4.

71 John-Alder, K., 'Paradise Reconsidered. The Early Design History of Pardisan Park in Tehran', in Gharipour, M. (ed.), *Contemporary Urban Landscapes of the Middle East*, London 2016, pp. 120, 128.

*

Iran's global civilisational-developmental positioning formed part of a pivotal, transformative era in world affairs and in domestic yet transnationally linked concerns around the world: the global long 1970s. As Poul Villaume put it:

> [T]he 'long 1970s' was a decisive international transition period during which traditional, collective-oriented socio-economic interests and welfare policies were increasingly replaced by the more individual and (neo)-liberally oriented value policies of the post-industrial period. … These socioeconomic and sociocultural processes also found their expression at the level of national and international political power.[72]

Similarly, Claudia Hiepel, in *Europe in a Globalising World*, identified the (long) 1970s as not simply a crisis but a restructuration, as 'the beginning of a multilateralisation that went beyond the Iron Curtain. … The [I]ssue of interdependence became increasingly important … . At the same time the nation-state in its function as a regulatory interventional state slipped into crisis. … With the oil crisis as "the birth pains of interdependence" (Henry Kissinger), even high level politicians increasingly perceived themselves as part of a game that they could less and less influence'.[73] Last but not least, this decade also witnessed the maturation of truly 'counter-hegemonic forces' to the politically and ideologically bi-polar logic of the Cold War, as Prasenjit Duara has stated – a development with roots reaching back at least to the early 1960s.[74]

While different in theme, these studies have something crucial in common. All pay attention only to forces emerging victorious from the 1970s: neo-liberalism, China's state capitalism, and Islamism. This is an important factor: historians and the public tend to be interested more in winners than losers. Still, our hindsight knowledge of the Pahlavi state's revolutionary demise does not diminish its relevance. Regarding Iran's post-1970s future, one may understand *tamaddon-e bozorg* as a precursor to the Islamic Republic's universalist aspirations. While

72 Villaume, P., Mariager, R., and Porsdam, H. 'Introduction', in idem (eds.), *The 'Long 1970s'*, Abingdon 2016, p. 1.

73 Hiepel, C., 'Introduction', in idem (ed.), *Europe in a Globalising World*, Baden-Baden 2014, pp. 10, 11.

74 Duara, P., 'The Cold War as a Historical Period', in *Journal of Global History*, vol. 6, no. 3, 2011, pp. 477–479. See also Westad, O. A., *The Global Cold War*, Cambridge 2005.

their contents differed, both were framed as new, alternative approaches beyond the Cold War's two main ideological camps. One of the most famous revolutionary slogans was *na sharqi, na gharbi, jomhuri-ye eslāmi*, 'neither Eastern nor Western, [but] an Islamic republic'. The Islamic Republic's success as a regional power and the universalist self-view that underlay its global aspirations built on a pattern established in the late Pahlavi period.[75]

Turning to the global long 1970s themselves, the case of Iran's global projection of *tamaddon-e bozorg* and *tamaddon* broadens our understanding of this transformative era: it was characterised not simply by the genesis of a neoliberal hegemony, and not only by challenges like political Islam or China's state capitalism.

First, as observed in the Iranian case, the global long 1970s evinced two interlocking pairs of characteristics. One pair concerned empire. Dreams of empire waxed in the guise of civilisation in Iran just as memories of empire silently and in transmuted shapes echoed throughout European ex-imperial countries like Britain. In his fascinating trilogy, *Memories of Empire*, Bill Schwarz calls that echo 'remembering-forgetting'. Britons talked less openly about empire by the late 1960; empire was present only as memory and story, not as lived experience. Still, to many, 'colonial order remained the natural order of things. ... Memories of an ordered past ... were driven by a powerful, if displaced, recollection of the forms of authority which had been deeply shaped by the experience of empire'. Although such imperial memories were not simply grafted one-to-one onto contemporary post-imperial Britain, they helped to give form to contemporary fears about societal decomposition. In the mid- to late 1960s, i.e. in early post-imperial Britain, whiteness was encoded as order, blackness (of recent immigrants) as disorder. More broadly, countless 'everyday acts of insubordination', most often by youngsters disobeying symbols and persons of authority, 'threatened the very existence of civilised life and, at home, the very existence of the nation' to anxious Britons, transgressing ideas and ideals of an older, more ordered, (implicitly imperial-time) life.[76]

75 For Africa, see Lob, E., 'The Islamic Republic of Iran's Foreign Policy and Construction Jihad's Developmental Activities in Sub-Saharan Africa', in *International Journal of Middle East Studies*, vol. 48, no. 2, 2016, pp. 313–338. As Ansari, A., *Politics*, p. 298, has argued:

> If the fall of the Soviet Union and the Caucasus revived memories of empire... the transformations which followed the launch of the Global War on Terror in 2011 [*sic*] were to prove even more dramatic. Iranians had hitherto dreamed of *Iranshahr*; now they appeared on the verge of realising it. With Iranian influence extending into Afghanistan and Iraq, the political identity of Sasanian Iran appeared to be re-emerging.

76 Schwarz, B., *Memories of Empire, volume 1: the White Man's World*, Oxford 2011, pp. 3, 6, 8, 9. For France, see for example Shepard, T., *The Invention of Decolonisation: The Algerian War and the Remaking of France*, Ithaca 2006.

Iran constituted a parallel to early post-imperial European countries like Britain; together, they formed a pair. In both, empire was present. In both, too, (the) 'time' (of empire) was curious: what one may call 'dream-time'. To be sure, in Britain this time referred to dreams of an empire past, while in Iran it concerned a past that was becoming present again. But in neither country was the dreamt of empire directly invoked. Rather, in Iran's case it was re-framed as civilisation, as Iran's ability to guide the world and bridge different world regions. Iran's subtle but self-confident global presentation of its past empire – and now, anew, its imperial present – as an ordering, civilising force in a world described as chaotic mirrored early post-imperial British fears that loss of empire equalled loss of order and civilisation. These two developments did not happen at the same time by chance, then. Rather, their simultaneity reflected the global connectedness of imperial fates. The very era that looked like dusk and chaos from the perspective of conservatives in Europe in the late 1960s, looked like a new dawn and new-found power from the viewpoint of Iran's establishment. The shah both reflected this parallel development and gave it form when he launched some of his most vitriolic attacks on what he saw as the degenerating West in interviews on British TV, for instance with BBC's Peter Snow, whom he told: '[I]f you continue this unruly and indisciplined [*sic*] social system, your country will explode.'[77]

The other pair of characteristics concerned a wave of political-cultural anti-establishment unrest in the Global North, on the one hand, and, on the other, a conservative push-back against that unrest. The United States and the Soviet Union – the bastions of the world's foremost universalist ideologies, liberal capitalism and communism – were, like their respective allies in Europe, rocked by sustained domestic, yet transnationally linked, cultural-political unrest.[78] Erupting in 1968, this unrest was deeply felt throughout the 1970s. For the Soviets, it took the form also of a fight within the communist world: from the early 1960s, Peking contended with Moscow for the crown of true communism. To make matters worse, the United States and the Soviet Union were weighed down by failures and interventions abroad, most momentous in Vietnam and Czechoslovakia, respectively.[79] And, in 1973, a quarter century of continuously fast economic growth in

77 Ansari, A., *Iran*, p. 184.

78 Fink, C., Gassert, P., and Junker, D., 'Introduction', in idem (eds.), *1968: The World Transformed*, Washington 1998, p. 1.

79 Fink, C., 'Introduction', pp. 3–8. See also Ferguson, N., Maier, C., Manela, E., and Sargent, D. (eds.), *The Shock of the Global: the 1970s in Perspective*, Cambridge, MA 2010.

the Global North came to a halt.[80] Iran's geostrategic rise and its accompanying projection of itself as a civilisational-developmental model complemented this multi-dimensional crisis besetting the United States, the Soviet Union, and their allies. Iran could be presented as a beacon for the world – the shah and Iran's state establishment could praise *tamaddon* and *tamaddon-e bozorg* not only as a domestic success but as an inspiration for a world in crisis – *because and as* the American and Soviet centres of the two hitherto leading ideologies, liberal capitalism and communism, experienced sustained domestic cultural-political unrest.

As Jeremy Suri has shown, the conservative push-back against the anti-system protests of the 1960s/1970s helped bring about the superpower Cold War détente of the 1970s.[81] It was deeply felt in key countries of the Global North domestically, too. In the United States, for example, the famous 'silent majority' was conjured up and culturally sharpened by US President Richard Nixon; and in the United Kingdom, to add another example, the right-wing Tory Enoch Powell racialised British post-imperial political discourse deeply into the 1970s.[82] That conservative push-back was felt also in the Third World, where conservative regimes diagnosed a moral if not existential weakening of the Global North. Iran was a case in point, as this chapter's first part has shown: the Iranian establishment's civilisational-imperial move included moral(ist) judgments of the West as lazy if not immoral, materialist, and past its prime.

This brings me to a second reason why the Iranian case helps us see the global long 1970s from a wide angle. What is fascinating about Iran's moral critique is that it targets 'the West' and places itself outside 'the West' while speaking a moral(ist) language similar to that of Western conservatives criticising their own anti-establishment populations in the 1960s/1970s. There were some differences, of course. While Iran's establishment experienced global interdependence as increased power, statesmen in the Global North like Kissinger felt a decreasing ability to influence world affairs. Also, the former's 'Eastern' notions of identity were foreign to Western conservatives. Still, in a twentieth-century-adjusted version of the 'homogenisation of differences' that Chris Bayly famously

80 Especially for the United States, see Borstelmann, T., *The 1970s: A New Global History from Civil Rights to Economic Inequality*, Princeton 2012.

81 Suri, J., *Power and Protest: Global Revolution and the Rise of Détente*, Cambridge 2003.

82 Brinkley, A., '1968 and the Unraveling of Liberal America', in *1968: The World Transformed*, pp. 220n4, 228–233; Schwarz, *Memories of Empire*; Fink, C., 'Introduction', p. 12n41. See also Goltz, A. and Waldschmidt-Nelson, B. (eds.), *Inventing the Silent Majority in Western Europe and the United States: Conservatism in the 1960s and 1970s*, Cambridge 2017.

diagnosed for nineteenth-century globalisation, the two expressed *difference* in a *shared* language. That is, they shared a language, while asserting to belong to entirely distinct parts of the world. In the 1970s though that situation had a post-imperial twist. 'Western' countries were not supremely dominant anymore, and a few 'Third World' countries like Iran even were able to see themselves as distinctly ascendant.[83] This development characterised also (various forms of) state welfarism, which was alive and kicking even though the 1970s gave birth to neo-liberalism. Unlike earlier decades, however, democracies and communist countries in the Global North were no longer the only state welfarist models. Now, Third World countries like autocratic Iran became self-appointed models. In the 1970s, then, a global, and globally felt, crisis produced different domestic answers that however were deeply transnational, i.e. inspired by other countries' policies. Ascendant countries in the Global South played an active part in this conversation. Indeed, it was this conversation about the world's future that helped make Iran, in the eyes of its establishment, a global player rather than 'only' a Third World country by the 1970s.

Bibliography

Adas, M., 'Contested Hegemony: The Great War and the Afro-Asian Assault on the Civilising Mission Ideology', in *Journal of World History*, vol. 15, no. 1, 2004, pp. 31–63.

Alam, A., *The Shah and I*, London 1991.

Alvandi, R., *Nixon, Kissinger, and the Shah: The United States and Iran in the Cold War*, New York 2014.

Amanat, A., 'Historiography ix. Pahlavi period', in *Encyclopedia Iranica*, available at: <www.iranicaonline.org/articles/historiography-ix>.

Amanat, A., *Pivot of the Universe: Nasir al-Din Shah and the Iranian Monarchy*, London 2008.

Ansari, A., *Modern Iran since 1921*, London 2003.

Ansari, A., 'The Myth of the White Revolution: Mohammad Reza Shah, "Modernisation", and the Consolidation of Power', in *Middle East Studies*, vol. 37, no. 3, 2001, pp. 1–24.

Ansari, A., 'Taqizadeh and European Civilisation', in *Journal of the British Institute of Persian Studies*, vol. 54, no. 1, 2016, pp. 47–58.

83 Bayly, C., *The Birth of the Modern World*, Malden 2004.

Aryanpur (Kashani), A. (ed.), *A Translation of the Historic Speeches of His Imperial Majesty Shahanshah Ayamehr*, Tehran 1975.

Ashraf, A., 'Iranian Identity', in *Encyclopedia Iranica*, available at: <www.iranicaonline.org/articles/iranian-identity-iv-19th-20th-centuries>.

Bayly, C., *The Birth of the Modern World*, Malden 2004.

Belmonte, M. (ed.), *Foreign Relations of the United States, 1969–1976, Volume E–4, Documents on Iran and Iraq, 1969–1972*, Washington, DC 2006.

Belmonte, M. (ed.), *Foreign Relations of the United States, 1969–1976, Volume XXVII, Iran; Iraq, 1973–1976*, Washington, DC 2012.

Berger, S., and Miller, A. (eds.), *Nationalising Empires*, Budapest 2015.

Borstelmann, T., *The 1970s: A New Global History from Civil Rights to Economic Inequality*, Princeton 2012.

Boroujerdi, M., *Iranian Intellectuals and the West*, Syracuse 1996.

Bowden, B., *The Empire of Civilisation: The Evolution of an Imperial Idea*, Chicago 2009.

Brinkley, A., '1968 and the Unraveling of Liberal America', in Fink, C., Gassert, P., and Junker, D., (eds.), *1968: The World Transformed*, Washington 1998, pp. 219–236.

Burton, A. (ed.), *After the Imperial Turn: Thinking With and Through the Nation*, Durham 2003.

Castiglioni, C., *Gli Stati Uniti e la modernizzazione iraniana*, Milan 2015.

Castiglioni, C., 'No Longer a Client, Not Yet a Partner: the US-Iranian Alliance in the Johnson Years', in *Cold War History*, vol. 15, no. 4, 2015, pp. 491–509.

Chatterjee Miller, M., *Wronged by Empire: Post-Imperial Ideology and Foreign Policy in India and China*, Stanford 2013.

De Grazia, V., *Irrestistible Empire: America's Advance through Twentieth-Century Europe*, Cambridge, MA 2005.

Duara, P., 'The Cold War as a Historical Period', in *Journal of Global History*, vol. 6, no. 3, 2011, pp. 457–480.

Endy, C., 'Power and Culture in the West', in Immerman, R., and Goedde, P. (eds.), *The Oxford Handbook of the Cold War*, Oxford 2013, pp. 323–340.

Ferguson, N., Maier, C., Manela, E., and Sargent, D. (eds.), *The Shock of the Global: the 1970s in Perspective*, Cambridge 2010.

Fink, C., Gassert, P., and Junker, D., 'Introduction', in idem (eds.), *1968: The World Transformed*, Washington 1998.

Gemeinnütziger Verein Villa Hügel, *7000 Jahre Kunst in Iran*, Essen 1962.

Gheissari, A., *Iranian Intellectuals in the 20th Century*, Austin 1998.

Ghosh, D., 'Another Set of Imperial Turns?', in *American Historical Review*, vol. 117, no. 3, 2012, pp. 772–793.

Hakim-Elahi, N., *Dar rah-e tamaddon-e bozorg az Kurosh ta Pahlavi* [On the Path of the Great Civilization from Cyrus to the Pahlavi Dynasty], Tehran 1971.

Hiepel, C., 'Introduction', in idem (ed.), *Europe in a Globalising World*, Baden-Baden 2014, pp. 1–15.

Howe, S., 'Introduction', in idem (ed.), *The New Imperial Histories Reader*, Abingdon 2010, pp. 1–18.

Hung, H., 'From Qing Empire to the Chinese Nation: an Incomplete Project', in *Nations and Nationalism*, vol. 22, no. 4, 2016, pp. 660–665.

Iriye, A., 'Historicising the Cold War', in Immerman, R., and Goedde, P. (eds.), *The Oxford Handbook of the Cold War*, Oxford 2013, pp. 15–31.

Istituto italiano per il medio ed estremo Oriente, *Mostra d'arte iranica*, Milano 1956.

John-Alder, K., 'Paradise Reconsidered. The Early Design History of Pardisan Park in Tehran', in Gharipour, M. (ed.), *Contemporary Urban Landscapes of the Middle East*, London 2016, pp. 120–148.

Johns, A., 'The Johnson Administration, the Shah of Iran, and the Changing Pattern of U.S.–Iranian Relations, 1965–1967: "Tired of Being Treated like a Schoolboy"', in *Journal of Cold War Studies*, vol. 9, no. 2, 2007, pp. 64–94.

Kashani-Sabet, F., *Frontier Fictions: Shaping the Iranian Nation, 1804–1946*, Princeton 1999.

Keefer, E. C. (ed.), *Foreign Relations of the United States, 1958–1960, Near East Region; Iraq; Iran; Arabian Peninsula, Volume XII*, Washington, DC 1993.

Khachayar, A. -A., *Le culte d'Etat chez la Nation Iranienne (démontré à travers les âges en vue de la paix)*, Paris 1936.

Kramer, P., 'Power and Connection: Imperial Histories of the United States in the World', *American Historical Review*, vol. 116, no. 5, 2011, pp. 1348–1391.

Lob, E. 'The Islamic Republic of Iran's Foreign Policy and Construction Jihad's Developmental Activities in Sub-Saharan Africa', in *International Journal of Middle East Studies*, vol. 48, no. 2, 2016, pp. 313–338.

Maier, C., *Among Empires: American Ascendancy and its Predecessors*, Cambridge, MA 2006.

Matin-Asghari, A., 'The Pahlavi Era', in Daryaee, T. (ed.), *Oxford Handbook of Iranian History*, Oxford 2012, pp. 346–364.

McMahon, R. (ed.), *The Cold War in the Third World*, Oxford 2012.

McMahon, R., 'The Republic as Empire: American Foreign Policy in the "American Century"', in Sitkoff, H. (ed.), *Perspectives on Modern America*, Oxford 2001, pp. 80–100.

Milani, A., *The Shah*, New York 2011.

Miller, E., *Misalliance: Ngo Dinh Diem, the United States, and the Fate of South Vietnam*, Cambridge 2013.

Mirsepassi, A. and Faraji, M., 'De-politicising Westoxification: The Case of Bonyad Monthly', in *British Journal of Middle Eastern Studies*, vol. 45, no. 3, 2016, pp. 355–375.

Mohammadi Malayeri, M., *Farhang-e Irani va Ta'sir-e an dar Tamaddon-e Eslam va Arab* [Iranian Culture and its Influence on Islamic and Arab Civilisations], Tehran 1944.

Nabavi, N., *Intellectuals and the State in Iran*, Gainesville 2003.

Naraqi, E., *Ghorbat-e gharb* [The Alienation of the West], Tehran 1974.

Pahlavi, M. R, Bayanat, *Mosahebehha va Payamha-ye 'Alahazrat-e Homayun Shahanshah Aryamehr az Shishom-e Bahman 1351 ta Shishom-e Bahman 1352* [Declarations, Interviews, and Messages of H.I.H. Shahenshah Armyamehr from the sixth of Bahman 1351 to the sixth of Bahman 1352],Tehran 1973.

Pahlavi, M. R., *Be-su-ye Tamaddon-e Bozorg* [Towards the Great Civilisation], Tehran 1977.

Pahlavi, M. R, *Rahbari-ye Ostandaran va Farmandaran be-su-ye Dowran-e Tamaddon-e Bozorg* [Provincial Governors' and Governors' Guidance towards the Period of the Great Civilisation], Tehran 1973.

Pahlavi, M. R., *Selection from the Shahanshah Aryamehr's Speeches and Writings on Culture*, Tehran 1975.

Pahlavi, M. R., *Speeches and Messages by his Imperial Majesty Mohammad-Reza Pahlavi Aryamehr Shahanshah of Iran on the Occasion of the Celebration of the 2500th Anniversary of the Founding of the Persian Empire*, n.p. 1972.

Palais des beaux arts, *Sept mille ans d'art en Iran*, Paris 1962.

Pines, Y., *The Everlasting Empire: The Political Culture of Ancient China and its Imperial Legacy*, Princeton 2012.

Pirniya, H., *Iran-e Bastan* [Ancient Iran], Tehran 1938.

Pirniya, H., *Iran-e Bastani* [Ancient Iran], Tehran 1927.

Porter, B., *Empire and Superempire: Britain, America, and the World*, New Haven 2006.

Purdavud, I., *Farhang-e Iran-e Bastan* [The Ancient Culture of Iran], Tehran 1947.

Ramazani, R. K., 'Iran's Changing Foreign Policy: A Preliminary Discussion', in *Middle East Journal*, vol. 24, no. 4, 1970, pp. 421–437.

Ramazani, R. K., *Iran's Foreign Policy, 1941–1973*, Charlottesville 1975.

Ramazani, R. K., 'Emerging Patterns of Regional Relations in Iranian Foreign Policy', in *Orbis*, vol. 18, no. 4, 1975, pp. 1043–1069.

Razi Hamadani, A., *Tarikh-e Iran* [The History of Iran], Tehran 1938.

Sarkash, A., *Kudak-e ʿAsr-e Enqelab: Pishgam-e Tamaddon-e Bozorg* [The Child of the Age of Revolution: The Pioneer of the Great Civilization], Tehran 1973.

Schwarz, B., *Memories of Empire, volume 1: the White Man's World*, Oxford 2011.

Shakibi, Z., 'Pahlavism: The Ideologisation of Monarchy in Iran', in *Politics, Religion, and Ideology*, vol. 14, no. 1, 2013, pp. 114–135.

Shepard, T., *The Invention of Decolonisation: The Algerian War and the Remaking of France*, Ithaca 2006.

Siebertz, R., *Die Briefmarken Irans als Mittel politischer Bildpropaganda*, Wien 2005.

Smithsonian Institution, *7000 Years of Iranian Art*, Washington 1964.

Steinbach, U., 'Irans Rolle im Arabischen Nahen Osten und Indischen Ozean', in *Orient*, vol. 17:2, 1976, pp. 88–114.

Suri, J., *Power and Protest: Global Revolution and the Rise of Détente*, Cambridge 2003.

Takriti, A., *Monsoon Revolution: Republicans, Sultans, and Empires in Oman, 1965–1976*, Oxford 2013.

Van Vleck, J., *Empire of the Air: Aviation and the American Ascendancy*, Cambridge, MA 2013.

Villaume, P., Mariager, R., and Porsdam, H. 'Introduction', in idem (eds.), *The 'Long 1970s': Human Rights, East-West Détente, and Transnational Relations*, Abingdon 2016, pp. 1–12.

Wang, F., *The China Order: Centralia, World Empire, and the Nature of Chinese Power*, Albany 2017.

Westad, O. A., *The Global Cold War*, Cambridge 2005.

Zanchetta, B., *The Transformation of American International Power in the 1970s*, Cambridge 2014.

Contributors

Roham Alvandi is Associate Professor of International History at the London School of Economics and Political Science and Director of the LSE IDEAS Cold War Studies Project.

Claudia Castiglioni is a Research Fellow at the University of Milan and Adjunct Professor of Iranian History and Politics at the Institute d'études politiques de Paris (Sciences Po).

Houchang Esfandiar Chehabi is Professor of International Relations and History at the Frederick S. Pardee School of Global Studies at Boston University.

Maziyar Ghiabi is Associate Professor of Social Sciences and Medical Humanities, and the Director for the Centre of Persian and Iranian Studies (CPIS) at the University of Exeter.

Ramin Nassehi is a Teaching Fellow in the Department of Economics at University College London.

Cyrus Schayegh is Professor of International History and Politics (IHP) at the Graduate Institute of International and Development Studies in Geneva.

Robert Steele is a postdoctoral fellow at the Institute of Iranian Studies, Austrian Academy of Sciences.

Samine Tabatabaei is a PhD candidate in Art History and Communication Studies at McGill University.